T0135756

Studien zur Mustererkennung

herausgegeben von:

Prof. Dr.-Ing. Heinrich Niemann
Prof. Dr.-Ing. Elmar Nöth

Bibliografische Information der Deutschen Nationalbibliothek

Die Deutsche Nationalbibliothek verzeichnet diese Publikation in der Deutschen Nationalbibliografie; detaillierte bibliografische Daten sind im Internet über http://dnb.d-nb.de abrufbar.

ISBN 978-3-8325-2258-2
ISSN 1617-0695

Logos Verlag Berlin GmbH
Comeniushof
Gubener Str. 47
10243 Berlin
Tel.: +49 030 42 85 10 90
Fax: +49 030 42 85 10 92
INTERNET: http://www.logos-verlag.de

Automatic Assessment of Children Speech to Support Language Learning

Automatische Bewertung der Sprache von Kindern als Hilfe beim Fremdsprachenlernen

Der Technischen Fakultät der
Universität Erlangen–Nürnberg

zur Erlangung des Grades

DOKTOR–INGENIEUR

vorgelegt von

Christian Hacker

Erlangen — 2009

Als Dissertation genehmigt von der
Technischen Fakultät der
Universität Erlangen-Nürnberg

Tag der Einreichung:	18.12.2008
Tag der Promotion:	10.06.2009
Dekan:	Prof. Dr.-Ing. habil. J. Huber
Berichterstatter:	Prof. em. Dr.-Ing. H. Niemann
	Prof. M. Russell

Acknowledgements

I am very thankful to my supervisor Prof. em. Dr.-Ing. Heinrich Niemann. He gave me many useful advises and spent even after he retired and became emeritus much time for my dissertation. I learnt scientific work and accuracy from him as my lecturer, head of the Chair of Pattern Recognition, and supervisor and appreciate it much that I could finish my work under his guidance.

In the same way I am very grateful to Prof. Dr.-Ing. habil. Elmar Nöth the head of the speech group, who fascinated me for speech processing and all the different sub-areas I worked in. I like to thank him for his advises, motivations, the friendly relation, and the wonderful days at conferences and workshops, as well as for the acquisition of third-party funds for my position.

I'm very pleased that Prof. Martin Russell, an expert in the field of children speech recognition, agreed to be my second reviewer. His group recorded the data which I could use in my thesis. I like to thank him also that he came to Erlangen for my defence.

I further like to thank Prof. Dr.-Ing. Joachim Hornegger for his support during the second part of my thesis as he headed the Chair of Pattern Recognition. I thank him in particular that he renewed my contract. Furthermore, I like to thank my external examiner Prof. Dr.-Ing. habil. Rudolf Rabenstein.

Results of research are usually not the outcome of studies conducted by a single person. They are triggered by international research projects, and arise from the close cooperation with colleagues and students. In the case of this thesis additionally the cooperation with the Ohm-Gymnasium Erlangen and the Montessori school was very fruitful.

I like to thank Dr. phil. Anton Batliner and Dr.-Ing. Stefan Steidl for the cooperation within the Pf-Star project. Anton was the one who guided me through this European project and who gave me many advises. Our collaboration was also very closely in the SmartWeb project. Together with Stefan I recorded the corpus with non-native children which is investigated in this thesis and we started to analyse children speech. Anton, Stefan and me spent wonderful times at various project meetings.

STRin Ute Guthunz and OStD Dr. Bernd Grunwald provided us the possibilities to collect data at the Ohm-Gymnasium and to evaluate our demonstration system. In particular, I am very grateful to Ute and her colleagues for annotating the data used in this thesis. I like to thank her further for the hints and information regarding second language learning.

There have been major contributions of my students. I like to thank Dr.-Ing. Tobias Cincarek for his excellent work on pronunciation features and André Heßler for the nice demonstration system. Also parts of the diploma theses of Dr.-Ing. Andreas Maier, Florian Hönig and Werner Spiegl can be found in the present work. Later, as my colleague at the institute, Andreas designed and provided the client/server architecture of the demonstration system.

I like to thank all the other colleagues at the Chair of Pattern Recognition for the great time. In particular I like to mention the colleagues of the speech group: Axel Horndasch and Florian Hönig (collaboration in SmartWeb), Dr.-Ing. Georg Stemmer (speech recognition system), Viktor Zeißler (prosody module), and Dr.-Ing. Tino Haderlein (various scripts). Thank you, dear parents and dear Sabine for your support during the last years.

Abstract

Focus of this work are pattern recognition related aspects of computer assisted pronunciation training (CAPT) for second language learning.

An overview of commercial systems shows that pronunciation training is being addressed by the growing field of computer assisted language learning only to a small extend, although in the state-of-the-art section a number of such approaches for automatic assessment can already be presented. In the present thesis different approaches are extended and combined. In particular a large set of nearly 200 pronunciation and prosodic features is developed. By this approach pronunciation scoring is regarded as classification task in high-dimensional feature space.

Automatic speech recognition is the basis of most pronunciation scoring algorithms. In this thesis a system is presented, which supports second language learning in school, i.e. the target users are children. For this reason a state-of-the-art speech recognition engine is adapted to children speech, since young speakers are only hardly recognised by automatic systems. Phonetically motivated rules for typical mispronunciation errors are integrated into the system to make it suitable for pronunciation scoring.

Evaluating an algorithm for pronunciation assessment is more difficult than simply counting the correctly recognised mistakes, since there exists no objective ground truth. This can be shown by evaluating the annotations of 14 teachers. However, with different measures it can be verified that the accuracy of the system (in comparison with teachers) thoroughly reaches the agreement among teachers. The evaluation is conducted with native German speakers learning English.

Kurzfassung

Schwerpunkt dieser Arbeit sind mustererkennungsspezifische Aspekte für das computergestützte Aussprachetraining (CAPT) beim Erlernen einer Fremdsprache.

Eine Übersicht von kommerziellen Systemen zeigt, dass Aussprachetraining vom wachsenden Sektor des computergestützten Fremdsprachenerwerbs nur in geringem Maße adressiert wird, obwohl im Abschnitt über den Stand der Technik eine Vielzahl solcher Verfahren zur automatischen Bewertung bereits vorgestellt werden können. In der vorliegenden Abhandlung werden verschiedene Ansätze erweitert und kombiniert. Insbesondere wird eine große Menge von fast 200 Aussprachemerkmalen und prosodischen Merkmalen entwickelt. Bei diesem Ansatz wird Aussprachebewertung als Klassifikationsaufgabe im hochdimensionalen Merkmalsraum betrachtet.

Grundlage der meisten Aussprachebewertungsalgorithmen ist die automatische Spracherkennung. In dieser Arbeit wird ein System vorgestellt, das den Fremdsprachenerwerb in der Schule unterstützt, d.h. die Zielgruppe sind Kinder. Dazu wird ein Standard Spracherkenner auf Kindersprache adaptiert, da junge Sprecher gewöhnlich nur schwer von automatischen Systemen verstanden werden. Phonetisch motivierte Regeln für typische Aussprachefehler werden in das System integriert und machen es so zur Aussprachebewertung geeignet.

Einen Aussprachebewertungsalgorithmus zu evaluieren ist schwieriger als bloßes Zählen der korrekt erkannten Fehler, denn es gibt keine festen objektiven Kriterien. Dies zeigt sich durch die Evaluation der Annotationen von 14 Lehrern. Mit Hilfe verschiedener Maße kann aber gezeigt werden, dass die Akkuratheit des Systems (im Vergleich mit Lehrern) durchaus die Übereinstimmung der Lehrer untereinander erreicht. Die Auswertung wird mit nativen deutschen Sprechern, die Englisch lernen, durchgeführt.

Contents

List of Figures

List of Tables

Chapter 1

Introduction

In times of globalisation foreign language skills have become more and more important. *Computer-aided language learning* (CALL) makes it possible to improve and practise a foreign language without any teacher or human dialogue partner e.g. at home. Using mobile devices or MP3-players, training of vocabulary is even possible on a walk or while commuting to work. This can be useful for people who do not have the time to attend a regular evening class or for students as additional tuition or homework. Nowadays, CALL-systems for various languages are on the market; most of the systems focus on reading skills, listening comprehension, and writing.

> *"Speaking, however, remains the most difficult aspect of language learning to incorporate into a computer-based instruction system. Thus, the pivotal practice of active conversation skills is still restricted to live classroom instruction and real-life 'sink or swim' situations."*

This statement from Bernstein et al. [Ber90] in 1990 is still true. Unfortunately, even in school individual time per pupil to train the spoken language and its correct pronunciation and intonation is extremely short, although oral examinations and the ability to speak a foreign language properly have become more important. What is more, some students do not have the courage to speak aloud unless they feel confident with the foreign sounds. All in all, it still remains highly recommendable for foreign language students to go abroad and to learn from 'sink or swim' situations. Yet, this is often not possible; therefore, commercial tuition software is more and more integrating pronunciation exercises based on automatic speech processing.

1.1 Computer Assisted Language Learning

Let us first have a look at second language education in school. What tools are used by the teachers, e.g. in an English course in Germany? Usually lessons are given in English, text books are used, and sometimes tapes or CDs are played or videos are shown that go with the text book. In grammar schools additionally intensification courses are given, where in small groups (15 pupils) a computer lab can be used or role plays can be acted. Alternatively, a confusing amount of additional tools is offered via the Internet, e.g. educational programs from websites of British TV stations or museums[1]. With the help of CALL-software vocabulary, grammar, and sentence patterns are trained. However, no *computer-aided pronunciation training* (CAPT) is employed yet, since no appropriate software is available[2]. State-of-the-art CAPT technologies are a further development and extension of the conventional language laboratories and compare the learner with an average pronunciation calculated from native speakers; conventional language laboratories, however, have not been used any more, since in the last two decades teaching methods have focused on free text production, creative writing, and speaking tasks rather than on pattern drill and pure imitation. Summing up, to get more practice in the spoken language additional tuition with CALL-software that includes CAPT technology and exceeds the range of exercises offered in common language laboratories might be very helpful.

The design of a complete CALL application requires the consideration of several aspects and needs expert knowledge of teachers, pedagogues, psychologists, linguists, phoneticians, and computer scientists. However, in this thesis, many aspects of this large research field are only touched and not discussed in detail. The reader is referred to international journals or conferences[3] on *e-learning* which are published by international associations like *Calico* (Computer Assisted Language Instruction Consortium)[4], *EUROCALL* (European Association for Computer Assisted Language Learning)[5] , or *SLATE* (ISCA-SIG: Speech and Language Technology in Education)[6]. In general, the following topics are of interest: What target group is addressed (e.g. beginners, children), what content has significance (e.g. everyday conversations), what exercises should be designed to teach this content (e.g. building sentences from pre-built blocks), how to structure the graphical user interface, where to integrate multimedia content, how to motivate a student, how to evaluate the student, which pedagogical criteria have to be met, and, last but not least, what feedback should be given to the learner. Finally, for the complete system long-term studies are important to evaluate the progress of the users.

Those parts of the system where speech input is used require additional considerations: Does the utterance of the student have to be *phonetically* correct, does the exercise focus on particular phones or words, are regional variants of English allowed, or is it even sufficient

---

[1]e.g. http://www.bbc.co.uk/learning/subjects/english.shtml, http://www.museumoflondon.org.uk/English/Learning/Learningonline/

[2] Existing pronunciation training software is mainly aimed at adult education; no software that goes along with the text book of all school types and all regional varieties in different federal states is currently available.

[3]e.g. Calico (https://calico.org/), ReCall (http://www.eurocall-languages.org/recall/index.html), Computer assisted language learning (http://www.tandf.co.uk/journals/titles/09588221.asp), i-Jet (http://www.online-journals.org/index.php/i-jet), interactive computer aided learning (http://www.icl-conference.org/)

[4]http://www.calico.org/about.html

[5]http://www.eurocall-languages.org/

[6]The International Speech Communication Association Special Interest Group (ISCA SIG) on Speech and Language Technology in Education http://www.cs.cmu.edu/~max/mainpage_files/SLATE.htm

to be *intelligible* which would imply that a strong non-native accent is tolerated? Neri et al. [Ner02a] recommend to aim at speech intelligibility rather than at nativeness or accent-free pronunciation. Further, for future systems algorithms would be desirable that recognise systematic mistakes and adapt the exercises to the learner's skills.

An overview of *feedback* in CAPT systems is given by Neri et al. [Ner02b]. Very little research has been carried out on the effectiveness of feedback, and the available studies investigate only short-term effects up to now. Students should not only receive a score but also comprehend why they got this score.

> " [...] *feedback should first of all be comprehensible, should not rely solely on the learner's own perception, should allow verification of response correctness, pinpoint specific errors, and possibly suggest a remedy.* " [Ner02b]

Further pedagogical requirements that CAPT systems should meet in the future are discussed in [Ner02a]: The decision, which pronunciation errors to reject, should take into account four criteria: error frequency, error persistence, perceptual relevance, and robustness of error detection.

Finally, Eskenazi gives in [Esk99] the following general recommendations for foreign language learning: Learners should hear large quantities of speech in the foreign language, they should hear many different speakers, and they should produce large quantities of speech on their own. It is important that they receive pertinent feedback at just the right times. Intervening too often would discourage the student. Further, students should feel at ease and not be embarrassed to utter new sounds in the classroom. An ongoing assessment should monitor the student's progress. Unfortunately, not everything mentioned above can be satisfied in class which confirms the potential for CAPT systems.

The main focus of the present thesis is on CAPT. In particular, the following aspects related to pattern recognition are emphasised: recognition of *what* the user said and classification *how* it was spoken and whether it is correctly pronounced or not. Promising results will be discussed, which are based on investigations on acoustic modelling, prosodic features, and pronunciation features. Since in the case of a reading exercise the transcription of the speech input is known, the time alignment between the recorded speech signal and the text can be computed. It is compared with the hypothesis of an automatic speech recognition system or with a-priori estimated statistics, e.g. of the duration of phonemes. The experimental part will be limited to second language (L2) English. The mother tongue (L1) of the children who were recorded in the context of the present thesis is German. However, in [Hac05b] it was shown that the algorithms and features used in this thesis can also be successfully applied to adult speakers with other mother tongues.

The newly developed technologies are integrated in a demonstration system that will be introduced in Chap. 2.4. Selected exercises of this client/server system *Caller* (**C**omputer **A**ssisted **L**anguage **Le**arning from **Er**langen) are illustrated in Fig. 1.1. It shows an exercise where the learner has to build sentences from words, a vocabulary test, a reading test that requires speech input, and a "bonus" game, where misspelled words have to be found.

Figure 1.1: *Caller*: Computer assisted language learning from Erlangen.

A cooperation with a local grammar school[7] made it possible to record data, assess the recordings, and to evaluate the system in class (Fig. 1.1, bottom, left). Additional recordings were collected at a private general-education secondary school[8].

At the end of this thesis investigations are presented which even go a step further; the approaches aim at an improvement of human/machine interaction. Future systems are expected to place greater emphasis on *spoken* language training and will also respond to spoken instructions[9]. Thus it may become important to react to the user's emotions like anger and to classify his/her focus of attention: Does the learner talk to the system, to someone else, or is he/she just thinking aloud?

Cognitive systems that respond to the emotional user state are investigated in *Humaine*[10]. Within the *SmartWeb* project[11], a multimodal system that reacts to the user focus has been developed. Results from both projects and first and foremost from the *Pf-Star* project[12] (Speech technologies for children and emotion recognition, amongst others) are presented and discussed in the present work.

Recent research in CAPT for German and Italian learners of English was conducted within the *ISLE*-project[13] of the European Union, which is described in Chap. 2.3. The

---

[7]Ohm-Gymnasium Erlangen (grade 5–13)

[8]Montessori-Schule Erlangen (grade 5–9)

[9]Simple instructions to a virtual tutor are e.g. possible in the CALL-software from http://www.digitalpublishing.de/english/

[10]http://emotion-research.net/

[11]http://www.smartweb-projekt.de/

[12]http://pfstar.itc.it/

[13]Interactive Spoken Language Education: http://nats-www.informatik.uni-hamburg.de/~isle/

two-year project ended in 2000 and focused on data collection and the implementation of a demonstrator providing feedback on the phone-level. Fundamental algorithms for pronunciation scoring were investigated. The recordings that will be described and evaluated in the present thesis took place in 2003. Using this data, improved algorithms for pronunciation scoring were developed.

Nomenclature. To discriminate human assessment and automatic assessment, the following nomenclature is used throughout this work. Human experts or raters (e.g. teachers) *labelled* the data during an annotation phase. There are different kinds of labels: Marks (school grades) are numbers on a scale from 1 (best) to 6 (worst). In some cases also intermediate marks 1.3, 1.5, 1.7, 2.3, and so on are used. A binary label uses just the two categories wrong ($\mathcal{X}$) and correct ($\mathcal{O}$). Synonymously we use *rating* and *grading* if human experts give marks; *marking* is used if e.g. something is marked as wrong. In contrast, the computer *classifies* (discrete) or *scores* (continuously) an utterance. The user of the system is referred to as learner, student, or child.

1.2 Children Speech

For automatic pronunciation scoring, first of all the time alignment of the speech input and the intended word sequence (reference) is required. For this purpose *hidden Markov models* (HMMs) are applied. Second, the hypothesis of a speech recogniser (based on the same HMMs) is computed and in many cases compared with the time alignment. This means that robust automatic speech recognition (ASR) is a precondition for pronunciation scoring. Robust means on the one hand that a high word accuracy is desired, albeit not even the best second language learners have an approximately native accent. On the other hand, the speech recogniser must be able to reject wrong pronunciations, e.g. by making more errors for students that have poorer pronunciation. In the context of this thesis, robust also means that the recogniser has to deal with children speech. Wilpon and Jacobson report in [Wil96] up to 170 % higher error rates on children speech than on adult speech. In contrast to the ISLE project where adult speech was analysed, this work has to deal with both challenges non-native speech and children speech at the same time.

If we compare two languages, first of all the different phonetic inventory has to be considered. In German, there exist e.g. only closed vowels for the "a"-sound: the short /a/[14] in "Satz" and the long /a:/ in "Tat". In English, however, there exists an open vowel /A:/ in "stars" and the /V/ in "cut". Other similar vowels are /{/ in "pat" and the British /Q/ in "pot". The formants which are located at higher frequencies for children speech than for adult speech are characteristic of vowels. Tab. 1.2 shows the dependency on age and gender on the CID corpus[15] (after [Lee99]). For /A:/, the first formant is at 1170 Hz on the average for 5-year-old male children, at 970 Hz for 10-year-old children, and at 720 Hz for adults. The standard deviations for these age groups are 100, 90, and

---

[14]phonetic alphabet SAMPA [Sampa] as described in Appendix B.1
[15]Central Institute for the Deaf

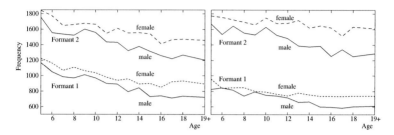

Figure 1.2: First and second formant for male and female speaker dependent on the age for the vowels /A:/ (left) and /V/ (right). After [Lee99].

70 Hz, respectively. The higher variability of the formant frequencies for younger children makes ASR more difficult. Higher variabilities can also be observed for the rate of speech. The reason for the higher frequency values of younger children is their shorter vocal tract. During puberty starting at around the age of 12, the differences between males and females become more significant. A detailed analysis of children speech is found in [Pot03, Lee99] and in Chap. 3.3. A comparison of Fig. 1.2 left and right shows the importance of the higher first formant and the lower second formant to discriminate /A:/ from /V/; this motivates the requirement of an analysis of the phonetic inventory which will be found in Chap. 2.

In the Pf-Star project substantial corpora with children speech have been recorded for the European languages German, Italian, Swedish, and British English [Rus03, Bat05a]. Results from the Pf-Star project are reported in [DAr04, Ele05, Ger04a, Ger06, Hac05a, Rus04, Ste03a, Ste03b]. In this thesis, the corpus of German children reading English sentences will be analysed and compared with British English data. Additionally the American YOUTH database will be employed.

1.3   Contribution of this Work

The present thesis focuses on the recognition of German children learning English and the automatic assessment of their pronunciation. Previous research can be found in the literature on different source and target languages, e.g. Japanese learners of English [Ber90, Tei00, Min04a], learners of Dutch [Cuc00b] or learners of French [Neu00]; only little research has focused on non-native speech from German people up to now. Investigations on automatic pronunciation training of Germans were mainly performed in the context of the European ISLE project [Her99b, Men00]. ISLE, however, had the goal to evaluate speech from adults. In the present work *children* learning English are studied.

Compared to adult speech, lower accuracy for the recognition of children speech has been reported in [Wil96, Pot03]. Yet, up to now, only little effort has been put on the development of *speech technology for children*. Whereas most research has been undertaken to investigate children speaking American English, the cooperation in Pf-Star with Italian,

Swedish, and British partners provided the opportunity to collect data in several European languages. Approaches (e.g. adaptation) to improve automatic speech and phone recognition of German children reading English texts are described and evaluated in the present thesis. The contribution of this work is the systematic evaluation of approved and modified approaches on this challenging recognition task with two sources of variability at the same time: non-native speech and children speech. When recognising non-native children, the error rate could be reduced by 17 %.

The corpus recorded in the context of this thesis was designed to provide *realistic data* for pronunciation scoring. Here, it was not the case that sentences have been read repeatedly until the pronunciation and reading was satisfactory. This is important for the tuition of children since they are usually less patient than adults. As a consequence, the sentences also contain reading errors, word fragments, and repetitions. On this data, the *agreement of up to 14 teacher ratings* is evaluated using different measures. The target is an objective pronunciation scoring that imitates the teachers and learns their way of marking and their selective intervention. In contrast, phoneticians who are employed in other studies usually precisely mark every phone deviation; a CALL-system that has learned those detailed references is likely to confuse or demotivate young beginners of English with too many and too detailed markings. Up to now, there is no other corpus with this kind of realistic data available, nor with such a spectrum of annotations.

Different approaches to assess the learner's pronunciation are investigated. First, a high dimensional set of text independent *pronunciation features* is developed. These features have been developed for German children learning English but have proven to work L1 independent [Hac05b]. The features are then combined with *prosodic features*. Finally, approaches using acoustic models for mispronounced words are investigated. HMMs are a statistic approach to model the pronunciation; in more error-prone approaches the spoken signal is directly compared with the utterance of one reference speaker. Further, the integration of a speech decoder makes the system more flexible, in particular if the user's utterance does not exactly match the reference sentence. State-of-the-art approaches use forced alignment and always map the reference text onto the acoustic input, no matter if words are skipped, uttered repeatedly, or if something completely different is said. The corpus described above is evaluated on different levels reaching from a phone-based analysis to more comprehensive levels, e.g. giving one mark for all sentences read by a speaker. The contribution of this thesis is to show that classification is an applicable method for pronunciation scoring. The input to the classifier is a large set of in part newly developed features; feature selection is applied to determine which of them are appropriate for an automatic assessment similar to teachers. Further, it is shown that the combination of this text independent approach with the text dependent approach integrating acoustic mispronunciation models improves the agreement with teachers. Further new approaches are presented which are based on boundary classification or which require only native data for training. The accuracy of the final automatic system reaches up to 90 % of the human experts and even outperforms some of the experts.

In the context of the present thesis, a client/server-based CALL application (*Caller*) has been developed, which can be used either at home or in class. It provides possibilities for the teacher to monitor the students' learning, and has qualities of a computer game to motivate the students. Pronunciation scoring and speech technologies are integrated into this system. Some multimodal extensions for future edutainment systems like the automatic classification of the focus of attention and the consideration of the user state are investigated. It will be shown, that with video and acoustic/prosodic information the focus of attention can be correctly classified in 85 % of the utterances.

Summing up, *realistic data* has been collected and assessed by several *teachers*. The focus is on *Germans* speaking English and on *children*. Children speech is harder to recognise with state-of-the-art *speech technology* which requires the investigation of different *adaptation techniques*. *Pronunciation scoring* approaches are developed, evaluated, and integrated into the CALL application *Caller*. Contributions to future multimodal systems are investigations of the *focus of attention* and *emotional user states*.

1.4   Structure of the Thesis

The thesis begins with a description of computer assisted pronunciation training (Chap. 2). First, an overview of existing phones in German and English and expected mispronunciations are discussed. To evaluate automatic scoring systems, expert labels are required. Section 2.2 introduces different common measures to evaluate the agreement among different experts (and automatic scores) and gives an overview of approaches from the literature to automatically score pronunciation using speech recognition technology. Different existing CAPT systems from earlier research projects and systems on the market are introduced in Section 2.3. In Section 2.4 the system *Caller* that has been developed in the context of this thesis is presented.

Chap. 3 gives an overview of automatic classification and speech recognition including a discussion of different evaluation measures. Problems that occur with children speech are addressed and solutions from the literature are given. Algorithms like vocal-tract length normalisation (VTLN) or adaptation, which are integrated in the speech recognition system of the Chair of Pattern Recognition (LME), are described.

Different adults and children speech corpora are investigated. Data that includes native English and non-native English speech are introduced in Chap. 4. The main focus is on a database with German children reading English texts. Newly developed approaches for automatic assessment, in particular a large set of pronunciation features, are introduced in Chap. 5. Here, also approaches based on meta-features, prosody and boundary classification are described.

After this theoretic and algorithmic part, three experimental chapters follow. In Chap. 6 the agreement of human experts is analysed. In Chap. 7 a speech recogniser for children is developed that is employed in Chap. 8. Here, experiments on automatic scoring of the pronunciation of non-native speech from children are described. The most important results are marked with an index and summarised in Appendix E.

Chap. 9 reports contributions to a multimodal extension of systems like *Caller* that integrates up to now only the aspects found in Chap. 7 and Chap. 8. The thesis ends with outlook (Chap. 10) and summary (Chap. 11).

Chapter 2

Computer Assisted Pronunciation Training

Computers are not able to replace any human teacher, but can assist the L2-learner to practise on his own in a foreign language. These days, software for computer aided language learning (CALL) is provided by many publishing companies of English textbooks. In some exercises, speech technologies make it possible that learners can train their pronunciation. In the beginning of this chapter it is discussed, which pronunciation errors are made frequently by German students learning English. There, also an overview of phonemes of both languages is given. In the succeeding section established approaches to compare expert and machine ratings are explained and the procedure, how those automatic scores are obtained for L2-learners. Finally, an overview of existing systems is given and the system of the LME is explained that was developed in the context of this thesis.

2.1 Overview of Pronunciation Errors

In this section common pronunciation errors of German speakers of English are analysed. First, the phonetic alphabet of both languages is compared. Then, general errors from the viewpoint of phoneticians or comparative philologists are summarised. After this, errors that are typically dealt with in the field of automatic pronunciation scoring are addressed.

2.1.1 English and German Phones

To be able to compare the German speakers of English with native speakers, the phonetic alphabets of both languages have to be taken into consideration. Since in Germany British English (BE) is taught in school, this variety is focused on. In the experiments in Chap. 8, data from German children is "compared" with British children data. However, since all German children are beginners of English, their pronunciation is quite more distinct from English than American and British English are. Thus, we also "compare" the German children with American data, particularly since more American children speech corpora are

	English	German
plosives	p, b, t, d, k, g	p, b, t, d, k, g
affricates	tS, dZ	pf, ts, tS, dZ
fricatives	f, v, s, z, S, Z h, T, D	f, v, s, z, S, Z h, C, x
nasals	m, n, N	m, n, N
liquids	l, r	l, R
semi-vowels	j, w	j

Table 2.1: Consonants in English (same for British and American) and German.

available (cf. Chap. 4). Consequently, phonetic differences between German and American English (AE) have to be shortly addressed, too.

In this thesis, the phonetic alphabet SAMPA [Sampa] is employed in order to transcribe all example words. All *phonemes* (smallest units in a language which are necessary to distinguish meaning) are written between slashes /./. A *phone* is a phonetic event and written in brackets [.]. A detailed overview and comparison of British English, American English, and German phonemes can be found in Appendix B.1.

All phones result from air that flows through the glottis and is modified by the articulators like the velum, tongue and palate, the lips, and the teeth. When the glottis is wide open, turbulences appear on the vocal chords and unvoiced *fricatives* like /f/ arise whose characteristics are the clearly visible higher frequencies in the spectrogram of a speech signal. A narrower glottis is the reason for periodic oscillation of the vocal chords; voiced phones like all *vowels* or *nasals* (e.g. /m/) are generated. A blocked airflow causes *plosives* or *stop consonants*. *Affricates* are sequences of stops and fricatives, e.g. /tS/. *Nasals* or *nasal stops* occur when the oral cavity is occluded and all air passes through the nose. *Liquids* are /r/ and /l/; /j/ and /w/ are *semi-vowels*.

An overview of the English and German consonant systems can be found in Tab. 2.1. For the consonant inventory, there are no differences between AE and BE. The relation between SAMPA notation and graphemes is for the most part intuitive except for /S/ (the fricative in "shin"), and /N/ (the nasal stop in "thing"). The voiced forms of /s/ and /S/ are /z/ and /Z/. There are some consonants that only exist in English and not in German: "th" (/T/ ,/D/), the English /r/ (in this work, the corresponding German phone is consistently denoted as /R/[1]) and the English semi-vowel /w/ (in "what"; the German word "war" is transcribed with /v/ like in "very"). Only in German exist /R/, /x/ (in "ach"), and /C/ (in "ich"). Not considered in the SAMPA alphabet is the *dark* /l/ that can be observed in British English before consonants or at the end of words ("hill") and in American English in principle. In German only clear /l/ (BE in "let") is known [Grz].

---

[1]The recordings of the data described in Chap. 4 were made in southern Germany, thus [r] is pronounced and not the northern German [R]; to discriminate the corresponding phoneme from the English phoneme in "wrong", we rename it to /R/.

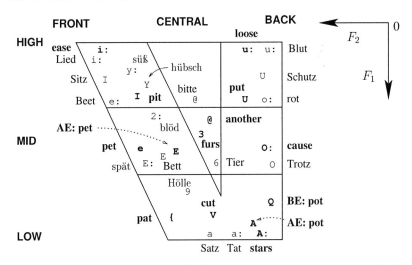

Figure 2.1: German (light) and English (bold) vowels. Approximate position after [Sch86].

More differences can be observed for the vowels. Long vowels are marked with colon, open vowels are written in capital letters. However, for American English no colon is used at all in [Sampa], since the notation remains unique. Nevertheless, in this thesis colons are used to show similarities between different languages. Vowels are characterised by their place of articulation. In the vowel space in Fig. 2.1 both dimensions correlate with the position of the highest point of the tongue: the horizontal axis defines whether the highest point of the tongue is in the back, the centre, or in the front. This dimension correlates with the second formant F_2. The vertical axis shows the vertical position of the tongue (high, medium, or low) and correlates with the formant F_1. English vowels are /V/ in "cut", /{/ in "pat", and the British /e/[2] in "pet" and /Q/ in "pot"; standard American English uses instead /A/ in "pot". Also the open English vowels /A:/ in "stars" and /O:/ in "cause" differ from the closed German vowels /a:/ ("Tat") and /o:/ ("rot"). The British /3r/ in "furs" is in American English pronounced as /3'/ or /@r/ and substitutes in [CmuDict] the final /@/ in "corner".

Vowels existing only in German are /a/ ("Satz"), /O/ ("trotz"), /e:/ ("Beet"), /E:/ ("spät") as well as the phonemes related to the umlauts /9/ ("plötzlich"), /2:/ ("blöd"), /Y/ ("hübsch"), and /y:/ ("süß"). The schwa /6/ occurs at the end of German words ("besser") or as diphthong in all combinations with vowels and a following "r" like in "Tier", "Haar" or "Berg". Common vowels in both languages are besides /E/ (see above): /I/ ("pit", "Sitz"), /i:/ ("ease", "Lied"), /U/ ("put", "Schutz"), and /u:/ ("loose", "Blut") as well as the schwa

---

[2]Americans and some Britons use /E/ instead, like in German "Bett"

English	aI (rise), aU (rouse), OI (noise)
British Eng.	@U (nose), I@ (fears), e@ (stairs), U@ (cures)
American Eng.	oU (nose)
German	aI (Eis), aU (Haus), OY ("Kreuz")
	i:6 (Tier), I6, y:6, Y:6, e:6,...

Table 2.2: Diphthongs in English and German.

/@/ ("another", "bitte"), although the positions in Fig. 2.1 are sometimes slightly different. However, small distances are not exactly represented in Fig. 2.1 and are not relevant in order to detect far distant mispronunciation of non-native beginners in the present thesis.

The diphthongs /aI/ ("rise", "Eis") and /aU/ ("rouse", "Haus") can be found in both languages. Similar diphthongs in English and German are /OI/ and /OY/ in "noise" and "Kreuz", respectively. Some diphthongs can be only observed in English[3]: /@U/ (AE[4]: /oU/) in "nose", /eI/ in "raise", and for BE /I@/ ("fears"), /e@/ ("stairs"), and /u@/ ("cures")[5]. An overview of existing diphthongs in English and German can be found in Tab. 2.2.

A speech recogniser for non-native English should not only be able to recognise all English phones; it should also be able to deal with phones from the speaker's mother tongue in order to detect pronunciation errors. In Bonaventura et al. [Bon00b] it is recommended to train acoustic models for a sufficiently rich set of phonetic symbols, more than actually used in the ISLE system (cf. Sect.2.3). There, models for phonemes that relate to German umlauts were added, as well as for /R/ and the German /U/. Other German phonemes were mapped to British ones: /A/ ← /a:/, /Q/ ← /O/, /V/ ← /a/, /e/ ←/e:/, /@U/ ← /o:/, /OI/ ← /OY/, and /tS/ ← /x/. In the next section we consider pronunciation errors which are mappings (→) from the correct English pronunciation to a wrong one.

2.1.2   Germans Speaking English

Typical pronunciation errors of non-native English from German speakers are described in [Grz, Dre85, Bie02, Bon00b]. An overview of the reported pronunciation mistakes and further typical phone confusions investigated in [Her99b, Tep05b] is given in Tab 2.3. The function that defines the rule based error i is denoted as e_i.

The survey in Dretzke [Dre85] investigates which frequent mistakes are rated as objectionable by native speakers. First, in German only unvoiced consonants can be found at the end of a word. Consequently, terminal devoicing is observed when Germans speak English ($e_1 - e_3$, e_{13}, e_{14} in Tab 2.3); "feed" and "peas" are often pronounced as "feet" and "piece". Even final /N/ is sometimes pronounced as [Nk] (e_5). Further, mispronunciation occurs for phones that are rare in German or do not exist at all. Those are primarily /T/ and /D/ that

---

[3]Albeit /@U/ is not observed in standard German, it arises from /o:/ through diphthongisation in some regional dialects, e.g. in the Upper Palatinate

[4]only notational difference

[5]AE: /fIrz/, /stErz/, /kjUrz/

pronunciation error			example	pronunciation error			example
e_1:	/..b/	→	[..p]	cab	e_{15}:	/Z/	→	[S]	pleasure
e_2:	/..d/	→	[..t]	feed	e_{16}:	/dZ/	→	[tS]	age
e_3:	/..g/	→	[..k]	big	e_{17}:	/v/	→	[f]	give
e_4:	/g/*	→	[dZ]	anger	e_{18}:	/w/	→	[v]	what
e_5:	/..N/	→	[..Nk]	song	e_{19}:	/v/	→	[w]	very
e_6:	/Ng/	→	[N]	finger	e_{20}:	/{/	→	[E]	bat
e_7:	/r/	→	[R]	right	e_{21}:	/I/***	→	[aI]	river
e_8:	/D/	→	[s]	mother	e_{22}:	/0:/	→	[@U]	bought (BE)
e_9:	/D/	→	[z]	they	e_{23}:	/Q/	→	[0:]	office (BE)
e_{10}:	/T/	→	[s]	think	e_{24}:	/Q/	→	[@U]	produce (BE)
e_{11}:	/s/**	→	[z]	said	e_{25}:	/V/	→	[a]	but
e_{12}:	"sch"	→	[S]	scheme	e_{26}:	/V/	→	[@]	cut
e_{13}:	/..z/	→	[..s]	peas	e_{27}:	/@U/	→	[o:]	toast
e_{14}:	/..Z/	→	[..S]	garage	e_{28}:	/I@/	→	[i:]	hearing

Table 2.3: Rules e_i to generate pronunciation error i. Mapping of correct pronunciation onto wrong pronunciation; overview from [Grz, Dre85, Bie02, Bon00b, Her99b, Tep05b]. (⋆) unless /g/ is followed by a front vowel; (⋆⋆) only for speakers from northern Germany; (⋆⋆⋆) if /I/ is between consonants.

are often substituted by [s] (e_8 – e_{10})[67]. The English /r/ is wrongly pronounced as [R][8] as defined by e_7. The semi-vowel /w/ cannot be found in the German language at all; it is replaced with the fricative [v]. Due to overgeneralisation, even /v/ can be mispronounced as [w] (e_{18}, e_{19}). /Ng/ like in "finger" or "English" does not exist in German; it is often pronounced as [N] like in "singer" (e_6). Since /Z/ and /dZ/ are scarcely to be found in German words, they are often pronounced as [S] and [tS] (e_{15}, e_{16}).

Distances between vowels in the vowel space are shown in Fig 2.1. In [Grz] the following possible confusions are pointed out (e_{20}, e_{23}, e_{25}): [{] sounds for German similar to [E], [Q] similar to [0:], and [V] to [a]. /@U/ might be wrongly pronounced as [o:] (e_{27}). In German, initial vowels are preceded by a glottal stop (/?aNst/: "Angst") but never in English. Last but not least in the survey [Dre85], natives favour the weak-forms e.g. "an" [@n] ∼ [n] or "to" [tU] ∼ [@] that are standard English but not used by most Germans.

Biersack [Bie02] compares in her M.A.-thesis systematic pronunciation mistakes. Recordings of six German students of English language and literature are phonetically analysed and compared with six native speakers. Differences in the pronunciation are discussed and exemplified with spectrograms. The author investigates differences between

---

[6] Commercial of a language school in German TV: "Mayday, mayday, [...] we are sinking!" - German coast guard, slightly absent-minded: "Hello [...] what are you s[instead of th]inking about?"

[7] A substitution with [t] and [d] or [f] and [v] would be more tolerable for natives [Grz].

[8] The recordings of the data described in Chap. 4 were made in southern Germany, thus [r] is pronounced and not the northern German [R]; to discriminate the corresponding phoneme from the English phoneme in "wrong", we rename it to /R/.

dark [l] and clear [l] (cf. Sect. 2.1.1) and spectral qualities of English /e/ and /{/ in "bed", "bet", and "bat": The phone in the utterances of Germans is similar to the German /E/ and in all cases closer to /e/ than to /{/ (e_{20}). Further, e_6 is investigated. In read English, reduction and *linking* is observed. For example, "for your" in the sentence "...you normally use for your coffee" is pronounced as [fOjO] or [fOrjU] by the German speakers and as [fjO] by the natives. Often *elision* of /@/ occurs, like in "entering" (/ent@rIN/ → [entrIN]); however, this is e.g. not allowed in "London" /lO:nd@n/. In "where it is" [wE:rItIz] the linking /r/ is important. For Germans, however, the linking between the last two words is a bigger problem and a glottal stop is wrongly inserted ([It?Is]). Further examples can be found in Delmonte [Del00]. He addresses *homorganic stop deletion* ("you want some" [ju:wQns@m]) and *palatalisation* that affects /t/, /d/, /s/, and /z/ ("meet you": [mi:tSj@]).

In the phonetic transcription of the ISLE database, Bonaventura et al. [Bon00b] observed besides e_6, e_{18}, e_{19} the following pronunciation mistakes of Germans: /s/ is confused with [z] in "said" (e_{11})[9] , and /Q/ with [@U] in "produce" (e_{24}). Other mistakes were to pronounce silent letters "b" or "p" e.g. "thumb" as [TVmb] or "pneumatic" as [pnOIm{tIk], where in the latter example additionally "pneu" is pronounced like a German syllable.

In [Bon00a], Bonaventura et al. describe pronunciation rules like e_2, e_8, e_{10}, e_{16}, e_{18} in Tab. 2.3. Additionally it was found that diphthongs are often realized as one long single sound (cf. e_{27}). Another example is /I@/ → [i:] in "hearing" (e_{28}). "Anger" might be pronounced as [eIndZ@]. This is an overgeneralisation of the rule that "g" is spoken as [dZ] (e_4) when followed by a front vowel like in "George". In "river", /I/ is mispronounced as [aI] (e_{21}). The grapheme sequence "sch" is incorrectly pronounced as [S] ("scheme", e_{12}). In the framework of ISLE, Herron et al. [Her99b] automatically detect nine different pronunciation mistakes, among them the error /O:/ → [@U] (e_{22}). Tepperman et al. [Tep05b] investigate on the same corpus e.g. /v/ → [f] (e_{17}) and /V/ → [@] (e_{26}).

Tab 2.3 shows 29 possible rules for mispronunciation from the literature. Many further rules can be imagined. Further publications are available for other languages than German, e.g. Italians learning English [Bon00b] or people learning Dutch [Tru05]. In the next section approaches to *automatically detect* wrong pronunciation are described.

2.2   State-of-the-Art

Several approaches to automatically assess non-native speakers' pronunciation will be summarised in this section. In some approaches mispronounced words or phones are detected (binary rating), whereas in other approaches marks are given, either on a continuous or on a discrete scale. Few approaches additionally give a diagnosis of *what* is spoken wrongly and *how* to correct it. The performance of all these approaches has to be checked by comparing the automatic result with expert ratings. First, measures for the assessment of ratings are summarised; then approaches for automatic scoring will be discussed.

---

[9]This confusion, however, is only expected in northern Germany. The German partner in ISLE was in Hamburg.

2.2.1 Evaluation Measures

To measure the correctness of an automatic evaluation scoring, it has to be compared with the *ground truth*. In the case of pronunciation scoring, the latter is not immediately given. To get an objective reference, experts like e.g. teachers, native speakers, or phoneticians have to be consulted. Different criteria are evaluated, e.g. fluency, speech rate, segmental quality, and overall pronunciation in [Cuc00b] or rhythm in [Suz04]. A reference rating that approximates the ground truth is e.g. given by the average of the ratings from many experts. Usually, even human experts are far away from an agreement of 100%. However, very different kinds of disagreement can occur: Strong deviations are observed, if one expert marks a spoken word or sentence as wrongly and the other as correctly pronounced; weak disagreement occurs, if two adjacent values on a scale of discrete marks are chosen, possibly also systematically higher or lower scores. The agreement between different raters of the data that has been recorded in the context of this thesis (Chap. 4) will be analysed in Chap. 6. Here, the reliability of each expert will be analysed. The inter-rater reliability will be measured in terms of correlation, with the Cohen κ, the Krippendorff α, and the classification rate. The different measures will be explained in the following after a short introduction of different correlation coefficients. The standard deviation of a random variable X_r that represents the ratings of expert r is defined as

$$\sigma_r = \sqrt{E((X_r - E(X_r))^2)} = \sqrt{E(X_r^2) - E(X_r)^2} \tag{2.1}$$

where $E(X_r)$ is the expectation. The domain of X_r is $\mathcal{M} \subseteq \mathbb{R}$. It is the set of possible ratings and is typically a finite set, e.g. $\mathcal{M} = \{x \in \mathbb{N} | 1 \leq x \leq 6\}$, the six marks used in German schools, or $\mathcal{M} = \{1.0, 1.3, 1.5, 1.7, 2.0, 2.3, 2.7, \ldots, 6.0\}$ if also intermediate marks are used[10].

The Pearson Correlation Coefficient [Fer71, p.101]. To compare two ratings X_r and X_l the correlation[11]

$$\rho(X_r, X_l) = \frac{\text{cov}(X_r, X_l)}{\sigma_r \sigma_l} \tag{2.2}$$

can be used that measures the linear relation between two random variables X_r and X_l, where the covariance is defined as

$$\text{cov}(X_r, X_l) = E[(X_r - E(X_r)) \cdot (X_l - E(X_l))] = E(X_r \cdot X_l) - E(X_r) \cdot E(X_l). \tag{2.3}$$

As the true distribution of X_r and X_l is unknown, the correlation is estimated from samples: the vector $\boldsymbol{x}^{(r)} \in \mathcal{M}^N$ contains a set of N measurements $x_i^{(r)}, i = 1 \ldots N$ of X_r, e.g. the ratings of the rater r for all samples i. $\rho(\boldsymbol{x}^{(r)}, \boldsymbol{x}^{(l)})$ is calculated similar as in Eq. 2.2, however, the sample correlation and the sample standard deviation are used [Fer71, p. 61]. $\rho(\boldsymbol{x}^{(r)}, \boldsymbol{x}^{(l)}) = 0$ means that there is no linear relation between r and l; they are uncorrelated in terms of the Pearson correlation. $|\rho(\boldsymbol{x}^{(r)}, \boldsymbol{x}^{(l)})| = 1$ shows that there exists a linear function that exactly maps each rating from r onto the respective rating from l.

---

[10]In schools, often replaced with $\mathcal{M} = \{1, 1\text{-}, 1\text{-}2, 2+, 2, 2\text{-}, \ldots, 6\}$

[11]In the literature, often r is used to denote the Pearson correlation; in this thesis ρ is used instead.

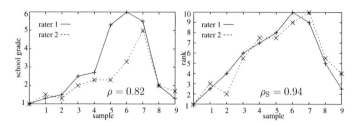

Figure 2.2: Pearson correlation (left) and correlation for the rank order after Spearman (right).

The Spearman Rank Correlation [Fer71, p. 303]. It may be the case, that the data is graded on an ordinal scale. Now, $\mathcal{M}$ comprises all possible grades. However, between the elements of the set $\mathcal{M}$ only relations $<$, $=$, or $>$ are defined, but it is not possible to make any assertion concerning the distance of the elements. The rating is not any more metric, but categorial. This is true for school grades where e.g. mark 2 is worse than mark 1 but the distance cannot be interpreted as being the same as the distance between mark 4 and mark 3. In this case, the Spearman rank correlation is used instead of the Pearson correlation coefficient. The data is first converted into ranks and then the correlation for the rank order is calculated according to Eq. 2.2. For instance, the sequence $(3, 4, 7, 8)$ and the sequence $(1, 2, 5, 9)$ are both mapped onto the ranks $(1, 2, 3, 4)$. The ratings $(11, 21, 19, 15, 19)$ are mapped onto $(1, 5, 3.5, 2, 3.5)$ since in the case of tied ranks, where certain data values are equal, the average rank is assigned (here 3.5 and 3.5 instead of 3 and 4 for the two occurrences of 19). The Spearman correlation will be denoted in the following as ρ_S[12]. An example is illustrated in Fig. 2.2.

Reliability. In Linn et al. [Lin95], and in the "Assessment Handbook" [Mer95] the quality of assessment in teaching is analysed with statistical measures. The reliability [Fer71, p. 365] measures the consistency or stability of the ratings of a single expert. If a rating $X_r = X_r^t + X^e$ consists of the true rating X_r^t of teacher r and an error X^e, the reliability is defined as

$$\text{rel}_r = \frac{(\sigma_r^t)^2}{\sigma_r^2}. \tag{2.4}$$

Estimates of the reliability, in particular of the consistency of the testing procedure, can be obtained e.g. with the *split-half* approach or the *Cronbach* α, that will be explained in the following paragraphs. These methods are used to evaluate the consistency of a test where the test score is the sum of the scores from several items. If all items of the test (testlets) have a high correlation, they measure the same attribute, and the reliability of

---

[12]In the literature, often r is used for the Pearson correlation and ρ for Spearman

the test is high. The reliability (and the correlation between testlets) is low, if the items measure different attributes or if the measurement is erroneous.

In the context of this thesis, test means evaluating the pronunciation of a speaker with the help of a rater r. The testlets are the spoken words that measure the attribute good/bad pronunciation; each speaker has to read the same set of N_{testlet} words. If the testlets do not correlate at all, they measure different things. In this case some testlets do not measure the goodness of the pronunciation, which means that the test based on the ratings of r is little or not reliable.

The Split-Half Reliability   [Fer71, pp. 366]. Let $\boldsymbol{X}_{\text{testlet}}^{(r)}$ be a matrix with $Z \times N_{\text{testlet}}$ ratings of an arbitrary but fixed rater r. Each row j represents a testlet ($j = 1, \ldots, N_{\text{testlet}}$) and contains Z ratings (evaluating e.g. Z speakers). The test itself is the combination of the testlets: $\boldsymbol{x}_{\text{test}}^{(r)}$ contains the $i = 1, \ldots, Z$ test results, where component i is the sum of the elements in the i-th column of $\boldsymbol{X}_{\text{testlet}}^{(r)}$.

The reliability of this test and the expert r can be calculated with the split-half approach by dividing the testlets into two sets that are equivalent in content and difficulty. Often, the testlets are divided in even and odd numbered items. Let $\boldsymbol{x}_{\text{test}}^{(r)-}$ contain the Z test results, where component i is the sum of the $N_{\text{testlet}}/2$ odd elements in the i-th column of $\boldsymbol{X}_{\text{testlet}}^{(r)}$, and let $\boldsymbol{x}_{\text{test}}^{(r)+}$ contain the Z test results, where component i is the sum of the $N_{\text{testlet}}/2$ even elements. Then the correlation $\rho(\boldsymbol{x}^{(r)+}, \boldsymbol{x}^{(r)-})$ measures the reliability. Usually the *Spearman-Brown formula* [Fer71, p. 367]

$$\rho_{\text{SB}}(\boldsymbol{x}^{(r)+}, \boldsymbol{x}^{(r)-}) = \frac{2\rho(\boldsymbol{x}^{(r)+}, \boldsymbol{x}^{(r)-})}{1 + \rho(\boldsymbol{x}^{(r)+}, \boldsymbol{x}^{(r)-})} \tag{2.5}$$

is applied. The *Kuder-Richardson formula 20* [Fer71, S.367] is equivalent to the split-half approach on all possible splittings. However, it allows only binary ratings (e.g. wrongly/correctly pronounced). A generalisation for arbitrary ratings is the *Cronbach* α [Lin95, S. 89].

The Cronbach α**.**   The most common index to measure reliability was defined in 1951 by Cronbach [Cro51]. Again, it measures the reliability of a test that is based on N_{testlet} testlets and evaluated by an arbitrary but fixed rater r. It is

$$\alpha = \frac{N_{\text{testlet}}}{N_{\text{testlet}} - 1} \cdot \left(1 - \frac{\sum_{j=1}^{N_{\text{testlet}}} \left({}_{\text{testlet}}\sigma_r^j \right)^2}{{}_{\text{test}}\sigma_r^2} \right) \tag{2.6}$$

where ${}_{\text{testlet}}\sigma_r^j$ is the standard deviation of the testlet j calculated from the elements of the j-th row of $\boldsymbol{X}_{\text{testlet}}^{(r)}$. ${}_{\text{test}}\sigma_r$ is calculated from $\boldsymbol{x}_{\text{test}}^{(r)}$. Values of α are equal or smaller than 1. The Cronbach α measures the reliability of the test based on one expert's gradings. Next, evaluation measures for the *inter-rater* reliability are discussed.

Inter-Rater Correlation. In the following paragraphs, the agreement and consistency between two or more human experts will be analysed. The same measures can obviously also be applied for the assessment of the agreement of an automatic system and a human expert. This means, that the *decoder* of a speech signal with the encoded information of wrong or correct pronunciation is in one case a human expert and in the other case a machine.

To calculate this inter-rater reliability, a common measure is again the correlation $\rho(\boldsymbol{x}^{(r)}, \boldsymbol{x}^{(l)})$ between raters r and l. For R raters the open correlation [Neu00] of rater r is defined as

$$\rho(\boldsymbol{x}^{(r)}) = \rho\left(\boldsymbol{x}^{(r)}, \frac{1}{R-1}\sum_{l \neq r} \boldsymbol{x}^{(l)}\right). \tag{2.7}$$

Rater r is compared with the mean of all other experts. Using the Spearman correction for attenuation formula [Fer71, p. 370]

$$\rho_{\text{cor}}(\boldsymbol{x}^{(r)}, \boldsymbol{x}^{(l)}) = \frac{\rho(\boldsymbol{x}^{(r)}, \boldsymbol{x}^{(l)})}{\sqrt{\text{rel}_r \cdot \text{rel}_l}} \tag{2.8}$$

the correlation can be normalised with each rater's reliability to get rid of measurement errors (cf. Eq. 2.4). In [Wit00] the correlation ρ_{Witt} is calculated only for units that are rejected by at least one rater.

The Cohen κ. In the following, we claim $\mathcal{M} \subset \mathbb{R}$ to be a finite set that consists of $\text{card}(\mathcal{M}) =: K$ labels or marks. In the context of classification (cf. Sect. 3.1) $k \in \mathcal{M}$ is the common label of all units belonging to the same class. Since there is a one-to-one mapping between classes and their labels, label k and class k are used synonymously.

When measuring the agreement between raters, one could simply count the number of cases where all raters have assigned identical labels. κ takes additionally into account the percent agreement that would be predicted by chance P_c. The observed percent agreement of R raters for K classes is denoted as P_o. Cohen [Coh60] introduced 1960 the formula[13] in terms of P_c and P_o which can be rewritten to

$$\kappa = \frac{P_o - P_c}{1 - P_c} = 1 - \frac{\bar{P}_o}{\bar{P}_c} \tag{2.9}$$

using the disagreement probabilities $\bar{P}_o = 1 - P_o$ and $\bar{P}_c = 1 - P_c$. The value of κ is zero, if the observed agreement is equal to chance ($P_o = P_c$), and 1 if P_o is 100 %. This measure originally has been defined for two rater r and l ($R = 2$) and for $K = 2$:

$$\kappa^{(r,l)} = \frac{P_o^{(r,l)} - P_c^{(r,l)}}{1 - P_c^{(r,l)}} \tag{2.10}$$

---

[13]Formulas to estimate the observed agreement and the chance agreement for the case with 2 raters will be presented in Eq. 2.12 and 2.13

For arbitrary numbers K, Fleiss et al. [Fle69] introduced 1969 the weighted κ, where the level of agreement between labels $c, k \in \mathcal{M}$ is weighted with $\omega_{c,k}$ [Kru99, pp 6-7]. Possible weightings after Cicchetti [Cic72] are

$$\omega_{c,k} = 1 - \left| \frac{c-k}{K-1} \right| \quad \text{or} \quad \omega_{c,k} = 1 - \left(\frac{c-k}{K-1} \right)^2. \tag{2.11}$$

For the original Cohen κ the weighting equals 1 for $c = k$ and 0 else. Let now $n_{ck}^{(r,l)}$ be the number of units that are labelled with c by rater r and with k by rater l and $n_c^{(r)}$ (total number of items labelled with c by r) and $n_k^{(l)}$ the marginal sums. Then the estimation of the observed agreement $\hat{P}_o^{(r,l)}$ for two raters r and l is

$$\hat{P}_o^{(r,l)} = \frac{1}{N} \sum_{c=1}^{K} \sum_{k=1}^{K} n_{ck}^{(r,l)} \omega_{c,k} \tag{2.12}$$

and the agreement by chance between two raters is calculated using a-priori probabilities $n_c^{(r)}/N$ calculated over N units

$$\hat{P}_c^{(r,l)} = \frac{1}{N^2} \sum_{c=1}^{K} \sum_{k=1}^{K} n_c^{(r)} n_k^{(l)} \omega_{c,k}. \tag{2.13}$$

For $R > 2$ raters, $\hat{P}_o^{(r,l)}$ and $\hat{P}_c^{(r,l)}$ are averaged over all $R(R-1)/2$ pairs of raters. Finally, κ after Davies and Fleiss [Dav82] is defined as

$$\kappa = \left[\sum_{r=1}^{R} \sum_{l=1, l \neq r}^{R} (1 - \hat{P}_c^{(r,l)}) \cdot \kappa^{(r,l)} \right] \Big/ \left[\sum_{r=1}^{R} \sum_{l=1, l \neq r}^{R} (1 - \hat{P}_c^{(r,l)}) \right] \tag{2.14}$$

in [Kru99, p. 12]. Inserting Eq. 2.10 in Eq. 2.14 we obtain

$$\kappa = \left[\sum_{r=1}^{R} \sum_{l=1, l \neq r}^{R} \hat{P}_o^{(r,l)} - \sum_{r=1}^{R} \sum_{l=1, l \neq r}^{R} \hat{P}_c^{(r,l)} \right] \Big/ \left[\frac{R(R-1)}{2} - \sum_{r=1}^{R} \sum_{l=1, l \neq r}^{R} \hat{P}_c^{(r,l)} \right] \tag{2.15}$$

for multiple raters. The structure of this equation is similar to Eq. 2.9.

The Cohen κ goes along with several disadvantages. It is not possible that raters grade only part of the data; all data has to be rated by all R experts. The κ-paradox is addressed in [Fei90, Kut03]:

- Even if $\sum_{k=1}^{K} n_{kk}^{(r,l)}$ is constant, a different distribution of $n_{kk}^{(r,l)}$ over all classes k causes different a-priori probabilities $n_k^{(r)}/N$, and consequently different κ.

- If the distribution of the marginals $n_k^{(r)}$ differs across raters, κ is greater than in the case of identical marginals across raters.

- The chance agreement is subtracted even for $P_o = 0$ which results in a negative κ

A solution to the κ-paradox for the unweighted case is formulated by Kutschmann et al. [Kut03]:

$$P_{c,ney}^{(l,r)} = \frac{1}{N^2} \sum_{k=1}^{K} \left(n_{kk}^{(r,l)} \right)^2 \tag{2.16}$$

Here, only this part of the chance agreement P_c is considered, that is also part of the observed agreement.

The Krippendorff α. The definition of α_{krip} [Kri03, Kri05] is identical to the definition of κ (Eq.2.9, right). However, now the calculation of n_{ck} includes all raters; it is the number of units rated by any rater r with c and by any other rater l with k. Consequently, the n_c and the a-priori probabilities n_c/N of label c are not rater-dependent any more. This approach also works if for some units labels of some raters are missing. Given the number of raters R^i for unit i and the rating $x_i^{(r)}$ for unit i from rater r, then

$$n_{ck} = \sum_{i=1}^{N} \frac{\sum_{r=1}^{R} \sum_{l=1,l\neq r}^{R} \chi_c(x_i^{(r)}) \chi_k(x_i^{(l)})}{R^i - 1} \tag{2.17}$$

with $\chi_c(x) = 1$ if $x = c$ and 0 else. With the marginal sums $n_c = \sum_k n_{ck}$ and $n = \sum_c n_c$, Krippendorff defines

$$\alpha_{krip} = 1 - \frac{(n-1) \sum_{c=1}^{K} \sum_{k=c+1}^{K} n_{ck} \text{dist}(c,k)}{\sum_{c=1}^{K} \sum_{k=c+1}^{K} n_c n_k \text{dist}(c,k)}, \tag{2.18}$$

where $\text{dist}(c,k)$ stands for different distance measures. For ordinal data,

$$\text{dist}(c,k) = \left(\frac{n_c}{2} + \sum_{i=c+1}^{k-1} n_i + \frac{n_k}{2} \right)^2 \quad \text{for } c \neq k \quad \text{and } \text{dist}(c,k) = 0 \text{ else,} \tag{2.19}$$

is used. On page 18 in the paragraph "Spearman rank correlation", the ordinal data is first converted into ranks; if one class is observed more often than once, a tied rank is used. The effect is a larger distance to the adjacent ranks. In other words, the conversion into ranks is skipped, but higher a-priori probabilities of ranks i that lie in between c and k in Eq. 2.19 result in greater numbers n_i and greater distances $\text{dist}(c,k)$. A distance measure for metric data is $\text{dist}(c,k) = (c-k)^2$.

Classification Rate. If the reference consists of discrete ratings, the decoder, e.g. a human expert, can be evaluated by measuring the classification rate , the proportion of correctly classified elements (agreement percentage), or the F_1-measure [Lan98], as will be discussed in Chap. 3.1. However, these approaches become problematic if more than two classes are considered, e.g. for the discrete marks 1 to 6: a confusion of mark 1 and 6 would be punished in the same way as a confusion of 1 and 2. Therefore, [Mer95] proposes to count also adjacent classes as agreement. Teixeira et al. [Tei00] measure the deviation of ratings with the *error*

$$\text{err}(\boldsymbol{x}^{(r)}, \boldsymbol{x}^{(l)}) = \frac{1}{N \cdot D} \sum_{i=1}^{N} |x_i^{(r)} - x_i^{(l)}|, \qquad (2.20)$$

where D is the difference between the highest ($k_{\max}$) and lowest ($k_{\min}$) mark $k \in \mathcal{M}$ and $\boldsymbol{x}^{(r)} \in \mathcal{M}^N$ the set of ratings from rater r. Witt et al. [Wit00] use $1 - D \cdot \text{err}(\boldsymbol{x}^{(k)}, \boldsymbol{x}^{(l)})$ as *agreement*.

Further Measures. The *strictness* of a rater is the percentage of marked items. Witt et al. [Wit00] compare two ratings $\boldsymbol{x}^{(r)}$ and $\boldsymbol{x}^{(l)}$ with the absolute difference of both raters' strictness. In the same paper, the *phoneme correlation* is defined as the correlation between two *phone rejection statistics*. The phone rejection statistic for rater r is a vector where the number of rejections of phoneme p is counted in the pth component. In [Suz04], the root mean square error (RMS) is calculated between automatic score and human rating and compared with the standard deviation between raters. If ratings are not elements of a metric space, Steidl et al. [Ste05a] propose an *entropy based measurement*.

2.2.2 Approaches for Automatic Assessment

In many publications automatic pronunciation scoring has been addressed. Data was collected, databases were rated by human experts, and raters and automatic scoring were compared using measures as defined in Sect. 2.2.1. In the following, selected approaches from the literature are summarised. Some studies focus on text dependent scoring; there, possible mispronunciations are defined for a certain text in advance, and sometimes, additionally, recordings from natives and non-natives reading this very text are required. Text independent approaches are more flexible and can easily be adopted to new reading exercises. A phoneme based detection of pronunciation mistakes is a segmental analysis of pronunciation errors; in other works, word, sentence, or speaker based marking is focused on. Supra-segmental analysis usually takes prosody into account. Scores derived from acoustic models (e.g. by Viterbi alignment cf. Sect. 3.2.4) and prosodic scores describing the fundamental frequency or pitch (F_0), the energy, and durations can be used to evaluate the agreement with human ratings. In the following, these scores are denoted as S_i and can be used in terms of features for automatic classification (cf. Sect. 3.1).

Pronunciation scoring has been evaluated on data of various speaker groups with different proficiencies; children have been investigated in [Esk02, Par04, Ban03]. In most publication the target language is English; some are specialised on non-native speech from Japanese learners e.g. [Ber90, Imo00, Tei00, Suz04, Min04a, Yam05], Italian learners [Del00, Her99b], Germans [Men00], or Greeks [Mou06]. Other research focuses on the target language Dutch [Cuc00b, Tru05], French [Neu00], Japanese [Oht05], Spanish [Ber04], or Swedish [Lan98]. Few approaches use data with artificial pronunciation errors [Her99b, Wit97]: for the investigation of an error e_i ($A \rightarrow B$), correctly pronounced utterances are used but the transcription in the dictionary is changed ($B \rightarrow A$). A rough summary of the approaches that will be described in detail can be found in Tab. 2.4.

Text-Dependent Approaches. In early work in 1990 Bernstein et al. [Ber90] present an approach to score non-native learners using speech recognition technology. Best results are obtained by aligning utterances with sentence models trained on native data.

For vowel analysis, Rooney et al. [Roo93] compare formants with data collected from native speakers. The two features are the normalised formants $F_1 - F_0$ and $F_2 - F_1$[14]. In this approach a simple visualisation of the articulatory position for each uttered vowel similar to Fig. 2.1 can be given. The gender of the user however has to be known in advance.

In Herron et al. [Her99b, Men00] (ISLE-project, cf. Sect. 2.3) normalised patterns of energy, pitch, and duration over vocalic regions are compared with clusters of stressed and unstressed vowels. To detect phone level mispronunciation, in a first step errors are localised using a speech recogniser in forced alignment mode. Confidence scores are calculated from the acoustic likelihood $P(\boldsymbol{f}|q^{\mathrm{a}})$ of the acoustic observation $\boldsymbol{f}$ given the reference phone q^{a} and some kind of upper and lower bound: the output probability $\max_q P(\boldsymbol{f}|q)$ of the most likely model q and the likelihood $P(\boldsymbol{f}|\bar{q})$ given a background model $\bar{q}$. Using these three predictors, Gaussian classifiers are trained on different classes of phones like vowels, fricatives, etc. separately on correctly and incorrectly pronounced data. The likelihood ratio of the Gaussian classifiers trained on correct and incorrect data results in a confidence score; segments with low confidence are passed to the diagnosis module.

In the diagnosis module, a second, word based forced alignment is performed, in which models with expected errors that are frequently observed in the candidate's mother tongue are added to the recogniser. Since only one alternative pronunciation is considered in the demonstrator, which has to run in real time, and only for selected words, this approach is here ranked as text dependent.

To minimise the number of false alarms, while optimising the reading miscue detection using a speech recogniser, the choice of alternative pronunciations that are added to the recogniser was optimised at the Carnegie Mellon University [Ban03]. Improvement has been obtained by ignoring miscues when the target word is a function word and by adding truncated versions of each word to the recogniser's vocabulary. Additionally, errors that have been made by at least two children in the past, should be predicted by the system. However, since data with reading miscues is sparse, several criteria had to be defined which are used to classify the top n most appropriate regular words to be further added to the recogniser as possible substitutes of the target word. Those criteria are e.g. frequencies of and Levensthein distance [Lev66] between target and miscue word.

In both publications [Her99b, Ban03] predicted reading miscues are added into the lexicon; all reading miscues have to be assigned with some small n-gram probabilities within the language model. A special decoding scheme for the speech recogniser was

---

[14]This normalisation replaces VTLN (cf. Sect. 3.3.2) since the size of the fundamental frequency is correlated with the size of the vocal tract.

developed in [Hag05]. Reading miscues (mispronunciations, repetitions, insertions, deletions, filled pauses) are detected efficiently in [Li07] where for each text a specific language-model is built on-line and combined with a general garbage language model. No manual adjustments are required any more in advance if new texts are added to the tuition-software.

Prosodic analysis is focused on by Delmonte [Del00]. Economy students learning English imitate a master signal. On the word level syllable duration is analysed; on the utterance level stress is detected and further a stylised contour is calculated from prosodic activities like energy and fundamental frequency. A visual feedback allows the user to compare his utterance with the master utterance ("golden speaker"). Prosodic analysis that aims at a comparison of a student's and a teacher's signal is described by Bagshaw [Bag94].

Yamashita et al. [Yam05] calculate prosodic features describing the difference between pre-recorded native speech and the learner's utterance: Features comparing F_0, energy, and duration of both signals are combined using linear regression. Unnatural F_0 and energy patterns of Japanese learners of English are either extremely flat with little dynamic changes, or a simple concatenation of word-based patterns where F_0 and energy drop at every word boundary.

Phone Level, Text-Independent Approaches. For phone level assessment, Witt et al. [Wit00, Wit99] introduce the *Goodness of Pronunciation* (GOP) measure. If the orthographic transcription is known, the posterior probability $P(q^a|\boldsymbol{f})$ of the phone q^a given the acoustic observation $\boldsymbol{f}$ of length $\dim(\boldsymbol{f})$ is used to calculate

$$S_{\text{GOP1}} = \frac{1}{\dim(\boldsymbol{f})} \left| \log\left(P(q^a|\boldsymbol{f})\right) \right| = \frac{1}{\dim(\boldsymbol{f})} \left| \log\left(\frac{P(\boldsymbol{f}|q^a)P(q^a)}{\sum_q P(\boldsymbol{f}|q)P(q)} \right) \right| \quad (2.21)$$

$$\approx \frac{1}{\dim(\boldsymbol{f})} \left| \log\left(P(\boldsymbol{f}|q^a)\right) - \log\left(\max_q P(\boldsymbol{f}|q)\right) \right| \quad (2.22)$$

where the a-priori probabilities of all phones are assumed to be equal in Eq. 2.22. The sum over all phones q in the denominator is approximated with the maximum that is obtained using an unconstrained phone loop trained on native data (subtrahend in Eq. 2.22). The minuend is obtained from a Viterbi alignment. For the classification, global and phone dependent thresholds that are obtained from native speech or from expert ratings are investigated. Low S_{GOP1} is obtained, if the likelihoods $P(\boldsymbol{f}|q^a)$ and $\max_q P(\boldsymbol{f}|q)$ are identical, which indicates good pronunciation; in the case of poor pronunciation the minuend in Eq. 2.22 is smaller than the maximal likelihood of the phone recogniser and the absolute S_{GOP1}-values become large. An extension is the S_{GOP2} measure, which additionally penalises high probabilities of common errors. In [Wit97] it was further shown that monophone acoustic models yield best performance.

In Franco et al. [Fra99] the minuend in Eq. 2.22 is replaced with the log-likelihood obtained from a Gaussian mixture model (GMM) trained on wrongly pronounced phones, whereas the subtrahend is obtained from a GMM trained on correct native pronunciation

(S_{GOP3}). Earlier work showed the advantage of log-posterior scores over log-likelihoods as in Eq. 2.22 [Kim97]. Log-likelihood and posterior scores are further compared for phone level assessment by Langlais et al. [Lan98].

To compare native and non-native pronunciation, Eskenazi [Esk96] contrasted in first experiments the scores that are obtained from forced alignment. A further measure is the duration of a voiced segment in comparison to the preceeding segment. In a similar way also the number of pitch peaks and the average of the first cepstrum coefficient were analysed. In [Esk02], Eskenazi et al. compare the phone based detection of pronunciation errors for children when using different speech recognisers, trained on either adults or children data.

Truong et al. [Tru05] investigate the discrimination of phones that are typically mispronounced by learners of Dutch. The paper focuses on the classification of /x/ vs. /k/ after a segmentation using forced alignment; best results are obtained with an LDA classifier using 4 features: The rate-of-rise (ROR) that describes the slope of the energy, the energy 5 msec before and 10 msec after the maximum ROR and the normalised duration.

A new approach based on Hidden-Articulatory Markov Models (HAMM) is investigated by Tepperman and Narayanan [Tep05b]. HAMMs are applied in parallel e.g. to model lip separation (4 discrete categories) or the tongue tip (5 discrete categories). Per vowel, the average HAMM output is computed for each HAMM stream. These values are combined in a feature vector that is used to classify typical mispronunciation errors. Phonological features (articulatory features, but obtained from phonological labels rather than from articulatory measurements) are also investigated in [Sto06]; forced alignment is used and for phones with low posterior probability conclusions can be drawn regarding the way of articulation.

Sentence or Speaker Level, Text-Independent Approaches. In Cucchiarini et al. [Cuc00b] sets of sentences of about 30 sec length are analysed. The automatic scores are obtained from the total duration of speech plus pauses S_{Dur1} and the rate-of-speech (ROS) S_{ROS1} which is the number of speech segments per duration. Another score is similar to S_{GOP1}: the *likelihood ratio* S_{LR} is the difference of the log-likelihood score obtained from the forced alignment and the one from a phone recogniser using unigram or bigram phone language models. [Cuc00a] compares read speech and spontaneous speech; for the latter, only low correlations with expert ratings are obtained. Here, temporal characteristics of speech have been investigated: S_{ROS1}, S_{ROS2} (number of speech segments per duration without pauses), the phonation-time-ratio S_{PTR} (length of speech without pauses / total duration), and the numbers of pauses, their mean length, and the mean length of intervals between pauses.

Several scores for sentence level assessment are proposed by Neumeyer et al. [Neu00]. Using native acoustic models, first the log-likelihood score $\log P(\boldsymbol{f}|q_i^{\mathrm{a}})$ for the i-th phone is obtained from forced alignment. The final globally averaged score $S_{\mathrm{LikeliGlob}}$ is strongly dependent on the match of the longer phones. Therefore also a locally averaged score $S_{\text{LikeliLoc}}$ is introduced.

$$S_{\text{LikeliGlob}} = \frac{\sum_{i=1}^{N} \log P(\boldsymbol{f}|q_i^{\text{a}})}{\sum_{i=1}^{N} d_i} \quad \text{and} \quad S_{\text{LikeliLoc}} = \frac{1}{N} \sum_{i=1}^{N} \frac{\log P(\boldsymbol{f}|q_i^{\text{a}})}{d_i} \tag{2.23}$$

are computed over N segments of individual length d_i. $S_{\text{LikeliGlob}}$ should include silence, $S_{\text{LikeliLoc}}$ should exclude silence [Neu96]. Less influenced by spectral characteristics of the speaker or the channel is the normalised score

$$S_{\text{LikeliNorm}} = \frac{1}{N} \sum_{i=1}^{N} \frac{\log P(\boldsymbol{f}|q_i^{\text{a}}) - \max_q \log P(\boldsymbol{f}|q)}{d_i} \tag{2.24}$$

when computing $\max_q \log P(\boldsymbol{f}|q)$ with a context independent phone model. With a different derivation, Neumeyer et al. found a sentence score similar to the phone level score in Eq. 2.22. Another approach to reduce the influence of speaker and channel is the use of the log-posterior probability $\log P(q_i^{\text{a}}|\boldsymbol{f})$ in Eq. 2.23 ($S_{\text{Posterior}}$). Further scores are the accuracy S_{Acc} of a phone recogniser (cf. Sect. 3.2.1) trained on native speech data, the timing between syllables $S_{SylTime}$ (English is here regarded as stress-timed language), and the log-probability of observed durations after normalisation to compensate the rate-of-speech ($\bar{d}_i$). This score

$$S_{\text{Dur2}} = \frac{1}{N} \sum_{i=1}^{N} \log P(\bar{d}_i|q_i^{\text{a}}) \tag{2.25}$$

uses duration statistics obtained from native data. Best correlation with human experts has been obtained with $S_{\text{Posterior}}$ and S_{Dur2}. For the speaker level it was investigated, how many sentence scores have to be averaged to obtain good correlation with human raters. Combinations of several scores with neural networks or linear regression are investigated in Franco et al. [Fra00].

Since in the case of an unknown text no forced alignment is possible, in Moustroufas et al. [Mou06] an extension is described in which scores from two recognisers based on acoustic models $\boldsymbol{\lambda}_{\text{target}}$ trained on the target language and acoustic models $\boldsymbol{\lambda}_{\text{source}}$ trained on the source language, respectively, are compared.

$$S_{\text{CDiff}} = \log P(\boldsymbol{w}|\boldsymbol{f}, \boldsymbol{\lambda}_{\text{target}}) - \log P(\boldsymbol{w}|\boldsymbol{f}, \boldsymbol{\lambda}_{\text{source}}) \quad \text{and} \tag{2.26}$$

$$S_{\text{CNorm}} = \frac{\log P(\boldsymbol{w}|\boldsymbol{f}, \boldsymbol{\lambda}_{\text{target}})}{\log P(\boldsymbol{w}|\boldsymbol{f}, \boldsymbol{\lambda}_{\text{target}}) + \log P(\boldsymbol{w}|\boldsymbol{f}, \boldsymbol{\lambda}_{\text{source}})} \tag{2.27}$$

are based on the confidence or log-posterior score of the word sequence $\boldsymbol{w}$. Another measure compares in a similar way the log-likelihoods of two Gaussian mixture models.

Combinations of scores to evaluate learners of Japanese are investigated in Ohta and Nakagawa [Oht05], e.g. the accuracy S_{Acc2} of a syllable recogniser and its insertion, deletion, and substitution rate (cf. Chap 3.2.1) as well as scores similar to Eq. 2.22, Eq. 2.27, or $S_{\text{LikeliGlob}}$ in Eq. 2.23. Best combination to score non-natives learning Japanese was the posterior probability, the substitution rate, S_{Acc2}, and the standard deviation of mora lengths.

In a real time scoring system for the telephone (PhonePass cf. Sect. 2.3), Bernstein et al. [Ber04] measure rate-of-speech, pauses, stress, and additionally the latency of the response.

A large set of prosodic features is investigated for pronunciation scoring in Teixeira et al. [Tei00] and combined with scores like $S_{\text{Posterior}}$ and S_{Dur2}. The prosodic features describe the duration of pauses, words and vowels, lexical stress information, and pitch variation. Further, gender and ROS are used as features; the latter turned out to encode important information. The best combination of features includes posterior scores, duration, ROS, and segmental information, but no features containing supra-segmental information like pitch and lexical stress.

Park et al. [Par04] use phone, phrase, and word based prosodic and acoustic features to compare the test speaker with a knowledge base obtained from native speaker statistics.

The influence of phone level durations on sentence scoring is investigated by Suzuki et al. [Suz04]. The authors analyse the duration of sentences, words, pauses, and function words, as well as syllable duration, vowel, and consonant duration. It turned out, that vowels are more appropriate than consonants, weak vowels more than strong vowels, and that function words are more relevant than content words. The explanation is that English is a stress-timed language, and learners (Japanese in [Suz04]) with lower proficiency tend to not reduce the vowel duration of function words.

Minematsu [Min04b] presents a very different approach to judge non-natives by computing a structural representation of phones from a small set of utterances. This representation is compared with a native structure. This structure is a distance matrix in cepstrum space that is visualised as a tree-diagram. The distances between phones, however, should be invariant to non-linguistic influences like microphone and room (multiplicative distortion i.e. shift of the resulting cepstrum) or the length of the vocal tract (linear transformation i.e. multiplication with matrix in cepstrum space). A solution is a distortion of the space by measuring distances of Gaussian distributions of different phones with the Bhattacharyya distance measure [Bha43]. Minematsu compares likelihood scores, posterior scores, and structural distortion scores; further investigations are focused on the intelligibility [Min04a], vowel confusion, stress, and articulatory effort [Asa05].

Another aspect of correct pronunciation is the right intonation. Tepperman and Narayanan [Tep05a] investigate stress detection with prosodic features derived from syllable nuclei. Besides energy, duration, and F_0, features that describe the slope and the range of energy and F_0 are investigated. Linguistic rules to normalise vowel durations dependent on their context are applied. After classifying stress vs. non-stress, in each word the stressed syllable with best posterior probability is decided for as the primary stress. Imoto et al. [Imo00] used features computed from fundamental frequency, energy, and vowel duration for a syllable-based classification of strong and weak sentence stress.

Tab. 2.4 gives an overview of several approaches. Early approaches compare the learner with prerecorded data, several authors create additional acoustic models for expected mispronunciations, and many calculate scores from log-likelihood probabilities, log-posterior

[Ber90], [Roo93]	alignment with sentence models/prerecorded data
[Her99b], [Men00]	mispronunciation models, stress-detection (ISLE)
[Ban03], [Hag05], [Li07]	mispronunciation models, language modelling
[Del00], [Yam05]	prosody: comparison with golden speaker
[Wit00], [Wit99], [Wit97], . [Fra99], [Kim97], [Lan98]	$S_{GOP1}, S_{GOP2}, S_{GOP3}$ log-posterior, log-likelihood
[Esk96], [Esk02]	log-likelihood, duration, pitch, cepstrum
[Tep05b], [Sto06]	articulatory/phonological features
[Cuc00b], [Cuc00a] [Tru05]	$S_{Dur1}, S_{ROS1}, S_{ROS2}, S_{LR}, S_{PTR}$: duration, ROS, log-likelihood, phonation-time-ratio, pauses; duration, rate-of-rise
[Neu00], [Neu96], [Fra00]	$S_{LikeliGlob}, S_{LikeliLoc}, S_{LikeliNorm}, S_{Posterior}, S_{Acc}, S_{SylTime}$ S_{Dur2} log-likelihood, log-posterior, phone accuracy, duration
[Mou06]	S_{CDiff}, S_{CNorm} log-posterior, log-likelihood (here: unknown text)
[Oht05]	$S_{Acc2}, S_{LikeliGlob}$: syllable accuracy, substitution rate, log-posterior, log-likelihood, duration
[Ber04]	ROS, pauses, stress, latency of response
[Tei00], [Par04]	prosodic and segmental scores
[Suz04]	duration (words, function words, weak/strong vowels)
[Min04b], [Min04a], [Asa05]	structural representation
[Tep05a], [Imo00]	stress detection

Table 2.4: Literature overview of pronunciation scoring in the order of appearance (except [Tru05]) in the text.

probabilities, and prosodic information such as pitch, energy, duration, pauses, and rate-of-speech. New approaches are based on articulatory features or phone distances. Besides pronunciation, also stress is evaluated.

Further Aspects on Pronunciation Scoring. For a different application than CALL (a tutoring system on physics) Forbes-Riley and Litman found in [For05] significant correlations between prosodic features obtained from the student voice and a posttest score that rates the learning success of the student. [Kra04] analyses uncertainty of children and adults using audio and video. For some medical application, the word accuracy of a speech recogniser and prosodic features are used successfully to evaluate tracheoesophageal speech [Had07, Sch05] or children with a cleft lip or palate [Mai09, Mai06b, Mai06c, Mai06e].

2.3   Existing Systems

After the introduction of general approaches to score the pronunciation of children, in this section an overview of existing systems is presented. First, systems from other research projects including ISLE are described. Then, an overview of selected commercial systems available in German bookstores is given. A list of tuition systems is shown in Appendix C.

Pronunciation Tuition Systems.   Neri et al. [Ner03] give an overview of different components of CALL systems and the role of ASR technology. In [Ner02c, Ner03] the type of feedback that is provided by state-of-the-art CAPT systems is examined and a critical overview of various products is given. The student speech and a reference signal are often contrasted and displayed as wave form (impossible to extract information how to improve pronunciation), as spectrogram (not easily interpretable for students), or as a pitch graph, where additionally syllable length and energy are visualised (meaningful, but no segmental errors). The challenge in developing systems that give a diagnosis on segmental errors is to provide an appropriate scoring: a diagnosis on smaller segments with more specific feedback is likely to include more errors [Ner02b].

In the following a short overview of systems developed at different universities is given. The SLIM-system that addresses Italian economy students learning English is described in [Del00]. The system developed in the STAR-project (1990) is described in [Rus00]. At the Centre for Speech Technology of the KTH, Stockholm, the ARticulation TUtoR (ARTUR) is being developed [Gra05]. Besides speech recognition and an analysis of phone duration and stress, multimodal information is used to calculate relations between facial and vocal tract movements [Bes04]. As feedback the user's articulation and the correct one are contrasted using 3D models of the face and the vocal cord.

The CALL system *Parling* [Mic04] has been developed at the ITC-irst, Trento, and addresses children of a primary school (aged 8 – 11). Different tales can be read and listened to. The pupils can click on anchor words, then the entry of the pictorial dictionary appears. Now the learners can listen to the words in the dictionary and repeat them. Wrong pronunciation is rejected. Each story is associated with a different type of game (e.g. the Memory game) that helps the user memorising the story vocabulary. In Germany, at the TU Dresden the platform *OpenVOC* has been developed [Hof05]. The system AzAR[15] was developed at the same time and addresses east European speakers learning German[16].

There are three sites in the USA, which developed major systems that are also launched as products. At the Center for spoken Language Research, Colorado, the *Colorado Literacy Tutor*[17] is being developed. WriteToLearn[TM] automatically evaluates both writing skills and reading comprehension and is brought on the market by Pearson Knowledge Technologies[18]. An extension on read speech of children based on the SONIC speech recogniser is described in [Hag04]. Details on the Italian version of the system can be found in [Cos05].

---

[15]Automat zur Akzent Reduktion, cf. http://www.ias.et.tu-dresden.de/institut/jb2005.pdf
[16]Demo system of voice INTER connect GmbH http://voiceinterconnect.de
[17]http://www.colit.org/
[18]http://www.pearsonkt.com/

At SRI international the systems VILTS[TM] and Autograder[TM] have been developed[19]. The underlying algorithms are described in [Neu96, Kim97, Neu98, Fra99, Neu00, Fra00, Tei00]. The authors also hold several patents[20]. Currently, EduSpeak®[21] is launched by Speech@SRI. Another patent at SRI was invented by J. Bernstein[22]. He developed the automated English test *PhonePass* for the telephone[23]. The system was developed by *Ordinate* and is now distributed by *Versant*[TM] (In Germany: http://www.versanttest. de/). Several exercises (e.g. repeating, finding opposites, and answering short questions) have to be solved; in the end a grade is calculated (cf. [Ber04]).

Listen[24] (Literacy Innovation that Speech Technology ENables) is a reading tutor developed at the Carnegie Mellon University [Ban03]. At the same University, the *Fluency* pronunciation trainer was developed that is described by Eskenazi et al. [Esk98, Esk00]. It is based on the SPHINX II speech recogniser. To make the students active speakers, elicitation techniques are used. The question *"When did you meet her? (yesterday)"* is intended to be answered by the user with *"I met her yesterday"*. It is possible to predict the student's response to make speech recognition more robust. Wrong syllable duration (relative to the preceeding syllable) and wrong pronunciation are marked. There is an advice in written form, how to place the articulators for correct pronunciation as well as illustrations (sidecut and front of the head). The user can further listen to a reference speaker that is automatically selected to fit best to the user speech. The system is evaluated with students of different nationality. NativeAccent[TM] is a product of Carnegie Speech[25].

Interactive Spoken Language Education (ISLE). The ISLE-project[26] was a European research project that focused on non-native German and Italian speech from adults. It started in 1998 and ended in 2000. The academic partners were the Universities of Leeds, Milan, and Hamburg. The commercial partners were *Didael*[27] and the *Ernst Klett Verlag*[28]. The underlying HMM based speech recogniser was developed by *Entropic*[29]. Publications on pronunciation scoring and non-native speech recognition in ISLE are among others [Atw99, Her99b, Her00, Men00, Bon00a, Bon00b].

---

[19]http://www.speech.sri.com/projects/language_instruction.html

[20] Method and apparatus for automatic text-independent grading of pronunciation for language instruction (SRI 2000), Method and system for automatic text-independent grading of pronunciation for language instruction (SRI, 2001), Method and apparatus for language training (Minds and Technologies. Inc, 2001),

[21]http://www.speechatsri.com/products/eduspeak.shtml

[22]Method and apparatus for voice-interactive language instruction (SRI, 1997)

[23]Interview: http://www.eltnews.com/features/interviews/021_jared_bernstein.shtml)

[24]http://www.cs.cmu.edu/~listen/

[25]http://www.carnegiespeech.com/speech_products.html

[26]http://nats-www.informatik.uni-hamburg.de/~isle/

[27]http://www.didael.it

[28]http://www.klett.de

[29]1999 acquired by Microsoft

Data has been collected from 23 German and 23 Italian intermediate learners of English, annotated on the phone level (insertions, deletions, substitutions), and labelled with stress errors. The data is distributed via ELRA[30] and e.g. investigated in [Tep05a, Tep05b].

The ISLE system provides detailed feedback on what the user pronounced incorrectly and how to improve the pronunciation. "Question answering" is an exercise where the answer needs to be constructed from sets of pre-defined building blocks [Men00]. A low perplexity speech recogniser that is tolerant to non-native data and adapted to the user determines the correctness of the answer. Then, the system re-recognises the utterance with less tolerant models in forced alignment mode; low confidence scores indicate possible pronunciation errors [Her99b]. The diagnosis module selects the most severe errors and adds models for wrongly pronounced words to the speech recogniser. Those error candidates are created rule based, applying letter-to-phone and phone-to-phone rules that describe mispronunciations that are typical of the respective L1-group. The most likely error candidate and consequently the most likely mispronunciation rule is found using a further word based forced alignment step that allows alternative pronunciations. To reduce complexity in the real time demonstration system, the number of errors per word was limited to one [Men00]. This way, the actual phone confusion is detected and remapped to the orthographic transcription. The feedback is e.g. a highlighted "ea" in "cheaper" with the remark "That should sound like *media* and not like *else*". The student can click on the words "media" and "else" to hear it. Additionally the lexical stress (putting the stress on the right syllable of a word) is classified.

Neri, Cucchiarini, and Strik assert in their overview on available CAPT systems [Ner02b] that although the feedback design in ISLE seems to be satisfactory, the performance is rather poor. "[...] a system that does not have the ambition of telling the student to which sound his/her pronounced version corresponded is likely to make fewer errors than the ISLE system". Further it is criticised that typical errors of specific L1/L2 pairs have to be available and "that such a system is not able to handle unexpected, idiosyncratic errors that may be frequently made by some learners and that may be detrimental to intelligibility" [Ner02b, p. 3].

The market analysis at the beginning of the ISLE project has shown that available systems offer only limited feedback. The report [Atw99, p.9] states: "The market for multimedia software for use at home is also considered to have extremely high potential. ISLE fills this gap in the market, but must be implemented quickly [...]". A comparison between [Atw99] and the following survey shows that on the one hand more and more systems use ASR technology now, but on the other hand they have made no breakthrough yet.

Commercial Systems Available in Germany.   From the large amount of commercial systems only a short selection of systems available for German children learning English that include pronunciation training can be given. From the website of the Bavarian Ministry of Education[31], the Bavarian School-Server can be addressed. Here, information on available

---

[30]European Language Resources Association `http://catalog.elra.info`
[31]Bayerisches Staatsministerium für Unterricht und Kultus, `http://www.km.bayern.de`

software is given that is appropriate to be used in class[32]. A list including those systems is shown in Appendix C. It includes *Tell Me More* and *Lernvitamine Englisch* (cf. below) but also applications which use rudimentary speech technology (record and play) only. Software reviews on *Tell Me More* (French, Chinese, and Japanese system) and *TripplePlayPlus* are summarised in [Ner03]. The following systems have been tested by the author of this thesis. The *digital publishing* company[33] was founded in 1994 and provides English courses in several languages, in particular advanced education in companies; it is currently the market leader in Germany. Leader in other European countries is *Auralog*[34] which was founded 1987. Further, *Klett/Pons* and *Langenscheidt* are offering pronunciation training software. The Langenscheidt system is based on the speech recogniser *lingDIALOG* by LingCom[35].

- *Lernvitamine Englisch*[36] (digital publishing, Cornelson) and *Interaktive Sprachreise Englisch* (digital publishing) are based on *Intellispeech*: The learner can listen to his own speech and to a reference speaker. Both signals are shown and a score is calculated. "With *Intellispeech*, the learner can focus on matching native speech through comparisons with multiple male and female speakers. Intellispeech not only uses a phonemic database, but character feature sets to determine how well something was said in comparison to real speech. The result: The closer the learner's pronunciation is to that of native speakers, the higher the score. Continued use leads to a dramatic improvement in pronunciation" (from `http://www.digitalpublishing.de/english/`). Further speech recognition allows the selection of sentences, and a "voice pilot" reacts to some user commands if they start with the name of the virtual tutor "Tim, translate, please!". Barge in is detected automatically; no push-to-talk is necessary.

- *Tell Me More* and *Talk to Me* (Auralog, Cornelsen)[37]: S.E.T.S.® -technology (Spoken Error Tracking System, based on the Nuance speech recogniser[38]) allows localisation and correction of pronunciation errors. The speech signal of the user and a reference signal are displayed together with the pitch. A pronunciation score is calculated and the 3D animation shows the speech production. Some kind of dialogue is possible, since the user can select among predefined answers.

- *Der große Kurs für Anfänger Englisch* (Pons[39]). Sentences have to be read to train special phonemes. To train the "w", e.g. "I work in a bank" has to be read. If "w" is

---

[32]Bayerischer Schulserver,
`http://www.schule.bayern.de/unterricht/schulfaecher/Englisch/software_englisch.htm`
[33]digital publishing AG, Munich,`http://www.digitalpublishing.de/english/`
[34]Auralog SA, France,`http://www.auralog.com`
[35]`http://www.lingcom.de/`
[36]`http://www.lernvitamine.de/cgi/WebObjects/Lernvitamine`
[37]`http://www.abitz.com/cornelsen/tellmemore_englisch.php3`
[38]`http://www.nuance.com/`
[39]`http://www.pons.de/`

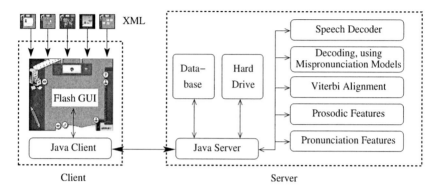

Figure 2.3: *Caller*-architecture: Computer assisted language learning from Erlangen.

mispronounced as fricative it is rejected very robustly. However, all other words in the sentence can be omitted or pronounced arbitrarily. "th" is discriminated from "s" but not from the fricative "f". Speech recognition is provided by the *Acapela* group[40].

The next section describes the software developed at the LME.

2.4 *Caller*: Computer Assisted Language Learning from Erlangen

The algorithms for pronunciation scoring presented in this thesis are integrated in *Caller* (**C**omputer **A**ssisted **L**anguage **L**earning from **Er**langen) together with other multimedia-based exercises designed for language learning. *Caller* is described in [Hes05, Hes06, Hac07a] and was developed and evaluated within a cooperation with a local grammar school (Ohm-Gymnasium Erlangen). The advantages of this system in comparison to commercial products are (i) that it is a client/server system, which can be accessed in class and from home, and which enables the teachers to monitor the students, (ii) that this client/server architecture allows to run complex newly developed scoring algorithms on the server (i.e. the algorithms that will be described in Chap. 5), which are based on the *LME* speech recogniser described in Chap. 3.2, and (iii) that all contents are defined in external xml-files that can easily be modified. Further, the modular concept of the system makes it easily extendable. This made a project possible, where at Ohm-Gymnasium some 11th grade students designed new exercises for the 5th grade. The current system implements several exercises from the text book [Hel03] which addresses students learning English in the first year (grade 5). The system is described in [Hac07b].

---

[40]http://www.acapela-group.com/

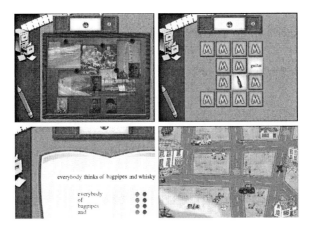

Figure 2.4: *Caller*, selected exercises: the listening test, the memory game, an analysis of the reading exercise, the maze.

The first version of *Caller* was a program that runs locally on a computer [Hes05]. It was applied in some English classes and was used for data collection. After this, the users were asked to answer some questionnaires about their impressions of the system. Version 2 is a client/server based system which is implemented in *Flash* and *Java*. Only a minimal installation is required locally on the clients to run the software. All exercises that are independent from speech input even run in a browser and require no installation at all. The architecture of *Caller* is shown in Fig. 2.3. All content is separated from structure, located on a web-server (xml-files), and loaded onto the clients dynamically. Also text, images and sound are loaded dynamically. Speech technology like a word recogniser and scoring algorithms run on a Linux-server, together with a database that contains e.g. user-information required for authentication or the users' progress and mistakes. The underlying client/server framework PEAKS (Program for the Evaluation of All Kinds of Speech disorders) was originally designed for a system to evaluate the speech of patients with speech disorder (e.g. with a cleft lip or palate) [Mai06a, Mai06b, Mai06c, Mai06e].

Besides the low effort to install the clients and the easy maintenance and update possibilities of the complex speech technology on the server, one of the greatest advantages of the client/server architecture is that students can access the system from home. Additionally, a control tool allows the teachers to log into the system in order to monitor the students' activities and look at the protocol of their mistakes that are stored in the database. All students' utterances are recorded, so that teachers can even listen to their spoken utterances. *Caller* is a language laboratory that can be used either in class or for homework and, in addition, has qualities of a "computer game" since a lot of *edutainment* is provided in some bonus exercises.

The Exercises.   *Caller* allows to define several chapters in `xml`-files. Each chapter consists of several exercises. Each of them has to be performed by the student, then he/she is allowed to play a bonus exercise. The student can collect points and an avatar (smiley) reacts positively or negatively depending on the user's input. In future, highscores of the best students will be shown on a website. Up to now, four *Flash*-modules are provided for the different exercises. The magnet board allows to drag and drop magnets (Fig. 2.4 top left), the desktop provides cards that can be used as file cards or game cards (Fig. 2.4 top right), the notebook (Fig. 2.4, bottom left) displays text and the "learnboy" (Fig. 1.1, right front) that has been designed like a Gameboy™ is an appropriate environment for the bonus games. Several of the exercises require speech input.

The listening test (Fig 2.4, top left) is practised on the magnet board. By clicking on people's pictures, they tell a story, what the region looks like, where they come from. Then the student has to drag the people to the picture of the respective countryside. In another exercise, the learner has to build sentences from words written on magnets (Fig 1.1, top left).

Playing the memory game (Fig 2.4, top right), the student has to turn any two cards face up. He succeeds if he turns up a word and the corresponding icon. If two cards are turned up which are not a pair, the player has to turn them face down again. In the spoken vocabulary test (Fig 1.1, top right), words written on file cards have to be translated. All words that are not correctly translated (or not recognised by the speech recogniser due to wrong pronunciation) have to be worked on again. Another written vocabulary test is found in the notebook environment. Now the user has to type the words to examine the correct spelling. In the notebook environment also the reading exercise is displayed (Fig 1.1, bottom centre), which is most interesting in the context of this thesis: The student has to read some sentences, then his/her pronunciation is analysed. The system marks words, phones or syllables that have been wrongly pronounced (Fig 2.4 bottom left). For the mispronounced words, the student now can listen to his own pronunciation and to a reference speaker. Currently, two bonus games are implemented. One allows the user to navigate a bouncing ball with voice commands through a maze and pass several obstacles (Fig 2.4, bottom right). Playing the other game, the user has to shoot off wrongly spelled words flying past (Fig. 1.1, right front). Firing at correct words causes negative scores.

There are many exercises which require speech input: the spoken vocabulary test, one bonus game, and the reading test. The student uses a head mounted microphone and starts the recording with a push-to-talk button. Alternatives to push-to-talk will be discussed in Chap. 9. On the server the recorded speech is analysed by a speech decoder (word recogniser) and several modules for pronunciation scoring as introduced in the next paragraph.

Architecture.   The client/server architecture is outlined in Fig. 2.3. The core of *Caller* is the server with speech technologies and a *MySQL*-database. From the client, different communication objects are transmitted to the server, e.g. to request a login, to request the turn-list for the current exercise, or to send the recorded audio data. On the server, the database is accessed, audio data is stored on the hard drive, and several speech recognition and analysis modules are invoked: the speech decoder or optionally a speech decoder based on additional mispronunciation models, which are modelling expected pronunciation errors (cf. Chap. 5), finds the most likely spoken word sequence (cf. Chap. 3). In the case of a reading exercise, additionally forced Viterbi alignment (cf. Chap. 3) is performed between the recorded utterance and the known word sequence the user had to read. Further modules for pronunciation scoring are based on pronunciation features and prosodic features (cf. Chap. 5).

In the database, user information, session information, exercise content, and user statistics can be found. The user information contains among others name, grade, and password. Passwords are transmitted and stored encrypted. A superuser-flag allows the teacher to monitor all activities of the specified class. Further, session information is stored in the database which maps a user to a unique session-ID to enable multi-user handling. The exercise content defines for each turn of the reading exercise the reference text, the vocabulary, and the language model that has to be used during recognition. With the *Caller GameBuilder* software, this data can be modified, when new exercises are created. Last but not least, the user statistics store all activities of a student, like references to the stored audio input, wrongly typed input, and the number of trials needed to complete an exercise. The teacher has access to all these statistics from the control tool.

Evaluation. 80 students have tested the language learning software in class. More than 70 % preferred speech input to keyboard input. 81 % liked the idea to work with the software at home whereas only 5 % disliked it. 67 % would train the same chapter more than two times. 79 % believe to have learned and improved somehow by using this software.

2.5 Summary

In the beginning of this chapter English and German phonemes were contrasted. Difficulties for Germans learners of English are terminal devoicing and the pronunciation of the unknown phones /D/, /T/, /w/, and /Ng/. The distance between vowels is shown in vowel space. /{/ is often incorrectly pronounced as /E/, /Q/ as /O:/, and /V/ as /a/.

State-of-the-art procedure to evaluate the agreement of raters or the agreement between automatic and human assessment is the Pearson correlation. If the data is graded on an ordinal scale, raters should be compared using the Spearman rank correlation. The Cronbach α measures the reliability of a rater; the Cohen κ and the Krippendorff α are used to evaluate the agreement between multiple raters. In both approaches the chance agreement is "subtracted".

Early work on automatic pronunciation scoring was published in 1990 [Ber90]. Various segmental features that can be obtained using speech recognition technology are investigated e.g. in [Wit00, Cuc00b, Neu00]. Further prosodic information is used in [Tei00, Suz04]. [Tep05a] employs prosody to classify the primary stress of a word. In newer approaches pronunciation scoring is performed with Hidden-Articulatory Markov Models [Tep05b] or a structural representation of distances in phoneme space [Min04a].

An overview of existing systems is given in Appendix C. ARTUR shows the correct pronunciation with 3D-models of the face, Fluency gives written advises and illustrations how to place the articulators. The Parling system has been developed for children. PhonePass is an automated English test on the telephone. ISLE addresses German and Italian adult learners. Mispronunciations are detected on the phone level and a diagnosis is given which phone has been uttered wrongly. This satisfactory feedback unfortunately turned out to be error-prone and does not handle unexpected pronunciation errors. Commercial systems are available e.g. by Auralog, Cornelsen, digital publishing, and Pons. At the LME, the system *Caller* has been developed. All contents can be dynamically modified in external `xml`-files. Only a minimal installation is required locally on the computer; speech recognition and scoring modules that will be described later in this thesis run on a server.

Chapter 3

Robust Classification and Speech Recognition

This chapter gives an overview of automatic classification and automatic speech recognition. The first section explains different classifiers and evaluation measures. Then, speech and phone recognition are described; here, in addition temporal context has to be taken into account. TRAP features are explained which can be used alternatively to the widespread MFCC features. In the last section difficulties in recognising children speech are addressed. Here, approaches from the literature are discussed and adaptation methods explained. Classification algorithms will be applied in Chap. 8 for automatic pronunciation scoring. Speech recognition for children and adaptation methods are subject of Chap. 7. The TRAP approach will be applied in this thesis for pronunciation scoring (Chap. 5 and Chap. 8).

3.1 Automatic Classification

The goal in automatic pattern recognition and analysis is to map a pattern f onto a class Ω_k. All classes Ω_k ($k = 1 \dots K$) have to be pairwise disjoint; the union $\bigcup_k \Omega_k$ is referred to as the field of problem. An example for a two class problem is the discrimination of correctly and wrongly pronounced words. To keep the formulae short and clear, in the following the class index k is used instead of Ω_k. After Niemann [Nie90], a classification system consists of the following modules: In a first step, the recorded signal f is *preprocessed*. Preprocessing comprises e.g. coding, normalisation or filtering. Then, *features* are extracted and stored in a vector c. *"Features of patterns of one class occupy a somewhat compact domain of feature space. The domains occupied by features of different classes are separated"* [Nie90, p.8]. The classification is the last step and will be described in this section in detail. It requires a preceding training phase and training data. Unsolved problems are to automatically find appropriate features for a specified field of problem. Manual work and inventive talent are necessary (cf. Chap. 5). It is further unsolved to find appropriate constituents of a complex problem. In the following, the optimal classifier is introduced, different classifiers that are used in this thesis are explained, and evaluation measures are discussed. Boosting is a meta-classifier that is explained at the end of this section.

3.1.1 Optimal Decision Rule

The optimal classifier is described in [Nie03]. Every classifier approximates the optimal classifier. In order to classify a feature vector $c \in \mathbb{R}^d$ with d components (features), a decision rule

$$\delta(k|c) \quad \text{with} \quad \sum_k \delta(k|c) = 1 \tag{3.1}$$

is applied that assigns c to a class k with a certain probability. $k = 0$ means, that the pattern is rejected. Let now be $p(k|l)$ the confusion probability (deciding for class k instead of class l) and r_{kl} the costs of this wrong decision. Then the risk of a decision rule is defined as

$$V(\delta) = \sum_k \sum_{l \neq 0} P_l p(k|l) r_{kl} \tag{3.2}$$

using the *priori probabilities* P_l. The optimal classifier is defined as the classifier which minimises the risk

$$
\begin{aligned}
V(\delta) &= \sum_k \sum_{l \neq 0} P_l \int_{\mathbb{R}^d} p(c|l) \delta(k|c) dc \quad r_{kl} \\
&= \int_{\mathbb{R}^d} \sum_k \left[\sum_{l \neq 0} r_{kl} P_l p(c|l) \right] \delta(k|c) dc \\
&= \int_{\mathbb{R}^d} \sum_k u_k(c) \delta(k|c) dc
\end{aligned}
\tag{3.3}
$$

with the test variables

$$u_k(c) = \sum_{l \neq 0} r_{kl} P_l p(c|l) \quad k = 0, 1, 2, \dots . \tag{3.4}$$

The optimal decision is the decision for the class whose test variable is minimal.

In the special case of a forced decision only classes $k > 0$ exist. If additionally a simple $(0,1)$-cost function with $r_{ll} = 0$ and $r_{kl} = 1$ for $k \neq l$ is employed, the calculation of the test variables is reduced to

$$u_k(c) = \sum_{l \neq 0, l \neq k} P_l p(c|l), \quad k = 1, 2, 3 \dots . \tag{3.5}$$

This term is minimised if the missing summand $P_k p(c|k)$ is maximum. Thus, the optimal classifier is defined through the decision rule

$$\delta(k|c) = \begin{cases} 1 & \text{if} \quad \bar{u}_k(c) := P_k p(c|k) = \max_l P_l p(c|l) \\ 0 & \text{else.} \end{cases} \tag{3.6}$$

The classifier based on this decision rule is the *Bayes classifier* or *maximum a posteriori* (MAP) classifier; it maximises the a posteriori probability

$$p(l|c) = \frac{P_l p(c|l)}{p(c)} \tag{3.7}$$

Since the denominator is independent of the class k it can be neglected in Eq. 3.6. Next, classifiers that approximate this optimal classifier are explained.

3.1.2 Classification Techniques

There are different types of classifiers that are distinguished [Nie90]. In statistical classification it is assumed that the class conditional densities $p(c|k)$ which are required for the calculation of the test variables u_k (cf. Eq. 3.4 and 3.5) can be modelled with a parametric family of densities, e.g. Gaussian densities. Distribution free classification does not require those assumptions; here, the discrimination function is estimated. Nonparametric classification hold for different families of densities but are memory and time consuming and not used in this thesis. The reason is that approaches like the n-nearest-neighbour classifier require all the training data to be kept in memory for the decoding process.

During the *learning* process the class conditional densities or the discrimination functions are estimated from the training data. For supervised training a class label (the ground truth) is required for each sample. Unsupervised learning algorithms are e.g. employed for the training of the codebook of a speech recogniser (cf. Sect.3.2). The classifiers used in this thesis which discriminate e.g. correct vs. wrong pronunciation and are introduced in the following are own implementations of the *LME*, except the package for neural networks.

The Gaussian Classifier. It is a statistical classifier that is based on the assumption that the data of each class k is approximately distributed normally. The distribution

$$p(c|k) = \mathcal{N}(c|\boldsymbol{\mu}_k, \boldsymbol{\Sigma}_k) \tag{3.8}$$

$$= |2\pi\boldsymbol{\Sigma}_k|^{-1/2} \exp\left(-\frac{(c - \boldsymbol{\mu}_k)^{\mathrm{T}}\boldsymbol{\Sigma}_k^{-1}(c - \boldsymbol{\mu}_k)}{2}\right) \tag{3.9}$$

of the feature vector c is modelled with one Gaussian density per class. The parameters that have to be determined e.g. using maximum likelihood estimation are the class conditional covariance matrices $\boldsymbol{\Sigma}_k \in \mathbb{R}^{d \times d}$ and the mean vectors $\boldsymbol{\mu}_k \in \mathbb{R}^d$ for each class k in d-dimensional feature space. Instead of maximising $\bar{u}_k = P_k p(c|k)$ from Eq. 3.6, it is faster and numerically more robust to maximise $2\ln\bar{u}_k$. From Eq. 3.9 and 3.6 we obtain

$$\bar{u}_k(c) = 2\ln P_k - \ln|2\pi\boldsymbol{\Sigma}_k| - (c - \boldsymbol{\mu}_k)^{\mathrm{T}}\boldsymbol{\Sigma}_k^{-1}(c - \boldsymbol{\mu}_k). \tag{3.10}$$

The last summand is the *Mahalanobis*-distance between samples c and the class centre $\boldsymbol{\mu}_k$. In Fig. 3.1, left, it is illustrated that the discrimination plane $\{c|\bar{u}_k(c) = \bar{u}_l(c)\}$ is polynomial of degree two; therefore this approach is also called *QDA - quadric discriminant analysis* (QDA) (e.g. in [Fri89]). In practise, the calculation of each test variable can be reduced to a scalar product of dimension $(d^2 + d)/2 + d + 1$. For further reading [Nie03, p.310, p.333] or [Sch95, p.79] are recommended.

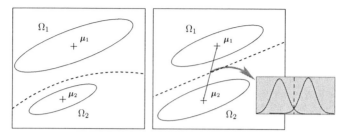

Figure 3.1: Gaussian and LDA classifier.

Linear Discriminant Analysis (LDA).   The LDA-classifier is very similar to the Gaussian classifier. The only difference is that the covariance matrices Σ_k have to be identical for all classes k. For this purpose all covariance matrices are substituted by the average matrix

$$\Sigma = \frac{1}{K} \sum_{k=1}^{K} \Sigma_k. \tag{3.11}$$

Equal covariances result in linear decision boundaries in feature space as illustrated in Fig. 3.1, right, since the quadratic terms $c^T \Sigma c$ in Eq. 3.10 are now independent of the class label k. LDA is the linear case of QDA; it is less sensitive to violations of the basic assumption of a normal distribution of the class samples [Fri89] and generally requires less training data [Wal77]. In the one-dimensional case the classification threshold between classes k and l is the midpoint $(\mu_k + \mu_l)/2$ between both class centres if no a priori weightings (P_k) are applied. Details of the implementation can be found in [Zor05]. LDA is the most frequently applied classifier in Chap. 8.

In contrast, the LDA-transformation is used in the same way as the principal component analysis (PCA) to transform features c and to reduce their dimensionality: The PCA is a global rotation of the data of all classes; the eigenvectors of the global covariance matrix form the basis of the target space. The directions with the least scattered data are indicated by the eigenvectors with the lowest eigenvalues. These directions might be least significant for classification. In contrast, the LDA-transformation separates the agglomeration areas while keeping them compact.

Gaussian Mixture Models (GMM).   If the data does not satisfy a unimodal distribution, each class k can be modelled with m Gaussian densities

$$p(c|k) = \sum_{m=1}^{M} c_m^k \mathcal{N}(c|\mu_m^k, \Sigma_m^k), \quad \sum_{m=1}^{M} c_m^k = 1. \tag{3.12}$$

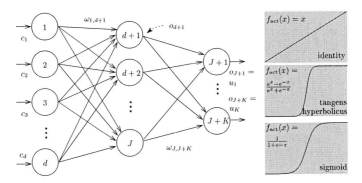

Figure 3.2: Structure of a multi-layer perceptron (left) and different activation functions (right).

Each density m is weighted with a factor c_m^k that has to be estimated additionally during training. All parameters are estimated with the EM-algorithm (expectation–maximisation, cf. [Nie03, p. 36]).

Neural Networks. Artificial neural networks (ANN) are distribution free classifiers that work similar to neural processing in the brain. ANNs consist of units (neurons) and directed, weighted links between units. From the weighted sum of all its inputs the activation of a neuron is determined; active neurons emit an output.

There are different topologies used for ANNs. The following description is restricted to the *multi-layer perceptron* (MLP) which arranges the units in layers, is forward directed (left to right), and allows only links between adjacent layers. Fig. 3.2 shows an example with one input layer (left), one hidden layer, and one output layer. A weight $\omega_{i,j}$ is assigned to the link between units i and j. In the resulting weight matrix W only entries in the upper triangular matrix are allowed; the block structure encodes the topology. The example

$$
W = \begin{pmatrix}
0 & 0 & 0 & * & * & 0 \\
0 & 0 & 0 & * & * & 0 \\
0 & 0 & 0 & * & * & 0 \\
0 & 0 & 0 & 0 & 0 & * \\
0 & 0 & 0 & 0 & 0 & * \\
0 & 0 & 0 & 0 & 0 & 0
\end{pmatrix}
\tag{3.13}
$$

with weights "$*$" for $\omega_{i,j} \neq 0$ encodes an ANN with 3 input nodes, one hidden layer with 2 nodes and 1 output node. In [Mak89] it has been proven that any arbitrary decision boundary can be modelled with an ANN with two hidden layers, only. However, training ANNs with more layers possibly converges faster [Nie03, S.370].

The d input units receive the d components of the feature vector $\boldsymbol{c}$ and perform a simple branching of the input to the units of the first hidden layer. All other neurons j are characterised by

- an activation state $a_j(\tau)$ at time τ

- an activation function

$$a_j(\tau + 1) = f_{\text{act}}(a_j(\tau), \text{net}_j(\tau), \vartheta_j) \tag{3.14}$$

  to determine the activation state at time $\tau + 1$ dependent on the current activation state, the net input, and a threshold ϑ_j. Examples are shown in Fig. 3.2, right.

- an output function f_{out} to determine the output $o_j = f_{\text{out}}(a_j(\tau))$; f_{out} often is the identity.

The propagation or net input

$$\text{net}_j(\tau) = \sum_i o_i(t) \omega_{i,j} \tag{3.15}$$

is calculated from the weighted outputs of all preceding units i with connections leading to j. The outputs o_j of the units in the right most layer are the scores u_k ($k = 1, \ldots, K$) for the K classes of the field of problem.

Training of ANNs is for instance performed with the *backpropagation algorithm*. It computes the error on the output layer by comparing the scores u_k with the ground truth and propagates the error back onto the other layers. According to the error, the weights $\omega_{i,j}$ are adapted by means of gradient descent. In the present work the more robust variant *Rprop* (resilient backpropagation) is used that only takes into account the sign and not the value of the derivative during gradient descent (described in [Rie94]). Different chance initialisations are used for the training and different *weight-decay* values that avoid overfitting by driving the weights to zero unless reinforced by backpropagation [Wer88]. As activation function the tangent hyperbolicus is applied (Fig. 3.2, right). All those settings are available in the SNNS package (Stuttgart Neural Network Simulator)[1] described in [Zel95, Zel97].

Resampling of the Data.   To robustly train and evaluate classifiers with sparse data the easy albeit computationally intensive *cross-validation* approach is applied. For the n-fold cross-validations data is partitioned into n disjoint subsets. $n-1$ partitions are used for the training of the classifier and one for testing. By systematically leaving out one subset at a time all the data is used exactly once for evaluation; training of statistics using different subsets is called the *jackknife* approach. To guarantee speaker disjoint training and test sets the maximum allowed number n is the number of speakers in the corpus. This case is in the following referred to as *leave-one-speaker-out* training (loo).

---

[1]SNNS: freely available at `http://www-ra.informatik.uni-tuebingen.de/SNNS/`

		decoder	
		wrong pron. $(\mathcal{X})$	correct pron. $(\mathcal{O})$
reference	wrong pronunciation $(\mathcal{X})$	**hits,** true positives (n_{tp})	**miss,** false negatives (n_{fn}), type 2 error
	correct pronunciation $(\mathcal{O})$	**false alarms** (n_{fa}), false positives, type 1 error	**correct acceptance** true negatives (n_{tn})

Table 3.1: Binary classification with the H_0-hypothesis "wrongly pronounced".

3.1.3 Evaluation Measures

In this thesis the 2-class problem wrongly pronounced vs. correctly pronounced plays an important role. Mispronounced units are labelled with $\mathcal{X}$ and correct pronunciation with $\mathcal{O}$. The decoder (automatic classifier) predicts the hidden information $\mathcal{X}$ or $\mathcal{O}$ for each unit (e.g. spoken word); the prediction is compared with the ground truth or reference that is obtained from human labellers. Tab. 3.1 shows a confusion matrix for binary classification. If we test the H_0-hypothesis "wrongly pronounced", all elements with wrong pronunciation that are classified as $\mathcal{X}$ count to the *true positives* (n_{tp}). The proportion of correctly classified elements with label $\mathcal{X}$ with respect to all elements labelled with $\mathcal{X}$ is defined as the *recall* of class $\mathcal{X}$, or *sensitivity*, or *hit-rate*

$$\text{REC}_{\mathcal{X}} = \frac{n_{\text{tp}}}{n_{\text{tp}} + n_{\text{fn}}}. \tag{3.16}$$

The number of correctly pronounced words that are classified as $\mathcal{O}$ is denoted as *true negatives* (n_{tn}) with respect to this H_0-hypothesis. The recall of class $\mathcal{O}$ or *specifity* is

$$\text{REC}_{\mathcal{O}} = \frac{n_{\text{tn}}}{n_{\text{tn}} + n_{\text{fa}}}. \tag{3.17}$$

There are two kinds of possible errors: *False alarms*, *false positives*, or *type 1 errors* occur, if a correctly pronounced word is classified as mispronounced. Those errors are counted with n_{fa}. The *type 2 error* counts all mispronounced words that are not detected (false negatives, n_{fn}). Since it is confusing to use in the case of pronunciation scoring e.g. true positives for detected mispronunciation (which is actually something negative), the term *hit* is used (bold in Tab. 3.1); *correct acceptance* is used instead of true negatives. The type 1 and type 2 error is referred to as *false alarm* and *miss*.

There are different measures to describe the overall performance of a classification. To calculate the overall recognition rate

$$\text{RR} = \frac{n_{\text{tp}} + n_{\text{tn}}}{n_{\text{tp}} + n_{\text{fn}} + n_{\text{fa}} + n_{\text{tn}}} \tag{3.18}$$

all correctly classified elements are considered. However, in the case that there are much more elements in either class (e.g. $|\mathcal{X}| \ll |\mathcal{O}|$) good recognition rates would be obtained,

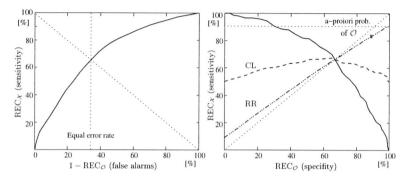

Figure 3.3: Left: ROC-curve (smoothed) and equal error rate. Right: ROC-curve, recognition rates RR, and CL. Maximisation of RR results in the a priori probability of the more frequent category.

if everything was classified as $\mathcal{O}$. A better measure is consequently the class-wise averaged recognition rate

$$\mathrm{CL} = \frac{\mathrm{REC}_{\mathcal{X}} + \mathrm{REC}_{\mathcal{O}}}{2}, \qquad\qquad (3.19)$$

which neglects the a priori probabilities of both classes. CL is the unweighted average recall; using the a priori probabilities as weights instead of equal weights $(1/2)$, RR is obtained. A ROC-curve (Receiver Operating Characteristic) is computed by shifting the discrimination threshold. Different thresholds result in high n_{tp} and low n_{tn} or vice versa; this influences $\mathrm{REC}_{\mathcal{X}}$ and $\mathrm{REC}_{\mathcal{O}}$ in a similar way as appropriate class weightings would do (which corresponds to "manipulated" a-priori probabilities $\tilde{P}_k = \omega_k P_k$ or – after Eq. 3.7 – weighted a posteriori probabilities $\omega_k P(k|\boldsymbol{c})$). A ROC-curve plots the sensitivity (y-axis) dependent on different false alarm rates (x-axis). The intersection with the straight line $y = 1 - x$ leads to the *equal error rate* that is e.g. used to evaluate pronunciation scoring in [Fra99]. At this point, the probability of false detection is equal to the probability of missing a target. A ROC-curve and the equal error rate (34 % in this example) are illustrated in Fig. 3.3, left. For many applications it might be important to specify the false alarm rate, that is maximally acceptable. Then an appropriate threshold is chosen and the sensitivity can be measured.

The ROC-curve in Fig. 3.3, right, shows sensitivity vs. specifity. The recognition rate RR varies between 10 % and 90 % since these are in the illustrated example the a priori probabilities of the categories $\mathcal{X}$ and $\mathcal{O}$. If everything is classified as $\mathcal{O}$, RR reaches 90 % whereas CL is equal to chance (50 %). The ROC-curve, RR, and CL meet in one common point, which is 1 - *equal error rate*. Note, that this point is not the maximum of CL, but very close to it. The figure shows that it is not reasonable to maximise RR if the data of both categories is not expected to be distributed equally; by maximising CL, however, a point close to the equal error rate can be found. In the experimental part of this thesis, the procedure in the 2-class case to obtain a CL-value that is close to the equal error rate is the following:

1. Classification: soft decision, e.g. posterior probabilities $P(k|\boldsymbol{c})$ of class k given the observation $\boldsymbol{c}$.

2. Multiplication of $P(k|\boldsymbol{c})$ with weight $\omega_k \in [0,1]$, $\sum_k \omega_k = 1$.
   The weights ω_k are chosen on the validation data so that RR $\approx$ CL, which implies, that the recalls for both classes have the same size.

3. On the test data: Decision for the class with maximum score $\omega_k P(k|\boldsymbol{c})$; calculation of CL and RR

Another common measure for the 2-class problem is the *positive predictive value* or *precision*

$$\mathrm{PREC}_{\mathcal{X}} = \frac{n_{\mathrm{tp}}}{n_{\mathrm{tp}} + n_{\mathrm{fa}}}. \tag{3.20}$$

It shows, how many of all detected errors are indeed mispronounced. The *F-measure* [Rij79] is a measure which is maximum, if both, precision and recall, are large.

For classification problems with multiple classes $k = 1 \ldots K$ the recalls in Eq. 3.16 and Eq. 3.17 are obtained by dividing diagonal elements of the confusion matrix with the sum of all elements in the respective line (REC_k for line k). CL is now the mean of all recalls; for K-class problems, CL will in the following often be renamed to

$$\mathrm{CL}\text{-}K = \frac{\sum_{k=1}^{K} \mathrm{REC}_k}{K}. \tag{3.21}$$

RR is the relation of the correct items (diagonal elements of the confusion matrix) to the total number of items. An example for a classification problem with multiple classes is the classification of phonemes. An example in pronunciation scoring is the classification of school grades while neglecting their values. Instead of calculating an equal error rate it is in the case of multiple classes much faster to simply maximise CL[2]. In many cases it is even impossible to get the same error rates for all classes using e. g. a linear classifier.

3.1.4   Boosting

Boosting is a meta-classifier that utilises *weak classifiers* or *weak learners* to build a *strong classifier*. The AdaBoost (adaptive boosting) algorithm is a relatively new approach and was invented by Freund and Schapire [Fre95, Fre99a]; a first boosting algorithm by Schapire was developed 1989 and is described in [Sch90].

---

[2]An additional constraint could be, that the deviation of each recall from CL has to be smaller than a specified threshold.

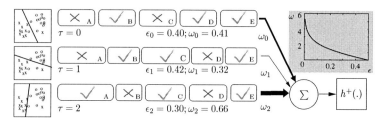

Figure 3.4: AdaBoost. Weak classifiers (left) at 3 different time steps τ. Each line with rectangles (centre) represents the training set with 5 samples A–E. The width of the rectangles indicates the weight ϕ of the sample. 'X'/'$\checkmark$' stands for wrong/correct classification of the sample. Wrong classification results in a larger weight in the next line $(\tau + 1)$. The combination to a strong classifier $h^+(.)$ is based on weights ω_τ (right).

Given a training set $\{c^v | v = 1 \ldots n\}$ with n samples of the distribution $\mathcal{D}$ and known binary labels $x^v \in \{0, 1\}$, weights $\phi_{\tau,v}$ can be assigned to each sample $c^v \in \mathbb{R}^d$. The basic idea is now, to calculate for each binary, weak classifier $h_\tau : \mathbb{R}^d \to \{0, 1\}$ an error ϵ_τ and to increase then the weights of wrongly classified samples dependent on ϵ_t. This results in a different distribution $\mathcal{D}_{\tau+1}$ of the data that forces in the next iteration a weak classifier $h_{\tau+1}$ to be selected that focuses on hard examples in the training set. In detail, the algorithm is the following:

1. Assign uniform weights $\phi_{0,v} = 1/n$ to each sample c^v.

2. For each iteration $\tau = 0 \ldots t$

    (a) Train the weak learner $h_\tau(.)$

    (b) Calculate the error $\epsilon_\tau \in [0; 1]$, stop if $\epsilon_\tau > 0.5$

$$\epsilon_\tau = \sum_{v=1}^{n} \phi_{\tau,v} |h_\tau(c^v) - x^v| \tag{3.22}$$

    (c) Use greater weights for all wrongly classified words:

$$\phi_{\tau+1,v} = \phi_{\tau,v} \cdot \exp(\omega_\tau) \quad ; \quad \omega_\tau = \log\left(\frac{1 - \epsilon_\tau}{\epsilon_\tau}\right) \tag{3.23}$$

    For $\omega(\epsilon)$ refer to Fig. 3.4, right top.

    (d) Normalise the weights for $\sum_v \phi_{\tau+1,v} = 1$

3. Output of the strong classifier

$$h^+(c^v) = \begin{cases} 1 & \text{if} \quad \sum_\tau \omega_\tau h_\tau(c^v) \geq \frac{1}{2}\sum_\tau \omega_\tau \\ 0 & \text{else} \end{cases} \tag{3.24}$$

The final strong classifier $h^+(.)$ is a linear combination of the weak classifiers; it decides for the output 1, if the majority of the weak classifiers decides for 1, where each classifier votes with its weight ω. Fig. 3.4 illustrates the weighting of the data; smaller ϵ result in greater ω. AdaBoost has turned out to be very robust against overfitting to the training data [Fre99a]. Even if there is a certain training iteration from which on ϵ_τ does not decrease any more, further iterations can have a positive effect on the test data. The algorithm described works only in the 2-class case, but there are extensions for multi class and regression problems [Fre95]. AdaBoost is also able to identify outliers (samples with the highest weights ϕ) [Fre99a]. *BrownBoost* puts less emphasis on those outliers [Fre99b].

In the same way, as one single weak classifier can be boosted to increase its classification rate, it is also possible to combine different classifiers. In this case, in step (2a) of each iteration τ *many* classifiers h_τ^i are trained and the one with lowest error ϵ_τ is selected as classifier h_τ. In the case of face detection, Viola and Jones [Vio04] go even a step further: Here, a weak classifier is trained for each feature component $\{c_i^v | v = 1 \ldots n\}$. Choosing $t < d$ classifiers $h_0 \ldots h_t$ can be seen as a *feature selection* of t out of d components: The best feature and the 2nd best feature that performs optimal on the data where the first has failed and so on. In other words, due to the new weights, the second best feature (weak classifier) uses complementary information and so on. In [Vio04] each weak classifier further consists only of a threshold ϑ_i^τ and a polarity, that shows, which side of ϑ_i^τ is 1 and which 0. In this case, the step (2a) is replaced with a loop over all features and all possible thresholds to find the weak classifier $h_\tau(c_i, \vartheta_i^\tau)$ with lowest error ϵ_τ.

In this thesis, an AdaBoost algorithm with two further modifications will be applied in Chap. 8. First of all a *global* threshold ϑ_i is calculated on the *initial* distribution $\mathcal{D}$ for all weak classifiers. Each weak classifier $h^i : \mathbb{R}^d \to \{0, 1\}$ selects feature component c_i and applies ϑ_i to decide for class 0 or 1. This way, in each iteration a feature is selected that is optimal on the *original* distribution $\mathcal{D}$; optimal means here that it can classify data samples well which previous weak learners failed to classify rather than that it can best learn the new distribution $\mathcal{D}_\tau$ (which is defined by the current set of weights). The second modification is to start with initial weights which guarantee that the first feature being selected is optimum in terms of CL instead of RR (cf. [Vio04]). The modified AdaBoost for feature selection is outlined in Fig. 3.5. Classification with the selected feature components and the corresponding weak classifiers is performed in the same way as described in Eq. 3.24.

3.2 Speech Recognition

After the previous introduction to classification, in the following speech recognition will be illuminated. Here, it is not any more sufficient to classify at discrete time steps e.g. phonemes; now the temporal progression has to be taken into account, too. The speaker independent continuous speech recogniser which is employed in the following chapters has been developed at the *LME* since 1978 and is described by Schukat-Talamazzini [Sch95]. It is e.g. integrated in the train time-table system *Evar* [Eck93] and was the first conversational system for continuous speech connected to the phone network. Recent changes to

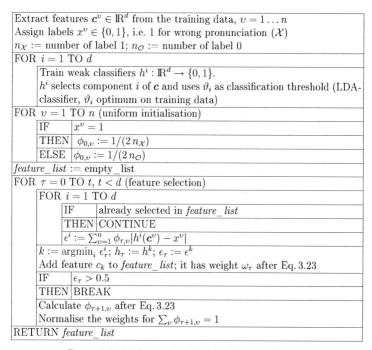

Figure 3.5: AdaBoost algorithm for feature selection.

the recogniser are explained in Stemmer [Ste05b]. The biggest advantage compared to the freely available HTK system[3] is the faster decoding (Sect. 3.2.4), further characteristics are e.g. polyphone based acoustic models (Sect. 3.2.3). In Sect. 3.2.2 different approaches for the feature extraction are explained. First of all, evaluation measures like the *word error rate* are defined.

3.2.1 Evaluation Measures

For continuous speech or phone recognition, sequences of words or phones are evaluated. Now, it cannot only be the case, that a word or phone is correct or wrong (substituted by another word/phone) as in Sec. 3.1.3, but it can also be deleted or inserted. The Levensthein distance [Lev66] specifies the minimal number of insertions n_{ins}, deletions n_{del}, and

---

[3]http://htk.eng.cam.ac.uk/

substitutions n_{sub} that are necessary to map the recognised sequence onto the reference sequence. It is obtained by dynamic time warping. The *word accuracy* is

$$\mathrm{WA} = \left(1 - \frac{n_{\mathrm{sub}} + n_{\mathrm{ins}} + n_{\mathrm{del}}}{n_{\mathrm{all}}}\right) \cdot 100\% \tag{3.25}$$

where n_{all} is the total number of words or phones in the reference. The *word correctness* is

$$\mathrm{WC} = \left(1 - \frac{n_{\mathrm{sub}} + n_{\mathrm{del}}}{n_{\mathrm{all}}}\right) \cdot 100\%. \tag{3.26}$$

Note, that the WA becomes negative, if a sufficient number of words is inserted. This is not the case for WC. However, WC becomes large not only by recognising everything correctly but also by performing a number of insertions (in the unlikely case, when every word in the reference is recognised as a sequence of all possible words it reaches even 100 %). In this thesis for all speech recognition experiments the *word error rate*

$$\mathrm{WER} = 100\% - \mathrm{WA} \tag{3.27}$$

is given as well as its relative reduction (improvement).

3.2.2 Feature Extraction

The *LME*-recogniser currently uses a 24-dimensional feature vector, which contains the short-time energy, 11 Mel frequency cepstrum coefficients and 12 first-order derivatives. In this thesis, also *TRAP* features (**TempoRAl P**atterns) are investigated in Chap. 5. A detailed description of the feature extraction is necessary to understand the adaptation approaches applied in Chap. 7.

Cepstral Features. In [Rie95] the feature extraction module has been developed. In [Ste05b], amongst others, changes of the filter bank were investigated and vocal tract length normalisation (VTLN, cf. Sect. 3.3.2) was added. In the following, a brief outline of the current module is given:

1. Every 10 msec a window of 16 msec length of the speech signal $\boldsymbol{f}$ is analysed. This corresponds to a window size of $N = 256$ samples if 16kHz data is used (short-time analysis). The data is quantised with 16 bits.

2. Each short-time window is pointwise multiplied with a Hamming window.

3. The short-time spectrum is calculated using the Fast Hartley Transform (FHT).

4. The magnitude-squared spectrum is multiplied with a bank of B filters uniformly spaced on the *Mel scale*, which results in an auditory based, coarser resolution of the higher frequencies. The result is the *Mel spectrum*. This approach is equivalent to three consecutive processing steps: (i) Mel frequency warping of the power spectrum, (ii) convolution (i. e. smoothing), and (iii) down-sampling. Originally $B = 18$

overlapping trapezoid filters have been used, that covered the frequency range from 62.5 – 6250 kHz. It was replaced by a filter bank with $B = 25$ triangular filters in [Ste05b]. Example filter banks are shown in Fig. 3.11; filter i and $i + 2$ touch each other on the frequency axis. In the following chapters different numbers of filters and different ranges of frequency covered by the filterbank are investigated. However, when using large numbers of filters (up to 256 in [Hon05]), one should ensure that the bandwidth of the filters is kept constant (much more than 50 % overlap), since their size influences the smoothing of the power spectrum.

5. The short-time energy is the sum of all Mel spectrum coefficients. An auditory based energy value is obtained when taking the logarithm (after setting zero-values to a small positive value $\varepsilon = 10^{-6}$).

6. To keep the short-time energy on a constant level it is subtracted from the median filtered time contour of the energy maxima.

7. To calculate the *Mel frequency cepstral coefficients* (MFCC), first each of the B band energy values is mapped onto the interval $[\varepsilon; 1.0]$ and log-transformed.

8. The *Discrete Cosine Transform* (DCT) is applied to the sequence of B band energy values. Of the resulting *Mel cepstrum* the 12 lowest coefficients are selected, which encode the low frequencies of the Mel spectrum.

9. Last but not least, a dynamic adaptive cepstral subtraction (DACS) is applied to eliminate characteristics of the channel, the room, or the physiology of the speaker's vocal tract. Each MFCC coefficient is subtracted from the mean that has been calculated adaptively over the preceding 2000 frames that have been classified as speech.

10. The first of the 12 cepstrum coefficients is replaced by the short-time energy value. Each of these 12 static features is smoothed with a triangular filter (Tyrolean hat) which is an interpolation of the current MFCC with its two neighbours.

11. The final 24 dimensional cepstral feature vector additionally contains 12 first-order derivatives of the 12 static features (regression line within the surrounding time interval of 56 msec [Ste01] which is 5 frames).

In the *LME* recognition system up to now no improvements have been achieved with additional 2nd-order derivatives. However, additional context features were investigated in [Ste01, Hac01]: The calculation of the 1st-order derivatives using multiple time resolutions could raise the recognition rates.

PLP, RASTA, and Modulation Spectrogram.   Another widely used approach to obtain acoustic features is *Perceptual Linear Prediction* (PLP). In [Hon05] PLP and MFCC are compared and different computation steps are combined. The main differences in PLP are the following: First, the Bark filter bank is used after applying the Hamming window

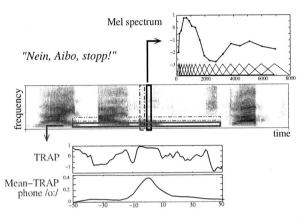

Figure 3.6: Spontaneous speech of a child (in German). Example of a TempoRAl Pattern (TRAP).

and the Fast Fourier Transform (FFT). Next, an equal-loudness transform weights the filter bank coefficients to simulate the sensitivity of hearing. This corresponds to a pre-emphasis $f'_\tau = f_\tau - 0.95\, f_{\tau-1}$ often applied to the time-signal f in MFCC computation. In PLP, the equalised bark filter values are further transformed by raising each to the power of 0.33 [Her90]. This auditorily warped line spectrum is finally processed using linear prediction (LP); one obtains a smoothed curve, the *model spectrum*, that approximates the envelope of the filter bank spectrum. Usually the first e.g. 13 cepstrum coefficients (*model cepstrum*) are used as features.

Hermansky et al. introduced in 1991 RelAtive SpecTrAl (RASTA) processing [Her91] for speech enhancement in noisy speech. It is originally applied to the log spectrum and in later work as well to the cepstrum. A filter is applied to the temporal progression of each frequency band which is implemented by computing the temporal derivative and a re-integration step. This is equivalent to smoothing plus sliding mean subtraction as shown in [Hon04].

MFCC features are calculated using only one short-time analysis window that contains e.g. 16 msec of speech; temporal context is included by calculating the derivatives e.g. over 56 msec. There are many approaches that look onto a larger temporal context, e.g. RASTA processing. Frequencies that do not satisfy the physical constraints on the rate-of-change are filtered out; those frequencies result from speaker or recording conditions (low frequencies) or noise (high frequencies). The temporal changes of the log-spectrogram (time vs. frequency) around time τ are illustrated in the *modulation spectrum* (modulation frequency vs. frequency). The contribution of different modulation frequency ranges to the speech recognition performance is investigated in [Tib97]. It turned out that an important range is 2 – 8 Hz; the syllabic rate in speech is around 4 Hz. Further investigations of the modulation spectrum are found in Atlas et al. [Atl04]; the *modulation spectrogram* shows the 4 Hz modulation at any time step and for all frequency bands in a spectrographic format and was introduced by Greenberg [Gre97]. Phoneme, speaker, and channel variabilities per frequency band are analysed in [Kaj99].

TRAP Features.   A multi-stream approach using TempoRAl Patterns (TRAP) was introduced by Hermansky in [Tib97, Her98] and in the PhD-Thesis of Sharma [Sha99]. A TRAP is the temporal evolution of the logarithmic energy within a critical band as illustrated in Fig. 3.6. Up to 1 sec. time trajectories centred around the frame under consideration are taken into account. The *mean TRAP* is obtained by averaging per filter bank all TRAPs belonging to the same phoneme regardless of the context. [Her98] focuses on 29 phoneme classes. The temporal window is Hanning-filtered to reduce the influence of the temporally more distant frames.

Classification with TRAPs is performed as follows: In a first step, the surrounding TRAP of each frame is compared with all mean TRAPs of the respective filter bank. The scores that measure the similarity (e.g. the correlation) are stored in a vector (1 component per phone). In later investigations, neural networks are used to calculate phone scores (class conditional log-likelihood), instead. In a second step vectors are build which contain the correlation scores with each phoneme (later investigations: log-likelihood scores, cf. Fig. 3.7). Such vectors are obtained for all critical bands (15 from 0 - 4 kHz in [Sha99], 22 from 0 - 7.5 kHz in the experimental part of this thesis, cf. page 155) and combined using another huge neural network (*merger* or *combiner*). This two-step approach is referred to as *tandem* approach and outlined in Fig. 3.7. The results are phone posterior scores which are used for frame recognition or as features. The latter are usually combined frame based with conventional features like MFCCs.

In [Sha99] the TRAP approach is motivated with the human way of speech processing analysed 1953 by Fletcher [Fle53] (reviewed in [All94]). Fletcher's articulation index characterises speech intelligibility under conditions of low-pass and high-pass filtering. It was measured in a perceptual study with nonsense syllables. Using B band-pass filters the overall articulation error $e = e_1 e_2 \ldots e_B$ was shown to be the product of the partial articulation errors e_i in frequency band i. Allen's [All94] interpretation is that humans process phones in independent frequency sub-bands and that the resulting phone estimates are then combined to the final recognition. As a consequence, one corrupted frequency band does not affect the overall recognition.

There are several modifications of the TRAP approach described in Fig. 3.7, in particular, the inputs of the merger do not have to be posterior scores of phonemes. In [Jai03] TRAPs from adjacent critical bands are combined (3 at a time); now, the resulting input to the combiner are 75 features per band. In [Her03] the set of mean TRAPs for all phones and in all energy bands is reduced to 9 universal patterns (UTRAPs) by clustering. The band-dependent ANNs (phoneme recognisers) are replaced with a recogniser for those

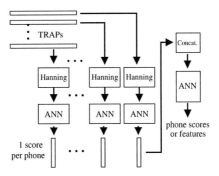

Figure 3.7: TRAP tandem approach as described by Hermansky [Tib97, Her98].

9 patterns. Chen et al. [Che04, Che03] introduce and compare different 2-stage tandem approaches and 1-stage setups.

Using TRAPs better recognition results are obtained under different conditions of noise in [Her98, Her99a]. An extension for conversational speech is investigated in [Mor04]. Recognition of reverberated data is investigated in [Mai05c, Mai05b]. TRAPs generalise better if training and test is performed with mismatched, differently reverberated data. It was investigated to combine recognisers using information of different frequency bands with ROVER [Fis97]. In the present thesis TRAPs are for the first time employed for pronunciation scoring (Chap. 5.3).

3.2.3 Acoustic and Language Modelling

The standard approach for acoustic modelling in speech recognition is based on *hidden Markov models* (HMM), a statistical representation of the words contained in the lexicon of the speech recogniser. Additionally *language models* (LM) are employed to incorporate a priori knowledge of the occurrence of word sequences. Details on the *LME* recognition system can be found in Schukat-Talamazzini [Sch95] and a compact overview in English including recent changes in Stemmer [Ste05b].

Acoustic Modelling. Difficulties in speaker-independent speech recognition arise from the fact that sounds are uttered slightly differently at any time, differently by any person, and that additionally words are non-linearly distorted in time. HMMs are stochastic models for words or sub-word units that take those issues into account. A Markov chain is a discrete-time stochastic process (at time steps $\tau_1 < \tau_2 < \tau_3 \ldots$) with the *Markov property*. This property means, that the future is conditionally independent of the past and only dependent on the presence. A Markov chain is given by

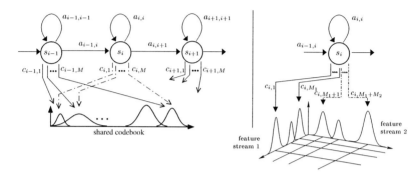

Figure 3.8: Left: structure of a semi-continuous HMM. Right: Combination of 2 codebooks for independent feature streams.

- a state variable $q_\tau \in \{s_1, s_2, \ldots, s_I\}$ that is a random variable which describes the state at time τ,

- initial state probabilities $\boldsymbol{\pi} = (\pi_1, \pi_2, \ldots, \pi_I)$ with $\pi_i = P(q_1 = s_i)$, and

- a matrix $\boldsymbol{A}$ with transition probabilities $a_{ij} = P(q_{\tau+1} = s_j \,|\, q_\tau = s_i)$, $a_{ij} \geq 0$ which is the probability of the transition $s_i \to s_j$ ($\sum_j a_{ij} = 1$).

In speech recognition Markov chains are used but superimposed by a second stochastic process: Whereas the state q_τ remains hidden, in HMMs an output o_τ can be observed that satisfies a state dependent distribution $p(o_\tau|q_\tau)$. The output distribution of state s_i is symbolised with $b_i(o_\tau)$; the densities of all states are combined in $\boldsymbol{b}$. For *continuous HMMs* the observation is the feature vector ($o_\tau = \boldsymbol{c}^\tau$) calculated from the speech signal $\boldsymbol{f}$ at time τ; the densities $b_i(\boldsymbol{c}^\tau) \in \mathbb{R}^d$ are called the state dependent *codebook* which is obtained by vector quantisation. For *discrete HMMs* o_τ is a discrete symbol and $b_i(o_\tau) = P(o_\tau|q_\tau)$ a discrete random distribution. The definition of the HMM $\boldsymbol{\lambda}$ is complete, once $\boldsymbol{\pi}$, $\boldsymbol{A}$, and $\boldsymbol{b}$ are determined:

$$\boldsymbol{\lambda} := (\boldsymbol{\pi}, \boldsymbol{A}, \boldsymbol{b}) \tag{3.28}$$

Most common topologies are left-to-right HMMs ($a_{ij} = 0$ for $j < i$), in particular linear HMMs ($a_{ij} = 0$ for $j > i + 1 \vee j < i$). The output densities for continuous HMM are Gaussian mixtures with M densities (a codebook with M densities) where each of them is weighted with $c_{i,m}$:

$$b_i^{(\mathrm{cont})}(\boldsymbol{c}^\tau) = \sum_{m=1}^{M} c_{i,m} \, \mathcal{N}(\boldsymbol{c}^\tau | \boldsymbol{\mu}_{i,m}, \boldsymbol{\Sigma}_{i,m}). \tag{3.29}$$

Continuous HMMs are typically limited to diagonal covariance matrices. The *LME-*recogniser is based on *semi-continuous HMMs* as shown in Fig. 3.8, left. Generally much more densities are available per state (e.g. $M = 500$). Full covariance matrices can be estimated very robustly since the codebook is shared among all states s_i and all data can be used to estimate its densities. In

$$b_i^{(\text{semi})}(\boldsymbol{c}^\tau) = \sum_{m=1}^{M} c_{i,m} \mathcal{N}(\boldsymbol{c}^\tau | \boldsymbol{\mu}_m, \boldsymbol{\Sigma}_m) \tag{3.30}$$

only $c_{i,m}$ depends on i and causes a state-dependent weighting of the Gaussian densities. Discrete HMMs would require a discretisation of the feature vectors in advance employing also a state independent codebook. In this case, the discrete symbols obtained by vector quantisation are the observations o_τ.

In [Hac03], the *LME*-recogniser was extended in a way, that it cannot only process one sequence of feature vectors (stream), but also multiple streams from independent information sources. Assuming statistical independence of static and dynamic features, two *feature streams* are obtained. In this case $b_i^{(\text{semi})}(\boldsymbol{c}^\tau)$ can be calculated from the product of two streams, where $\boldsymbol{c}_{\text{stat}}^\tau$ and $\boldsymbol{c}_{\text{dyn}}^\tau$ are the $d/2$ static and dynamic feature components of the feature vector $\boldsymbol{c}^\tau$.

$$\begin{aligned} b_i^{(\text{semi})}(\boldsymbol{c}^\tau) &= b_i^{(\text{semi})}\left(\boldsymbol{c}_{\text{stat}}^\tau, \boldsymbol{c}_{\text{dyn}}^\tau\right) \\ &= b_i^{(\text{semi})}\left(\boldsymbol{c}_{\text{stat}}^\tau\right) \cdot b_i^{(\text{semi})}\left(\boldsymbol{c}_{\text{dyn}}^\tau\right), \qquad \boldsymbol{c}_{\text{stat}}^\tau, \boldsymbol{c}_{\text{dyn}}^\tau \in \mathbb{R}^{d/2} \end{aligned} \tag{3.31}$$

Additionally, each factor can be exponentially weighted (codebook exponents). This approach is outlined in Fig. 3.8, right; it shows two orthogonal feature spaces for two feature streams with M_1 and M_2 densities. This way, a codebook with $M_1 \times M_2$ densities in the hatched area is modelled, although less parameters have to be estimated: the $M_1 + M_2$ covariance matrices have the smaller size $d/2 \times d/2$. A related approach is to integrate the output of a phone recogniser as in Stemmer et al. [Ste03c, Ste03d].

Isadora. For the training of the acoustic models the *ISADORA* system is employed [Sch95, pp. 271]. It is based on *recursive HMMs* (RMM): Each state of an RMM contains an elementary state like in HMMs or a whole RMM. This way, models that build a tree hierarchy can be trained. A monophone forms the root of the tree e.g. /e/, specialised models are e.g. /e/t, /e/r, or /e/k. More specialised models of /e/k would be r/e/k, then r/e/k@, and perhaps up to r/e/k@gn if enough words like "recognition" and "recogniser" exist in the training data. In the present thesis, such polyphones (with arbitrary context length) have to occur at least 50 times during training to be generated. Generalised polyphones additionally use categories like vowels V+ or plosives P+ in order to model e.g. r/e/P+. Each polyphone is defined as an HMM of 1–4 states as defined for all occurring centre phones in Appendix B.2. It follows the entry for /e/ and /eI/[4]

```
S:    /e/    [e]  [e]  [e]  ;
S:    /eI/   [e]  [e]  [e]  [I]  ;
```

The symbols on the right side ([e], [I]) are sub-phonemic units to name the HMM states.

---

[4]"S" denotes sequential states, "A" atomic states, details in [Sch95, pp. 281]

Training.   To train the HMMs only a word based transcription of the data and a pronunciation dictionary containing all occurring words is required. No manual alignment between phones and time intervals of the speech signal is necessary. The training starts with a codebook estimated with the k-means algorithm, a uniform initialisation of the HMMs and an initial training of the acoustic models. Then the following procedure is repeated always 10 times:

- training of the codebook

- soft vector quantisation: scores are calculated for each density m; all densities with scores greater than a threshold are kept in the beam (not only the one with the best score as for hard vector quantisation).

- automatic labelling with sub-phonemic labels (forced alignment cf. 3.2.4)

- training of the acoustic models

The training steps are performed with the *Baum-Welch* algorithm [Bau66]: 10 iterations are applied in each loop to the acoustic models. The formulae to estimate π and A, all M densities (μ_m, Σ_m), and the $I \times M$ weightings $c_{i,m}$ can be found e.g. in [Ste05b, pp. 68]. Given a tree hierarchy of acoustic models like in ISADORA, the A.P.I.S. training (accumulation, propagation, interpolation, and smoothing) described in [Sch95, pp. 303] is applied.

Language Modelling.   A language model (LM) is a probability distribution

$$
\begin{aligned}
P(\boldsymbol{w}) &= P(w_1 w_2 \dots w_L) \\
&= P(w_2) \cdot P(w_2|w_1) \cdot P(w_3|w_1 w_2) \cdot \dots \cdot P(w_L|w_1 \dots w_{L-1})
\end{aligned}
\tag{3.32}
$$

over all word sequences $\boldsymbol{w}$ of individual length L. This stochastic grammar is approximated with n-gram probabilities

$$
P(w_i|w_1 \dots w_{i-1}) \approx P(w_i|w_{i-n+1} \dots w_{i-1}).
\tag{3.33}
$$

A bigram language model is achieved for $n = 2$ and a unigram for $n = 1$. More robust estimates can be obtained by mapping words w_i onto more general categories C_i. Then the conditional n-gram probability can be rewritten to

$$
P(w_i|w_{i-n+1} \dots w_{i-1}) = P(w_i|C_i) \cdot P(C_i|C_{i-n+1} \dots C_{i-1}).
\tag{3.34}
$$

Further approaches to avoid the sparse data problem like interpolation are summarised in [Ste03c, pp. 71].

The *perplexity* of a language model measures its performance. In the case of an unknown distribution P_{LM} that is estimated from samples ($\hat{P}_{\mathrm{LM}}$) the perplexity given L words is defined as

$$
2^{\left(-\frac{1}{L} \sum_{i=1}^{L} \log_2 P_{\mathrm{LM}}(w_i)\right)}
\tag{3.35}
$$

where the exponent can be seen as the crossentropy

$$H(P_{\mathrm{LM}}, \hat{P}_{\mathrm{LM}}) = -\sum_{i=1}^{L} P_{\mathrm{LM}}(w_i) \cdot \log_2 \hat{P}_{\mathrm{LM}}(w_i) \tag{3.36}$$

The lower the perplexity, the better is the performance of the language model.

3.2.4 Decoding and Forced Alignment

In HMM-based recognition two types of evaluations are possible. Given an HMM $\boldsymbol{\lambda}_i$, the probability that the observed acoustic signal is produced by $\boldsymbol{\lambda}_i$ is required when deciding for the HMM with highest a posteriori probability. Given also the transcription of the acoustic observation, that implicitly defines a sequence of HMMs, the most likely sequence of hidden states $q_1 \ldots q_t$ can be computed in order to obtain a time alignment between the acoustic observation and words, phonemes, or sub-phonemic units (Viterbi alignment). Combining the a posteriori probabilities of the acoustic model AM with the language model probabilities, the final speech decoder is obtained. Phoneme recognition is explained at the end of this section.

A Posteriori Probabilities. The probability $p_{\mathrm{AM}}(o_1 \ldots o_t | \boldsymbol{\lambda})$ of an acoustic model $\boldsymbol{\lambda}$ can be computed efficiently by applying either the *forward algorithm* or the *backward algorithm*. For the first algorithm the forward probability at time τ

$$
\begin{aligned}
\alpha_\tau(j) &= p(\boldsymbol{c}^1, \ldots, \boldsymbol{c}^\tau, q_\tau = s_j | \boldsymbol{\lambda}) \\
&= \left(\sum_{i=1}^{I} \alpha_{\tau-1}(i) a_{ij} \right) b_j(\boldsymbol{c}^\tau) \quad \text{with } \alpha_1(j) = \pi_j b_j(\boldsymbol{c}^1)
\end{aligned}
\tag{3.37}
$$

is recursively computed to obtain finally

$$p_{\mathrm{AM}}(\boldsymbol{c}^1 \ldots \boldsymbol{c}^t | \boldsymbol{\lambda}) = \sum_{j=1}^{I} \alpha_t(j), \tag{3.38}$$

where t is the total number of frames τ.

Viterbi Probabilities. The Viterbi algorithm is more efficient, since the sum in Eq. 3.38 is replaced by the maximum operator. Now, the score is calculated from exactly one path, the most likely path. It is again recursively computed in

$$
\begin{aligned}
\theta_\tau(j) &= \max_{q_1, \ldots, q_\tau} p(\boldsymbol{c}^1, \ldots, \boldsymbol{c}^\tau, q_1, \ldots, q_{\tau-1}, q_\tau = s_j | \boldsymbol{\lambda}) \\
&= \max_{i=1 \ldots I} (\theta_{\tau-1}(i) a_{ij}) \, b_j(\boldsymbol{c}^\tau) \quad \text{with } \theta_1(j) = \pi_j b_j / \boldsymbol{c}^1)
\end{aligned}
\tag{3.39}
$$

to obtain finally

$$p_{\mathrm{Viterbi}}(\boldsymbol{c}^1 \ldots \boldsymbol{c}^t | \boldsymbol{\lambda}) = \max_{j=1 \ldots I} \theta_t(j) \tag{3.40}$$

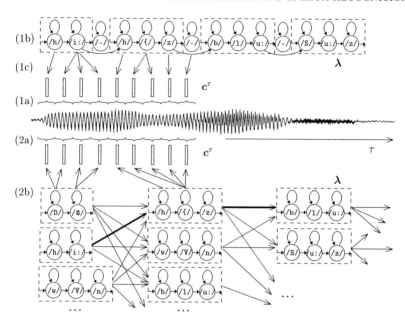

Figure 3.9: Forced alignment (top) vs. speech recognition (bottom). Feature extraction (1a), concatenation of annotated/expected word models (1b), and time alignment (1c) in a way, that the features $\boldsymbol{c}^{\tau}$ are generated with maximum probability given the word models and a codebook. For speech recognition the feature extraction (2a) is identical, but from all word models and possible word sequences the one is searched which maximises the probability of the feature sequence $\boldsymbol{c}^{\tau}$ (2b).

and implicitly the optimal path, similar to dynamic time warping. This path is the optimal state sequence $q_1 \ldots q_t$; t denotes the length of the sequence. The knowledge about the optimum sequence allows this algorithm to be applied for forced alignment, where the time alignment of a given transcription of the speech signal has to be calculated.

Forced Alignment.   For forced alignment, a transcription of the data is required. In a first step, features are extracted from the speech signal (Fig. 3.9, 1a). Then the word HMMs of the words in the transcription are connected to a sentence HMM while allowing additional silence models /-/ between words (1b, for "He has blue shoes"). Then the time alignment between sentence model and feature sequence is calculated using the Viterbi algorithm. The simple acoustic model resulting from the known transcription keeps the search-space compact. From the most likely state sequence the state at each time τ can be easily found as well as its sub-phonemic label (described in Sect. 3.2.3, ISADORA)[5]. The one-to-one mapping between states and the transcription gives information about the starting and end points of the words or phones..

The Speech Decoder. The optimal word sequence $\boldsymbol{w}^{(\text{opt})}$ given an acoustic observation $o_1 = \boldsymbol{c}^1, \ldots, o_t = \boldsymbol{c}^t$ is calculated by the speech decoder that combines the probabilities of the acoustic models and the language model

$$\boldsymbol{w}^{(\text{opt})} = \operatorname*{argmax}_{L, \boldsymbol{w} = (w_1, \ldots, w_L)} \ p_{\text{AM}}(\boldsymbol{c}^1 \ldots \boldsymbol{c}^t | \boldsymbol{w}) \cdot P_{\text{LM}}(\boldsymbol{w})^{\gamma_{\text{lw}}} \cdot (\gamma_{\text{ip}})^L. \tag{3.41}$$

Thereby, p_{AM} is calculated for all possible word sequences $\boldsymbol{w}$ i.e. the corresponding HMM $\boldsymbol{\lambda}$ that is obtained from the concatenation of word HMMs[6]. The transition probability between the final state of a word based HMM with the initial state of another word based HMM is given by the bigram probability. Fig. 3.9 compares forced alignment and speech recognition. In step (2a), again feature vectors are computed, but the alignment with the acoustic models (2b) is combined with an extensive graph search over all combinations of word models.

The heuristic parameter $\gamma_{\text{lw}} > 0$ is the *language weight* or *linguistic weight* that adjusts the influence of the language model letting the influence of the acoustic model constant. Usually γ_{lw} is greater than 1; this way in particular small values of P_{LM} are strongly scaled down as will be discussed in the experimental part (Fig. 7.5). The insertion penalty $0 < \gamma_{\text{ip}} < 1$ prevents the decoder from inserting too many words: the greater the length L of the word sequence, the smaller is the factor $(\gamma_{\text{ip}})^L < 1$. $\gamma_{\text{ip}} > 1$ increases the whole term being maximised in Eq. 3.41 (stronger for longer word sequences); the overall score now may take values that are greater than 1 but not necessarily since the product of probabilities becomes often very small for long sentences, anyway.

To accelerate the extensive search in Eq. 3.41 over all possible word sequences and all possible state sequences as in Eq. 3.38, first p_{Viterbi} is used instead of p_{AM}. Next, a beam search is used to prune the word graph [Ste05b]. Finally, an $A^\star$-search [Nil82] is applied to find the best matching word sequence. It re-scores the word graph with a 4-gram language model; the costs of the remaining paths which have to be estimated for each partial path are obtained from the bigram LM.

Phoneme Recognition. Recognition of phonemes can be performed in the same way as in Eq. 3.41. $\boldsymbol{w}$ is now a sequence of phonemes w_i. The decoder uses not any more acoustic models for all words in the vocabulary, but acoustic models for each phoneme (monophone models instead of polyphones). The "language model" is estimated from phoneme sequences. Another approach without using HMMs is the *frame classifier*. Every frame of 16 msec is classified without utilising temporal context information with an arbitrary classifier (cf. Sec. 3.1.2).

---

[5]The figure is simplified and shows only the phonemes; each state is in truth a sequence of 2-4 states with sub-phonemic labels i.e. [h] [h] [h] [i] [i] [i]. for /hi:/

[6]Which are again a concatenation of polyphone HMMs

In the following section problems appearing in the particular case of recognising speech from young people are discussed.

3.3   Robust Recognition of Children Speech

The focus in this thesis is computer assisted language learning for children. After the sections about classification and speech recognition it will now be discussed whether different algorithms have to be applied when the users are expected to be children. The following section starts with a literature review on analysis and recognition of children speech. In the second part, the algorithms that will be applied in this thesis are explained.

3.3.1   Children Speech: Analysis and Recognition

Characteristics of Children.   In 1996 Wilpon and Jacobsen [Wil96] reported word error rates that are 170 % higher for children (but also for the elderly) than those for adults. It was argued that the higher pitch could be a reason, however, by testing children with a recogniser trained on women, also higher error rates were obtained. The reason seems to be the smaller vocal tract, which stops growing a couple of years after puberty, around age 15. In this study also better results were obtained with MFCC features than with linear prediction. Early investigation in adaptation to children speech can be found in [Bur96]. Details on differences in vowels or fricatives can be found in [Lee99, McG88].

An overview of the characteristics of children speech for different age groups and in comparison with adult speech is given by Potamianos et al. [Pot03, Pot97a]. Difficulties in recognising children originate from several facts: anatomical and morphological differences in the vocal tract geometry cause higher fundamental and formant frequencies; the F_1/F_2 vowel-space as shown in Fig. 2.1 becomes more compact with increasing age and the formant values decrease. Further, children cannot control their articulators as precisely as adults, have a less refined ability to control super-segmental aspects such as prosody, and have a slower speaking rate. At the same time the variability in speaking rate, vocal effort, and degree of spontaneity is higher for younger speakers. Intra-speaker variability is measured with the *mean cepstral distance*, i.e. the Euclidean distance between MFCC vectors (static components) of two repetitions of the same vowel. For children, intra-speaker variability is higher, which means that the overlap among phonemic classes is greater and automatic classification harder. The average sentence duration was longer as well for read speech as for spontaneous speech evoked in a Wizard-of-Oz scenario. Spontaneous speech further contains more disfluencies and extraneous speech and the frequency of mispronunciations (here in the mother tongue) is higher. Breathing noises occur more often in speech of younger children whereas filled pauses occur more often in utterances from children of age 11 and older. Conversational speech is investigated in [Nar02]. The linguistic inter-speaker variability in child-machine voice interaction was twice as high as the intra-speaker variability. This indicates that speaker adaptation to the language model could raise the classification performance. A child LM is investigated in [Das98].

As shown by Gerosa [Ger06], the recognition performance is not uniformly poor across all children but there exists a wide variation. Only a limited number of children has very high error rates, i.e. children whose pronunciation (in their mother tongue) is judged to be poor [Li02]. [Ger06] further points out, that not only the acoustic intra-speaker variability, but also the inter-speaker variability is higher for children. It is measured per age group by calculating the Bhattacharyya distance of densities in cepstral space (one density per phone). As the densities are estimated from many speakers, high inter-speaker variability results in higher variances and a smaller average Bhattacharyya distance of the codebook. Further, an analysis of the coarticulation of consonant/vowel-pairs reveals that the relative duration of the transition is smaller for younger children; the ability of coarticulation is limited.

The shift of the fundamental frequency and the formants in children speech can be observed in Tab. 3.2 (after Peterson and Barney [Pet53]). In their work 15 children of age around 8 were investigated. For a larger corpus, age dependent analysis of the formants can be found in Lee et al. [Lee99], cf. Fig. 1.2. Vowels are also investigated in [Pal96, Hub99]. Note that for speech with telephone bandwidth only 2–3 formants exist in the range 0.3–3.2 kHz whereas 3–4 exist for adults. The effect of bandwidth reduction is investigated in [Li01]. An approach to learn bandwidth extension (additive effect in cepstral space) from a small amount of wideband data is presented in [Sel05].

[Lee99] shows that vowel duration becomes minimum at age 15. Also sentence duration and the duration of fricatives (/s/ in this study) are larger for children until the age of 13 is reached. F_0-differences between male and female speaker start around age 12, since the pitch changes for males during puberty around age 12 – 15. Female pitch drops from 7 to 12 but not after age 12. Also F_0 variation decreases; it reaches adult level at 14 (female) or 15 (male). The formant frequency variability reaches adult level simultaneously for all formants at 14. For females, however, F_1 decreases again after age 18 (sociolinguistic phenomenon). Only little work can be found on infants [Lin05, Mar02, Zaj05, Zma05].

Speech Recognition. A common approach to compensate the mismatch of filter bank energy values in children and adult speech resulting from the longer vocal tract and different formant frequency values is *vocal tract length normalisation* (VTLN) [Bur96, Cos05, Ele05, Giu03, Gus02, Hag04, Mol00, Pot97b, Cla98, Das98, Ste03b, Ger06]. The warping factor β scales the distances of the filters in the Mel filter bank. Additionally various adaptation and normalisation approaches are applied [Cos05, DAr04, Ele05, Ger06, Hag04, Pot97b, Ste03a]. In the following an overview of algorithms and investigations from the literature is given. In part, they are applied and verified in Chap. 7 using the corpora described in Chap. 4. VTLN, MAP, and MLLR are explained in detail in the next section.

In [Pot03], experiments on digit recognition are described. For young speakers of age 12 and below best results are achieved with acoustic models trained on children, whereas for children of age 13 and older acoustic models from adults perform best. Recognition rate is poor for children younger than 9 and reaches adult level at around 13 or 14.

		i:	I	E	{	A:	O:	U	u:	V
F_0	male	136	135	130	127	124	129	137	141	130
	female	235	232	223	210	212	216	232	231	221
	children	272	269	260	251	256	263	276	274	261
F_1	male	270	390	530	660	730	570	440	300	640
	female	310	430	610	860	850	590	470	370	760
	children	370	530	690	1010	1030	680	560	430	850
F_2	male	2290	1990	1840	1720	1090	840	1020	870	1190
	female	2790	2480	2330	2050	1220	920	1160	950	1400
	children	3200	2730	2610	2320	1370	1060	1410	1170	1590
F_3	male	3010	2550	2480	2410	2440	2410	2240	2240	2390
	female	3310	3070	2990	2850	2810	2710	2680	2670	2780
	children	3730	3600	3570	3320	3170	3180	3310	3260	3360

Table 3.2: Fundamental frequency F_0 and Formants $F_1 - F_3$ for English vowels and different speaker groups after Peterson and Barney [Pet53]. The age of the children was around 8 [Lee99].

The optimal warping factor β for VTLN is obtained by measuring the mean cepstral distance between adult and children vowels (Euclidean distance in cepstral space). In an exhaustive search the optimal β is found that minimises the distances in cepstral space. This warping factor is age dependent; for five-year-old children it is 0.7 for males and 0.65 for females with acoustic models trained on male adults. For male children of age 15 the warping factor reaches adult level ($\beta = 1.0$); with age 12 it starts growing stronger then the female warping factor. For females, adult level ($\beta = 0.85$) is reached with age 14. The remaining after-warping-distance in cepstral space decreases with increasing age. Phoneme dependent analysis shows that the same type of warping factor can be used for all phones. However, phone dependent warping can further reduce spectral mismatch. Potamianos et al. [Pot03] suggest a class dependent warping factor for phonemic classes.

A maximum likelihood approach for speaker normalisation is proposed in [Pot03, Pot97b]. The acoustic input is warped with the most likely β, given an HMM λ and an initial transcription obtained in a first recognition pass. This way, similar warping factors are obtained as in the case of minimising cepstral distances. This approach is extended by additionally maximising the likelihood with respect to spectral shaping and model selection. In [Pot03], spectral shaping is performed by applying a linear bias to the means μ_m of the codebook and model selection by choosing between acoustic models trained on 2 different age groups. Experiments showed that on average only three digits are necessary to estimate warping factor and linear bias, and that the improvements obtained on both influencing factors are additive with respect to the improvements obtained for each individual factor.

Gerosa investigates in his Phd-Thesis acoustic modelling of children speech [Ger06]. In a first step, cepstral mean and variance normalisation is applied (transcription task only, if all data of a speaker is available). Then, 3 approaches for VTLN are investigated; in all approaches the training is performed on speaker normalised (VTLN) utterances. The *two-pass VTLN* uses an initial transcription obtained in a first recognition pass (see above) to select the optimal β. The *fast VTLN* uses GMMs to estimate the optimal β and does not require word hypotheses on the test set. In the case of data augmentation age dependent models are trained with children data that has been warped to fit best to the respective age group. After this, full decoding is applied, which means, that successively models of all age groups are applied before finally the models with highest likelihood are selected.

CMLSN (Constrained MLLR based Speaker Normalisation) to estimate an affine transformation of the codebook by means of the EM algorithm is described in [Giu04, Ger06]. Again, the training data is normalised per speaker applying the optimal affine transformation. For testing the two-pass approach is applied. CMLSN always outperforms VTLN and shows similar performance as SAT (speaker adaptive training [Gal98]). Combinations VTLN plus SAT or VTLN plus CMLSN perform best.

[Pot03] and [Ger06] both report that for children worst recognition rates are obtained on adult HMMs; significantly better rates are reached after normalisation and best results on children models plus normalisation. Strongest improvement could be achieved on children younger than 12 [Pot03]. In the mismatched case, children perform better on adult female HMMs; utterance dependent warping is not better than speaker dependent warping [Ger06]. In the case of speaker normalised training [Ger06], high recognition rates are also obtained with models trained on adults *and* children.

At the KTH in Stockholm, children interacting with the animated talking agent *Pixie* are analysed. A different interaction behaviour of children is reported in [Bel03]; the transformation of children speech (with standard algorithms used for speech synthesis, e.g. PSOLA) to generate an appropriate input for a black-box recogniser is described in [Gus02]. The width of the short analysis window and the width of the filters in the Mel filter bank have no effect on the recognition rate as has been shown in [Li01].

Since the present thesis includes results from the Pf-Star project, a short overview of the research from all project partners is given next, to complete this literature survey. All investigations are summarised in the Pf-Star report [Rus04]. In [Ele05] VTLN is applied as well as MLLR and MAP adaptation. Undesirable effects on warping non-speech segments are reported. The effect of age-dependent and age-independent acoustic models as well as model retraining and MAP-adaptation is investigated in [DAr04] for read, spontaneous, and emotional speech. The corpus with read speech data will be described in Chap. 4. In [Ste03b, Ste05b] an approach for non-linear VTLN is developed and the speaking rate of read children speech is analysed. [Ste03a] investigates HMM interpolation with adult acoustic models. Improvements on German data were reported, when adding normalised adult data ($\beta = 1.2$) to the children training data [Rus04, Mai06b].

[Pot03], [Pot97b]	VTLN: mean cepstral distance; maximum-likelihood estimation: two-pass VTLN, spectral shaping, model selection
[Ger06], [Giu04]	two-pass VTLN, fast VTLN (GMM); data augmentation (warped data from other age groups); VTLN + CMLSN, VTLN + SAT
[Bel03]	interaction of children
[Gus02]	PSOLA to transform children speech
[Li01]	analysis of the filter bank
[Rus04], [Ele05], [DAr04], [Ste03a], [Ste03b], [Ste05b], [Ger04a], [Ger04b]	Pf-Star-project: VTLN, non-linear VTLN, MLLR, MAP, HMM-interpolation, age (in)dependent models; read, imitated, spontaneous, emotional, and non-native speech, speaking rate normalisation, augmentation with adult data

Table 3.3: Literature overview of children speech recognition in the order of appearance in the text.

Non-Native children are investigated in [Ger04a, Ger04b]. The word error rate achieved for Italian children speaking English on a recogniser trained on British English is 100 - 600 % higher than for British children. Recognition on *imitated speech*[7] is significantly better than on read speech. Lower error rates using non-native acoustic models confirm that there are systematic differences between native and non-native speech. Similarly low error rates are achieved by applying MLLR on native acoustic models. More details on MLLR can be found in the following section.

A summary of this literature overview can be found in Tab. 3.3.

3.3.2   Applied Adaptation Techniques

Gales discriminates in [Gal01] between three broad classes of adaptation: model indepen-dent schemes (i) are directly applied to feature vectors c. The most common forms are cepstral mean and cepstral variance normalisation. Feature transformation (ii) like vocal tract length normalisation (VTLN) also act on the features, but are usually optimised with respect to the likelihood or the word accuracy of the acoustic models. Finally (iii), model transformation is directly applied to the acoustic models. e.g. mean and variances of the codebook. Examples are speaker adaptive training (SAT), maximum likelihood lin-ear regression (MLLR), and maximum a posteriori adaptation (MAP). Further approaches to adaptation of acoustic models can be found in [Oh06, Ste03a, Ste04b]. Next, those approaches are described which will be applied in the following section of this thesis to

---

[7]Imitated speech means, that the candidate had listened to a prerecorded speaker before his utterance was recorded. In this case, the pronunciation of foreign words is improved; errors resulting from a wrong grapheme-to-phoneme-mapping (e.g. pronunciation of the silent 'e' at the end of the word) do not occur. However, mispronunciations still do occur, if the candidate is not familiar with a foreign sound and if he is not able to discriminate similar phones he perceives.

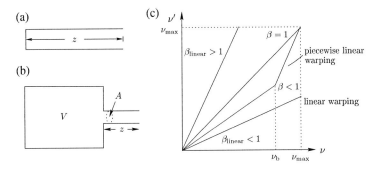

Figure 3.10: (a) Uniform tube model of the vocal tract, (b) Helmholtz resonator; (c) warping function $\nu \to \nu'$ for different factors β_{linear} (linear warping) and β (piecewise linear warping). Figures after [Eid96, Mol01].

improve recognition of children. First, vocal tract length normalisation is discussed (after [Ste05b]); then, adaptation techniques follow that have been implemented in the context of this thesis (after [Mai05a]).

VTLN. Microphone or room characteristics are distortions that are multiplicative in the spectrum domain and additive in the cepstrum domain. VTLN, however, tries to compensate for the effect of speaker specific vocal tract lengths by warping the frequency axis of the spectrum[8]. A uniform tube of length z as shown in Fig. 3.10 (a) is a very crude approximation of the human vocal tract. However, according to [Eid96], this model is appropriate for open vowels like /A:/; the mean frequency of the i-th formant F_i is approximately [Wak77]

$$F_i \approx \frac{(2i-1)\,c}{4z}, \tag{3.42}$$

where c denotes the velocity of sound. It can be seen in the formula, that a smaller z causes higher F_i. A more complex model is the *Helmholtz Resonator* that is appropriate for closed front vowels like /i:/. It is a tube of volume V with a narrow orifice with a cross section surface of size A as shown in Fig. 3.10 (b). Here, the first formant frequency (unit 1/sec) is *proportional* to $\sqrt{A/(V\,z)}$ (unit 1/m). Scaling each dimension with β while keeping z constant results in formants scaled with $1/\sqrt{\beta}$. This shows, that changes of the vocal tract affect formant frequencies of different phonemes in a different way. Fig. 3.10 (c) shows linear warping

$$\nu' = \beta_{\text{linear}}\,\nu \tag{3.43}$$

---

[8]VTLN is equivalent with a linear transformation (matrix multiplication) in cepstrum space [Pit03].

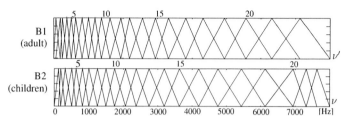

Figure 3.11: Top: Mel filter bank with 22 filters; the frequency-axis is sampled with 128 values. Bottom: bi-linear expanded filter bank. When using B2 instead of B1, this implies a mapping $\nu \to \nu'$ which satisfies piecewise linear VTLN with $\beta = 0.8$.

for different values of β_{linear}. $\beta_{\text{linear}} < 1$ means that the Mel filters are shifted to higher frequencies and the highest filters even to frequencies $\nu > \nu_{\text{max}}$. Piecewise linear warping constrains all filters to the interval $\nu_{\text{min}} \leq \nu \leq \nu_{\text{max}}$. It is defined as

$$\nu' = \begin{cases} \beta\,\nu & 0 \leq \nu \leq \nu_b \\ \frac{\nu_{\text{max}} - \beta\,\nu_b}{\nu_{\text{max}} - \nu_b}\,(\nu - \nu_b) + \beta\,\nu_b & \nu_b < \nu \leq \nu_{\text{max}} \end{cases} \qquad (3.44)$$

where ν_b is the boundary frequency that falls above the highest significant formant frequency (e.g. $7/8\,\nu_{\text{max}}$ as in [Ste05b]) and where ν_{max} is not greater than half the sampling rate.

Fig. 3.11, top, shows an example of a Mel filter bank with 22 filters[9]. Mel filtering of the spectrum means indirectly (cf. Sect 3.2.2) that it is first warped, then smoothed, and finally sampled (at the points defined by the peaks of the filter bank that are uniformly spaced in Mel space). The degree of smoothing is given by the common width of all filters in Mel space. To match e.g. the higher formant frequencies of children and the formant frequencies of adults, different sampling points must be chosen. When filterbank B1 is used for adult speech, then filterbank B2 may be appropriate for children. B2 is an expanded filterbank obtained from a mapping $\nu' \to \nu$. However, when applying B2 instead of B1, it is equivalent to map frequencies $\nu \to \nu'$ before applying the original bank B1. This second mapping (not the expansion of the filterbank) is described by $\nu' = \beta\nu$ and is referred to as vocal tract length normalisation. For children warping factors $\beta < 1$ are applied, which is exemplified for $\beta = 0.8$ and piecewise linear warping in Fig. 3.11. Given an adult filter bank B1 which e.g. has been used for training, the children filter bank B2 (e.g. for evaluation with children) is received by the expansion $\nu = (1/\beta)\,\nu'$. Each of the 20 lower bandpass filters in Fig. 3.11, bottom, can be found in Fig. 3.11, top, covering a lower frequency range; the filters 21 and 22 are above the boundary ν_b. Further reading on VTLN can be found in [Mol00, Cla98].

---

[9]Since in the *LME* feature extraction frontend 16 msec short time analysis windows are used ($= 256$ samples), the magnitude-squared spectrum consists of 128 samples, only. This is the reason for the artifacts visible for the narrow filters.

MAP. The maximum a posteriori adaptation is also known as Bayes adaptation [Hua01]. It computes a posteriori the parameters θ of the codebook from the set of observed test data $c^1, c^2, \ldots$. The Bayes estimate is obtained by maximising the equation

$$\theta_{MAP} = \underset{\theta}{\operatorname{argmax}}\, p(\theta | c^1, c^2, \ldots) = \underset{\theta}{\operatorname{argmax}}\, p(c^1, c^2, \ldots | \theta)\, p(\theta). \tag{3.45}$$

The adaptation of the means of the codebook as applied in Chap. 7 is given by the equation

$$\hat{\mu}_m = \frac{\phi_{MAP}\mu_m + \sum_v P(m|c^v, \lambda)\, c^v}{\phi_{MAP} + \sum_v P(m|c^v, \lambda)} \tag{3.46}$$

where $\phi_{MAP} \geq 0$ is a heuristic weight for the initially estimated mean μ_m. MAP estimation converges against the maximum likelihood estimate if enough adaptation data is available or for small ϕ_{MAP} [Woo01]. It is faster because initial models are used. The disadvantage is, that much data is required to robustly re-estimate all mean vectors in the codebook, however, this is alleviated when using semi-continuous HMM that have less parameters to estimate than continuous HMM. Details can be found in [Mai05a, Kul02, Sch96].

MLLR. If not enough balanced adaptation data is available, a more robust transformation is a global linear transformation that is applied to all densities in the codebook. This means that also a density m can be transformed that is not observed in the adaptation data. The most common transformation is MLLR using a set of linear regression functions to maximise the likelihood of the adaptation data [Leg95]. Each set of Gaussians sharing a transformation build a regression class; in the following all Gaussians will share the same transform: To estimate the mean of density m, the original mean is transformed with A and shifted with b. This can be rewritten with a single matrix multiplication

$$\hat{\mu}_m = A\mu_m + b = \widehat{W} \begin{bmatrix} \mu_m \\ 1 \end{bmatrix} \quad \text{with} \quad \widehat{W} = [\; Ab \;] \tag{3.47}$$

According to [Gal97] the matrices $\widehat{W}$ can be estimated with the EM-algorithm. In the E-step (estimation) the likelihood function

$$\mathcal{L}(\mathcal{C}, \mathcal{C}') = \eta - \frac{1}{2} \sum_m \sum_\tau \zeta_\tau(m) \left[\eta_m + \log \left| \hat{\Sigma}_m \right| + (c^\tau - \hat{\mu}_m)^{\mathrm{T}} \hat{\Sigma}_m^{-1} (c^\tau - \hat{\mu}_m) \right] \tag{3.48}$$

is computed, where the original model $\mathcal{C}$ is adapted to $\mathcal{C}'$; η is a constant only dependent on transition probabilities and η_m a normalisation constant for the Gaussian component m.

$$\zeta_\tau(m) = P(m|c^1, c^2, \ldots, c^t, \lambda) \tag{3.49}$$

is the probability that the density m has been used at time τ to produce the acoustic observation of length t. $\mathcal{L}(\mathcal{C}, \mathcal{C}')$ increases the likelihood of the adaptation data. By setting the derivative to zero the optimum transformation can be found.

When adapting $\boldsymbol{\mu}_m$, only, we can set $\widehat{\boldsymbol{\Sigma}}_m = \boldsymbol{\Sigma}_m$. Further, if the transformation is a translation ($\boldsymbol{A} = \boldsymbol{I}$, identity), the equation 3.47 can be directly solved and $\boldsymbol{b}$ is obtained [Sch96, Mai05a]. To calculate $\widehat{\boldsymbol{W}}$ in the general case we have to solve

$$\sum_\tau \sum_m \zeta_\tau(m) \boldsymbol{\Sigma}_m^{-1} \boldsymbol{c}^\tau \begin{bmatrix} \boldsymbol{\mu}_m \\ 1 \end{bmatrix}^{\mathrm{T}} = \sum_\tau \sum_m \zeta_\tau(m) \boldsymbol{\Sigma}_m^{-1} \widehat{\boldsymbol{W}} \begin{bmatrix} \boldsymbol{\mu}_m \\ 1 \end{bmatrix} \begin{bmatrix} \boldsymbol{\mu}_m \\ 1 \end{bmatrix}^{\mathrm{T}} \tag{3.50}$$

A solution for diagonal covariance matrices $\boldsymbol{\Sigma}_m$ is given in [Gal97, p.6]. For arbitrary (positive definite) covariance matrices a solution is obtained by applying the *Cholesky* decomposition

$$\boldsymbol{\Sigma}_m^{-1} = \boldsymbol{C}_m \boldsymbol{C}_m^{\mathrm{T}} \tag{3.51}$$

By the transformation $\tilde{\boldsymbol{\mu}}_m = \boldsymbol{C}_m^{\mathrm{T}} \boldsymbol{\mu}_m$ and $\tilde{\boldsymbol{c}}^\tau = \boldsymbol{C}_m^{\mathrm{T}} \boldsymbol{c}_\tau$ the MLLR can be applied in normalised domain in which all Gaussians have identity covariance matrices $\tilde{\boldsymbol{\Sigma}}_m = \boldsymbol{I}$ [Gal97, p.12].

Given the updated mean vectors $\widehat{\boldsymbol{\mu}}_m$ the covariance matrices can be adapted in a second pass. The new covariance matrices are

$$\widehat{\boldsymbol{\Sigma}}_m = \widehat{\boldsymbol{H}} \boldsymbol{\Sigma}_m \widehat{\boldsymbol{H}}^{\mathrm{T}} \tag{3.52}$$

Again, this is solved in normalised domain and we yield

$$\widehat{\boldsymbol{H}} = \frac{\sum_m \left\{ \boldsymbol{C}_m^{\mathrm{T}} \left[\sum_\tau \zeta_\tau(m) \left(\boldsymbol{c}^\tau - \widehat{\boldsymbol{\mu}}_m \right) \left(\boldsymbol{c}^\tau - \widehat{\boldsymbol{\mu}}_m \right)^{\mathrm{T}} \right] \boldsymbol{C}_m \right\}}{\sum_k \sum_\tau \zeta_\tau(m)} \tag{3.53}$$

Further details on MLLR can be found in [Mai05a, Mai06d, Gal97, Gal98].

3.4   Summary

The optimal decision rule in automatic classification given a (0,1)-cost function is given by the Bayes classifier. It is approximated e.g. by statistical classifiers. In this chapter, the Gaussian classifier (quadric discriminant analysis), the LDA-classifier (linear discriminant analysis), and GMM are described. Artificial neural networks (ANN) are distribution free classifiers. Leave-one-speaker out (loo) evaluation is explained as well as ROC evaluation. The class-wise averaged recognition rate (CL) is in the case of unbalanced data a more meaningful evaluation measure than the overall recognition rate (RR). CL is the unweighted average of the recalls. For the two-class case, an algorithm to optimise CL on the validation data set is given. Boosting combines weak classifiers to a strong classifier; a modification of the AdaBoost algorithm is used for feature selection.

Speech recognisers are evaluated with the word accuracy (WA) or word error rate (WER). In a first step, features are extracted from the speech signal. The *LME* recogniser uses standard cepstral features (MFCC) and their first order derivative. TRAP-features

(TempoRAl Patterns) describe the temporal progression considering a wide temporal context but only a small frequency band. The tandem approach combines scores of band-dependent TRAP-classifiers to feature vectors. Acoustic modelling with HMMs and language modelling (LM) using the *LME* software ISADORA is described in [Sch95, Ste05b]. Polyphone based recursive semi-continuous HMMs, feature streams, and n-gram LMs have been explained. The Viterbi algorithm computes a score for the acoustic observation based on the most likely state sequence. Forced alignment calculates based on the Viterbi probabilities the time intervals of words for a known transcription and a given speech signal. Speech decoding searches for the most likely word sequence. The combination of scores obtained from acoustic and language models is dependent on the parameters language weight γ_{lw} and insertion penalty γ_{ip}. Phone recognition is performed in a similar way or by means of a frame classifier.

On children, up to 170 % higher error rates are reported. Differences between children and adults are the shorter vocal tract of children and the resulting higher formants, as well as higher inter- and intra-speaker variabilities. Speaking rate differs as well as the amount of extraneous speech or breathing noises. [Lee99] reports differences up to age 15. Worst recognition for children is obtained on adult HMMs; best performance is achieved with children HMMs. If not enough training data is available, the recogniser has to be adapted to the children, or vice versa. Vocal tract length normalisation (VTLN), maximum likelihood linear regression (MLLR), and maximum a posteriori adaptation (MAP) are described in detail.

Chapter 4

Data and Annotations

To evaluate non-native English, a corpus of German children reading English sentences has been recorded in two different schools. The recordings took place in the context of the Pf-Star project and are described in [Bat05a, Rus03, Bat04a]. To compare the non-native English with native speech, another children corpus has been recorded in Birmingham [DAr04]. Besides this BE data, data from American children will additionally be investigated in the present thesis. A children speech recogniser will be the basis of all algorithms developed for pronunciation scoring of children. Such a recogniser can also be received by adapting an adult speech recogniser to children. These investigations require further corpora with adult data. At the end of this chapter, Tab. 4.11 will summarise all details of the six databases used in this thesis.

4.1 Non-Native English from Children

In this section, the data recorded from German children reading English texts is presented. In the first part the NONNATIVE database and its three subsets will be described. It follows in the second part an overview of the annotations of this corpus. In the last part, a description of additional recordings of good German readers of English texts can be found.

4.1.1 The NONNATIVE Database

The NONNATIVE database comprises recordings of German children reading English texts. It has been recorded during the Pf-Star project and is described in [Bat05a, Rus03]. After a general overview of the corpus, its three subsets will be presented in detail.

The database was recorded in Erlangen and contains 3.4 hrs. of realistic speech from 57 children (26 male and 31 female) from a grammar school[1] (Ohm-Gymnasium) and a general-education secondary school[2] (Montessori-Schule Erlangen). In the following OHM and MONT is used to name the data from the two schools. A superset of OHM that includes

---

[1]Grade 5–13
[2]Grade 5–9

additional data from older pupils is denoted as OHMPLUS. All recordings include reading errors, repetitions of words, word fragments, and nonverbals. For the recording, a headset with preamplifier was used (dnt Call4U Comfort), which was connected to the sound card of the data collection computer. The signals were recorded with 44.1 kHz and 16 bit quantisation but downsampled to 16 kHz for all experiments in this thesis. The data collection took place in a classroom, where only the child and an instructor were present. The reference texts the children had to read consist of 18,597 words and are divided in 4,627 sentences or phrases (4,627 files). The size of the vocabulary of the reference texts is 934 words. Originally it was intended that all partners of the Pf-Star project should record the same sentences and word lists. However, most children recorded in Erlangen had been learning English for half a year only and thus had very poor English skills. Therefore, only a few word and sentence lists containing known words were used and supplemented with known texts from the text book used in the respective school. For all data, the reference text (which had to be read) is available as well as a manual transliteration.

The age of the children is 11.1 years on average; most children in MONT were 10–12 (grade 5–6), most in OHM were 10–11 (grade 5). OHMPLUS includes 4 additional children of the 7th grade. Detailed information on the speakers can be found in Tab. A.1 and A.2 in Appendix A).

The pronunciation of the data has been labelled by up to 14 experts on the word level, on the sentence level, and partially on the text and speaker level. On average, each pupil read about 3.8 texts. Each text contains around 11 sentences or short phrases. Additionally, some children read lists of words. The lists have not been graded on the text level, since those gradings are usually "more" than just counting all mispronounced words: The experts e.g. also assess, whether the student understood the text he is reading. Detailed information for each subset of the corpus is given in the following. A detailed description of the annotations can be found in Sect. 4.1.2.

The MONT Data and its Annotations (1 Expert). The MONT subset of the NON-NATIVE corpus (recorded at the Montessori-Schule) consists of recordings from 25 children (17 female and 8 male). Their age was 10 – 13 (grade 5 and 6). The recordings comprise 1.6 hrs. of speech; 2,108 sentences have been read which contain 7,640 words. The vocabulary consists of 621 types[3]. Part of the material that has been read are word lists with 951 tokens (76 types) which were read by 14 children.

The data has been graded by one expert on the word, the sentence, and on the speaker level. The expert (rater S) was a German student of English (graduate level). On the word level, she marked all mispronounced words. In some cases also the transcription of the wrong pronunciation is given in SAMPA [Sampa]. A comparison of Tab. A.1 and A.2 in Appendix A suggests that the MONT children have worse pronunciation since much more words have been marked. All sentences have been graded with school grades (marks) 1 (best) to 5 (worst pronunciation).

---

[3]Each word in the vocabulary is referred to as type. Each occurrence of a word in the spoken sentences is a token

level	MONT		OHM		OHMPLUS ($\supset$ OHM)	
	tokens	experts	tokens	experts	tokens	experts
word	7,640	S, M	8,088	$S, T_1 - T_{12}, N, M$	10,957	$S, T_1 - T_{12}, N, M$
sentence	2,108	S	1,303	S	2,519	S
text	98	–	97	$T_1 - T_{12}, N$	123**	$T_1 - T_{12}, N$
speaker	25	S	28	$S, (T_1 - T_{12}, N)^\star$	32	$S, (T_1 - T_{12}, N)^\star$

Table 4.1: Overview of available ratings of the NONNATIVE data. ($\star$) the average of the 3.8 text ratings is used; ($\star\star$) word lists have not been labelled at the text level.

After this, the data has been rated on the speaker level. The speaker annotation is also performed with marks 1–5. In this second pass, the annotations of the first pass were not visible. Tab. 4.1 shows the number of tokens that are annotated per level. Additionally, rater M (German student of linguistics, graduate level) annotated syntactic boundaries on the word level. He annotated for each word the category of the syntactic boundary [Bat98] which would follow, if the reader used the correct prosody for the sentence. Details on the annotations will follow in Sect. 4.1.2.

The OHM Data and its Annotations (14 Experts). Recordings of the OHM-subset of the NONNATIVE corpus (28 pupils) have been recorded at Ohm-Gymnasium. The 15 male and 13 female children were all 10 – 11 years old and read 1,303 sentences and phrases (1.2 hrs. of speech). The number of words is 8,088 tokens and 323 types. All children had been learning English for half a year only (grade 5).

This part of the corpus has been annotated by 14 experts. The first expert is again rater S. In the same way as for the MONT data, she has annotated the data on the word, sentence, and speaker level. Again, also rater M annotated syntactic boundaries. Additionally, the data has been annotated by 12 teachers of English (raters $T_1 - T_{12}$) on the word and text level. The teachers $T_8 - T_{12}$ are student teachers who have less than 2 years of teaching experience. The 14th rater is a native teacher (rater N). N is British and was working as an exchange teacher, who taught German children at Ohm-Gymnasium. An overview of available ratings is given in Tab. 4.1. Some of the experts rated the data again half a year later: T_2, T_3, T_4, T_6, and the student teacher T_8. This makes it possible to measure not only the inter-rater agreement but also the intra-rater agreement (cf. Chap. 6).

Summing up, the following annotations are available: On the word level, mispronounced words have been marked by 14 raters ($T_1 - T_8$, N, and S). Rater S carefully marked all phone deviations (cf. Sect. 4.1.2), whereas the teachers marked all those words, where they would have stopped and corrected the students in class. This means that a teacher does not mark all mispronounced words but only some selected cases in order to avoid asking too much of the children and frustrating them. M labelled categories of syntactic boundaries. On the sentence level, only S graded the data with marks 1 – 5. All other experts rated the data on the text level. On the speaker level, ratings are again available from S. For $T_1 - T_8$ and N speaker level ratings are automatically generated by averaging the text level gradings (3.8 on average). There was no calibration labelling for the experts: The teachers rated in the way like they are used to do it in their daily work. Ratings of 12 teachers on the text level have been reported in [Hac05a]; the word level marking of the first 10 teachers is analysed in [Hac07a].

The OHMPLUS Data and its Annotations (1–14 Experts). There are some more recordings available that are only included in the OHMPLUS data and not in the OHM-set. This additional data is separated from the OHM-set, since the children were on the one hand older than 11 (and had been learning English for more than one year), on the other hand, they additionally read word lists where ratings are only available from rater S and not from all 14 experts. OHMPLUS is a superset of OHM

$$\text{OHM} \subset \text{OHMPLUS} \subset \text{NONNATIVE} \tag{4.1}$$

The 4 additional children in OHMPLUS are not grade 5 as the children in OHM but grade 6 and 7. The 3 male pupils were of age 12 – 13 and the female speaker 14. The 32 speakers read in total 2,519 sentences with 10,957 words. The vocabulary consists of 605 words. OHMPLUS consists of 1.6 hrs. of speech that is annotated by the experts S, M, T_1 – T_{12}, and N. As for OHM, 5 teachers rated the data half a year later again.

The word lists[4] read by the 4 additional children consist of 879 tokens (220 types). For this data, word level annotations are only available from S and M; text level rating was not performed.

4.1.2   Annotations of the NONNATIVE Database.

In this section, the annotations on word, sentence, text, and speaker level are described in detail. As explained in the previous section, not all ratings are available for all parts of the data. An overview, which part is annotated by which rater is given in Tab. 4.1.

Word Level: Mispronounced Words. For the OHM-subset and the largest part of OHMPLUS, word level ratings are available from 14 experts, for the MONT subset only from S. Mispronounced words have been marked with $\mathcal{X}$. On default, all words are labelled as correctly pronounced ($\mathcal{O}$). The teachers marked words of the reference text. S, however, marked the words while she was transliterating the data. Consequently, she marked words of the spoken word sequences. Strictly speaking, she used several labels, that are mapped onto the broad category $\mathcal{X}$ in the present thesis. The 3 examples

    (a) Liz it's [**is] one [**on] o'clock
    (b) On &Monday Claire visited [*/vIT@/] visited [*/vIsi:d@t/] a
    farm with the Kellys
    (c) Paul [**$Paul] has got a white cat

corpus	S	T_1	T_2	T_3	T_4	T_5	T_6	T_7	T_8	T_9	T_{10}	T_{11}	T_{12}	N	μ
MONT	1,005	–	–	–	–	–	–	–	–	–	–	–	–	–	–
OHM	341	372	378	320	312	579	589	**298**	355	384	380	325	331	**572**	395
OHMPLUS	566*	527	525	452	418	794	781	462	495	525	517	429	479	711	549

Table 4.2: Word level annotation: Number of $\mathcal{X}$ labels for different subsets of the NONNA-TIVE data from 14 experts. (⋆) incl. word lists, 481, else.

corpus	M_0	M_1	M_2	M_3
MONT	4,585	568	66	2,421
OHM	5,455	830	104	1,699
OHMPLUS	6,881	967	157	2,952

Table 4.3: Word level annotations of syntactic boundaries by rater M.

exemplify the different annotations:

- The prefix "&" denotes a deviation of one phone within the word (360 words).

- The prefix "&&" denotes deviations of two phones (28 words).

- [**is] denotes a substitution of the preceding word (475 words).

- [**$Paul] denotes a substitution with a German pronounced word (61 words).

- [*/vIsi:d@t/] gives a phonetic transcription of a mispronounced word (495 words).

To compare the annotation of S with the other experts, first the spoken utterance had to be aligned with the reference sentences. Deletions (words in the reference text that have been omitted by the speaker) are additionally marked as mispronounced (51 words). Further $\mathcal{X}$-labels have been generated for adjacent words of insertions (101 words). Tab. 4.2 shows the number of words, which have been marked by each expert. For the OHM set in the mean (μ) 395 out of 8,088 words are mispronounced (5 %): T_7 marked only 298 words whereas the native speaker marked 572 words. In the OHMPLUS set, also 5 % are marked on average. For MONT 1,005 words out of 7,640 are mispronounced (13 %). Numbers per speaker can be found in Appendix A, Tab. A.1 and A.2.

Word Level: Syntactic Boundaries. On the word level, also syntactic boundaries have been annotated by rater M. However, he did not listen to the utterances but performed the labelling on the reference sentences applying solely linguistic knowledge. After that, the reference text was mapped onto the spoken word sequence. The boundaries are introduced as M_1, M_2, and M_3 in [Bat98, Kie96, Bat96], with M_3 being the strongest boundary. In short, the following rules were followed:

---

[4]Text ID T138 an T139, cf. page 193

corpus	1	2	3	4	5	μ
MONT	283	892	487	270	176	2.6
OHM	205	701	312	68	17	2.2
OHMPLUS	228	883	400	95	34	2.3

Table 4.4: Sentence level annotation: Marks 1 (best) to 5 (worst) as well as the average mark (μ) from expert S for different subsets of the NONNATIVE data (OHMPLUS without word-lists).

- to cause a boundary, each constituent has to consist of at least 3 words

- M_1 boundaries occur ahead of a prepositional phrase, ahead of a predication ("is", "are"), within enumerations, often before names (e.g. "thank you, Dave"), and e.g. before "too" or after "hello"

- M_2 boundaries occur at the comma for appositions, at the dash, and e.g. after "please" in the beginning of a sentence.

- M_3 boundaries occur at the end of a sentence (full stop, exclamation mark) and e.g. after "yes" or "no"

The default label is M_0 (no boundary). As can be seen in Tab. 4.3, the most frequent boundary is M_3. Between 33 % and 40 % of the words are followed by some boundary.

Sentence Level: Marks 1 – 5. Sentence level ratings have been only given by rater S, but for all sentences of the NONNATIVE corpus. She gave discrete marks from 1 (best) to 6 (worst). However, mark 6 occurs only in a few cases, so it has been mapped onto 5. Tab. 4.4 shows that the most frequent mark is 2 followed by 3. The average mark is 2.6 for the MONT subset and 2.3 for the OHMPLUS data.

Text Level: Marks 1 – 5. 12 teachers (T_1 – T_{12}) and a native teacher N graded the data on the text level. As for the sentence level, marks 1 – 6 were used and the few occurrences of 6 mapped onto 5. Here, also some intermediate marks were allowed: 1, 1.3, 1.5, 1.7, 2, 2.3 .... Not all teachers, however, made use of the intermediate marks to the same extent. For the OHMPLUS data, the distribution of the ratings for 13 experts is shown in Tab. 4.5. For the OHM set, a similar overview can be found in Appendix A (Tab. A.4). The average mark is between 2.1 (rater N) and 3.3 (rater T_5). Some experts did not assign the mark 5 at all, T_7 did not use the mark 1. Five teachers reevaluated the data half a year later. For these cases the exact numbers are shown in Tab. A.3. The mean rating per teacher is slightly better in the second pass, but the relation among each other is preserved. The mean text-rating for each speaker of the OHMPLUS data is summarised in A.2 .

expert	1	1 + x	2	2 + x	3	3 + x	4	4 + x	5	μ
T_1	12	0	42	0	**51**	2	14	0	2	2.6
T_2	11	18	22	21	**30**	11	8	0	2	2.5
T_3	27	0	40	0	**42**	0	12	0	2	2.4
T_4	25	14	**27**	20	23	5	8	1	0	2.2
T_5	5	0	22	0	**41**	0	41	0	14	**3.3**
T_6	10	28	**30**	28	10	8	7	2	0	2.2
T_7	0	5	14	25	**31**	21	14	4	9	3.1
T_8	7	0	25	0	**66**	0	22	0	3	2.9
T_9	11	0	47	0	**55**	0	10	0	0	2.5
T_{10}	10	10	**33**	22	27	10	6	5	0	2.4
T_{11}	14	0	**43**	9	28	6	20	0	3	2.6
T_{12}	25	1	**41**	6	39	0	7	1	3	2.3
N	15	**39**	17	20	19	11	1	1	0	**2.1**

Table 4.5: Text level annotation: marks 1 (best) to 5 (worst) for OHMPLUS from 13 experts, $x \in \{0.3, 0.5, 0.7\}$. Per line, the most frequent mark is shown in bold.

Speaker Level: Marks 1 − 5. A speaker level grading is only performed by S (marks 1 − 5). The mean rating is 3.4 for the MONT data (4 speakers with 2; 10 with 3; 9 with 4; 2 with 5). For OHMPLUS the mean grade is 2.6 (3 with 1; 12 with 2; 13 with 3; 3 with 4; 1 with 5). For the experts T_1 − T_{12} and N the speaker rating is generated from the text ratings of the respective speaker. The average of the speaker ratings per expert is between 2.0 and 3.3. Except for T_5, no rating worse than 4 can be found. The speaker level ratings are summarised in Appendix A (per expert: Tab. A.5; per speaker: Tab. A.1 and A.2)

4.1.3 NONNATIVERC: Additional Data from the Reading Contest

During the reading contest at Ohm-Gymnasium additional 5 children reading English texts could be recorded (age 11 − 14). The reading contest is a competition among the best readers of the lower grades of the school. Each participant had to read one known and one unknown text. The winner (male) was from the 8th grade, all other readers were from the 6th grade (1 male, 3 female). The amount of collected data in NONNATIVERC is only 0.4 h but 3,692 words; the reading is more fluent than in the NONNATIVE data. The vocabulary contains 423 words only, since all children read the same unknown text, and also the known text was the same for the 4 readers from the 6th grade.

This corpus will be used for training, only. The purpose is to put non-native speech from children with rather good pronunciation to the training of the native English speech recogniser (Tab. 4.6). Also the syntactic boundaries will be trained using this database. For this reason, M annotated this corpus with the boundaries M_1 (327 words), M_2 (265 words), and M_3 (460 words). 2,636 words are not followed by a syntactic boundary (M_0). The rater annotated the reference texts without listening to the recordings; after that, the reference text was mapped onto the spoken word sequence.

	# speakers	# sentences	# words
training	5	350	3,177
validation	5	55	515
all	5	405	3,692

Table 4.6: Partition of the NONNATIVERC data: total number of speakers, sentences, and words. This databases will be only used for training.

4.2   Native English from Children

To evaluate non-native speech from German children speaking English, native acoustic models are required. There will be two corpora employed, one with American children (YOUTH) and one with British children (BIRMINGHAM).

4.2.1   YOUTH: Native, American Data

The YOUTH corpus[5] (© 2002, Carnegie Speech Company, Inc.) contains more than 14 hrs. of speech from 135 American children of age 8 – 10. The 56 boys and 79 girls are from two different schools and have been recorded with 16 kHz. They wore Andrea NC-72 headsets attached to a preamplifier. Only one child was recorded a second time, where the second recording is not used in this thesis. Thus, 24,947 out of 25,122 sentences are used. The corpus also comprises some speakers with a cold and some non-native speakers. The non-natives, however, grew up in the states and have only little or no perceptible accent. The children read sentences from nursery rhymes and tales such as Peter Pan. The texts consist of short sentences, phrases, and single words. Recordings that did not correspond exactly to the expected phonetic content were eliminated or re-recorded. There was a set of 179 utterances, which had to be read by all children. The second set each child had to read was repeated for every 10th child (25 utterances). There was a fixed 45 min. session for each child, thus most children did not finish the texts. The number of words is 85,009. The vocabulary consists of only 778 words, since the texts were read repeatedly.

Tab. 4.7 shows the partition of the YOUTH corpus into training, validation and test data. This partition was used in the Pf-Star project by all partners and is balanced with respect to the school and the gender. 82 speakers are in the training set, 26 in the validation set, and 27 in the test data set. In some experiments, where YOUTH is combined with other corpora during training, the subsets training-2 and validation-2 of training-1 and validation-1, respectively, are used. The three sets are speaker disjoint. For automatic speech recognition 39 phonemes are used to model the American English words. This requires a phonetic transcription of all words. In most cases, the transcription could be found in the CMU pronunciation dictionary [CmuDict]; however, since the *LME*-recogniser cannot handle pronunciation alternatives, a manual selection of the most standard English

---

[5] A license of the database was bought during the Pf-Star project.

	# male	# female	# speakers	# sentences	# words
training-1	34	48	82	15,180	51,807
validation-1	10	16	26	4,868	16,701
test	12	15	27	4,899	16,501
training-2	34	48	82	7,500	25,543
validation-2	10	16	26	500	1,688
all	56	79	135	24,947	85,009

Table 4.7: Partition of the YOUTH database: number of male and female speakers, total number of speakers, number of sentences, and number of words. Training, validation, and test set are disjoint. Training-2 and validation-2 are subsets of training-1 and validation-1.

pronunciation was necessary. A list of the phonemes and its sub-phonemic units is shown in Appendix B.2.

The YOUTH database has been evaluated in [Par04, Esk02]. Other available American children corpora are the Colorado kids corpus that is analysed in [Ban03] and the CID corpus (Central Institute for the Deaf) analysed in [Lee99, Ger06].

4.2.2 BIRMINGHAM: **Native, British Data**

Another database with native English speech from children is the BIRMINGHAM corpus. This database comprises speech from British children recorded at the University of Birmingham and in two local primary schools in Birmingham and Malvern [DAr04]. Part of the recordings was made in an open library area and contains background noise, part was made in a closed class room, and part in a soundproof audiometric recording booth. The corpus was collected in the context of the Pf-Star project. It has been recorded with 22.05 kHz using an Emkay 3565 head mounted microphone. For this thesis, all data is downsampled to 16 kHz.

The corpus is described in [DAr04, Bat05a] and contains speech from 152 children[6]. of age 4 – 14. However, the largest part of the corpus are speakers of age 6 – 11. The children read 19,451 sentences, phrases, word lists, and digits. Each child read 20 SCRIBE sentences (an anglicised version of the phonetically balanced US TIMIT 460 sentence set), a standard text that can be used for accent classification, 20 digit triples, and finally word lists, phonetically rich sentences, and generic phrases that had been provided for all Pf-Star partners by the ITC-irst in Trento. Those files, which contain solely word fragments have been removed, so that only 18,701 utterances are used in this thesis (7.8 hrs.): This set consists of 54,182 words; the number of types is 1,740.

The partition of the BIRMINGHAM data in speaker disjoint training, validation, and test sets is shown in Tab 4.8. The validation-1 set contains 1 speaker per gender and age (6 –11).

---

[6] This is a preliminary version of the corpus. The final set (described in [DAr04, Bat05a]) contains after further recordings a total number of 159 speakers. Since the increase is negligible, the experiments in this thesis were not repeated using the larger set.

	m	f	age											# spk.	# sent.	# words
			4	5	6	7	8	9	10	11	12	13	14			
training	45	36	1	1	3	4	20	2	36	5	3	3	3	81	11,111	32,992
validation-1	6	6	0	0	2	2	2	2	2	2	0	0	0	12	864	1,858
validation-2	43	38	0	0	5	6	22	4	37	7	0	0	0	81	1,800	4,940
test	27	33	0	0	10	10	10	10	10	10	0	0	0	60	6,726	19,332
all	77	75	1	1	15	16	32	14	47	17	3	3	3	152	18,701	54,182

Table 4.8: Partition of the BIRMINGHAM database: number of male/female speakers, number of speakers per age group, total number of speakers, number of sentences, and number of words. Training, validation-1, and test set are disjoint.

BE	AE	BE example	
/Q/	/A/	/pQt/	
/e/	/E/	/pet/	not for /eI/
/@U/	/oU/	/n@Uz/	
/A:/	/{/	/A:sk/	beginning of word, only
/A:/	/A/	/plA:nt/	
/@/	/V/	/@baUt/	

Table 4.9: Mapping BE → AE. BE pronunciation has to be modelled with AE phonemes when evaluating BE speakers on AE acoustic models.

The test set consists of 60 speakers, 10 per age (6 – 11). Only the training data additionally contains some children of age 4, 5, 12, 13, 14. In Chap. 7 a second, larger validation set will be used: From the union of the training and the validation-1 data, randomly 300 sentences have been selected per age group for the validation-2 set.

For automatic speech recognition 44 phonemes are used to model the British English words. A list of the phonemes and its sub-phonemic units is shown in Appendix B.2. The transcription of most words could be found in the Beep pronunciation dictionary [Beep]. However, in some cases in Chap. 7 the BIRMINGHAM data will be evaluated with American English acoustic models. In this case, all BIRMINGHAM words are not built from the 44 British English phonemes but from the 39 American English phonemes. This case should be motivated with an example: Whereas Beep suggests to transcribe "apart" with /@pA:t/, the CMU pronunciation dictionary for AE [CmuDict] would suggest /VpArt/. However, in the described case, the *British pronunciation* of "apart" should be modelled with *AE phonemes*. As discussed in Sect. 2.1.1 and summarised in Sect. B.1 /@/ and /A:/ are not among the AE phones. A possible modelling would be /VpAt/[7]. The mapping of the British pronunciation onto AE phones is described in Tab. 4.9.

_____
[7]also /Vp{t/ and /VpVt/ were tried, but resulted in lower performance

	# speakers	# sentences	# words
training-1	233	13,604	190,140
training-2	172	1,850	27,232
training-3	191	1,822	25,648
validation	7	173	1,827
test	27	191	5,181
all	233	13,968	197,148

Table 4.10: Partition of the VERBMOBIL database: total number of speakers, number of sentences, and number of words. Training, validation, and test are disjoint but not speaker disjoint. The training-1 set contains 49 non-native speakers. Training-2 and training-3 are small subsets of training-1, where training-2 contains only native speakers.

4.3 Adult Speech

As native English adult speech corpus, the VERBMOBIL corpus is employed[8]. It comprises 22.5 hrs. of spontaneous speech from 233 American speakers and is described in [Ste05b]. The 13,965 utterances consist of 197,148 words; the sentences have an average length of 14 words which is significantly longer than for all other corpora ($\leq$ 4 words, except NONNATIVERC). Annotations of the gender are not available.

The partition of the data is the same as in [Ste05b] and can be found in Tab. 4.10. Unfortunately, the data sets turned out to be not speaker disjoint[9]. Further it turned out that – despite the fact that there is an additional VERBMOBIL DENGLISH corpus with German speakers of English sentences (not used in the present thesis) – also the VERBMOBIL training set contains 49 non-native speakers (972 utterances), mostly Germans. Training-2 is a small subset of training-1, which contains solely native speakers; the other subset training-3 contains around 50 % data from non-native speakers.

The phonetic transcription has been revised and the version from the Verbmobil project is not used. The new transcription was obtained from the CMU pronunciation dictionary [CmuDict]. Further, the same phoneme inventory with 39 phonemes (cf. Appendix B.2) as in YOUTH is used. This preprocessing of the VERBMOBIL corpus makes it now comparable with the YOUTH database.

VMGERMAN is a corpus with German speech from adult speakers. In this thesis a subset with the size of 4.5 hours is used to train acoustic models of German phonemes. Details on this corpus can be found in Tab. 4.11.

4.4 Summary

There will be different databases evaluated in this thesis. NONNATIVE consists of 3.3 hrs. of German children reading English texts (beginners); NONNATIVERC contains additional

---

[8]Recorded during the *Verbmobil* project [Wah00]

[9]Thus, the total number of speakers is 233 and not 260 = 233 + 27 as reported in [Ste05b]

corpus	# spk.	L1	L2	age	voc. size	size [hrs.]	# words/sent.		# exp.
NONNATIVE	57	G	E	10 – 14	934	3.3	18,597	4,627	1–15
MONT	25	G	E	10 – 13	621	1.6	7,640	2,108	2
OHM	28	G	E	10 – 11	323	1.2	8,088	1,303	15
OHMPLUS	32	G	E	10 – 14	605	1.6	10,957	2,519	1–15
NONNATIVERC	5	G	E	11 – 14	423	0.4	3,692	405	1
YOUTH	135	AE	AE	8 – 10	778	14.2	85,009	24,947	-
BIRMINGHAM	152	BE	BE	4 – 14*	1,740	7.8	54,182	18,701	-
VERBMOBIL	233	AE**	AE	adult	3,946	22.5	197,148	13,965	-
VMGERMAN	82	G	G	adult	2,676	4.5	34,343	1,880	-

Table 4.11: Overview of the corpora: number of speakers, their languages L1 and L2 (G for German, E for English, and AE/BE for American/British English), age, size of the vocabulary, size in hours, number of spoken words and sentences, and number of experts who labelled the data. (⋆) The test set of BIRMINGHAM contains only children of age 6 – 11. (⋆⋆) The training set also contains 49 non-native speakers.

0.4 hours speech from good readers. YOUTH is a collection of 14.2 hrs. of American children, BIRMINGHAM contains 7.8 hrs. of British children. 22.5 hours spontaneous speech from American adults are collected in the VERBMOBIL database. VMGERMAN contains 4.5 hours of German speech. An overview of all corpora can be found in Tab 4.11. Children younger than 8 are only contained in the BIRMINGHAM database. There is data from 62 German children, 135 American children, 152 British children, and 315 adults; 181 of the adult speakers are native American and 49 are non-native speakers, who are solely contained in the VERBMOBIL training set. 82 speakers are used additionally to train German acoustic models (VMGERMAN). The NONNATIVE and the BIRMINGHAM speech database have been collected during the Pf-Star project. The vocabulary of the English corpora is largest for VERBMOBIL (3,946 words) and BIRMINGHAM (1,740 words). The longest English sentences are spoken in VERBMOBIL (around 14 words per sentence).

The NONNATIVE data consists of three parts that are annotated by a different number of experts. For the MONT set, rater S graded the data on the sentence and speaker level and marked mispronounced words at the word level. M annotated syntactic boundaries only based on linguistic knowledge and without listening to the spoken utterances. The OHM set has been annotated by 15 experts, again rater S and M, and additionally 13 teachers including one native speaker (rater N). The teachers marked mispronounced words and graded the data on the text level. The speaker grading is obtained by averaging the marks from the text level (3.8 texts per speaker). 5 teachers rated the data again half a year later. The OHMPLUS set is a superset of OHM which additionally contains 4 older children. The NONNATIVERC corpus only contains ratings from M.

Chapter 5

Assessment of Pronunciation and Reading

Given the data that has been described in the previous chapter, in the following algorithms for the automatic assessment of the pronunciation are being developed. A survey on such algorithms in the literature has already been given in Sect. 2.2.2. In this chapter, after some general considerations in the first section three different approaches are described: The first is based on special acoustic models for wrongly pronounced words, the second on pronunciation feature extraction, and the third and final approach is based on prosodic feature extraction. At the end, an algorithm is given to automatically detect prosodic boundaries, which can be used additionally to measure the reading proficiency of the students.

5.1 General Considerations

In the preceding chapter, the data has been described, which will be analysed in the experimental part of this thesis. Annotations are available that judge the pronunciation of the children on the word, sentence, text, and speaker level. In the present chapter automatic approaches to assess the data are presented. The performance of the presented algorithms can be measured by analysing the agreement between the expert annotation and the hypotheses of the system. Additional expert annotations are the expected syntactic boundaries. Those annotations are also word based: it has been labelled which word is followed by a boundary. Approaches will be presented to automatically estimate whether an expected boundary is present or not. It will be investigated whether there is a correlation between the goodness of a child's pronunciation and the classification rate of prosodic boundaries.

To automatically assess the pronunciation on the word level, word based features are calculated which will be described in the following sections. Additionally a context of few words might be helpful to detect local changes of the pronunciation. The high dimensional feature vectors are the basis for a statistical classification as described in Chap. 3.1.

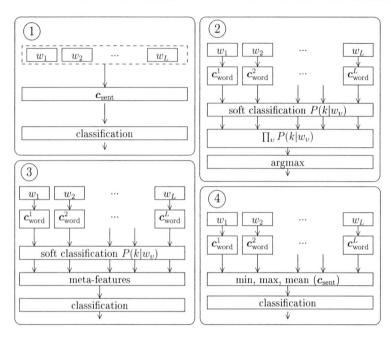

Figure 5.1: Sentence level classification using sentence features (1), averaged word classification (2), meta-features (3), and average word features (4). Word level features $\boldsymbol{c}_{\text{word}}^v$ are calculated from words w_v and sentence features $\boldsymbol{c}_{\text{sent}}$ from the whole sentence. $P(k|w_i)$ is the posterior probability of class k.

Approaches to assess the data on the sentence level are outlined in the following and illustrated in Fig. 5.1. K is the number of classes, L the total number of words w_v ($v = 1, \ldots, L$), $\boldsymbol{c}_{\text{word}}^v$ the respective d_{word}-dimensional word level feature vector, and $\boldsymbol{c}_{\text{sent}}$ the d_{sent}-dimensional sentence feature vector.

1. Sentence features: Calculate specific features $\boldsymbol{c}_{\text{sent}}$ from the larger time interval sentence. $\boldsymbol{c}_{\text{sent}}$ is input to a statistical classifier.

2. Averaged word classification: Features $\boldsymbol{c}_{\text{word}}$ are calculated word based, and classified on the word level. The output of the soft classification are K posterior scores $P(k|w_v), k = 1, ..., K$, for the K classes given the word w_v. Assuming statistical independence of the words w_v, the decision rule

$$\delta(k|\boldsymbol{w}) = \text{argmax}_k P(k|\boldsymbol{w}) = \text{argmax}_k \left(\prod_{v=1}^{L} P(k|w_v) \right) \tag{5.1}$$

is applied for a sentence $\boldsymbol{w} = w_1 w_2 \ldots w_L$. However, the pronunciation of the words w_v is usually not independent. Heuristic approaches to calculate the sentence a posteriori probabilities $P(k|\boldsymbol{w})$ are the calculation of $\sum_v P(k|w_v)$, $\min_v P(k|w_v)$, or $\max_v P(k|w_v)$. This way, the sentence pronunciation score reflects the average word score, or it is solely dependent on the worst mispronunciation or the best pronunciation observed for the underlying words.

3. Meta-features: An improved mapping of word level pronunciation scores onto sentence level scores utilises a second classification stage based on *meta-features* as proposed in [Bat07]. Minimum, maximum, and mean of the word based posterior scores $P(k|w_v)$, are calculated for each of K classes over all w_v and combined in a $3K$-dimensional feature vector:

$$c_{k,\text{meta}} = \min_{v=1}^{L} P(k|w_v), \qquad k = 1, \ldots, K \tag{5.2}$$

$$c_{K+k,\text{meta}} = \max_{v=1}^{L} P(k|w_v), \qquad k = 1, \ldots, K \tag{5.3}$$

$$c_{2K+k,\text{meta}} = \frac{1}{L} \sum_{v=1}^{L} P(k|w_v), \quad k = 1, \ldots, K \tag{5.4}$$

The components $c_{i,\text{meta}}$ of the resulting feature vector are referred to as *meta-features* since they are based on a prior classification step. In the next step, the meta-features are again input to another classifier. The intermediate step that calculates minimum, maximum, and mean of the word based classification results is necessary, since the number of words L varies per sentence. Otherwise, the word based scores could be simply concatenated to serve as input for the second classification stage.

4. Averaging of the word-based features: A compromise between approach (1) and (2) is the use of sentence features $\boldsymbol{c}_{\text{sent}}$ that are obtained from the calculation of minimum, maximum, and mean of each component of the word level feature vectors $\boldsymbol{c}_{\text{word}}^v$

$$c_{i,\text{sent}} = \min_{v=1}^{L} c_{i,\text{word}}^v, \qquad i = 1, \ldots, d_{\text{word}} \tag{5.5}$$

$$c_{d_{\text{word}}+i,\text{sent}} = \max_{v=1}^{L} c_{i,\text{word}}^v, \qquad i = 1, \ldots, d_{\text{word}} \tag{5.6}$$

$$c_{2d_{\text{word}}+i,\text{sent}} = \frac{1}{L} \sum_{v=1}^{L} c_{i,\text{word}}^v, \quad i = 1, \ldots, d_{\text{word}} \tag{5.7}$$

are the components of the resulting $3d_{\text{word}}$-dimensional feature vector which is input to a sentence level classification.

For the first approach, one has to make an effort for the development of specialised sentence level features. In (4), those features are calculated automatically, but the resulting feature vectors have a high dimension which might require more training data or a prior feature reduction. The advantage of the approaches (2) and (3) is that on the word level much more training data is available. The second, sentence level classification stage in (3) is performed in low dimensional space, e.g. $d_{\text{sent}} = 15$, if e.g. 5 school grades are classified.

Also for the text and speaker level classification the approaches (1) to (4) can be applied. However, due to sparse data on the higher levels, the approaches (1), (3), and (4) won't be used. On the word level, not only the approach based on features $c_{\text{word}}^{\upsilon}$ will be investigated, but also an approach on mispronunciation word models, which additionally allows pronunciation analysis on the phone level. This approach is described in the following section.

5.2   Acoustic Models for Wrongly Pronounced Words

Speech recognisers decode a given speech signal into a sequence of words. This sequence is the most likely speech sequence given a set of acoustic models (HMMs) and a language model (LM) as described in Sect. 3.2.4. This sequence contains only words that are part of the recogniser's vocabulary. Furthermore, for each word of the vocabulary a phonetic transcription is specified in the *lexicon* of the recogniser (in SAMPA). It is a common approach in pronunciation scoring (cf. Sect. 2.2.2) to add mispronunciation models to the recogniser which have to be additionally specified in the lexicon. An example system implementing this approach is ISLE (Sect. 2.3). Investigations in the context of the *Caller* system are described in [Hac07b, Hes06, Hes05].

The following example shows, how acoustic models for wrongly pronounced words can be applied: German learners of English have difficulties in pronouncing the English "th", since the phoneme /T/ is not present in the German language. If the correct pronunciation ought to be trained with the word "this", the lexicon of the speech recogniser could contain several pronunciation alternatives, e.g.

```
this       /TIs/
this~e10   /sIs/
```

where the first one is correct and the second one wrong. All entries of the lexicon with wrong pronunciations are tagged with suffixes which encode the error rule e_i as defined in Tab. 2.3. In this example, the rule e_{10}: /T/ → [s] has been applied to the right column.

It is essential that acoustic models for mispronunciations can be generated automatically. For this purpose, for each language pair (here: German/English) rules have to be collected from the literature. From the 28 rules e_1 to e_{28} summarised in Tab. 2.3, 22 are systematically applied to the vocabulary of the speech recogniser. The six rules that are omitted are e_9 and e_{11} substituting /D/ and /s/ with the voiced [z] which is only expected to occur for children from the northern part of Germany. Further, the confusion of /V/ with [@] is not used which is problematic if AE and BE training data is mixed (in AE, /@baUt/ is for example indeed modelled as /Vbout/; /@/ does not exist in AE). e_4 is omitted, since words like "angle" do not occur in the NONNATIVE data, and e_{14} and e_{16} are only specialised cases of e_{15}.

To further reduce the number of resulting mispronunciations, restrictions are imposed on the rules e_5, e_7, and e_{12}: /..N/ → [..Nk] is not applied to the final syllable "ing", /r/ → [R] is not applied to the final sound [r] (in German [6] is used instead of [R])[1], and "sch" → [S] is restricted to /sk/ → [S] in the beginning of words, like in "school".

The 22 mispronunciation rules are supplemented with the rules e_{29} to e_{50}: While grading the NONNATIVE data, the graduate student of English (rater S) was summarising which phoneme deviations have been observed. This survey comprises a number of weak deviations together with 38 strong deviations. Strong deviations that occur at least five times and are not part of Tab. 2.3 are summarised in Tab. 5.1. Any restrictions on the rules can be found in column four. Six rules affect consonants and 16 rules vowels. e_{50} appends the schwa [@] if the grapheme sequence ends with a grapheme 'e' which is not pronounced (*silent 'e'*). Rule e_{49} discriminates the English and German [u:][2], which has different formant frequencies for F_2 (cf. Fig. 2.1).

The 44 rules are applied to the vocabulary of the NONNATIVE database. This way, the original vocabulary of 934 words grows to 2698 words. e_7, e_{13}, e_{20}, and e_{37} are each applied more than 100 times; less than 10 times occur e_1, e_3, e_5, e_6, e_{12}, e_{32}, e_{34}, and e_{41}. To enable modelling the complete extended vocabulary with a given set of polyphone HMMs — that are e.g. trained on native data from the BIRMINGHAM corpus — this set has to contain also non-native phonemes like the German /R/, /o:/, /6/, or /u:/$_{German}$.

In the following it is explained, how those HMMs for wrongly pronounced words are integrated into the recognition framework. In general, a larger vocabulary makes confusions between words more probable and reduces the word recognition rate. However, the category based approach for language modelling after Eq. 3.34 allows an integration of mispronunciation models without drastically increasing the number of possible word confusions. No manual category system has been built for the recogniser in the present thesis. The reason is that the content of the pronunciation exercises has to be easily exchangeable without such manual adjustments. Thus, each word is automatically mapped onto a separate category, e.g. "this" onto C_i = "C=THIS", and only rare words are combined into one category C_j = "C=RARE". The 4-gram probabilities are now estimated from the sequence of categories by calculating $P(C_i|C_{i-3}C_{i-2}C_{i-1})$. Additionally the word probabilities given their category $P(w_i|C_i)$ are estimated, which are 100% if only one word w_i is part of the category C_i. If now additional mispronunciation models are used (e.g. "this∼e10"), then they are added to the same category as the respective correct pronunciation (e.g. "C=THIS"). This means that the n-gram probabilities can be kept unchanged, and only the probabilities $P(w_i|C_i)$ have to be adjusted. In this thesis a heuristic weight is used to balance the probability of correct and mispronounced words.

---

[1] Additionally not applied to /3r/, since [3] is only modelled in this very context and otherwise undefined.

[2] [u:]$_{German}$ is in all files that are necessary to describe the recogniser configuration replaced with [U:]

pronunciation error		example	restriction
e_{29}	/D/ → [d]	they	
e_{30}	/T/ → [d]	think	
e_{31}	/tS/ → [S]	cheap	beginning of word
e_{32}	/ndZ/ → [N]	sponge	end of word
e_{33}	/st/ → [St]	stall	beginning of word
e_{34}	/sp/ → [Sp]	sponge	beginning of word
e_{35}	/3/ → [e@]	early	
e_{36}	/3/ → [o:6]	early	
e_{37}	/{/ → [a]	bat	
e_{38}	/I@/ → [E:]	hearing	
e_{39}	/0:/ → [o:6]	bought	
e_{40}	/0:/ → [a]	ball	grapheme 'a'
e_{41}	/U/ → [@U]	put	grapheme 'u'
e_{42}	/V/ → [0]	come	grapheme 'o'
e_{43}	/V/ → [U]	cut	grapheme 'u'
e_{44}	/@/ → [E]	another	beginning of word
e_{45}	/aI/ → [I]	rise	
e_{46}	/aU/ → [@U]	rouse	
e_{47}	/eI/ → [i:]	great	graphemes 'ea'
e_{48}	/ju:/ → [u:]	pupil	
e_{49}	/u:/ → [u:]$_{german}$	tooth	
e_{50}	→ [@]	rise	end of word, silent 'e'

Table 5.1: Rules e_i to generate pronunciation error i: Mapping of correct pronunciation onto wrong pronunciation. These rules are applied additionally to the rules taken from the literature and defined in Tab. 2.3.

5.3   Pronunciation Features

Pronunciation features were designed for the evaluation of the pronunciation of non-native learners. This comprises first and foremost segmental features which are based on the output of a speech recogniser. The recognised word or phoneme sequence is compared with the reference sequence while taking likelihood scores, posterior scores, and duration information into account. A frame by frame comparison of both sequences is possible if the speech recogniser computes the time frame for each phone in the speech signal, and if the same information is available for the reference sequence (forced alignment).

The pronunciation features can be calculated with the *pronfex module* (**pron**unciation **f**eature **ex**traction), which is explained in the following. Prosodic features, which are based on energy, fundamental frequency, and duration, are part of the *prosody module* that will be introduced in the next section. The overlap of both modules is the analysis of durations: whereas the *prosody module* computes features that have been developed task independently and have been applied to the detection of boundaries or the classification of

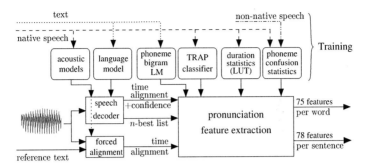

Figure 5.2: Pronunciation feature extraction.

emotions, the features in the *pronfex module* have been developed especially for pronunciation scoring. There are 75 word level pronunciation features and 78 sentence level features. The pronunciation features have been introduced in [Hac05b, Cin04a, Cin04b, Cin09]. The application for sentence level pronunciation scoring is described in [Hac05a][3] and for word based scoring in [Hac07a][4].

The pronunciation feature extraction is illustrated in Fig. 5.2. The inputs are the recognised word and/or phoneme sequence together with time alignment and confidences, and the reference text with time alignment. The time alignment is performed phoneme based. The alignment requires acoustic models estimated on native speech and for speech recognition additionally a language model. During training, 4 further sorts of statistics and classifiers have to be estimated: The phoneme bigram LM can be estimated from any English text and the frequency band dependent TRAP classifiers (cf. Chap. 3.2.2) and the duration statistics are estimated on native speech. The phoneme confusion statistics are estimated on both native and non-native data, where the non-native data has to be annotated with the word labels $\mathcal{X}$ or $\mathcal{O}$ indicating wrong or correct pronunciation. All features of the *pronfex* module are optional and can be specified in a configuration file. Some features additionally require n-best lists of the speech recogniser. Depending on the speech recogniser used (HTK[5] or the *LME recogniser*), different information can be received from the n-best lists and different features can be calculated.

The 4 kinds of statistics and their applications are explained in the following, where q_i is the phoneme number i in the phoneme sequence $\boldsymbol{q}$, q_τ the phoneme in time frame τ, and q^i the i-th out of Q phoneme symbols. q_i^{a} indicates the i-th phoneme in the reference (**a**lignment) and q_i^{r} the i-th phoneme in the sequence obtained from the speech **r**ecogniser.

- With the help of *phoneme bigrams* $P(q_i|q_{i-1})$, the a priori probabilities of observed phoneme sequences are estimated. The selection of an unlikely phoneme bigram dur-

---

[3]28 out of 78 features.
[4]63 of the 75 features.
[5]http://htk.eng.cam.ac.uk/

ing decoding is a hint for a pronunciation error, if the speech decoder in Fig. 5.2 is an unconstrained phoneme recogniser. This is also the case if a word based speech recogniser is used, which integrates mispronunciation models as explained in Sect. 5.2. However, a word recogniser without such mispronunciation models is only able to recognise words which are specified in the vocabulary. Such words do not contain uncommon phoneme sequences. Nevertheless, features based on bigram probabilities might be helpful in combination with other mispronunciation features, since infrequent phoneme sequences are more likely to be wrongly pronounced. The phoneme bigram LMs are estimated with the HTK-toolkit from the transliteration of the BIRMINGHAM data and the reference texts of the NONNATIVE data.

- *TRAP classifiers* are frequency band dependent classifiers for each of the B Mel filter banks. Unlike in Fig. 3.7, the merging step in the TRAP tandem approach is skipped, and only the band dependent results are evaluated for pronunciation scoring. The input to the classifiers are 816 msec[6] log-energy time-trajectories centred around the frame of interest. The performance of band dependent classifiers is rather low, since fricatives are hard to recognise in the lower frequency bands and vowels cannot be recognised in higher frequency bands; further, no classification information from the context is used like phoneme n-grams. However, for pronunciation scoring likelihood scores of the reference phone are taken into account and normalised with the maximum likelihood over all phonemes. The likelihood of the reference phone is expected to be high, even if the TRAP classifier would decide for another phone, with perhaps only little higher score. The TRAP scores are a band dependent extension of the GOP score introduced in Eq. 2.22.

- *Phoneme duration statistics* are used to calculate the expected duration of words and phones or to estimate the probability of an observed length of time. The distribution of phoneme durations is estimated on the BIRMINGHAM database after forced alignment. The estimation of mean and variance of the duration of each phone is performed with tools from the prosody module. $d_{\mathrm{LUT}}(q_i^{\mathrm{a}})$ is the expected duration of phoneme q_i^{a} from these duration statistics (look-up-table, LUT). To calculate the log-probability

$$\log P_{\mathrm{LUT}}(d_i | q_i^{\mathrm{a}}) = \log \left(\frac{1}{\sqrt{2\pi \cdot \sigma_{q_i^{\mathrm{a}}}}} \right) - \frac{(d_i - \mu_{q_i^{\mathrm{a}}})^2}{2\sigma_{q_i^{\mathrm{a}}}^2} \tag{5.8}$$

of an observed duration $d_i := d(q_i^{\mathrm{a}}, \boldsymbol{f})$ of a phone q_i^{a} and speech input $\boldsymbol{f}$, a normal distribution with mean $\mu_{q_i^{\mathrm{a}}} := d_{\mathrm{LUT}}(q_i^{\mathrm{a}})$ and standard deviation $\sigma_{q_i^{\mathrm{a}}}^2$ is assumed.

- *Phoneme confusion matrices* are used for a frame based comparison of the word hypothesis of the speech decoder and the forced alignment. A phoneme confusion

---

[6]Center frame plus 2×40 frames context. Due to a time shift of 10 msec of the short time analysis window and due to the 3 msec overlap with both adjacent frames (cf. Sect. 3.2.2), the time interval is 10 msec + 40 × 10 msec + 40 × 10 msec + 3 msec + 3 msec = 816 msec

occurs, if the reference phoneme and the recognised phoneme differ. Phoneme confusion matrices are estimated separately for correctly pronounced words ($M_\mathcal{O}$), for mispronounced words ($M_\mathcal{X}$), and for native British speech ($M_\mathcal{B}$). These matrices contain for all pairs of phonemes q^i, q^j the probabilities $P(q^i|q^j)$ that phoneme q^j is recognised as q^i. The entries of the $Q \times Q$ matrices are

$$
\begin{aligned}
m_\mathcal{O}^{i,j} &= P(q^i|q^j, \mathcal{O}), \\
m_\mathcal{X}^{i,j} &= P(q^i|q^j, \mathcal{X}), \\
m_\mathcal{B}^{i,j} &= P(q^i|q^j, \mathcal{B}), \quad 1 \le i, j \le Q,
\end{aligned}
\tag{5.9}
$$

given a set of Q phonemes and the events $\mathcal{O}, \mathcal{X}, \mathcal{B}$. The confusion matrices $M_\mathcal{X}$ and $M_\mathcal{O}$ are estimated on a subset of the NONNATIVE data which is not used for pronunciation evaluation. $M_\mathcal{B}$ is estimated on the BIRMINGHAM corpus.

Using the different statistic files, a high dimensional set of pronunciation features can be calculated. Word and sentence features are described in the following two sections. First, some notations have to be introduced: Let q_i^a be the reference phoneme at position i of the phoneme sequence $\boldsymbol{q}^a$, which is obtained by forced alignment, as defined above. Then $d_i = d(q_i^a, \boldsymbol{f})$ is the duration of phoneme q_i^a in the sentence given the speech input $\boldsymbol{f}$. D_{s+p} is the duration of the sentence including pauses and

$$
D_s = \sum_{i=1}^{n_p^{(\text{sent})}} d(q_i^a, \boldsymbol{f}) \le D_{s+p}
\tag{5.10}
$$

is the sentence duration without pauses with $n_p^{(\text{sent})}$ being the number of phones of the respective sentence. Let further $n_w^{(\text{sent})}$ be the number of words per sentence, then the rate-of-speech is defined as

$$
R^{(\text{phone})} = n_p^{(\text{sent})}/D_{s+p} \quad \text{or} \quad R^{(\text{word})} = n_w^{(\text{sent})}/D_{s+p}
\tag{5.11}
$$

From a word with $n_p^{(\text{word})}$ phonemes and its duration D_w, the rate of speech

$$
R_j^{(\text{local})} = n_p^{(\text{word})}/D_w
\tag{5.12}
$$

can be further calculated locally for each word j. A common way to measure the rate-of-speech is to count the number of syllables per time. However, preliminary investigations have shown lower correlation with human experts[7]. Moreover, syllables are language dependent and their automatic determination is not trivial for many languages. Language independent aspects of the pronfex module are investigated in [Cin09, Hac05b, Cin04a] Next, the features will be described.

---

[7]As will be described in Sect. 5.3.2, the development of the pronfex-module started with sentence based features [Cin04a]. Only those features were implemented which showed a high correlation to experts on the ATR-corpus [Gru04]. In a second step, similar word level features were designed.

5.3.1 Word Based Features

First of all, the word level features will be explained: For each of the words in the reference text 75 heuristic features are calculated. From these features, 12 groups are built. Within such a feature group, the elements often differ only in the way of normalisation.

Rate-of-speech Features (*PronRos*). 3 features are extracted that are based on the rate-of-speech (ROS) given the forced time alignment: *PronRos-1* is the number of phonemes $n_{\mathrm{p}}^{(\mathrm{word})}$, *PronRos-2* the local rate-of-speech $R^{(\mathrm{local})}$ after Eq. 5.12, and *PronRos-3* the reciprocal $1/R^{(\mathrm{local})}$.

Pauses Features (*PronPauses*). The 2 features *PronPauses-1* and *PronPauses-2* measure the length of pauses in frames before the current word and after the current word given the forced time alignment. The pause before the first word per sentence is set to the same value as after the first word and the pause after the last word to the same value as before the last word. For one-word sentences both pauses are set to zero.

Duration Features (*PronDurLUT*). 5 features are computed that use the duration statistics (look-up-table, LUT). It is the expected duration of the word *PronDurLUT-1*, the observed word duration *PronDurLUT-2* (= sum of mean phoneme durations from the time alignment) and the ratio of both durations (*PronDurLUT-3*). Further, the mean and standard deviation of the phoneme based duration deviation $\delta_i^{(\mathrm{phon})}$ are used as *PronDurLUT-4* and *PronDurLUT-5*, where $\delta_i^{(\mathrm{phon})} = |d(q_i^{\mathrm{a}}, \boldsymbol{f}) - d_{\mathrm{LUT}}(q_i^{\mathrm{a}})|$.

Duration Score (*PronDurScore*). To calculate duration score features, first the observed phoneme duration (obtained through forced alignment) is multiplied with the rate-of-speech; we receive the phoneme durations $\bar{d}_i$. The log-probability $\log P(\bar{d}_i|q_i^{\mathrm{a}})$ for phoneme q_i^{a} can be calculated after Eq. 5.8. Summing up these scores of all phones of the word *PronDurScore-1* is obtained. The feature *PronDurScore-2* is normalised by multiplication with $1/n_{\mathrm{p}}^{(\mathrm{word})}$ and *PronDurScore-3* by multiplication with $1/R^{(\mathrm{phone})}$.

Likelihood Features (*PronLikeli*). This category contains 7 features based on log-likelihood scores $L_\tau^{\mathrm{a}}(\boldsymbol{f}) := \log P(\boldsymbol{f}|\lambda_{q_\tau^{\mathrm{a}}})$ of the acoustic observation $\boldsymbol{f}$ given the HMM $\lambda_{q_\tau^{\mathrm{a}}}$ of the phone q_τ^{a} in frame τ. The word score *PronLikeli-1* can be approximated by the sum of all phoneme log-likelihood scores $L_\tau^{\mathrm{a}}(\boldsymbol{f})$ assuming statistical independence. *PronLikeli-2* and *PronLikeli-3* are obtained after normalisation with $n_{\mathrm{p}}^{(\mathrm{word})}$ and $R^{(\mathrm{phone})}$. The sum of duration normalised phoneme log-likelihoods is *PronLikeli-4*. Finally, the minimum, maximum, and standard deviation of phoneme log-likelihoods are the features *PronLikeli-5*, *PronLikeli-6*, and *PronLikeli-7*.

The following feature groups compare forced alignment and word recognition.

Likelihood Ratio Features (*PronLikeliRatio*). The next 3 features compare the log-likelihood scores $L_\tau^a(\boldsymbol{f}) = \log P(\boldsymbol{f}|\lambda_{q_\tau^a})$ received from the forced alignment and the scores $L_\tau^r(\boldsymbol{f}) := \log P(\boldsymbol{f}|\lambda_{q_\tau^r})$ received from a word or phoneme recogniser in each frame τ. q_τ^a and q_τ^r are the phones observed in frame τ, given forced alignment and recognition, respectively. In log-space both values are subtracted and summed up over the entire word (N frames).

$$PronLikeliRatio\text{-}1 = \frac{1}{n_p^{(\text{word})}} \sum_{\tau=1}^{N} \frac{L_\tau^a(\boldsymbol{f}) - L_\tau^r(\boldsymbol{f})}{d_\tau^a} \tag{5.13}$$

For *PronLikeliRatio-2* and *PronLikeliRatio-3* the normalisation factor is $(D_w)^{-1}$ and $(\sum_\tau d_{\text{LUT}}(q_\tau^a))^{-1}$ instead of $(n_p^{(\text{word})})^{-1}$.

TRAP Features (*PronTrap*). 6 features are calculated by employing band dependent TRAP classifiers. The extraction of the TRAP from the i-th frequency band ($i \le B$, given a Mel filter bank with B filters) of the speech input $\boldsymbol{f}$ is denoted with the operator $\text{trap}_i(\boldsymbol{f})$. Similar to *PronLikeliRatio*, a ratio of log-likelihood scores is used as feature. Here, likelihood ratios $L_\tau^a(\text{trap}_i(\boldsymbol{f})) - L_\tau^r(\text{trap}_i(\boldsymbol{f}))$ are calculated and averaged over all frames τ of the word. *PronTrap-1* to *PronTrap-3* are mean, minimum and maximum over the likelihood ratios of all B frequency bands. *PronTrap-4* is the mean over all frequency bands but normalised with the word duration. *PronTrap-5* and *PronTrap-6* are the mean over the frequency bands 1 to $\lfloor \frac{B}{2} \rfloor$ and $\lfloor \frac{B}{2} \rfloor + 1$ to B, respectively.

Recogniser Accuracy (*PronAcc*). The 6 accuracy features are the phoneme accuracy *PronAcc-1* (cf. Eq. 3.25)[8] between reference and overlapping (simultaneous) recognised phoneme sequence and the phoneme correctness *PronAcc-2* after Eq. 3.26. The mean confidence [Ste02] of all recognised words that overlap with the current word, is the feature *PronAcc-3*. The percentage of mispronunciation words (words with $\sim$ which separates the original word from the suffix indicating a mispronunciation rule, cf. Sect. 5.2) in the recogniser output, which overlaps with the current word is *PronAcc-4*. If additionally a phoneme recogniser is available, *PronAcc-5* and *PronAcc-6* are computed analogously to *PronAcc-1* and *PronAcc-2*, but from the phone recogniser output instead of using the underlying phonemes of the word recogniser output.

Phoneme Sequence Probabilities (*PronPhoneSeq*). 6 features are based on the phoneme bigram LM. It is the prior probability of the recognised phoneme sequence which overlaps with the current word (*PronPhoneSeq-1*). *PronPhoneSeq-2* and *PronPhoneSeq-3* are additionally divided by the length of the recognised phoneme sequence and by $R^{(\text{phone})}$. Those features are calculated from the phoneme sequence which forms the word sequence received by word recognition. If additionally a phoneme recogniser is available, *PronPhoneSeq-4* to *PronPhoneSeq-6* are obtained analogously.

---

[8]Instead of dividing with the total number of phones in the reference, the maximum of the number of phones in the reference and the number of phones in the recognised sequence is used. This avoids negative values.

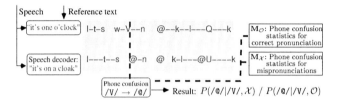

Figure 5.3: Illustration of the phone confusion features.

Confidence Features (*PronConfidence*). The confidence is in addition to feature *PronAcc-3* after [Ste02] (for each recognised word) directly calculated form the n-best lists of the speech recogniser for each reference word[9]. 3 features are available for the n-best lists of the HTK speech decoder. Those features are not used in the present thesis, but only *PronConfidence-4* and *PronConfidence-5* which are calculated from the n-best lists of the *LME* recogniser. They are implemented as the average frequency of all reference words within the n-best lists in the given time interval and their average confidence. The assumption is: the better the pronunciation of a particular word, the higher is its posterior probability, which is approximated by the probability of occurrence in the n-best hypotheses of the speech recogniser.

Phoneme Confusion Features (*PronPhoneConf*). 13 features are based on the phoneme confusion matrices $\mathbf{M}_{\mathcal{O}}$, $\mathbf{M}_{\mathcal{X}}$, and $\mathbf{M}_{\mathcal{B}}$ after Eq. 5.9 as illustrated in Fig. 5.3. The feature *PronPhoneConf-1* is the average over all $\tau = 1 \ldots N$ frames of the word

$$\frac{1}{N} \sum_{\tau=1}^{N} \log \frac{P(q_{\tau}^{r}|q_{\tau}^{a}, \mathcal{X})}{P(q_{\tau}^{r}|q_{\tau}^{a}, \mathcal{O})} \tag{5.14}$$

Instead of averaging, additionally the minimum, maximum, standard deviation, and median are calculated in *PronPhoneConf-2* to *PronPhoneConf-5*. These features normalise the a posteriori probability of the observed phone confusion given the assumption of wrong pronunciation by the probability of observing this very phone confusion in correctly pronounced words. The features *PronPhoneConf-6* and *PronPhoneConf-7* are the average of the probabilities $P(q_{\tau}^{r}|q_{\tau}^{a}, \mathcal{X})$ and $P(q_{\tau}^{r}|q_{\tau}^{a}, \mathcal{O})$, respectively.

If a confusion matrix from native speakers $\mathbf{M}_{\mathcal{B}}$ is available, we normalise with the probability of the observed phone confusion given native data. The average, minimum, maximum, standard deviation and median are now calculated from $\log[P(q_{\tau}^{r}|q_{\tau}^{a}, \mathcal{X})/P(q_{\tau}^{r}|q_{\tau}^{a}, \mathcal{B})]$; together with the average of the probabilities $P(q_{\tau}^{r}|q_{\tau}^{a}, \mathcal{B})$ one receives *PronPhoneConf-8* – *PronPhoneConf-13*.

---

[9]The calculation of those features requires the time consuming calculation of n-best lists with the speech decoder.

Context Features (*PronContext*). Last but not least, there are 19 features that take into account the context of the current word. The first 11 context features are differences of the current word's feature value and the value from the preceding word. Those features are calculated for the first feature of each group[10] and additionally for *PronPhoneConf-8*. The context feature of the first word per speaker is 0, if *pronfex* is invoked speaker based like in the present thesis. *PronContext-12* is a second order derivative, capturing the context of *PronContext-13*, which is the relation of the log-likelihood score of the current word and the score of the remaining words of the sentence. The other features measure the fluctuation of either ROS or duration, e.g. for $R_j^{(\text{local})}$

$$PronContext\text{-}14 = \frac{2R_j^{(local)_j}}{R_{j-1}^{(local)} + R_{j+1}^{(local)}}. \tag{5.15}$$

Here a context window of 3 words is used, other features are based on the context of up to 5 words (*PronContext-15 – PronContext-19*).

5.3.2 Sentence Based Features

The *pronfex* module additionally provides 78 heuristic sentence based features, divided into the same 12 groups. Whereas the word based features have been newly developed for this thesis, a couple of sentence based features is implemented according to the scores S_i from the literature, which are summarised in Tab. 2.4. All features were developed on the ATR-corpus [Gru04]. Among the innumerable possible features which eventually can be obtained by using arbitrary normalisation factors, 78 were implemented in the *pronfex* module. The criterion for the selection of those features was the correlation with human experts on the ATR-corpus [Cin04a, Hac05b].

Rate-of-speech Features (*SentRos*). 5 features *SentRos-1* to *SentRos-5* are based on the rate-of-speech: $R^{(\text{word})}$, $R^{(\text{phone})}$, both reciprocals, and the phonation-time-ratio $D_{\text{s+p}}/D_{\text{s}}$, cf. S_{ROS1}, S_{ROS2}, and S_{PTR} in Chap. 2.2.2.

Pauses Features (*SentPauses*). The 2 features *SentPauses-1* and *SentPauses-2* are the total duration of between-word pauses and the number of between word pauses longer than 0.2 sec.

Duration Features (*SentDurLUT*). 3 features are based on the duration. *SentDurLUT-1* and *SentDurLUT-2* are the mean and standard deviation of the duration deviation $|d(q_i^{\text{a}}, \boldsymbol{f}) - d_{\text{LUT}}(q_i^{\text{a}})|$ over all phonemes q_i^{a} of an utterance. *SentDurLUT-3* is the ratio of the expected duration of the sentence and the observed duration.

---

[10] For *PronTrap* the context feature is implemented but not yet used in this thesis

Duration Score (*SentDurScore*). The 3 sentence based duration score features are calculated analogously to the word based features. At first, the observed phoneme durations (obtained by forced alignment) are normalised with the rate-of-speech to receive $\bar{d}_i$. The probability $\log P(\bar{d}_i | q_i^{\mathrm{a}})$ for phoneme q_i^{a} can be obtained after Eq. 5.8. By summing up these probabilities over all phones of the sentence one receives *SentDurScore-1* (cf. S_{Dur2} in Eq. 2.25). After normalisation with $1/n_{\mathrm{p}}^{(\mathrm{sent})}$ *SentDurScore-2* is obtained and after normalisation with $1/R^{(\mathrm{phone})}$ *SentDurScore-3*.

Likelihood Features (*SentLikeli*). This group contains 9 features based on log-likelihood scores. $L_i^{\mathrm{a}}(\boldsymbol{f}) = \log P(\boldsymbol{f} | \boldsymbol{\lambda}_{q_i^{\mathrm{a}}})$ of the acoustic observation $\boldsymbol{f}$ given the HMM $\boldsymbol{\lambda}_{q_i^{\mathrm{a}}}$ of the phoneme q_i^{a}. The sentence likelihood *SentLikeli-1* is the sum of all phoneme log-likelihoods $L_i^{\mathrm{a}}(\boldsymbol{f})$. By multiplying with $1/n_{\mathrm{p}}^{(\mathrm{sent})}$ or $1/n_{\mathrm{p}}^{(\mathrm{word})}$ *SentLikeli-2* and *SentLikeli-3* are obtained.

The global and local sentence likelihood $S_{\mathrm{LikeliGlob}}$ and $S_{\mathrm{LikeliLoc}}$ calculated from phoneme likelihoods after Eq. 2.23 is also implemented but additionally normalised with $R^{(\mathrm{phone})}$ (*SentLikeli-4* and *SentLikeli-5*). *SentLikeli-6* is the local sentence likelihood, but calculated from word likelihoods: First, each word likelihood is normalised by the word duration and then the average is calculated over all words; for *SentLikeli-7*, each word score is normalised by the number of phones of the respective word. By replacing the observed phoneme duration d_τ with $d_{\mathrm{LUT}}(q_\tau^{\mathrm{a}})$ in *SentLikeli-6* and *SentLikeli-5*, one obtains *SentLikeli-8* and *SentLikeli-9*. These features calculate the sentence likelihood independent from deviations of the expected duration.

Likelihood Ratio Features (*SentLikeliRatio*). The following 3 features compare the log-likelihood scores $L_\tau^{\mathrm{a}}(\boldsymbol{f}) = \log P(\boldsymbol{f} | \boldsymbol{\lambda}_{q_\tau^{\mathrm{a}}})$ received from the forced alignment and the scores $L_\tau^{\mathrm{r}}(\boldsymbol{f}) = \log P(\boldsymbol{f} | \boldsymbol{\lambda}_{q_\tau^{\mathrm{r}}})$ received from a word or phoneme recogniser in each frame τ. q_τ^{a} and q_τ^{r} are the phones observed in frame τ, given forced alignment and recognition, respectively. *SentLikeliRatio-1* is analogous to Eq. 5.13 (cf. S_{LR} and S_{GOP1} in Chap. 2.2.2) but summed up over all frames of a sentence and multiplied with with $(n_{\mathrm{p}}^{(\mathrm{sent})})^{-1}$. For *SentLikeliRatio-2* and *SentLikeliRatio-3* the normalisation factor is $(D_{\mathrm{w}} \cdot R^{(\mathrm{phone})})^{-1}$ and $(R^{(\mathrm{phone})} \cdot \sum_i d_{\mathrm{LUT}}(q_i^{\mathrm{a}}))^{-1}$.

TRAP Features (*SentTrap*). 10 features are calculated by employing band dependent TRAP classifiers. Here, the likelihood ratios $L_\tau^{\mathrm{a}}(\mathrm{trap}_i(\boldsymbol{f})) - L_\tau^{\mathrm{r}}(\mathrm{trap}_i(\boldsymbol{f}))$ are calculated per frequency band $\mathrm{trap}_i(\boldsymbol{f})$ and averaged over all frames τ of the sentence. Since on the sentence level enough different phonemes occur, robust values can be estimated per frequency band i. The average values from each 3 band scores of the bands $1-3$, $3-5$, ..., $19-21$ are the features *SentTrap-1* to *SentTrap-10*.

Recogniser Accuracy (*SentAcc*). The following 10 features evaluate the recognition result. *SentAcc-1* and *SentAcc-2* are the phoneme and word accuracy (cf. Eq. 3.25 and

S_{Acc} in Chap. 2.2.2)[11]; *SentAcc-3* and *SentAcc-4* are the phoneme and word correctness (cf. Eq. 3.26). *SentAcc-5*, *SentAcc-6*, and *SentAcc-7* are the minimum, maximum, and average confidence [Ste02] over all recognised words in the sentence. The percentage of mispronunciation words (words with $\sim$, which separates the original word from the suffix indicating a mispronunciation rule, cf. Sect. 5.2) in the recogniser output is *SentAcc-8*. If a phoneme recogniser is available, the resulting phoneme sequence is used to measure accuracy and correctness in *SentAcc-9* and *SentAcc-10*.

Phoneme Sequence Probabilities (*SentPhoneSeq*). 6 features are based on the phoneme bigram LM and calculated analogously to the word based features. It is the a priori probability of the recognised phoneme sequence *SentPhoneSeq-1*. *SentPhoneSeq-2* and *SentPhoneSeq-3* are divided by the length of the recognised phoneme sequence and by $R^{(\text{phone})}$. *SentPhoneSeq-1* – *SentPhoneSeq-3* are obtained by employing an additional phoneme recogniser.

Confidence Features (*SentConfidence*). The confidence is calculated with 3 features form the n-best list of the *LME* speech recogniser. *SentConfidence-1* is the minimum frequency of any reference word in the n-best lists. *SentConfidence-2* is the maximum frequency, and *SentConfidence-3* the mean confidence averaged over all occurrences of any reference word in the n-best list.

Phoneme Confusion Features (*SentPhoneConf*). The 13 phoneme confusion features are the same features as on the word level but average, minimum, maximum, standard deviation, and median are calculated from the whole sentence, while skipping pauses in both phoneme sequences (forced alignment and recognised phoneme sequence).

Context Features (*SentContext*). 11 features take into account the context of the current sentence. They calculate the differences of the feature value of the current sentence and the value from the preceding sentence for the first feature of each group[12] and additionally for *SentPhoneConf-8*. The context features of the first sentence per speaker are all 0 if the module is invoked speaker based.

In the following chapter, word based prosodic features will be described.

5.4 Pronunciation Scoring with Prosodic Features

Speech contains more than the information *what* is said. Among others, it encodes e.g. speaker information and prosody. Prosody is the information, *how* something is said, and

---

[11]Instead of dividing with the total number of phones in the reference, the maximum of the number of phones in the reference and the number of phones in the recognised sequence is used. This avoids negative values.

[12] For *PronTrap* the context feature is implemented but not yet used in this thesis

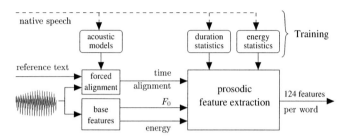

Figure 5.4: Prosodic feature extraction.

comprises *rhythm*, *stress*, and *intonation*. Prosodic information is attached to speech units which are larger than phonemes, e.g. syllables, words, or sentences. The *LME* has a profound experience in the analysis of prosody. The *prosody module* was developed during the *Verbmobil* project [Wah00] and extended during the SmartKom project [Wah06]. It is used to analyse accents, boundaries, sentence mood, and the emotional user state. Different applications are described in [Bat00, Not02, Zei06], a detailed description of prosodic features for emotion recognition can be found in [Bat03b, Hub02, Kie97]. New research areas in the field of prosodic analysis are the evaluation of pathological speech [Had07] and the classification of the user focus [Bat07]. The prosodic analysis in these various applications comprises the analysis of the fundamental frequency F_0, which correlates to *pitch*, the short time energy of the signal, which correlates to *loudness*, and the duration of word and phone segments. Further, jitter is investigated which is the local variation of the fundamental frequency (within neighbouring periods) and shimmer which is the local variation of the amplitude of the speech signal. An additional segmental analysis measures the duration of pauses, syllables, and words.

In this thesis, 124 prosodic features are calculated per word. In a first step, the short time energy, the fundamental frequency (values are stored per short time analysis window), and the pitch synchronous fundamental frequency are computed. From the speech recogniser an hypothesis of the spoken word sequence together with the time alignment is required to calculate the features in a word based manner. However, in the case of pronunciation scoring, the reference word sequence, that had to be spoken, can also be used as word hypothesis. In this case the recogniser has to work in forced alignment mode (cf. Sect. 3.2.4) to obtain information about the timing of the words. In contrast to the *pronfex* module, the forced alignment is word based, and in a second step each word interval is aligned with the underlying phonemes of the respective word. The word and phoneme based time alignment is also required to extract prosodic information from the duration of words and pauses. For this reason, additional statistics are required that contain mean and variance of duration and energy per phoneme, syllable, and word. Exploiting these information sources, a (highly redundant) set of 124 prosodic features can be calculated. The feature extraction is outlined in Fig. 5.4. Duration statistics, energy statistics, and acoustic models for forced alignment are estimated in the training phase from native data.

The feature calculation is exemplified in Fig. 5.5 for the F_0 features. From each word, several features are calculated, e.g. the maximum of the F_0 contour. Those features have the suffix "$[0, 0]$". The same features are additionally calculated from the context in order to model the variation between neighbouring words. The suffix "$[-2, -1]$" denotes that the respective feature (e.g. the maximum F_0) is calculated from the two preceding words, and "$[1, 1]$" denotes that the feature is calculated from the succeeding word. In general, intervals "$[i, j]$" with $-2 \leq i \leq j \leq 2$ are used. In contrast to the pronfex module, the context ends in the present thesis with the sentence boundary. On top of this, 15 global prosodic features are calculated over the whole sentence or utterance; components of the word based feature vectors, which contain global features, are constant over all words of a sentence. The 124 features are divided into 9 groups, which are described in detail in the following.

Energy Features (*ProsEne*). 25 features are based on the energy of the signal. *ProsEneMin*, *ProsEneMax*, and *ProsEneMean* are the minimum, maximum, and mean of the energy within a given interval "$[i, j]$". *ProsEneRegCoeff* is the regression of the energy, and *ProsEneNorm* the normalised energy. The normalisation is described in [Bat00] and is performed with respect to the mean and variance of the energy of the current word (obtained from the energy statistics) and with respect to the global sentence energy τ_{ene}. These 5 features are extracted from the current word, and from different context windows (19 features). The global energy τ_{ene} is the sentence energy normalised with the expected values from the energy statistic (*ProsEneTauLoc*[13]).

Fourier Analysis (*ProsFFT*). Additional 10 features based on the energy are summarised in *ProsFFT*. These features are the first 10 Fourier-coefficients of the energy trajectory within the respective word, describing changes of the energy in the range of 1 - 8 Hz.

Pitch Features (*ProsF$_0$*). 27 features are calculated from the fundamental frequency. *ProsF$_0$Min*, *ProsF$_0$Max*, and *ProsF$_0$Mean* are the minimum, maximum, and mean of the energy within a given interval; *ProsF$_0$On* and *ProsF$_0$Off* are the F_0 values at the onset and offset, i.e. the beginning of the first and the end of the last voiced region per word. *ProsF$_0$RegCoeff* is the regression of the energy and *ProsF$_0$MseReg* the mean square error between the regression line and the actual F_0 as shown in Fig. 5.5. These 7 features are extracted from the current word, and from different context windows (18 features). Two global features measure the mean (*ProsF$_0$MeanGlobal*) and standard deviation (*ProsF$_0$SigmaGlobal*) of the pitch per sentence.

---

[13]"Loc" indicated the local normalisation of this global feature: Each word is normalised, the mean of all words is the global feature.

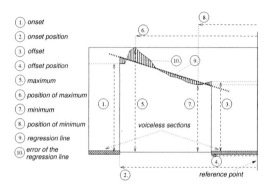

Figure 5.5: Prosodic features: 10 possible features per word for F_0. Figure from [War03, p.68]

Voiced/Unvoiced Features ($\boldsymbol{ProsVUV}$).   The F_0 can only be calculated from voiced regions of the speech signal. 10 global features measure the number of voiced/unvoiced segments ($ProsVuvNum+Global$, $ProsVuvNum\text{-}Global$), the duration of voiced/unvoiced segments ($ProsVuvDur+Global$, $ProsVuvDur\text{-}Global$) in frames, and the maximum duration of the voiced/unvoiced segments ($ProsVuvMax+Global$, $ProsVuvMax\text{-}Global$). The ratio of voiced and unvoiced segments in terms of duration and number ($ProsVuvRelNumGlobal$, $ProsVuvRelDurGlobal$), and the ratio of voiced/unvoiced sections and the total sentence duration ($ProsVuvRelSig+Global$, $ProsVuvRelSig\text{-}Global$) round off this feature set.

Duration Features ($\boldsymbol{ProsDur}$).   7 features are calculated based on the duration of words. It is the normalised word duration $ProsDurNorm$, which is extracted from the current word and from 5 different context windows. The normalisation is described in [Bat00] and is performed with respect to the mean and variance of the duration of the current word from the duration statistics and with respect to the global sentence duration τ_{dur}. The global duration τ_{dur} is the duration of the sentence normalised with the expected values from the duration statistic. It is the global feature $ProsDurTauLoc$.

Position of Extrema ($\boldsymbol{ProsPos}$).   Duration is also measured with 22 features describing e.g. the position of the extrema of the F_0 or energy with respect to a reference point at the time axis, which is the end of the word. These features are the position of the F_0 onset, offset, maximum, and minimum ($ProsPosF_0On$, $ProsPosF_0Off$, $ProsPosF_0Min$, $ProsPosF_0Max$) as illustrated in Fig. 5.5, as well as the position of minimum and maximum of the energy ($ProsPosEneMin$, $ProsPosEneMax$). $ProsPosEneMinRel$ and $ProsPosEne\text{-}MaxRel$ are the relative position with respect to a normalised word length of one. These

8 types of features are extracted from the current word (8 features) and from different context windows (14 features).

Length of Pauses Features (*ProsPause*). 7 features are used which measure the length of pauses; *ProsPauseBefore* is the length of a silent section before the current word, and *ProsPauseAfter* after the current word. Both features are similar to the *PronPauses* features from the previous section except for the first and final word per sentence, but calculated from the slightly different word based time alignment (not from the phoneme based alignment). 5 further features are calculated from different context windows, for *ProsPauseBefore* only from the left context, and for *ProsPauseAfter* from the right context[14].

Jitter Features (*ProsJit*). Jitter is described with 8 features: *ProsJitMean* and *ProsJitSigma* are the mean and standard deviation calculated from the current word (2 features) and from different context windows (4 features). 2 further features compute the global mean and standard deviation: *ProsJitMeanGlobal* and *ProsJitSigmaGlobal*.

Shimmer Features (*ProsShim*). Shimmer is described with 8 features: *ProsShimMean* and *ProsShimSigma* are the mean and standard deviation calculated from the current word (2 features) and from different context windows (4 features). 2 further features compute the global mean and standard deviation: *ProsShimMeanGlobal* and *ProsShimSigmaGlobal*.

The standard feature set used in many investigations at the *LME* consists of 95 prosodic features. This feature set does not contain the recently implemented features [Zei10] *ProsFFT*, *ProsJit*, and *ProsShim* nor the global features *prosVUV* [Hub02]. Neither does it contain the features *ProsEneMin*, *ProsPosEneMin* *ProsPosEneMinRel*, *ProsPosEneMaxRel* but it contains additional features based on the absolute energy or absolute duration (not relevant to evaluate the correct pronunciation), the regression error of the (absolute) energy, and filled pauses.

5.5 Detection of Prosodic Boundaries

The detection of prosodic and syntactic boundaries has been investigated at the *LME* in [Bat01, Bat99, Bat98, Kie96, Bat96]. The data being investigated in the present thesis, has been tagged with syntactic boundaries M_0, M_1, M_2, and M_3 (cf. page 77 in Chap. 4) on the word level. The label indicates, whether after the respective word a strong boundary M_3 is expected, or no boundary at all (M_0). These annotations could also have been performed

---

[14]Filled pauses are not considered separately, since they are not present after forced alignment of the reference text (present only after speech recognition or after forced alignment of the manually transcribed data).

automatically, if syntactical knowledge in terms of rules or stochastic grammars had been available.

To automatically detect prosodic boundaries, the 124 prosodic features as described in the previous section are employed. The present boundary will be detected by analysing the prosody within a word and its context of ± 2 words. The F_0, the energy, duration, and pauses will reveal, whether there is a boundary or not. Unfortunately, it has not been annotated, if the expected boundary occurs indeed. Consequently the approach in this thesis will be to train the characteristics of boundaries from native speakers and good readers on the supposition that there the expected M-boundary does indeed occur, i.e. is at the same time a prosodic boundary. The resulting classifier will then be applied to non-native data. This means that it is measured how well the expected syntactic boundaries are automatically detected, i.e. how great the chance is that they indeed occur. The algorithm is the following:

1. Train a classifier for M-boundaries on good readers (NONNATIVERC) using 124 word based prosodic features. It is classified for each word, whether it is followed by M_0, $\{M_1, M_2\}$, or M_3.

2. Classify each word of the test data which is followed by an expected M_1 or M_2 (Occurrences of M_1/M_2 have to be known for each text which has to be read.). Store the a-posteriori scores.

3. Average the scores over a sufficient large amount of sentences, e.g. all data of a speaker.

4. The resulting score measures pronunciation and reading proficiency of the speaker. In Chap. 8.4.2 this score is compared with ratings of human experts.

Summing up, it will be analysed whether this evaluation of reading proficiency correlates with pronunciation labels.

5.6 Summary

In this chapter different approaches for pronunciation scoring were explained. Some approaches are based on feature extraction followed by a classification step. If word based features are available, three algorithms for sentence level scoring are described in Fig. 5.1: combination of word based classification results (2), extraction of meta-features from word based classification results that are input to a second classification step (3), and combination of word based features (4). Approach (1) is the design of special sentence features. Similar approaches can be applied to obtain text or speaker scores from the word level. However, due to sparse data only (2) will be applied.

A common approach for L1- and text-dependent word level pronunciation scoring is to add mispronunciation models to the vocabulary of the speech recogniser. If the most likely word sequence the decoder has decided for contains a mispronunciation model with annotated phoneme deviations, one can even draw conclusions which phoneme is actually being wrongly pronounced. Mispronunciation models can be easily integrated in a speech recogniser based on word categories. For largely text independent applications it is essential to have rules e_i which automatically generate mispronunciations. In this thesis 44 rules are applied, which is a subset of the 50 rules from Tab. 2.3 and Tab. 5.1.

The second approach is based on newly developed high dimensional pronunciation feature vectors. For word level scoring up to 75 features can be calculated with the *pronfex module* (**pron**unciation **f**eature **ex**traction), and up to 78 sentence level features. These features are based on durations, pauses, rate-of-speech, and the log-likelihood of the speech input given the forced alignment with acoustic models (HMMs), as well as features that compare the recognised word sequence and the reference word sequence. Those features are e.g. the phoneme accuracy and confidence features, as well as the likelihood ratio between the log-likelihood score obtained by forced alignment and the one obtained by speech recognition. TRAP-based features calculate this likelihood-ratio per frequency band. Phone confusion features analyse, based on frame level, the a priori probability of an observed confusion (whether the recognised phoneme differs from the reference phoneme), which is different for wrongly pronounced words and for correctly pronounced words.

In a third approach 124 prosodic features are calculated per word using the *prosody module*. This module already has been applied successfully for the analysis of e.g. sentence mood and emotional user states. Prosody is the information *how* something is said. The prosodic features analyse, based on the word level, the energy, fundamental frequency, duration, length of pauses, jitter, and shimmer.

The prosodic features will not only be applied for the word based classification of the goodness of pronunciation, but also for the assessment of reading proficiency by classifying prosodic boundaries. The amount of automatically detected prosodic boundaries that match a manually annotated syntactic boundary is used as a measure of the reading proficiency.

Chapter 6

Analysis of the Expert Ratings

In the previous chapters, the algorithms and the data were described, that will be employed in this thesis. In the present and the following chapters all the experiments which were conducted on the data from Chap. 4 will be explained and the results discussed. This sequence of experimental chapters starts with an analysis of the expert ratings in the following. Applying different measures, it will be discussed to which extend the human experts agree on their annotations on different levels (from word level annotations to speaker level annotations).

6.1 Examined Measures

The experts ratings are evaluated applying different measures in Sect. 6.2. After this, the different measures will be compared in Sect. 6.3. In the present section, the applied measures are motivated and specified. Common measures have already been introduced in Sect. 2.2.1 and Sect. 3.1.3. On the word level, the data has been annotated with $\mathcal{X}$ (wrongly pronounced) or $\mathcal{O}$ (correctly pronounced). On the sentence, text, and speaker level the annotations are the school grades (marks) denoted as $c, k \in \mathcal{M} \subset \{x \in \mathbb{R} | 1 \leq x \leq 5\}$. The following measures are applied to the word level:

1. The *strictness* of an expert is defined on the word level. It is the percentage of marked words (% $\mathcal{X}$) of each expert. It is also analysed which strictness can be measured after the combination of annotations from different raters.

2. The *class-wise averaged classification rate* CL after Eq. 3.19 is calculated on the word level. In this two-class case, we rename CL to CL-2.

3. Further, word level labels are evaluated in terms of κ and α_{krip}. A description is found below (text and speaker level measures) and in Sect. 2.2.1.

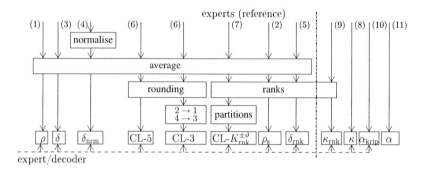

Figure 6.1: Different evaluation measures on the text and speaker level and the preprocessing of the data input. The numbers in brackets establish a relationship to the description in the text. Most measures compare the reference with a decoder (same preprocessing, no averaging). The measures (8) – (10) allow to compare multiple experts (no averaging step required). α (11) analyses the consistency of one expert.

The following measures are applied to the text and speaker level (also on the sentence level in Chap. 8[1]). Additionally, the *average grade* and *standard deviation* are calculated and will be compared in Fig. 6.3.

1. On the text and speaker level, the *Pearson correlation* ρ (Eq. 2.2) is computed. It analyses whether there is a linear relation between the gradings of different experts.

2. The *Spearman correlation* ρ_S measures the interrelation between the ranks of the grades: The data is first converted to ranks and then the Pearson correlation coefficient is calculated[2].

3. As the Pearson correlation ρ analyses only the relation between two sets of ratings ignoring their absolute values, additionally the *error* is calculated on the text level in a similar way as defined in Eq. 2.20. The error $\mathrm{err}(\boldsymbol{x}^{(r)}, \boldsymbol{x}^{(l)})$ between two sets of ratings from the raters r and l was introduced in [Tei00]. In the following a slightly different measure is calculated, since Eq. 2.20 can never become 1, unless the ratings contain solely the minimum and maximum mark. They are denoted as $k_{\min}, k_{\max} \in \mathcal{M}$ with $\forall k \in \mathcal{M} : k_{\min} \leq k \leq k_{\max}$. For $\mathcal{M} = \{x \in \mathbb{R} | 1 \leq x \leq 5\}$ a deviation of one mark would count $1/4$, but the maximum possible deviation for mark 3 is $2/4$.

---

[1]On the sentence level there are only ratings from a single expert available

[2]The approximation formula after [Fer71, p. 306] is not used. This formula results in falsified values, if the number of ranks is strongly differing for different raters. This is particularly the case, if only some of the raters often make use of intermediate marks.

The revised measure introduced in [Hac05a] calculates the mean *deviation* or *error* of the rater r from N samples with

$$\delta(\boldsymbol{x}^{(r)}, \boldsymbol{x}^{(l)}) = \frac{\sum_{i=1}^{N} |x_i^{(r)} - x_i^{(l)}|}{\sum_{i=1}^{N} \max(x_i^{(l)} - k_{\min}, k_{\max} - x_i^{(l)})} \tag{6.1}$$

where the sum of deviations is normalised with the maximum possible deviation. The disadvantage here is the asymmetrical behaviour: e.g. the confusion of the true mark 3 with mark 4 counts 2 in the denominator and 1 in the numerator, whereas the other way round a confusion would count 3 in the denominator.

4. δ_{nrm} calculates the deviation as in Eq. 6.1, but for the rater normalised data: After normalisation the mean is identical for each rater.

5. δ_{rnk} is also based on Eq. 6.1, but it is calculated after mapping the ratings to ranks. The minimum and maximum rank $k_{\min}, k_{\max}$ are calculated rater dependent. This way, raters that use different ranges of $\mathcal{M}$ are normalised as well.

6. The *class-wise averaged classification rate* CL after Eq. 3.19 and Eq. 3.21 can be calculated, if the elements of the set $\mathcal{M}$ are considered as data on a nominal scale (defined properties: $=, \neq$) and neither on an ordinal scale ($=, \neq, <, >$) nor an interval scale ($=, \neq, <, > +, -$). First, the marks are rounded to digits. In the five class case $\mathcal{M} = \{1, 2, 3, 4, 5\}$ we rename CL to CL-5. CL-3 gives the accuracy after mapping $2 \to 1$ and $4 \to 3$. Note that CL is not symmetrical. If two experts are compared, it has to be defined which of them is the reference and which one is being evaluated (decoder).

7. CL punishes a confusion of the marks 1 and 2 in the same way as the confusion of 1 and 3. To alleviate this effect, one could also count confusions as correct, if the difference between the annotated mark and the reference mark is not greater than a threshold ϑ. In the applied approach, the marks are first converted to ranks to get a larger number of classes K. At the same time the number of possible values for ϑ becomes larger and allows a more precise tuning. The algorithm to calculate CL-$K_{\mathrm{rnk}}^{\pm \vartheta}$ for rater r is the following:

   (a) Calculate for all samples $\{x_i^{(l)} | i = 1, \ldots, N\}$ the average mark $\bar{x}_i$ from all experts $l \neq r$.

   (b) Convert $\bar{x}_i$ into ranks x_i^{rnk}. Since many of the $\bar{x}_i$ are intermediate marks, the total number of ranks is high. The maximum rank value is approximately N, because tied ranks are used as described on page 18.

   (c) Divide the ranks in K partitions: Rank 1 to $\frac{N}{K}$ are renamed with 1, $\frac{N}{K} + 1$ to $2\frac{N}{K}$ are renamed with 2 and so on.

(d) Convert also the decoder's annotations x_i^r to ranks (again the maximum rank is $\approx N$, but usually less values between 1 and N are used) and divide them into K partitions.

(e) Calculate CL; confusions $\pm\vartheta$ count as correct.

The steps (b) and (c) are similar to histogram equalisation; the resulting K partitions are almost uniformly distributed.

8. The Cohen κ after Eq. 2.9 is an approach that calculates the observed agreement from a set of raters and subtracts the chance agreement. κ for multiple raters is defined in Eq. 2.15. For nominal data on the word level, no weighting function (cf. Eq. 2.11) is used, since only $(=, \neq)$ are defined. On the other levels, the square distance (Eq. 2.11, right) is applied if different labels are assigned from disagreeing raters.

9. κ_{rnk} is calculated like κ but after converting the ratings to ranks.

10. The Krippendorff α_{krip} (Eq. 2.18) also subtracts the chance agreement from the observed agreement. However, the way of calculation is different. For κ with square distance weighting and for α_{krip} with the distance function $\mathrm{dist}(c, k) = (c - k)^2$, the values are almost identical. In the following, the distance function for ordinal data after Eq. 2.19 is applied. For the nominal data on the word level the distance

$$\mathrm{dist}(c, k) = \left\{ \begin{array}{l} 0 \text{ for } c = k \\ 1 \text{ for } c \neq k \end{array} \right. \tag{6.2}$$

is applied.

11. The reliability of each rater is measured with the Cronbach α (Eq. 2.6). It can be calculated on the text level by assuming that each text level grading can be built from the word level annotations. The true interrelationship between ratings of different levels is discussed in Sect. 6.2.6

Only κ, κ_{rnk}, and α_{krip} are defined for multiple raters. All other measures compare pairs (r, l) of experts. The evaluation of a fixed (but arbitrary) rater r can be computed by averaging over all pairs (r, l). Another and more robust way is to replace the reference l by the average of all other experts. This way, the open CL and open δ are obtained – similar to the open correlation in Eq. 2.7. An overview of the different computation steps on the text and speaker level is given in Fig. 6.1. The left part shows the pre-processing for the reference in one iteration of the open correlation, open CL, or open δ. The same pre-processing steps but without averaging are applied to the decoder (rater r). ρ and δ require solely averaging, CL-5 and CL-3 additionally rounding. For CL-K_{rnk}, ρ_{S}, and δ_{rnk}, ranks have to be calculated after averaging. In addition (similar to the rounding step for CL-5), the calculation of CL-K_{rnk} includes a partitioning step. For δ_{nrm} the average is computed from the normalised ratings.

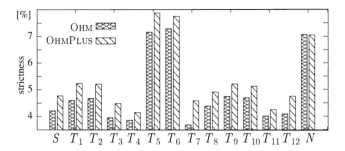

Figure 6.2: Strictness of the 14 experts (word-level).

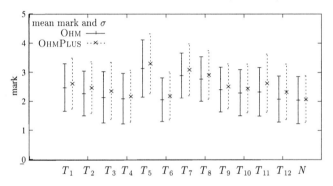

Figure 6.3: Average grade and standard-deviation of 13 experts on the text level.

The right part of the figure shows measures which allow to evaluate multiple raters (no averaging required): κ, κ_{rnk}, and α_{krip}. The Cronbach α analysis the reliability of a single expert. In all tables, instead of δ, δ_{nrm}, and δ_{rnk} the complements $1 - \delta$, $1 - \delta_{nrm}$, and δ_{1-rnk} will be shown, to make consistently large values become an indication of high agreement.

6.2 Evaluation of the Multi-Rater Annotations

6.2.1 Strictness and Average Rating

A comparison of the strictness of the 14 experts (graduated student S, teachers $T_1 - T_{12}$, and native teacher N) is shown in Fig. 6.2. All experts marked on the word level between 4 % and 5 % of the words, except rater T_5, T_6, and N who marked 7 % and more. All experts (except N) have marked a higher percentage of words on the OHMPLUS data. The average strictness on the OHM data is 4.9 % and on OHMPLUS 5.4 %.

For the text level, the average grade and standard deviation are shown in Fig. 6.3. On this level no annotations are available for rater S. The mean is for most experts between 2 and 3 and the standard deviation nearly one. The teachers who gave the worst (highest) marks are T_5 and T_7. T_5 is as well on the word level as on the text level very strict. Best marks are given by the native teacher. For OHMPLUS, the marks are worse than for OHM.

A robust reference on the text level can be obtained by calculating the average grade over many raters. On the text level, a word will be only regarded as mispronounced, if at least ϑ experts vote with $\mathcal{X}$. If all 14 experts had to agree ($\vartheta = 14$), only 50 words out of 10078 would be marked with $\mathcal{X}$. For $\vartheta = 1$, a large portion of 23 % would be marked as mispronounced. Tab 6.1 shows the percentage of marked words for different ϑ. An appropriate threshold is $\vartheta = 5$ which results in 4.6 % marked words on the OHM data and 5.1 % marked words on OHMPLUS. These numbers are close to the average strictness; thus a more robust reference is obtained while keeping the number of marked words nearly constant.

A more reliable reference could possibly be obtained, when taking only the teachers with more than 2 years of teaching experience and the native teachers as reference into account. Considering only these 8 *experienced teachers* T_1 – T_7, and N, 5.3 % and 5.9 % of the words are marked[3] for $\vartheta = 3$ on the OHM and OHMPLUS data, respectively[4]. Tab. 6.2 gives a closer look onto the most frequently occurring words that are marked by at least 3 of the 8 experienced raters. In many cases, the "th" causes difficulties, and is pronounced as /s/, e.g. in "the", "that", or "this". In father, /T/ is confused with /t/ and in "with" with /f/. Difficult frequently occurring words seem to be further "every" and "garage". Vowels are uttered wrongly in "old", "house", or "hurry".

The MONT set of the NONNATIVE data has only been marked by rater S. She has marked 9.2 % of the words: The English of the pupils from the general-education secondary school is worse than the English of the children from the grammar school (OHM).

6.2.2 Word Level Agreement

On the word level CL-2, κ, and α_{krip} are calculated to measure the agreement among the 14 raters. CL-2 is only defined for pairs of raters. Consequently, to calculate the agreement between rater r and the other raters, either CL-2 has to be calculated for all pairs of raters and then be averaged, or CL-2 has to be calculated between r and the "average" of the

---

[3]The experienced teacher do not contain any student teacher. However, it will turn out that not all of them show high agreement with the other experts on all levels of annotation: Whereas all 8 experts have high agreement scores on the word level, T_5 and in particular N have low agreement values on the text level. On the speaker level, some agreement scores are low for T_5, T_7, and N. In the following sections the results are presented in detail.

[4] In leave-one-expert-out experiments, where only the 8 experienced teachers are considered, 3 out of 7 teachers have to agree. Then, the strictness on OHMPLUS drops to 5.2 %; however, this is still in the desired range of each rater's strictness.

data	experts	$\vartheta = 1$	$\vartheta = 2$	$\vartheta = 3$	$\vartheta = 4$	$\vartheta = 5$	$\vartheta = 6$	$\vartheta = 7$
OHM	14 experts	22.5	11.7	7.6	5.8	**4.6**	3.7	3.1
OHMPLUS	14 experts	23.3	12.3	8.2	6.4	**5.1**	4.2	3.7
OHM	T_1 – T_7, N	18.1	8.5	**5.3**	3.8	2.7	2.0	1.4
OHMPLUS	T_1 – T_7, N	18.8	9.0	**5.9**	4.4	3.3	2.4	1.7

Table 6.1: Percentage of mispronounced words for different thresholds ϑ: Label $\mathcal{X}$ is assigned, if $\geq \vartheta$ experts vote with $\mathcal{X}$. The bold numbers are in the range of each expert's strictness. The bold cases will be denoted in the following as "5 of 14 teachers" and "3 of 8 experienced teachers". Each experienced teacher has more than one year teaching experience.

6	every	/efErI:/ /efri:/	9	o'clock	/OklOk/
6	it's	/is/	9	Sales	/s{lz/, /s{l@s/
6	no	/naU/, /nQt/	9	Thursday	/s3rsdeI/
6	there	/se@/	10	they	/seI/, /De@/
6	voices	/vOIsIs/, /voUsIs/	11	birthday	/b3rsdeI/
6	weather	/wes@/, /wed@/	11	thanks	/s{Nks/
7	father	/fA:s@/, /fA:t@/	13	is	/Its/
7	house	/hoUs/	14	old	/O:ld/
7	hurry	/hEri:/	30	garage	/gEr@dZ/
7	that	/s{t/, /d{t/	23	that's	/s{ts/, /d{ts/
7	this	/sIs/, /dIs/	45	the	/s@/
7	with	/vIf/, /wIs/			

Table 6.2: Most difficult words in OHMPLUS marked with $\mathcal{X}$ by at least 3 experienced teachers. Arranged according to the observed frequency. Shown are those words, that are more than 5 times mispronounced together with the most frequent mispronunciation (pronunciation errors in bold).

	S	T_1	T_2	T_3	T_4	T_5	T_6	T_7	T_8	T_9	T_{10}	T_{11}	T_{12}	N	μ
O	*65.1*	70.5	**71.2**	71.1	69.0	**73.1**	70.7	70.0	71.1	*64.9*	**72.4**	69.1	**72.0**	71.1	70.1
P	*67.0*	**73.0**	72.7	**73.0**	70.2	**74.7**	72.9	72.7	72.6	*67.6*	**73.9**	69.3	**73.7**	71.9	71.8[6.1]

Table 6.3: Pairwise agreement of the experts on the word level and average μ per line: mean CL-2 for 14 experts on the OHM corpus (O) and the OHMPLUS corpus (P). Maxima are shown in bold, minima in italics.

	S	T_1	T_2	T_3	T_4	T_5	T_6	T_7	T_8	T_9	T_{10}	T_{11}	T_{12}	N	μ
O	*68.8*	78.1	**80.9**	**80.5**	77.3	**81.1**	78.9	78.0	78.6	*69.9*	**81.7**	75.7	**81.4**	78.4	77.8
P	*71.0*	81.0	**81.7**	**82.3**	77.9	**82.1**	81.4	81.1	79.7	*72.6*	**82.8**	75.1	**82.7**	78.3	79.3$^{6.2}$

Table 6.4: Agreement of the experts on the word level and average μ per line: Open CL-2 for 14 experts ("at least 5 of the other experts vote for $\mathcal{X}$", $\vartheta = 5$) on the OHM corpus (O) and the OHMPLUS corpus (P). Maxima are shown in bold, minima in italics.

	S	T_1	T_2	T_3	T_4	T_5	T_6	T_7	T_8	T_9	T_{10}	T_{11}	T_{12}	N	μ
O	*67.6*	**78.6**	80.0	79.0	75.5	80.4	78.2	76.7	72.8	*66.8*	77.0	70.7	76.4	**78.9**	75.6$^{6.3}$
P	*69.2*	**80.8**	80.5	80.5	75.7	**81.2**	80.1	79.4	74.2	*69.6*	78.2	70.7	78.1	78.0	76.8$^{6.4}$

Table 6.5: Agreement of the experts on the word level and average μ per line: Open CL-2 using the reference "at least 3 of the (other) experienced teachers vote with $\mathcal{X}$"($\vartheta = 3$). Evaluation on the OHM corpus (O) and the OHMPLUS corpus (P). Maxima are shown in bold, minima in italics.

other raters (open CL-2). This "average" is calculated by applying $\vartheta = 3$ or $\vartheta = 5$ as defined in Tab. 6.1.

Tab. 6.3 shows the agreement of experts with the other experts by averaging CL-2 of all pairs. For OHM, CL-2 is between 64.9 % and 73.1 %, lowest for T_9 and S (numbers in italics) and highest for T_5, T_{10}, and T_{12} (numbers in bold). The mean calculated from all experts is 70.1 %. It is higher for OHMPLUS (71.8%$^{6.1}$). Again, lowest agreement is observed for T_9 and S and highest for T_5. In the previous section, a higher strictness has been observed for OHMPLUS; here, it is CL-2 that higher for OHMPLUS. The pairs of experts with lowest agreement (< 65 % CL-2) are the following (reference–decoder): S–T_{11}, S–T_9, T_5–T_9, and T_5–T_{11}. The highest CL-2 (≥ 78 %) is obtained for the pairs T_1–T_2, T_3–T_6, T_3–T_{12}, T_3–T_{10}, and finally 83.5 % for T_8–T_{11}.

Tab. 6.4 shows the numbers when measuring the agreement between one expert and the "average" of all other experts. This "averaged" reference is more robust (a word is only marked with $\mathcal{X}$ if at least 5 experts agree) and results in higher CL-2. For OHM it is between 68.8 % CL-2 and 81.7 % CL-2, again lowest for S and T_9 and highest for T_5, T_{10}, and T_{12}. The average open CL-2 is 77.8 % for OHM and 79.3%$^{6.2}$ for OHMPLUS.

Low agreement does not in all cases mean that the rater under consideration is not reliable; low agreement can also occur, when the reference is wrong. Therefore, in the next step CL-2 is calculated by employing only the native speaker and the teachers with more than two years of teaching experience for the reference; among others, T_9 and S are excluded, who showed a relatively low agreement with the other experts. Now, a word is marked as mispronounced, if at least 3 of the 8 experienced teachers (3 of the 7 other experienced teachers in order to have a rater disjoint reference and decoder) vote with $\mathcal{X}$. Now, CL-2 is between 75.5 % and 80.4 % for all experienced teachers on the OHM data, and between 66.8 % and 77.0 % for the other experts (Tab. 6.5). There are clear differences between the two groups of experts present, but not for the teachers T_4 and T_7 vs. T_{10} and

measure	reference	OHM			OHMPLUS		
		min	mean	max	min	mean	max
CL-2	pairwise	65.1	70.1	72.9	67.3	$71.8^{6.1}$	74.3
CL-2	open, voting: $\vartheta = 3$	66.8	$75.6^{6.3}$	80.4	69.2	$76.8^{6.4}$	81.2
$\kappa/\alpha_{\text{krip}}$	-	$0.39^{6.5}/0.39$			$0.43^{6.6}/0.43$		

Table 6.6: Summary of the word level agreement of 14 experts for the OHM and OHMPLUS data.

	T_1	T_2	T_3	T_4	T_5	T_6	T_7	T_8	T_9	T_{10}	T_{11}	T_{12}	N	μ
ρ	0.67	**0.69**	**0.71**	0.63	0.65	0.63	**0.69**	0.61	*0.52*	0.66	0.56	**0.68**	*0.51*	$0.63^{6.7}$
$1-\delta$	**79.6**	**79.3**	**79.0**	74.4	*67.9*	75.3	73.0	75.9	76.5	**78.4**	75.3	78.0	*71.0*	$75.7^{6.8}$

Table 6.7: Pairwise agreement of the experts on the text level and average μ per line (OHMPLUS data): mean correlation ρ and deviation δ. Maxima are shown in bold, minima in italics.

T_{12}. However, CL-2 decreases for nearly all raters in comparison to Tab. 6.4. The average is $75.6\%^{6.3}$ for OHM and $76.8\%^{6.4}$ for OHMPLUS.

The most important results to measure the word level agreement are summarised in Tab. 6.6. The results on the pairwise CL-2 will later in Sect. 6.2.5 be compared with the intra-rater agreement. The results based on a more robust reference (open CL-2) will be the baseline to evaluate the performance of the automatic system. In general, teachers have a high agreement in terms of *correct acceptance* but a low *hit-rate* (cf. definitions in Tab. 3.1): The specifity $\text{REC}_{\mathcal{O}}$ after Eq. 3.17 is on average 97.7 % (between 95.8 and 98.7 %) whereas the sensitivity $\text{REC}_{\mathcal{X}}$ is on average 60.8 % (between 44.8 and 68.5 %). Teachers agree on the correctly pronounced words, but they do not mark all wrongly pronounced words, since this would be very demotivating for the students. As the strictness is only around 5 %, there are much more words labelled with $\mathcal{O}$. Consequently, the recognition rate RR is high and between 94.5 % and 97.0 %, but not meaningful, since a classification of all words with $\mathcal{O}$ would also result in around 95 % RR (discussed in Sect. 3.1.3).

When measuring the agreement in terms of κ, $0.39^{6.5}$ is obtained for the OHM data and $0.43^{6.6}$ for OHMPLUS. Taking only the 8 experienced teachers into account, a higher κ is obtained. It is on the OHMPLUS data 0.45 and without rater N even 0.47. It was found that there is no difference between κ and α_{krip} on this data.

6.2.3 Text Level Agreement

To evaluate the agreement on the text level, first ρ and $1 - \delta$ are analysed for the experts T_1 – T_{12} and N. For S there are no ratings on the text level available. High agreement can be observed, if the correlation is high and if additionally the deviation δ is low. This section focuses on OHMPLUS; results for OHM are presented at the end of this section in the summary table (Tab. 6.10).

	T_1	T_2	T_3	T_4	T_5	T_6	T_7	T_8	T_9	T_{10}	T_{11}	T_{12}	N	μ
ρ	**0.83**	**0.86**	**0.88**	0.77	0.79	0.77	**0.85**	0.75	*0.63*	0.82	0.68	**0.84**	*0.62*	$0.78^{6.9}$
$1-\delta$	**84.6**	**86.2**	83.6	78.1	*68.5*	80.3	76.7	79.1	80.7	**84.7**	79.7	82.1	*74.9*	$79.9^{6.10}$
$1-\delta_{\mathrm{nrm}}$	84.1	**85.9**	84.5	82.9	81.0	84.1	**86.5**	82.9	80.0	**84.8**	*78.5*	83.5	*79.2*	$82.9^{6.11}$
ρ_{S}	0.81	**0.85**	**0.89**	0.78	0.80	0.77	**0.85**	0.74	*0.60*	0.83	0.70	**0.83**	*0.65*	0.78
$1-\delta_{\mathrm{rnk}}$	81.7	**83.7**	**86.1**	80.7	81.3	80.9	**84.6**	79.1	*74.5*	**82.7**	77.3	**83.0**	*74.0*	$80.7^{6.12}$

Table 6.8: Agreement of the experts on the text level and average μ per line (OHMPLUS data): open correlation ρ, open deviation δ, open deviation after normalisation δ_{nrm}, open deviation after ranking δ_{rnk}, and the Spearman correlation ρ_{S}. Maxima are shown in bold, minima in italics.

	T_1	T_2	T_3	T_4	T_5	T_6	T_7	T_8	T_9	T_{10}	T_{11}	T_{12}	N	μ
CL-5	**71.9**	**71.2**	**74.5**	*37.8*	*33.4*	52.5	45.4	60.3	41.5	45.8	45.5	**67.6**	*38.2*	52.7
CL-3	**88.0**	**87.5**	**92.2**	*48.4*	60.1	62.6	67.2	**82.0**	*49.8*	54.0	52.5	**86.8**	*49.0*	67.7
CL-5$_{\mathrm{rnk}}^{\pm 0}$	44.5	**56.3**	**57.3**	45.8	44.3	49.8	**52.3**	42.9	*35.4*	**50.3**	*40.3*	**52.2**	*41.3*	47.1
CL-10$_{\mathrm{rnk}}^{\pm 2}$	85.1	**88.9**	**89.4**	78.7	**85.4**	84.7	**88.5**	75.9	*71.7*	**87.0**	79.4	84.9	*66.8*	$82.0^{6.13}$
CL-10$_{\mathrm{rnk}}^{\pm 3}$	**94.4**	**96.8**	**99.2**	91.1	92.8	89.7	**96.6**	91.9	*79.7*	93.3	89.6	**95.2**	*83.2*	$91.8^{6.14}$

Table 6.9: Agreement of the experts on the text level and average μ per line (OHMPLUS data): classification rate CL-3, CL-5, and CL-$K_{\mathrm{rnk}}^{\pm\vartheta}$ after ranking and when tolerating confusions of $\pm\vartheta$. Maxima are shown in bold, minima in italics.

The pairwise agreement of raters (averaged per rater) is analysed in Tab. 6.7. Lowest agreement in terms of correlation is observed for T_9 and N; low $1-\delta$ is observed for T_5 and N. Being native speaker does not necessarily mean that the agreement with teachers of English is high, since they might weight the mistakes in a different way. For T_1 and T_2 high values can be found for ρ and δ. On average, the correlation is $0.63^{6.7}$ and $1-\delta$ is $75.7\%^{6.8}$.

In Tab. 6.8 the open ρ and open δ are analysed. The agreement is higher, since a more robust reference is used: the mean of all other teachers. Now, the correlation is on average $0.78^{6.9}$ and $1-\delta$ is $79.9\%^{6.10}$. Maxima and minima are observed for the same experts as in Tab. 6.7. If the normalised *deviation* is used instead, the agreement $1-\delta_{\mathrm{nrm}}$ rises to $82.9\%^{6.11}$. It grows in particular for teacher T_5 an T_7 who gave on average extremely high marks and for T_4, T_6, and N who gave very low marks (cf. Fig. 6.3). In the next step, the marks are first converted to ranks and then analysed. Highest agreement in terms of ρ_{S} and $1-\delta_{\mathrm{rnk}}$ can be found for T_2, T_3, T_7, T_{10}, and T_{12}. On average, $\rho_{\mathrm{S}}=0.78$ and $1-\delta_{\mathrm{rnk}}=80.7^{6.12}$ is achieved. For the Spearman Rank Correlation ρ_{S} all values are very close to ρ. The numbers for $1-\delta_{\mathrm{rnk}}$ are lower than for $1-\delta_{\mathrm{nrm}}$ but higher than for $1-\delta$.

An alternative measurement for the agreement is the classification rate (Tab. 6.9). Since classification is usually applied only to nominal data, a confusion of 1 and 2 is punished in the same way as 1 and 5. Using CL-5, the rating task is regarded as classification on nominal data with 5 classes. Chance agreement would be 0.2. For CL-3 the classification

measure	reference	OHM			OHMPLUS		
		min	mean	max	min	mean	max
ρ	pairwise	0.48	0.61	0.68	0.51	$0.63^{6.7}$	0.71
$1 - \delta$	pairwise	68.7	76.9	80.2	67.9	$75.7^{6.8}$	79.0
ρ	open, av. of other raters	0.59	0.76	0.85	0.62	$0.78^{6.9}$	0.88
$1 - \delta$	open, av. of other raters	69.2	81.0	86.4	68.5	$79.9^{6.10}$	86.1
$1 - \delta_{\mathrm{rnk}}$	open, ranks of av. rater	74.2	80.2	84.8	74.0	$80.7^{6.12}$	86.1
$\mathrm{CL}\text{-}10^{\pm2}_{\mathrm{rnk}}$	$\left\{\begin{array}{c}\text{open, ranks of av. rater}\end{array}\right.$	71.7	80.4	87.6	66.8	$82.0^{6.13}$	89.4
$\mathrm{CL}\text{-}10^{\pm3}_{\mathrm{rnk}}$	$\left.\begin{array}{c}\text{10 partitions}\end{array}\right\}$	80.1	90.6	95.9	79.7	$91.8^{6.14}$	99.2
$\kappa/\alpha_{\mathrm{krip}}$	-	0.51/0.51			0.54/0.54		
κ_{rnk}	ranks	0.62			$0.64^{6.15}$		

Table 6.10: Summary of the text level agreement of 13 experts for the OHM and OHMPLUS data.

of 3 classes is analysed (chance: 0.33). Integrating the ordinal properties of the data into the classification approach, a confusion of neighbouring marks can be allowed. For this kind of evaluation, the marks are first converted into ranks. CL-5 is between 33.4 % (T_5) and 74.5 % (T_3). On average it is 52.7 % and after conversion to ranks 47.1 %. For CL-3, up to 92.2 % are reached (average 67.7 %). Allowing a confusion of two out of ten ranks, the classification rate rises on average to $82.0\%^{6.13}$, allowing a confusion of three marks it reaches $91.8^{6.14}$.

Comparing Tab. 6.8 and Tab. 6.9 it can be seen that the following raters are most consistent with the other raters: T_1, T_2, T_3, T_7, T_{10}, and T_{12}. The teacher T_5 has shown good agreement on the word level, but not on the text level, unless the marks are converted to ranks. The reason is that his ratings are consistently higher (high ρ but poor CL-5). Low agreement is observed for T_9 on word and text level. N has on word level a medium agreement, but is the most inconsistent rater on the text level.

The similarity of the different measures can be analysed by correlating the different lines in Tab. 6.8 and Tab. 6.9. A high correlation of more than 0.9 is observed among all measures based on ranks. Furthermore, ρ is highly correlated with ρ_S, δ_{rnk}, and $\mathrm{CL}\text{-}10^{\pm3}_{\mathrm{rnk}}$. CL-5 is highly correlated with CL-3. In general, all measures are correlated better than 0.8, except δ (correlated at most with CL-5) and CL-5/CL-3 (correlated at most with δ and $\mathrm{CL}\text{-}10^{\pm3}_{\mathrm{rnk}}$. Summing up, several measures can be used to evaluate the consistency of raters. CL-3 and CL-5 are barely applicable unless nominal data is available. δ gives useful additional information about the size of deviation, but not whether this deviation is consistent or not.

Tab. 6.10 gives a summary of selected measures applied to the OHM and the OHMPLUS data. The agreement on OHMPLUS is slightly higher. However, $1 - \delta$ is higher for OHM (lower deviations of marks). On the text level κ and α_{krip} show similar results (0.54 for OHMPLUS). It is highest after converting the marks into ranks ($\kappa_{\mathrm{rnk}} = 0.64^{6.15}$). Additionally, Tab. 6.11 shows the agreement of the 8 experienced teachers T_1 – T_7 and N: the agreement rises slightly and κ_{rnk} reaches $0.68^{6.22}$. For the OHM data, the worst corre-

		OHM			OHMPLUS		
measure	reference (open)	min	mean	max	min	mean	max
ρ	av. of other raters	0.69	$0.77^{6.23}$	0.84	0.64	$0.79^{6.16}$	0.87
$1-\delta$	av. of other raters	68.8	$80.2^{6.24}$	86.2	67.4	$79.0^{6.17}$	86.2
$1-\delta_{\mathrm{nrm}}$	av. of other raters	79.2	$83.6^{6.25}$	86.7	79.1	$83.2^{6.18}$	85.9
$1-\delta_{\mathrm{rnk}}$	ranks of av. rater	76.1	$80.7^{6.26}$	83.8	74.5	$81.2^{6.19}$	85.0
CL-3	av. rater, rounded	63.0	$74.0^{6.27}$	83.1	46.7	$71.8^{6.20}$	89.1
CL-$10_{\mathrm{rnk}}^{\pm2}$	ranks, 10 partitions	73.0	$81.2^{6.28}$	84.7	65.3	$82.7^{6.21}$	88.7
κ_{rnk}	ranks		$0.66^{6.29}$			$0.68^{6.22}$	

Table 6.11: Summary of the text level agreement of the 8 experienced teachers for the OHM and OHMPLUS data.

lation is 0.69 (0.58 when comparing the worst student teacher and the mean experienced teacher), the worst $1-\delta_{\mathrm{nrm}}$ is 79.2 % (student teachers 79.3 %), CL-3 has a minimum of 63.0 % (student teachers 70.8), and the worst CL-$10_{\mathrm{rnk}}^{\pm2}$ is 73.0 % (student teachers 70.1 %).

6.2.4   Speaker Level Agreement

Finally, the speaker level agreement of 14 experts will be analysed. The numbers per expert are shown in Appendix A.3. A summary of the results is shown in Tab. 6.12. The first lines show the pairwise agreement in terms of ρ and $1-\delta$ (for details, cf. Tab. A.6). The average values are $0.66^{6.30}$ and $77.4\%^{6.31}$, respectively; in the open case (cf. Tab. A.7), $0.80^{6.32}$ and $82.6\%^{6.33}$ are reached. In both cases the agreement is higher than the agreement on the text level (Tab. 6.10). $1-\delta_{\mathrm{rnk}}$ is in the open case on average 81.9 %.

Furthermore, the results are analysed in terms of the open classification rate (for details, cf. Tab. A.8). CL-3 is on average $78.8\%^{6.36}$ and CL-$10_{\mathrm{rnk}}^{\pm2}$ is $82.9\%^{6.37}$. For CL-$10_{\mathrm{rnk}}^{\pm3}$ very high agreement is obtained for all raters, which results in low correlation with the other error measures. All other agreement measures are highly correlated (as on the text level), except for CL-5, CL-3, and δ.

Highest consistency with the other raters can be measured for T_1, T_3, and T_{10}, low agreement for S, T_5, T_8, T_9, and N. Tab. 6.12 further compares the agreement on 14 experts and on 8 experienced teachers. On average, $1-\delta$ is higher for the 14 experts, the other measures are higher for the experienced teachers. κ is around 0.47. After conversion to ranks $\kappa_{\mathrm{rnk}} = 0.67^{6.38}$ is achieved for the 14 experts and even $\kappa_{\mathrm{rnk}} = 0.73^{6.45}$ for the 8 selected experts. The results on OHM are rather similar as the results on OHMPLUS.

6.2.5   Reliability

It the previous sections it was shown that the agreement is not even among human experts 100 %. The maximum agreement, that one can expect, is the agreement that occurs between a rater r and his own rating from a previous evaluation phase and vice versa (intra-rater agreement). The results are shown in Tab. 6.13. The correlation ρ is symmetrical; for CL-2

measure		OhmPlus 14 experts			OhmPlus 8 exp. teachers			Ohm 8 exp. teachers	
		min	mean	max	min	mean	max	min	mean	max
ρ	(pairwise)	0.53	$0.66^{6.30}$	0.77	0.64	0.73	0.80	0.65	0.72	0.79
$1-\delta$	(pairwise)	67.2	$77.4^{6.31}$	81.6	67.0	76.5	81.2	67.5	77.1	81.3
ρ	(open)	0.63	$0.80^{6.32}$	0.94	0.72	$0.83^{6.39}$	0.92	0.74	$0.83^{6.46}$	0.92
$1-\delta$	(open)	67.7	$82.6^{6.33}$	90.6	66.8	$81.4^{6.40}$	90.3	67.5	$81.8^{6.47}$	89.8
$1-\delta_{nrm}$	(open)	78.7	$86.3^{6.34}$	90.7	81.5	$87.1^{6.41}$	90.4	81.3	$86.9^{6.48}$	89.7
$1-\delta_{rnk}$	(open)	73.5	$81.9^{6.35}$	90.6	74.9	$82.9^{6.42}$	87.6	76.5	$82.0^{6.49}$	87.1
CL-3	(open)	59.4	$78.8^{6.36}$	93.8	56.7	$76.6^{6.43}$	93.8	60.2	$76.5^{6.50}$	92.8
CL-10$_{rnk}^{\pm2}$	(open)	69.2	$82.9^{6.37}$	96.7	69.2	$85.7^{6.44}$	100.0	73.3	$86.1^{6.51}$	97.5
CL-10$_{rnk}^{\pm3}$	(open)	86.7	93.5	100.0	87.5	94.8	100.0	86.7	93.7	100.0
κ/α_{krip}			0.46/0.45			0.47/0.46			0.46/0.44	
κ_{rnk}			$0.67^{6.38}$			$0.73^{6.45}$			$0.70^{6.52}$	

Table 6.12: Summary of the speaker level agreement of the experts: Agreement of 14 experts (OhmPlus data) vs. 8 experienced teachers (OhmPlus and Ohm data).

level	measure	T_2	T_3	T_4	T_6	T_8	intra-rater (μ)	inter-rater (μ)
word	CL-2	78.4	80.4	82.0	79.7	77.2	79.5	$71.8^{6.1}$
text	ρ	0.82	0.83	0.75	0.82	*0.62*	0.77	$0.63^{6.7}$
	$1-\delta$	84.9	84.6	83.5	85.3	83.0	84.3	$75.7^{6.8}$
speaker	ρ	0.89	0.91	0.79	0.87	0.63	0.82	$0.66^{6.30}$
	$1-\delta$	87.6	86.9	86.3	87.9	84.1	86.6	$77.4^{6.31}$

Table 6.13: Reliability of the raters: Agreement of their first and second rating, average intra-rater agreement, and mean pairwise inter-rater agreement (OhmPlus data).

and δ, the evaluation was performed in both directions and averaged. For a comparison of the intra-rater and the inter-rater agreement, not any of the open cases based on a robust average rating can be used; the appropriate inter-rater results are obtained by a pairwise comparison of raters and are shown in Tab. 6.3, 6.7, and A.6 (and repeated in the rightmost column of Tab. 6.13). Each of the 5 raters who graded the data again half a year later, shows a high intra-rater agreement, that is in particular clearly higher than the mean pairwise inter-rater agreement. The only exception is rater T_8, who is a student teacher with less than 2 years teaching experience: on the text level his ratings correlate only with 0.62. On average, the word-level intra-rater CL-2 is 79.5 (inter-rater: $71.8^{6.1}$), the text-level intra-rater ρ is 0.77 (inter-rater $0.63^{6.7}$), and ρ on the speaker level is 0.82 (inter-rater $0.66^{6.30}$). At the same time, $1-\delta$ increases e.g. on the speaker level 86.6 % vs. $77.4\%^{6.31}$.

The Cronbach α measures the reliability of a test, as described in Sect. 2.2.1. Unfortunately, α cannot be computed for the whole data, since there are only some texts that are read by more than one or two students: the two texts T145 and T146 are read by 8 children,

	T145			T146		
	min	max	mean	min	max	mean
Cronbach α	0.49	0.90	0.82	0.63	0.86	0.76

Table 6.14: Cronbach α: Average reliability of the ratings for text T145 and text T146 each read by 8 children.

all other texts are read by fewer speakers. The approach to measure α on these two texts is the following: The two texts are considered as two tests to measure the pronunciation of different children. Each test consists of several testlets (words): T145 consists of 242 words and T146 of 144 words. Each testlet measures the pronunciation, while the overall test is a combination of the testlet results, i.e. the number of mispronounced words. If the test has a high reliability, then it is consistent: all testlets measure the same attribute, the pronunciation. For sure, each test requires ratings. If we now repeat the test with different raters (14) leaving all other variables constant, and if now α reveals a different consistency in each of the 14 iterations, it can be concluded that the raters, the only varying factor, have a different reliability.

On average, α is 0.76 (T146) and 0.82 (T145), cf. Tab. 6.14. Unfortunately, the relation of the experts in terms of reliability is different for T145 and T146. In the first case, S, T_5, and T_9 show lowest reliability; for T146 α is minimum for T_1 and T_2. On top of this, all raters have a lower α on T146: This text consists of less testlets and the (rater independent) number of mispronounced words is higher. On average 6 % of the words spoken by one of the eight children are mispronounced, for T146 only 3 %. To robustly calculate the reliability of the experts, more such texts would be required, which are read by several children. However, it could be shown that the reliability values themselves are satisfactorily high.

6.2.6 Graphical Comparison

After the detailed analysis of the agreement of experts on word, text, and speaker level, finally the evaluation of different levels will be compared in Fig. 6.4. Here, text level ratings of the different teachers and rater N are shown in the ρ-$(1-\delta)$-plane. Many measures that were computed in this chapter are highly correlated; ρ and δ are an infrequent pair that is only little correlated. The figure shows for T_1 – T_{12} and N the open values of ρ and $1 - \delta$ by comparing each expert with the average of the other raters. The most consistent experts are in the upper right corner: T_1, T_2, T_3, T_{10}, and T_{12}. The rater T_5 has high δ values; he gave on average worse marks. T_9, T_{10}, and S are separated in the left part of the figure due to a low correlation.

As there are no text-level ratings available from S, they are automatically calculated by downsampling the sentence level ratings or upsampling the speaker level ratings. Then the ratings are compared with the text ratings from T_1 – T_{12} and N. S_{spkr} is downsampled by assigning the speaker level rating to each text; the correlation is very low. S_{sent} is obtained

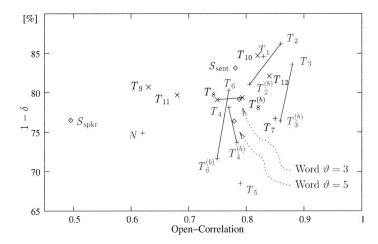

Figure 6.4: Text level agreement in terms of open ρ and open $1 - \delta$ for 13 experts T_1 –
T_{12} and N on the OHMPLUS data. The expert ratings and their second ratings (half a year
later) are connected with lines. The ratings from S are downsampled from the sentence
level (S_{sent}) or upsampled from the speaker level (S_{spkr}). Downsampled from the word level
are the annotations based on "at least $\vartheta = 5$ of 14 raters vote with $\mathcal{X}$" and "at least $\vartheta = 3$
of 8 experienced teachers vote with $\mathcal{X}$". Sampled ratings and $T_i^{(b)}$ are compared with the
mean of T_1 – T_{12} and N.

through upsampling: The grade of each text is the mean of the grades from the underlying
sentences. This rating is very close to those teachers having highest consistency.

High consistency with the experts' text level ratings is also obtained when downsampling the word level ratings. The correlation and $1 - \delta$ show high agreement with the text
level ratings, if the word level rating is used, that marks a word if at least $\vartheta = 3$ of the eight
experienced teachers vote with $\mathcal{X}$. Then the percentage of marked words is used as text
level rating. Slightly lower agreement is obtained, when the downsampled ratings are based
on the word level rating, that marks a word if at least $\vartheta = 5$ out of 13 raters vote with
$\mathcal{X}$. To calculate δ for upsampled and downsampled ratings, the ratings first are linearly
mapped onto the interval [1;5] which is the range of the text level ratings.

The second evaluation pass of teacher T_2, T_3, T_4, T_6, and T_8 is denoted as $T_2^{(b)}$, $T_3^{(b)}$,
$T_4^{(b)}$, $T_6^{(b)}$, and $T_8^{(b)}$. For $T_2^{(b)}$, and so on, ρ and δ are calculated with respect to the mean
of all other teachers. First and second rating of these 5 teachers are connected with lines in
the figure. The second ratings have lower agreement, in particular in terms of δ (Tab. A.3
shows that all teachers gave on average better marks in the second pass). The student

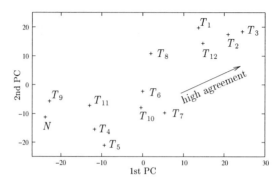

Figure 6.5: First two principal components of the 10 text-level ratings ρ, $1 - \delta$, $1 - \delta_{\mathrm{nrm}}$, ρ_S, $1 - \delta_{\mathrm{rnk}}$, CL-5, CL-3, CL-$5^{\pm 0}_{\mathrm{rnk}}$ CL-$10^{\pm 2}_{\mathrm{rnk}}$ CL-$10^{\pm 3}_{\mathrm{rnk}}$.

teacher T_8, however, shows constant δ and an improvement in terms of correlation. He was still learning the way of grading that is consistent with the experienced teachers.

A way to illustrate the agreement of the teachers using more than the two measures illustrated in Fig. 6.4 is outlined next: The 10 dimensional data based on the 10 text level measurements from Tab. 6.8 and Tab 6.9 can be easily visualised by eliminating highly correlated information. The principal component analysis is employed to extract the most important dimensions. If only one dimension is left, a ranking of the 13 raters is obtained in terms of the agreement with the remaining experts: T_3 has highest agreement, followed by T_2, T_{12}, T_1, T_7, T_8, T_6, T_{10}, T_5, T_4, and T_{11}. T_9 and N have the lowest agreement with other experts[5]. Two feature components are shown in Fig. 6.5: the first correlates among others highly with ρ and $1 - \delta_{\mathrm{rnk}}$, the second with CL-3, CL-5 and δ.

6.3   Discussion

In this chapter, the agreement of the experts and their reliability was analysed. On the word level, it was found that all experts have a similar strictness, i.e. that the percentage of marked words is for all raters around 5 %. A more robust reference rating is obtained, if only those words are marked as mispronounced, where at least ϑ experts vote with $\mathcal{X}$. Appropriate thresholds are $\vartheta = 5$ out of 14 experts or $\vartheta = 3$ out of 8 experienced teachers (without student teachers or students): In this cases, the strictness of the new reference is approximately 5 %, which corresponds to the strictness of most of the raters. The agreement on the word level is measured with the class-wise averaged classification rate CL-2. The average pairwise inter-rater agreement is 71.8%[6.1] CL-2 on the OHMPLUS data. The intra-

---

[5]Note, that N is among the 8 expert teachers with more than 1 year of teaching experience but does not show on all levels high agreement scores, as discussed on page 112 in the footnote.

rater agreement is obtained when comparing raters with their second rating that took place half a year later. It is on average 79.5 %. The open CL-2 averages the agreement between each expert and a combination of the other experts. This way, 79.3%$^{6.2}$ CL-2 are achieved.

As for the text level, it was found that some teachers gave (systematically) worse or better marks. To measure the agreement, not only the correlation ρ is calculated, but also the deviation δ in terms of marks. The average pairwise evaluation in terms of ρ and $(1-\delta)$ is 0.63$^{6.7}$ and 75.7%$^{6.8}$ in the inter-rater case and 0.77 and 84.3 % in the intra-rater case. The open inter-rater ρ and $(1-\delta)$ are 0.78$^{6.9}$ and 79.9$^{6.10}$, respectively. There are several other measures that turned out to be highly correlated with ρ: δ after normalisation of the ratings, and different measures that are not calculated on the marks themselves but on their ranks, e.g. $1 - \delta_{\mathrm{rnk}}$ and CL-10$_{\mathrm{rnk}}^{\pm\vartheta}$. The latter is the classification that is firstly based on 10 classes which can be obtained by ranking, and secondly tolerates a confusion of neighbouring marks. There is hardly any difference between Pearson correlation and the Spearman correlation. The classification rate CL-5 which punishes a confusion of neighbouring marks in the same way as far distant marks is not correlated with most other measures at all (little correlated with δ). Nevertheless, CL-5 = 52.7 % is obtained which is clearly higher than chance (20.0 %).

On the speaker level, the agreement of the experts is highest. Pairwise ρ and $(1-\delta)$ rise to 0.66$^{6.30}$ and 77.4%$^{6.31}$ for the inter-rater agreement and 0.82 and 86.6 % for the intra-rater agreement. The open inter-rater agreement is 0.80$^{6.32}$ and 82.6%$^{6.33}$, respectively. CL-10$_{\mathrm{rnk}}^{\pm 2}$ is on the text level 82.0%$^{6.13}$ and on the speaker level 82.9%$^{6.37}$.

A common measure to evaluate the agreement of ratings is κ. Nearly identical values are obtained for α_{krip}. On the word level $\kappa = 0.43^{6.6}$ is obtained. On the text and speaker level, ratings are first converted to ranks, then κ_{rnk} based on a square distance function between ranks is computed. It is 0.64$^{6.15}$ on the text level and 0.67$^{6.38}$ on the speaker level, based on 13 and 14 experts, respectively. Investigations based on Cronbach α have shown that ratings and testing procedure are reliable. The sum of word level marks per text can be used as text level rating. In Fig. 6.4 it is shown that this downsampled word level rating agrees highly with the text level gradings of different experts.

Summing up, it is recommended to evaluate the agreement with at least two measures: Measures correlated to ρ, which focus on the relation of the data samples, and measures like δ or CL, which focus on the correct value or category of the value. κ and mostly ρ are useful to compare results with the literature. Therefore, in Chap. 8 different measures will be used for evaluation. In this chapter it was shown that experts highly agree on their ratings: For different measures and different evaluation levels the inter-rater agreement reaches 82% – 90% of the intra-rater agreement. On the word level teachers highly agree on the number of words they mark as mispronounced. In order to not frustrate the student, not all wrongly pronounced words are rejected; the selection of marked words differs strongly. Based on several measurements it was also shown on the text level that high agreement does by far not mean 100 %.

The experts have not been calibrated, since they are teachers and it was intended to measure the way teachers assess students. Also in [Cuc00b], no instructions were given to the raters and a comparable agreement was obtained. With detailed instruction and calibration sessions, it certainly would be possible to further increase the agreement. However, an automatic system, which is able to achieve high correlations with those calibrated reference ratings can only detect mispronunciations specified in the rater instructions. Such a system can be built by implementing step by step modules for the specified phenomena. In this thesis, the approach based on pronunciation features is different: first, real ratings are collected from teachers, then a large set of pronunciation features is implemented, and finally it is investigated, which of the features are appropriate for a scoring similar to teachers, without any specifications what wrongly pronounced means in detail.

A robust rating is obtained by averaging ratings from a large set of teachers. Large means that in the literature no investigations based on a comparable amount of experts can be found. The objective of an automatic CAPT system should not be to achieve scores that are 100 % identical to *one* reference. They rather should be in the same range of the agreement of multiple experts based on different agreement measures. If N measurements span an N-dimensional space, where each human expert forms a point, then the centre of the point cluster would be an ideal CAPT system. The first two principal components of such a space are shown in Fig. 6.5. The principal components correlate to the ρ and $1 - \delta$ axes shown in Fig. 6.4; the final automatic recognition result will be projected into this plane and compared with the human experts (discussed in Chap. 8.4.1).

Chapter 7

Recognition of Adults and Children Speech

The algorithms for automatic pronunciation scoring presented in this thesis require automatic speech recognition. In this chapter, it is investigated how robustly speech from children can be recognised with state-of-the-art technologies, and to what extent these recognition rates can be improved. Various configurations of a speech recogniser are optimised for two children corpora and adaptation approaches are investigated. The target is to obtain in the end speech and phoneme recognisers that are not only improved to recognise children, but also to recognise non-native speech. Thereto, a recogniser comprehending acoustic models for English and German phonemes is trained from native and non-native data. Baseline results and improved results are compared in terms of word error rate (WER, cf. Eq. 3.27). The most important results are summarised in Appendix E. This chapter begins with an analysis of different characteristics of children speech.

7.1   Characteristics of the Children Data

In this section, children data from different corpora are compared with the adult speech from VERBMOBIL . The different children corpora are YOUTH (American English), BIRMINGHAM (British English) and NONNATIVE (non-native English). All plots are calculated from the training data; from VERBMOBIL only native speakers are used. To discriminate male and female speakers, parts of the VERBMOBIL data was auditorily classified to obtain 28 speakers per gender.

First of all, formants are calculated[1] from the data to confirm the results reported in Sect. 3.3.1. Fig. 7.1 indeed shows a shift of the formants to higher frequencies for all three children corpora. The figure analyses the distribution of F_1 vs. F_2 for several vowels. The means of the vowels [i:], [u:], [A:] (AE: [A]), and [{] build the vowel trapezoid as

---

[1]The freely available software PRAAT is used to calculate the formants. The software was developed by Paul Boersma and David Weenink, Institute of Phonetic Sciences, University of Amsterdam http://www.fon.hum.uva.nl/praat/.

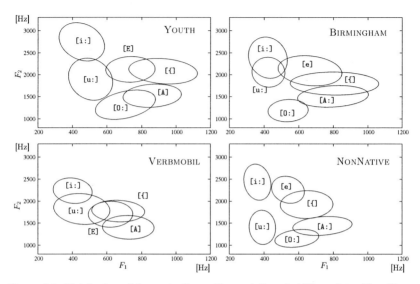

Figure 7.1: Distribution of formants F_1 vs. F_2 on adult and children data. The ellipses illustrate the standard deviation around the mean of the formants.

discussed in Chap. 2.1.1. In comparison to Fig. 2.1, the illustrations in Fig. 7.1 are rotated and inverted. Additionally to the corner vowels, [e] is shown for British English and [E] for American English. Also [O:] is plotted, but not for the VERBMOBIL data. On VERBMOBIL [O:] has a high variance and overlaps clearly with [A], cf. /bIkO:z/ and /bIkAz/.

For the VERBMOBIL data, it can be clearly seen that the vowels cover a more compact region of the F_1/F_2-plane. In comparison with the adults, it is true for all children databases that [A] and [{] have higher formants F_1 and [i:] has a higher formant F_2. Both formant frequencies are increased for [u:], but not for the NONNATIVE data. The German children seem to use a German [u:] which has a noticeably lower F_2 (cf. Fig. 2.1). Also [e] and [E] uttered by children have higher frequencies for both formants. The region covered by all vowels is on the F_1 axis from below 300 Hz to less than 900 Hz for adults, from 300 Hz to 1.1 kHz for native children and 300 – 900 Hz for the non-native children. On the F_2 axis the frequencies for all vowels from adults are below 2.5 kHz but in part even higher than 3 kHz for YOUTH. The distributions for NONNATIVE children's vowels is similar; exceptions are in particular [u:] and [{]. The variance in F_1 direction is smaller for most vowels.

In speech recognition the spectrum is calculated for each short-time analysis window. Then, the spectrum is smoothed and sampled (cf. Sect. 3.2.2). Using the example of a Mel

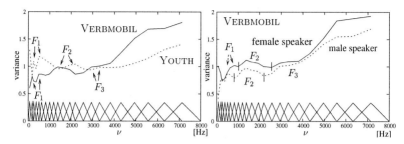

Figure 7.2: Intra speaker variability (average speaker): Variance of the energy per filterbank for American speakers. Comparison of children (YOUTH) vs. adults (VERBMOBIL) and male vs. female adults (VERBMOBIL).

filter bank with 22 filters covering the frequency range from 0 – 8 kHz, the variability of children speech is analysed next. For each Mel filter, the variance of the energy is analysed per speaker and then averaged over all speakers (intra-speaker variability). There can be two reasons for higher variability: on the one hand it can be caused by a higher between-class scatter, which would result in a better separability of the classes and a more robust classification. On the other hand, higher within-class scatter could be the reason which results in a higher overlap, which makes classification harder. It is not possible to conclude from higher variances, whether classification will be better or not. Consequently, we will only have a closer look on the place of relative maxima in variance on the frequency axis.

Fig. 7.2, left compares the American English corpora YOUTH and VERBMOBIL. The reason that the variances for the higher frequencies are lower for YOUTH could be that YOUTH has a much smaller vocabulary. However, the variability in the frequency range of formants is higher for YOUTH. Those higher variabilities have also been observed in Fig. 7.1. Furthermore, the relative maxima show the region of the three formants, that are clearly shifted to higher frequencies in comparison to VERBMOBIL, which motivates the essential use of VTLN: mixing both databases requires a filterbank for YOUTH that is expanded. In Fig. 7.2, right, the difference between female and male adult speakers is shown. For F_2 boundaries of the frequency interval are plotted which comprises higher frequencies for the female speakers; however, the shift is smaller than in Fig. 7.2, left, when comparing children and adults. Additionally it can be seen that variances for females are in general higher.

In Fig. 7.3, the intra-speaker variability is shown for the BIRMINGHAM and the NONNATIVE corpus. Here the peaks of the formants are not so clear; they are blurred and do not allow a discrimination between F_2 and F_3. When contrasting the 6–9 year-old native children and the 10 – 11 year-old children, variances for young children turned out to be greater and a shift of the formants towards higher frequencies can be found. The trajectory for the NONNATIVE data does not even have a peak for the F_1 formant. One reason for the overlap of the formants could be the large age range of the BIRMINGHAM

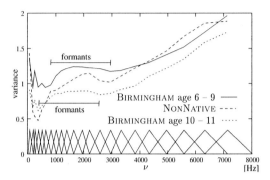

Figure 7.3: Intra speaker variability (average speaker): Variance of the energy per filterbank for non-native speakers (NONNATIVE) and native British speakers (BIRMINGHAM) of different age.

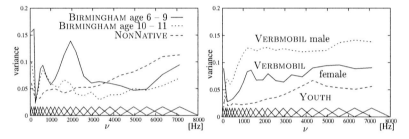

Figure 7.4: Inter speaker variability: Variance of the speaker mean of the energy per filterbank for VERBMOBIL, YOUTH, BIRMINGHAM, and NONNATIVE.

data and the inconsistent pronunciation in the NONNATIVE corpus.

The inter-speaker variability in analysed in Fig. 7.4. It measures per frequency band the variance of the speaker mean of the energy. The inter-speaker variability is in all cases smaller than the intra-speaker variability. High variances show that the elimination of speaker characteristics has failed. In automatic speech recognition, the only important information that is needed to be kept after feature extraction is the information *what* is said. Therefore it is desired to eliminate e.g. all information on *how* it is said and *who* said it. The figure shows maxima in variability for the formants and for high frequencies (fricatives). Fig. 7.4, left compares two age groups from BIRMINGHAM. The younger children show higher inter-speaker variances in particular for the fundamental frequency ($<$ 300 Hz) and the second formant (around 2 kHz). For the non-native speakers the inter-speaker variability is low in the region of the formants, the speech is more consistent among speakers, which of course can also mean that it is consistently wrong (cf. /u:/ in Fig. 7.1). In Fig. 7.4, right, greater variabilities are shown for male speaker. The reason for the low variabilities for YOUTH is certainly the fact that all speakers had to read the same texts.

The effect of the greater variabilities of younger children and the shift of the formants to higher frequencies will be analysed in the following sections in terms of word error rates.

7.2 Baseline Systems

7.2.1 General Considerations

In all experiments, the default setup is a semi-continuous HMM with a shared codebook with 500 densities (details in Sec. 3.2.3). For soft vector quantisation the beam is set to 0.1. For decoding, word accuracy is given for the unigram LM to show the performance of the acoustic models and additionally the performance using a 4-gram LM. In the next section, the optimal language weight for the LM is computed. For the A^*-algorithm, additionally a polygram language weight is used, that is in all experiments constant[2].

Acoustic models are built from those generalised polyphones (cf. Sect. 3.2.3) which are at least 50 times observed in the training data. Polyphones are specialised models of the monophone models. A monophone is built for each sub-phonemic unit. Phonemes and their sub-phonemic units are described in Appendix B.2. For British English 44 phonemes and polyhones are built from 44 sub-phonemic models[3], for American English 39 phonemes and polyphones from also 44 sub-phonemic models. The number of different sub-phonemic models given the union of both languages is 46; additionally four models are trained for silence, non-verbal sound and breathing.

As for the language modelling, no categories as described in Eq. 3.34 were explicitly designed for any of the databases and only all the rare words are merged into one category.

All speech recognisers are evaluated on the test data set in terms of WER (Eq. 3.27); the most important results are summarised in Appendix E. If we compare two systems, the baseline system A and another possibly improved system B, significance testing is essential to show, whether the results can be generalised. In the present thesis, the *matched pairs sentence-segment word error* (MAPSSWE) is employed [Gil89]. As in [Ste05b], a publicly available implementation from the *National Institute of Standards and Technology (NIST)* is used[4] [Pal90] for the statistical test for the null hypothesis that system A and B are identical. This hypothesis is rejected if the probability for the observed difference between A and B given the null hypothesis is ≤ 0.05. This upper boundary 0.05 is the *p-value*. The

---

[2]The polygram language weight is fixed to 7 in all experiments.

[3]It is pure chance that the number of phonemes and the number of sub-phonemic models is identical. One can expect more sub-phonemic models, since e.g. plosives can be subdivided into the phases silence, burst, and aspiration. However, a short and the corresponding long vowel is based on the same sub-phonemic model, which again reduces the total number.

[4]http://www.nist.gov/speech/tests/sigtests/mapsswe.htm

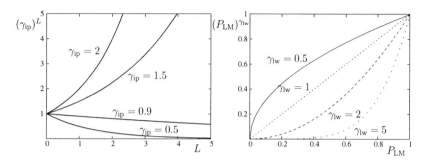

Figure 7.5: Effect of different γ_{ip} dependent on the sentence length L and of γ_{lw} dependent on the linguistic probability P_{LM} of the recognised word sequence. The speech recogniser decides for the word sequence $\boldsymbol{w}$ with maximum $p_{\mathrm{AM}}(\boldsymbol{c}^1 \ldots \boldsymbol{c}^t | \boldsymbol{w}) \cdot P_{\mathrm{LM}}(\boldsymbol{w})^{\gamma_{\mathrm{lw}}} \cdot (\gamma_{\mathrm{ip}})^L$ given a sequence of feature vectors $\boldsymbol{c}^1 \ldots \boldsymbol{c}^t$ after Eq. 3.41.

complement of the p-value is the probability, that the systems are different, i.e. that B is significantly better or worse.

7.2.2   Language Weight and Insertion Penalty

In this chapter the word error rate (WER) of recognisers trained on different corpora are reported. The recognition rate is e.g. dependent on recording conditions or the speaker group (worse recognition rates on children). However, important factors are in particular the size of the vocabulary and the perplexity (Eq. 3.35) of the language model. Dependent on the performance of acoustic models and the language model and dependent on the size of the sentences, a different language weight γ_{lw} and insertion penalty γ_{ip} as defined in Eq. 3.41 have to be chosen. In the following γ_{lw} and γ_{ip} are optimised on a validation data set to obtain baseline recognition results that are as good as possible and cannot be trivially outperformed with new algorithms.

The effects of γ_{ip} and γ_{lw} are shown in Fig. 7.5. Long sentences are punished with $\gamma_{\mathrm{ip}} \le 1$; $\gamma_{\mathrm{ip}} > 1$ punishes short sentences and additionally increases the overall scores which now can become much greater than 1.0. As a consequence, the beam search algorithm (cf. page 61) prunes less branches of the word graph given an unchanged threshold (beam) in all experiments. As for the language weight we observe the following: $\gamma_{\mathrm{lw}} < 1$ increases the influence of the language model; $\gamma_{\mathrm{lw}} > 1$ decreases its influence but less strongly for sentences with great LM score. In general, the influence of γ_{lw} is much stronger than the influence of γ_{ip}. Further, best performance can be observed for large values of γ_{lw} *and* large values of γ_{ip} or vice versa. The global optimum is usually found, when both configurations meet as can be seen in Fig. 7.6. It shows exemplarily on the YOUTH database the strong influence of γ_{lw}. Here and on other databases it was observed that there exists a threshold

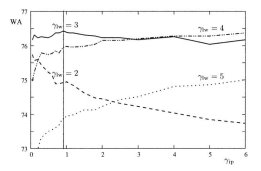

Figure 7.6: WA on the YOUTH validation data for different γ_{lw} and γ_{ip} using a unigram LM. WA strongly depends on γ_{lw}, optima are reached for small γ_{ip} given small γ_{lw} and for large γ_{ip} given $\gamma_{lw} \geq 4$.

$\bar{\gamma}_{lw}$ with the property, that for any larger γ_{lw} the WA increases with growing γ_{ip} ($\gamma_{lw} \geq 4$ in Fig. 7.6) whereas the opposite behaviour can be seen for $\gamma_{lw} < \bar{\gamma}_{lw}$. This observation motivates the following heuristic algorithm that is applied to find the optimal $(\gamma_{lw}, \gamma_{ip})$-pair:

1. Find the optimal $\gamma_{lw}^{(opt1)}$ (grid search in steps of ± 1 starting with $\gamma_{lw} = 3$) while keeping $\gamma_{ip} = 0.8$ constant. Stop, if the WA on the validation data set does not increase any more.

2. Find the optimal $\gamma_{lw}^{(opt2)}$ (grid search in steps of ± 1 starting with $\gamma_{lw} = \gamma_{lw}^{(opt1)}$) while keeping $\gamma_{ip} = 5.0$ constant. Stop, if the WA on the validation data set does not increase any more.

3. Choose the global optimum $\gamma_{lw}^{(opt)} \in \{\gamma_{lw}^{(opt1)}, \gamma_{lw}^{(opt2)}\}$ and look for the optimum[5] $\gamma_{ip}^{(opt)}$.

The optimal $(\gamma_{lw}, \gamma_{ip})$-pairs for different databases are summarised in Tab. 7.1. The language weights γ_{lw} is always greater than 1.0 and lowest for the YOUTH recognisers that have also lowest perplexity. γ_{ip} is only for YOUTH smaller than 1.0. The reason is that the sentences are very short (on average 3 words). The large γ_{ip} for VERBMOBIL and BIRMINGHAM raises the scores of the recogniser to keep more alternative word chains after the beam-search. Details on the different databases are discussed in the following.

---

[5]First, the optimum $\gamma_{ip}^{(opt1)} \in \{0.4, 0.6, 0.8, 1.0, 3.0, 5.0, 7.0, 9.0, 12.0\}$ is searched given this coarse resolution, then $\gamma_{ip}^{(opt)}$ is found by searching in a finer resolution around $\gamma_{ip}^{(opt1)}$.

LM	corpus	γ_{lw}	γ_{ip}	perplexity	ν_{min}	ν_{max}	B	WER [%]
unigr.	VERBMOBIL	4	13	165	62.5	6250	25	$52.3^{7.2}$
	YOUTH	3	0.9	141	62.5	6250	25	$23.8^{7.3}$
					0	8000	22	23.4
	BIRMINGHAM	5	7	168	62.5	6250	25	$52.2^{7.5}$
					0	8000	22	49.2
4-gr.	VERBMOBIL	4	10	33	62.5	6250	25	$34.6^{7.1}$
	YOUTH	2	0.9	3.5	62.5	6250	25	$3.3^{7.4}$
					0	8000	22	3.8
	BIRMINGHAM	4	9	13	62.5	6250	25	$26.1^{7.6}$
					0	8000	22	23.1

Table 7.1: Baseline systems: Optimal configuration of language weight γ_{lw} and insertion penalty γ_{ip}, perplexity of the LM on the test set, and WER on the test set. Results for the baseline Mel filter bank and an expanded filter bank for children. Number of filters B and frequency range in Hz.

7.2.3   Adult Speech

For the VERBMOBIL baseline system a similar setup as in [Ste05b] was applied. The filter bank consists of 25 triangular filters covering the frequency range from 62 – 6250 Hz. However, the training procedure as described in Sect. 3.2.3 is slightly different, the transcription of the lexicon was revised[6], and a consistent phone-hierarchy (cf. page 57) to build the acoustic polyphone models is used. The changes make the three speech recognisers for VERBMOBIL, YOUTH and BIRMINGHAM now comparable.

In [Ste05b] a word error rate of 35.0 % is reported with $(\gamma_{lw}, \gamma_{ip}) = (4, 10)$ and 4-gram language modelling. After all revisions, the new baseline of the VERBMOBIL recogniser is $34.6\%^{7.1}$ WER[7]. Although the optimal γ_{ip} calculated with the algorithm described above would be 9, in this thesis 10 is used as in [Ste05b][8]. With unigram LM $52.3\%^{7.2}$ WER are achieved. All baseline results are shown in Tab. 7.1.

7.2.4   Children Speech

The shift of the formants to higher frequencies for children speech may require a filter bank covering higher frequencies than necessary for adults. Further, broader filters could be more robust against the higher variability in children speech; to account this, the standard filter bank is used with less filters. Preliminary experiments on children speech showed best

---

[6]Now uses the same phonetic symbols as used in YOUTH. Basis is the CMU dictionary [CmuDict].

[7]about 1.5 percentage points are lost by a revised invoke of DACS adaptation during feature extraction. Now training and test is not mixed any more: the frontend module sees all the training data at first and after this the test data.

[8]To be comparable with [Ste05b], also the polygram language weight is in this case 4.5 and not like in all other experiments in this thesis 7

gender	age:	6–7	6–8	7–9	8–10	9–11	10–11
both		40.2	32.9	21.8	**15.3**	**15.4**	**15.9**

gender	age:	6	7	8	9	10	11
both		47.6	33.8	18.3	14.4	**14.0**	18.0
male		46.2	41.6	20.9	10.9	**9.9**	19.7
female		53.2	29.3	15.7	**15.3**	17.7	16.1

Table 7.2: Age dependent evaluation of the BIRMINGHAM test data on BIRMINGHAM acoustic models ($\nu_{\min} = 0, \nu_{\max} = 8000$). WER in %.

performance with a filter bank exploiting the whole range from 0 to 8 kHz with 22 filters [Rus04, p. 26], so γ_{lw} and γ_{ip} are being optimised for this very configuration.

For the YOUTH database can be seen in Fig. 7.6 that best word accuracy is reached with $(\gamma_{\mathrm{lw}}, \gamma_{\mathrm{ip}}) = (3, 0.9)$[9] in the case of a unigram LM; for 4-gram LM the optimum is achieved with a lower language weight $(2, 0.9)$. The word error rates are 23.4 % WER and rather low 3.8 % WER for the 4-gram LM, but with a perplexity of only 3.5 (Tab. 7.1). The unigram WER is 26.5 % for males and 21.3 % for females. Applying the same $(\gamma_{\mathrm{lw}}, \gamma_{\mathrm{ip}})$ but using the standard filter bank from VERBMOBIL (25 filters reaching from 62.5 Hz to 6250 Hz), the baseline error rates of 23.8%[7.3] (unigram LM) and 3.3%[7.4] (4-gram LM) are obtained.

As can be seen in Tab. 7.1, the performance of the BIRMINGHAM recogniser is noticeably worse, since a LM with higher perplexity is used and since the BIRMINGHAM data contains considerably younger children which are harder to recognise. The language weight is similar to the VERBMOBIL data and the insertion penalty slightly lower[10]. Applying a filter bank with 25 filters reaching from 62 – 6250 Hz, 52.2%[7.5] WER are reached with unigram LM and 26.1%[7.6] WER for 4-grams. With an alternative filter bank covering 0 – 8000 Hz with 22 filters, the error rates decreases to 49.2 % WER (unigram LM) and 23.1 % WER (4-gram LM). Again a gender dependent evaluation showed higher WER for males (26.2 %, 4-gram LM) than for females (20.5 %). In [DAr04] a continuous speech recogniser was trained with the HTK hidden Markov model speech recognition software toolkit[11] using a slightly larger training set but evaluated on the same test data with a unigram LM. With monophone acoustic models 60 % WER are achieved, with triphone acoustic models 44.6 % WER.

An age dependent evaluation of the BIRMINGHAM test set with $(\gamma_{\mathrm{lw}}, \gamma_{\mathrm{ip}}) = (4, 9)$ is shown in Tab. 7.2. On BIRMINGHAM acoustic models the WER is only 15.9 % for the 10–11 year-old children, but 40.2 % on the 6–7 year-old children. These smoothed results, where adjacent age brackets are combined, show an continuous decrease of WER with increasing age. When each age group is evaluated separately, the minimum WER is achieved for males

---

[9] 2nd optimum: $(\gamma_{\mathrm{lw}}, \gamma_{\mathrm{ip}}) = (4, 6)$

[10] Optima $(\gamma_{\mathrm{lw}}, \gamma_{\mathrm{ip}})$ on the validation data set are $(5, 7)$ and $(4, 0.8)$ for unigrams and $(4, 9)$ or $(3, 0.3)$ for 4-gram LMs

[11] http://htk.eng.cam.ac.uk/

		training data		
		VERBMOBIL	YOUTH	BIRMINGHAM
test	YOUTH	$41.3^{7.7}$	(3.8)	-
	BIRMINGHAM	$85.3^{7.8}$	-	(23.1)
	NONNATIVE	$72.6^{7.9}$	$50.3^{7.11}$	$43.5^{7.10}$

Table 7.3: Mismatched training and test for different corpora with 4-gram LM.

with age 10 and for females with age 9. The highest WER is found for 6-year-old female children. 7- and 8-year-old females can be better recognised than males, 9- and 10-year-old males better than females. Altogether, the error increases again slightly for age 11, since the distance to the centre age of the training data becomes maximum. It could be shown that a training restricted on 8 – 11 year-old children (children with low WER), results in no improvement. The evaluation on the 8 – 11 year-old children showed even slightly lower recognition rates than with the original acoustic models: More training data is the better data, even if it is from very young children.

7.2.5   Mismatched Training and Test

In the following, the VERBMOBIL adult speech recogniser is evaluated with children data. Here, automatic recognition becomes more difficult; besides different recording conditions, the main reason is the mismatch adults versus children which will be seen on the strongly age dependent performance of the recognisers. When testing with BIRMINGHAM, an additionally mismatch is BE vs. AE.

First, for each word of the children corpus under consideration acoustic models are built from the VERBMOBIL polyphone models. For BIRMINGHAM, additionally the transcription of the words is modified to better match with AE as described in Chap. 4 (Tab. 4.9): the new transcription of the words models the British pronunciation using the American phonetic inventory. The LM is solely trained on the transcription of the YOUTH or BIRMINGHAM training data, respectively. To obtain reasonable recognition results, the language weight is in all cases increased to $\gamma_{lw} = 5$; γ_{ip} is taken from Tab. 7.1 for the respective test corpus.

In comparison with children acoustic models (Tab. 7.1) the WER is noticeably higher when evaluating the YOUTH test data on VERBMOBIL. With 4-gram LM the WER reaches $41.3\%^{7.7}$. When testing the BIRMINGHAM data on VERBMOBIL, the error rates for the youngest children are around 100 %. In the best case (age 10 – 11) the WER is still around 75 %; on children acoustic models it is between 14 % and 18 %, only. The overall result when testing BIRMINGHAM on VERBMOBIL is $85.3\%^{7.8}$ WER. Results on mismatched training/test conditions are shown in Tab. 7.3, age dependent results in Tab. 7.6.

7.2.6   Non-Native English

Similar to the previous section describing mismatched training and test, now the NONNATIVE data is evaluated with acoustic models trained on native speech. Since the NONNA-

TIVE corpus provides no validation data to optimise any parameters, γ_{lw} is again set to 5 and γ_{ip} is taken from Tab. 7.1 for the respective training corpus. The language model is trained on the reference texts of the NONNATIVE corpus. The perplexity of the unigram LM is 161; with 4-grams it is 5.5. For evaluation the manual transcription[12] of the test set is used as reference, like in all previous experiments.

When testing NONNATIVE data on VERBMOBIL the WER is 72.6%[7.9], which is high but lower than for BIRMINGHAM on VERBMOBIL, where even 6-year-old children are tested with adult models. When evaluating the NONNATIVE children data on the BE BIRMINGHAM data the WER is 43.5%[7.10]. This is the optimum baseline system for the NONNATIVE data. Even with the YOUTH training data containing not so young children and data with a very clear pronunciation, only 50.3%[7.11] are achieved for non-native speakers. All results are summarised in Tab. 7.3.

7.3 Improved Systems

7.3.1 Optimisation of the Filter Bank

In the previous section it was shown that the WER is very high when testing children on adults data. Let's now consider the beneficial case that enough children training data is available which allows a matched training and evaluation. However, up to now it is not known, whether the baseline results in Tab. 7.1 can be improved by choosing a different filter bank that covers also higher frequencies, nor which number of filters should be chosen to obtain an optimal sampling of the Mel spectrum. With the right spacing of the filters the formants are extracted while the relative maxima in the spectrum resulting from the harmonic frequencies are eliminated. These harmonic frequencies are multiples of the fundamental frequency which is unfortunately rather high for young speakers.

In a first step, the maximum frequency ν_{max} covered by the filter bank is optimised while keeping the number of filters $B = 22$ and the minimum frequency $\nu_{min} = 0$ constant[13]. As can be seen in Fig. 7.7, the optimum on the validation set is $\nu_{max} = 7000$ Hz for YOUTH. In this case, on the test set 22.2%[7.12] WER are obtained with a unigram LM and 2.9%[7.13] WER in the 4-gram case. For BIRMINGHAM the optimum is $\nu_{max} = 7500$ which goes with the assumption that for younger children a larger frequency range is required. The WER on the test data is 49.7%[7.14] WER (unigram LM) and 23.7%[7.15] WER (4-gram LM). All results are summarised in Tab. 7.4. They are consistently better than in the $\nu_{max} = 6250$ case in Tab. 7.1. In contrast, the WER rises slightly if the filter bank is extended to $\nu_{max} = 7000$ for VERBMOBIL.

Next (and only for YOUTH) the number of filters B is optimised. As can be seen in Fig. 7.8, left, an optimum is indeed achieved for $B = 22$. The optimisation of the lower cut-off frequency ν_{min} shows two cases with minimal WER: to cut off the range below the

---

[12]in the case of foreign speakers the transliteration differs clearly from the texts that actually had to be read.

[13]also γ_{lw} and γ_{ip} are kept constant.

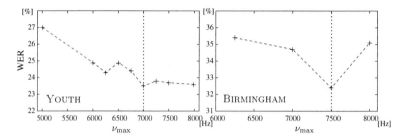

Figure 7.7: Optimisation of ν_{max} on the validation data set of YOUTH and BIRMINGHAM.

corpus	ν_{max}	B	WER unigram	WER 4-gram
YOUTH	7000 Hz	22	22.2[7.12]	2.9[7.13]
BIRMINGHAM	7500 Hz	22	49.7[7.14]	23.7[7.15]

Table 7.4: Children speech recognition after optimisation of the filter bank. WER in %.

fundamental frequency which has for children values up to 280 Hz (cf. Tab. 3.2), or to use all frequencies $\nu \geq 0$ leaving it to the cepstrum computation to extract the important information. Since both cases make sense, the configuration used above ($B = 22$ and $\nu_{min} = 0$) can remain unchanged. In comparison with the baseline results using the standard filter bank ($B = 25$, $\nu_{min} = 62.5$, $\nu_{max} = 6250$) a relative reduction of the WER of 9 % (BIRMINGHAM) and 12 % (YOUTH) is achieved with the new filter bank and 4-gram LM. Both improvements are significant; the p-value is smaller than 0.001 for BIRMINGHAM and 0.048 for YOUTH (with unigram LM on both corpora < 0.001).

A further improvement in the case that children data is available is obtained with the multi codebook approach described in Fig. 3.8, right. Using the optimal filter bank and 2 feature streams for static and dynamic features, the WER drops on YOUTH to 19.3%[7.16] (unigram LM) and 1.9 % WER (4-gram LM); for BIRMINGHAM the improved recognition rate with a unigram LM is 48.7%[7.17] WER. However no improvement is achieved for a 4-gram LM (24.8 % WER). In the following section, the case is considered, where not sufficient children data is available to train children acoustic models.

7.3.2   Vocal Tract Length Normalisation

To compensate for the mismatch between young speakers and adults, VTLN as described in Sect. 3.3.2 is applied. The scaling factor β is estimated age and/or gender dependent on the validation data set of the respective corpus. The optimal β is found by maximising the word recognition rate ($0.65 \leq \beta \leq 1.0$; steps of 0.025). After that, the test data is evaluated based on this optimum scaling factors (4-gram LM). The target was to obtain

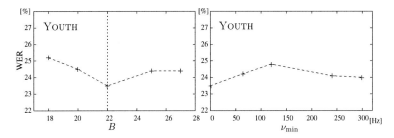

Figure 7.8: Optimisation of the Mel filter bank: number filters B (left) and $\nu_{\min}$ (right). WER on the validation data set of YOUTH.

$\nu_{\max}$	VTLN	all			male			female		
		WER	β_{linear}	β	WER	β_{linear}	β	WER	β_{linear}	β
6250	-	$41.3^{7.7}$			35.5			45.2		
6250	p.w.l.	21.0		0.75	21.9		0.825	20.8		0.75
7000	linear	31.0	0.89		28.1	0.89		32.9	0.89	
7000	linear + p.w.l.	$\mathbf{19.2}^{7.18}$	0.89	0.825	20.7	0.89	0.875	18.5	0.89	0.825

Table 7.5: Evaluation of the YOUTH test data (age 8 – 10) on VERBMOBIL acoustic models with and without VTLN: linear VTLN through filter bank extension and/or piece-wise linear (p.w.l.) VTLN through filter bank warping. WER in %.

a-priori knowledge of the expected distortion of the frequency scale given a certain speaker group.

Tab. 7.5 shows the results when testing the YOUTH corpus on VERBMOBIL acoustic models with and without VTLN. When using the same $\nu_{\max}$ as for VERBMOBIL, the optimum β for piecewise linear VTLN (Sect. 3.3.2) is 0.825 for males and 0.75 as well for females as for the gender independent optimisation. Optimum means minimum WER on the validation data. On the test data, the overall WER is reduced from $41.3\%^{7.7}$ to 21.0 %. Without VTLN it is harder to recognise with VERBMOBIL acoustic models females (45.2 % WER) than males (35.5 % WER). Therefore the β being chosen to get the best overall improvement is identical with the female β. After VTLN around 21 % WER are achieved for both genders.

In the next step, it is investigated, whether recognition can be improved by using a larger frequency range. Therefore $\nu_{\max} = 7000$ is chosen, which has been found to be optimal in Sect. 7.3.1. This expansion of the filter bank while keeping the number of filters constant implies a linear VTLN with $\beta_{\text{linear}} = 0.89$ and results in a WER of 31.0 %. After this extension of the frequency range, again a piecewise linear VTLN is conducted for an additional warping of the filter bank. Here, the optimum β is 0.875 for males and 0.825 else. Since these investigations are based on a filter bank extended to 7000 Hz (linear

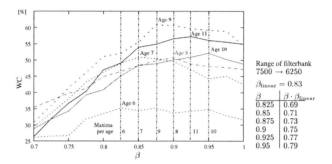

Figure 7.9: Age dependent optimisation of β on the validation data of BIRMINGHAM using VERBMOBIL acoustic models: increasing age results in increasing word correctness (WC in %). β for piece-wise linear VTLN ($\nu_{max} = 7500$) is shown age dependently. $\beta_{linear} = 0.83 =$ const. through filter bank extension.

gender	ν_{max}	VTLN	age: 6	7	8	9	10	11	all
both	6250	-	> 100	99.9	80.9	80.8	**74.6**	**74.6**	85.3[7.8]
male	6250	-	> 100	99.8	76.8	65.2	**58.0**	65.6	79.5
female	6250	-	> 100	> 100	**84.8**	**85.0**	89.9	**84.7**	90.5
both	7500	linear + p.w.l.	> 100	79.4	58.2	57.3	61.1	**56.2**	**67.6**[7.19]

Table 7.6: Age dependent evaluation of the BIRMINGHAM test data on VERBMOBIL acoustic models with and without linear/piece-wise linear (p.w.l.) VTLN. WER in %, β as shown in Fig. 7.9.

VTLN), β has to be multiplied with β_{linear} to get the overall scaling factor $\beta_{linear} \cdot \beta = 0.78$ for males and 0.74 for females; the error rate is reduced to 19.2%[7.18]. This is a significant improvement (p-value < 0.001) in comparison to the result without linear VTLN (21.0% WER, $\nu_{max} = 6250$ Hz)

On the BIRMINGHAM corpus β is calculated for each age group separately. Again the data is evaluated on VERBMOBIL acoustic models. The baseline results in Tab. 7.6 show very high WER that is even 100 % for young children. A comparison of Tab. 7.6 and Tab. 7.2 shows noticeably higher WER in particular for females in the case of mismatched training and test. WER decreases with increasing age. The decrease is more continuously as in Tab. 7.2 where an increase of WER for the 11-year-old children was observed.

The estimation of age dependent β on the validation data (validation-2 set, see Tab. 4.8) is shown in Fig. 7.9. It has been observed that the low WA of the young children (< 0 %) has been caused by a high number of insertions. The reason is that children read very slowly. Since it is not possible to get rid of the insertions by just using a smaller γ_{ip}, in the following experiments the insertions are simply not counted when optimising β: The word correctness (WC, cf. Eq. 3.26) is used instead. The optimia are shown in Fig. 7.9. For 6-year-old children WC is below 35 % and the maximum is reached for $\beta = 0.825$. For age 10 and 11 WC is much higher; the maximum is found for $\beta = 0.925$ and greater. The validation is based on a filter bank extended to 7500 Hz (linear VTLN) and therefore β has to be multiplied with $\beta_{\text{linear}} = 0.83$. This results in overall scaling factors between 0.69 and 0.79. The scaling factor increases with rising age. It is 0.75 for 8 year old children, which corresponds with YOUTH ($0.89 \times 0.825 = 0.73$ for 8–10-year-old children). On the test data the age dependent VTLN reduces WER from 85.3%[7.8] to 67.6%[7.19] (Tab. 7.6). The WER on 11-year-old children is only 56.2 %.

Using VTLN, the WER could be reduced by 54 % relatively on YOUTH, by 21 % on BIRMINGHAM, and by 29 % on the 9-year-old children from BIRMINGHAM. All three cases are highly significant (p-value < 0.001). In the next section, adaptation is used additionally.

7.3.3 Adaptation

VTLN is a feature transformation that makes the MFCC better fit to the codebook of the speech recogniser. This warping factor is estimated on the validation data (Sect. 7.3.2). In a next step optimisation is performed the other way round: now the densities of the codebook are re-estimated to better fit to the features. This transformation of the codebook parameters is estimated on the test data. Thereto, the recognised word sequence of a first recognition pass (with VTLN) is used for unsupervised adaptation. In the case of a reading exercise also supervised adaptation can be applied, since the spoken word sequence is very close to the known reference text. In the following the manual transliteration of the utterances is used in investigations with supervised adaptation.

Preliminary experiments have shown that adaptation after VTLN results in significantly lower WER than without VTLN. Using MAP (cf. Sect. 3.3.2), an individual shift of each mean vector of the codebook is calculated. MLLR is used to transform all mean vectors and covariance matrices of the codebook globally. In combination, first MLLR and after it MAP is carried out. Both transformations are estimated on the complete test data or on a subset, e.g. on an age group or on an individual speaker. Finally, an additional Baum-Welch (BW) re-training after the adaptation is investigated. It adapts the HMM parameters to the transformed codebook and/or the transformed feature vectors. In the case BW1 one BW iteration is conducted and for BW5 five iterations.

The investigations in the previous section have shown, that the combination of linear and piecewise linear VTLN results in lower WER than using piecewise linear VTLN alone. Further, preliminary experiments have shown that also adaptation after linear and piecewise linear VTLN is still better than adaptation after linear VTLN. Consequently in all experiments, that will be described in the following, the codebook is adapted to the feature vectors that are linearly *and* piecewise linearly warped.

The results of different combination of MLLR, MAP, BW1, and BW5 are summarised in Tab. 7.7 for the YOUTH database. All results are – as expected – clearly better when adapting with the transliterated utterances, than when adapting with the recognised, erroneous word sequence based on a recogniser with $19.2\%^{7.18}$ WER. Further, it can be seen that speaker adaptation is in most cases better than speaker independent adaptation. These are the results in detail: With the global transformation MLLR, the WER gets worse than the baseline. Little improvement can be obtained with MAP, but only in the speaker dependent case. The combination of MLLR and MAP is not superior to MAP alone[14]. With MAP and speaker dependent adaptation the WER is significantly reduced to 17.7 % (p-value < 0.001).

Baum-Welch re-training (BW5) is extremely important and improves recognition even in the speaker independent case: the WER drops to 13.9 % using solely BW5 and to 12.7 % in combination with MAP (significant improvement with MAP: p-value < 0.001). In the speaker dependent case, the best combination is MLLR, MAP, and BW5 when $12.5\%^{7.20}$ WER are achieved (significantly better than no adaptation or only BW5: p-value < 0.001; not significantly better than MAP + BW5). The less expensive investigations using BW1 yield worse results. However, in the best combination (MAP + BW1) 12.8 % WER are obtained with speaker dependent adaptation.

When the transliteration is given, the error rate even drops to $5.7\%^{7.21}$. This is achieved in the speaker dependent case using MAP and BW5 which is significantly better (p-value < 0.001) than the speaker dependent case (10.2 % WER). Results in combination with MLLR or BW1 are significantly worse (6.9 % WER, p-value < 0.001).

For the YOUTH data it can be concluded so far that BW is important, that the combination of MAP and BW performs best, and that MLLR is useful in exactly one case, only. However, what happens, if we have less data available, and not all the speaker's utterances have been seen in advance? Fig 7.10 shows for the speaker dependent, unsupervised adaptation, that the combination of MLLR, MAP, and BW5 is only optimum in the case when all data of a speaker is available. Assuming an average length of 2.05 sec. per utterance, 6.2 minutes of data is on average available per speaker when all test utterances are employed, and 0.5 minutes when only every 13th utterance is used. The approaches with BW5 require more than 1.6 minutes of data for adaptation (every 4th utterance) to achieve any improvement of the baseline result. With less data the risk of over-adaptation is too high. For the approaches based on BW1 there is no overadaptation and even every 10th utterance (0.6 min.) is enough. However, if less than 1.6 minutes of data are available, BW1 performs as good as without prior MAP adaptation.

With only 0.5 minutes of data (every 13th utterance) 18.9 % WER are achieved using BW1 re-training. The adaptation time[15] is on the average per speaker[16] in the best case with 6.2 min. adaptation data 141 sec. ($12.5\%^{7.20}$ WER, MLLR + MAP + BW5), in the best case with 3.1 min. adaptation data 64 sec. (13.4 % WER, MLLR + MAP + BW1), and if only 0.6 min. are used 0.8 sec. (17.6 % WER, only BW1).

---

[14]This approach has been used successfully in preliminary experiments based on worse baseline results.
[15]Adaptation time on a Intel Pentium with 3 GHz and 2 MB RAM
[16]only time for MLLR, MAP, and BW without vector quantisation

adaptation	manual translit	WER (speaker independent)	WER (speaker dependent)
no adaptation (VTLN only)	no	$19.2^{7.18}$	
MLLR	no	(28.2)	(26.5)
MAP	no	(20.2)	17.7
MLLR + MAP	no	(21.4)	18.4
BW5	no	**13.9**	14.2
MAP + BW5	no	**12.7**	**12.9**
MLLR + MAP + BW5	no	14.3	$\mathbf{12.5}^{7.20}$
BW1	no	15.1	14.3
MAP + BW1	no	15.2	**12.8**
MLLR + MAP + BW1	no	16.4	**13.1**
MLLR + MAP	yes	(21.0)	17.4
MAP + BW5	yes	**10.2**	$\mathbf{5.7}^{7.21}$
MLLR + MAP + BW5	yes	12.0	6.0
MAP + BW1	yes	12.6	**6.9**
MLLR + MAP + BW1	yes	13.7	7.4

Table 7.7: Evaluation of the YOUTH test data (age 8 – 10) on VERBMOBIL acoustic models after adaptation or speaker dependent adaptation and after linear/piece-wise linear VTLN as in Tab. 7.5. Supervised adaptation requires the transliteration of the utterances. Increased WER in shown in brackets. WER in %.

Results on the BIRMINGHAM data are shown in Tab. 7.8. Here, the adaptation was not performed speaker dependent but age dependent. Applying unsupervised MLLR, MAP and BW5 $54.1\%^{7.22}$ are achieved on average, and in the case without MLLR 55.4 % WER (significant difference with p-value 0.005). However the 8 year old children are better recognised without the global transformation MLLR and in all other cases results were improved using additional MLLR. Similar observations can be made for supervised adaptation: The best overall result is achieved with MLLR, MAP, and BW5 $(36.9\%^{7.23})$ but the age groups 6, 8, and 9 are better recognised without MLLR. Fig. 7.11 shows the first 7 densities of the codebook in the subspaces spanned by the energy and the 7th MFCC coefficient without adaptation (VERBMOBIL) and after adaptation to different age groups.

Summing up, with adaptation and BW re-training, the WER could be reduced by 35 % relatively for YOUTH and 20 % relatively for BIRMINGHAM in the unsupervised case (relative to the results based on VTLN: $19.2\%^{7.18}$ and $67.6\%^{7.19}$). In the supervised case the improvement is 70 % relatively for YOUTH and 45 % relatively for BIRMINGHAM. The improvement for the 9 year old BIRMINGHAM children is up to 48 %. All those improvements are highly significant with a p-value < 0.001.

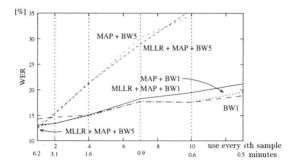

Figure 7.10: Speaker dependent, supervised evaluation of YOUTH on VERBMOBIL acoustic models after adaptation using a varying portion of adaptation data (varying average time of adaptation data per speaker). Configurations based on BW1 perform best for small amounts of data.

7.3.4   Further Improvements

In additional experiments it was investigated, whether WER for children can be reduced using more training data even if the training is from adults. For this purpose the adult speech was adopted to the children speech with the inverse VTLN. In the previous sections linear and piece-wise linear VTLN was applied to children data. The linear part was an extension of the filter bank from $\nu_{max} = 6250$ Hz to $\nu_{max} = 7000$ Hz for the children. Additionally the filter bank was piecewise linearly warped with age dependent β between 0.825 and 0.95 (mean: 0.888). In the following children models trained with BIRMINGHAM data using a filter bank with $\nu_{max} = 7000$ Hz are supplemented with adult speech from VERBMOBIL (native speakers only, small training-2 set from Tab. 4.10) using a filter bank with $\nu_{max} = 6250$ Hz and $\beta^{-1} = 1/0.888 = 0.13$.

As described on page 3.2.3, the training procedure consists of 10 iterations, where each of them consists of codebook re-estimation and several Baum-Welch iterations. The adult speech is not used for the codebook re-estimation and not in in the first and the last of the 10 training iterations[17]. With this approach the WER could be significantly reduced from 23.7%[7.15] to 23.2 % WER (p-value 0.011). The error rate can be reduced using more data, even if it is data from adults. A detailed analysis on inverse VTLN was conducted on German data and is described in [Rus04]. The resulting speech recogniser was employed in [Mai06b]. In [Ger06] a similar approach was investigated and referred to as data augmentation (cf. Tab 3.3).

The rate-of-speech has been observed to be much smaller for the younger children. In [Ste03b] PSOLA algorithm (Pitch-Synchronous Overlap and Add), that manipulates

---

[17]In the first training iteration, the number of polyphone models is defined: Acoustic models are built for each polyphone that occurs more than 50 times in the training data. To keep the number of polyphones constant, the VERBMOBIL data is not used in the first iteration

adaptation	translit	age: 6	7	8	9	10	11	all
no adaptation (VTLN only)	no	> 100	79.4	58.2	57.3	61.1	56.2	$67.6^{7.19}$
MAP	no	99.7	76.4	59.4	55.7	58.8	59.3	66.8
BW5	no	90.7	66.9	45.7	45.4	48.1	54.7	57.2
MAP + BW5	no	89.5	66.7	**44.2**	42.8	46.8	51.2	55.4
MAP + BW1	no	96.1	71.2	49.7	47.9	50.7	54.5	60.2
MLLR + MAP + BW5	no	**86.4**	**65.1**	45.7	**42.4**	**43.3**	**50.0**	$54.1^{7.22}$
MAP	yes	>100	75.8	58.9	54.2	58.1	58.8	66.2
BW5	yes	65.5	48.1	26.9	31.7	31.8	37.6	39.3
MAP + BW5	yes	**62.2**	47.2	**26.1**	**28.6**	31.5	34.6	37.4
MLLR + MAP + BW5	yes	63.2	**46.0**	28.0	29.6	**28.1**	**33.3**	$36.9^{7.23}$

Table 7.8: Evaluation of the BIRMINGHAM test data on VERBMOBIL acoustic models with age dependent adaptation after linear and piece-wise linear VTLN. Supervised adaptation requires the transliteration of the utterances. WER in %.

the speech signal and is widely used in speech synthesis, is employed to normalise the children speech. Similar results, however, can be obtained more easily by using a different frame shift time. For feature extraction, in all experiments a short-time analysis window of 16 msec was used; consecutive windows are shifted by 10 msec which are 160 frames for 16 kHz speech signals. A increased time shift of e.g. 250 samples ($\approx$ 16 msec) reduces the number of short time analysis windows per time and increases the rate-of-speech (speed-up of 160 %). This way, the results of Tab. 7.8 could be improved for the youngest children. In the unsupervised (MLLR + MAP + BW5)-case, the WER could be reduced to 80.0 for six-year-old children and 63.9 for seven-year-old children (significant for six-year-old children, only; p-value 0.001). For the older children WER was increased, strongest for the age 10 and 11. This larger frame shift was only applied during testing; during adaptation, this approach would reduce the adaptation data and possibly result in higher error rates.

7.3.5 Improved Recogniser for Non-Native English from Children

In the context of pronunciation scoring, a non-native speech recogniser has been developed (for adults) in the ISLE project [Bon00b]. In the present thesis, the hint will be followed that for non-native speech recognition the training of acoustic models should include a large set of native and non-native phonemes. The target of this section is the development of a speech recogniser for non-native children, that includes acoustic models for British, American, and German phonemes. A list of phonemes and sub-phonemic models for these languages can be found in Appendix B.2.

In Tab. 7.3, 43.5%[7.10] WER has been reported when evaluating the NONNATIVE data on BIRMINGHAM. In the first line of Tab. 7.9 the non-native children are evaluated on the improved recogniser from Tab. 7.4 using an extended filter bank with $\nu_{max} = 7500$ Hz. The WER on non-natives drops to 42.2 %. Given the case that only a small amount of BE

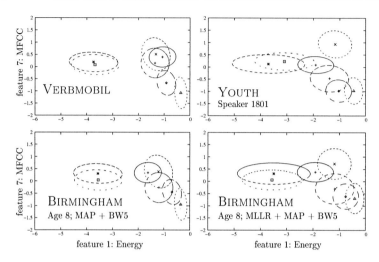

Figure 7.11: Transformation of the codebook (first 7 densities) when adapting VERBMOBIL models to YOUTH (speaker dependently) and BIRMINGHAM (age dependent for 8-year-old children, with and without MLLR).

data is available, the adult speech recogniser trained on VERBMOBIL can be adapted (here with the 10-year-old children from the BIRMINGHAM test set, cf. Tab. 7.8, last line). The WER for non-native children is 64.3 %; without adaptation it would be 72.6[7.9] (Tab. 7.3). A direct adaptation to the non-native data is not investigated, since acoustic models would be adapted to the wrong pronunciation. A further reduction of WER might be achieved in future research by applying additional ROS adaptation, cf. Sect. 7.3.4.

In the next step, the NONNATIVERC corpus is employed (cf. Chap. 4.1.3). Non-native children with good reading proficiency, which are in the same age as the children from the NONNATIVE corpus, are added to BIRMINGHAM training data. This way, the WER could be further reduced to 37.0 % WER for NONNATIVE, while the error rate for BIRMINGHAM increases only little.

YOUTH contains American English data, and is also added to the training of the speech recogniser, in order to train some additional American phonemes, and to investigate, whether training becomes more robust when using more data. Thereto, the small training set and validation set was employed (training-2 and validation-2 in Tab. 4.7). The additional phonemes are /E/ and /A/; /oU/ is mapped onto /@U/. All other phonemes are trained with American and British data. The intersection of the vocabulary from YOUTH and BIRMINGHAM contains many words with different phonetic transcription for American and British English (e.g. "answered" is pronounced /A:ns@d/ in BE vs. /{ns3rd/ in AE); this makes it necessary to mark all words from the YOUTH corpus with the suffix

training data	evaluation (WER in %)		
	NONNATIVE	BIRM.	YOUTH
BIRMINGHAM	42.2	$23.7^{7.15}$	–
VERBMOBIL $\nu_{max} = 6250$, supervised adaptation to BIRMINGHAM (age 10)	64.3	$36.9^{7.23}$	–
BIRMINGHAM, NONNATIVERC	37.0	23.9	–
BIRM., NONNATIVERC, YOUTH ($\nu_{max} = 7000$)	39.2	27.4	3.9
BIRM., NONNATIVERC, YOUTH ($\nu_{max} = 7500$)	37.4	27.9	3.7
BIRM., NONNATIVERC, YOUTH ($\nu_{max} = 8000$)	$\mathbf{35.9}^{7.24}$	$27.6^{7.25}$	$3.6^{7.26}$
BIRM., NONNATIVERC, YOUTH ($\nu_{max} = 8000$), VERBMOBIL ($\nu_{max} = 6250, \beta = 0.13$)	36.9	29.9	4.4
BIRM., NONNATIVERC, YOUTH ($\nu_{max} = 8000$), VMGERMAN ($\nu_{max} = 6250, \beta = 0.13$)	$38.9^{7.27}$	$30.2^{7.28}$	4.0

Table 7.9: Speech recognition for non-native speech: different training configurations for the acoustic models. Evaluation on different corpora with 4-gram LM. $\nu_{max} = 7500$ for the corpora BIRMINGHAM, NONNATIVERC, and NONNATIVE. The phonetic inventory of the different recognisers comprises British, American, and even German (last line) phonemes.

"$\sim$AM", e.g "answered$\sim$AM" (pronunciation alternatives, specified in the transcription). Furthermore, different ν_{max} are investigated for the YOUTH corpus. In a previous section, $\nu_{max} = 7000$ Hz was found to be optimal, however, in combination with BIRMINGHAM and NONNATIVERC $\nu_{max} = 8000$ turned out to perform best. The WER was reduced to 35.9%[7.24] on NONNATIVE data (significance level: p-value < 0.001 in comparison to $\nu_{max} = 7000$, p-value $= 0.029$ in comparison to the recogniser based only on BIRMINGHAM and NONNATIVERC), while it rises for BIRMINGHAM to 27.6%[7.25]. The error on YOUTH shows only a small absolute increase from 2.9%[7.13] WER to 3.6%[7.26] WER. This recogniser has reasonable word accuracy on non-native, British, and American children and will be employed in the next chapter for pronunciation scoring. The improved recognition of NONNATIVE data significantly reduces the WER in comparison to the baseline with 43.5%[7.10] by 17% relatively (p-value < 0.001).

In the final investigation, adult data from VERBMOBIL is added to the training to make it more robust. VMGERMAN is employed, to train additional German phones, like /R/, /C/, /x/. /6/, /a/, /a:/, /9/, /Y/, /y:/, /2:/, /o:/, and the German version of /u:/. For these experiments, the filter bank used for feature extraction from adult data is warped to better fit with children data as described in Sect. 7.3.4. Since no improvement could be achieved on any of the three test corpora when using the adult English data (VERBMOBIL, training-3 set), only adult German data is employed. This recogniser will be investigated in the next chapter, in order to recognise pronunciation errors, where the English phone is substituted by a German phone. However, the WER on NONNATIVE data rises to 38.9%[7.27] but is still significantly better than the baseline recogniser (p-value < 0.001). The word error rate on BIRMINGHAM rises to 30.2%[7.28] and on YOUTH to 4.0%.

corpus	γ_{lw}	γ_{ip}	perplexity	ν_{min}	ν_{max}	B	PER [%] native	PER [%] NONNATIVE
YOUTH	2	4	2.1	0	7000	22	$18.5^{7.29}$	$56.5^{7.31}$
BIRMINGHAM	2	12	4.1	0	7500	22	$47.6^{7.30}$	$61.7^{7.32}$

Table 7.10: Phoneme recognition: Optimal configuration of language weight γ_{lw} and insertion penalty γ_{ip}, perplexity of the LM on the test set, and phoneme error rate PER on the test set. Number of filters B and frequency range in Hz.

7.4 Phone Recognition

This final section on children speech recognition focuses on phoneme recognition. In word recognition experiments, the 4-gram WER was $2.9\%^{7.13}$ when training and testing on YOUTH and $23.7\%^{7.15}$ WER when training and testing on BIRMINGHAM (Tab. 7.4). Employing these acoustic models for non-native speech recognition, strongly increased WER was observed, but better results on BIRMINGHAM acoustic models (Tab. 7.3).

In the following the *phoneme error rate* (PER) will be measured on phoneme recognisers that are based on the same acoustic models as the recognisers mentioned above. Only the vocabulary has been exchanged: it now consists of 39 phonemes and diphthongs in the American case and 44 in the British English case. When testing the NONNATIVE corpus on American acoustic models, analogous to Sect. 7.2.5 some phonemes have to be changed as described in Tab. 4.9 in order to model British pronunciation with American phonemes.

Then a 4-gram *phoneme language model* is trained on the respective training data set (perplexity 2.1 for YOUTH and 4.1 on BIRMINGHAM). Before testing, γ_{lw} and γ_{ip} have been optimised as discussed in Sect. 7.2.2. The results are summarised in Tab. 7.10: $18.5\%^{7.29}$ PER are received for YOUTH and $47.6\%^{7.30}$ PER for BIRMINGHAM.

Now these phoneme recognisers are tested with the NONNATIVE data. As in Sect. 7.2.6, the LM is trained on the NONNATIVE reference texts and γ_{lw} is increased to 5. The PER is $56.5\%^{7.31}$ on YOUTH acoustic models and $61.7\%^{7.32}$ on BIRMINGHAM. Using the acoustic models trained on American, British, and non-native data from Tab. 7.9 (result $35.9\%^{7.24}$ WER) the PER reaches 100 %. The optimum phoneme recogniser is not based on the acoustic models from the optimum speech recogniser; the best result in phoneme recognition is achieved when clearly and homogeneously pronounced training data without reading errors is employed, like the YOUTH database. The percentage of errors is in all cases clearly greater than in word recognition, yet the number of tokens in the vocabulary is rather small in phoneme recognition. Relief can be produced with higher order phoneme language models; however, computation time would rise strongly due to the exponentially increased search space.

7.5 Discussion

This chapter has focused on the recognition of children speech, with the final goal to obtain a speech recogniser that even performs well on non-native children data. In the beginning of this chapter, it was found that the formants in three children databases – the British English corpus BIRMINGHAM, the American English corpus YOUTH, and the non-native speech corpus NONNATIVE– show higher frequencies for all vowels in comparison to adult speech (VERBMOBIL). For /u:/, however, both formants F_1 and F_2 have lower frequencies when it is pronounced by non-native children from Germany. The shift of the formant frequencies can also be shown by a novel approach that analyses the variances of the filter bank energies. This analysis of band energies shows higher inter- and intra-speaker variabilities for younger children, in particular in the region of formants. From this analysis, higher word error rates can be expected for children and the requirement of an expanded filterbank (VTLN) becomes obvious.

Three baseline systems are described for the three databases after an optimisation of the parameters language weight (γ_{lw}) and insertion probability (γ_{ip}). With 4-gram LM, on VERBMOBIL a WER of 34.6%[7.1] can be achieved, which is slightly improved in comparison to [Ste05b]. The phonetic transcription of all words in the vocabulary has been revised in order to make the lexicon compatible with the AE YOUTH database. The WER is high, since the LM has a high perplexity. The WER on BIRMINGHAM is 26.1%[7.6] and on YOUTH (in this corpus all speakers partly read the same texts; consequently the perplexity is rather low) 3.3%[7.4]. The highest WER is achieved for the youngest children. Using unigram LM, the error rates are 52.3%[7.2], 52.2%[7.5], and 23.8%[7.3]. The word error rates increase steeply, if YOUTH or BIRMINGHAM is tested on adult acoustic models (41.3%[7.7] and 85.3%[7.8] WER, 4-gram LM). Testing the NONNATIVE data on the three different recognisers, highest error rates are again achieved in the case, where the mismatch adult/children is present. Lowest error rates are obtained using BE acoustic models trained on BIRMINGHAM (43.5%[7.10] WER).

There were several approaches investigated to improve the recognition of children speech. If enough training data is available to train acoustic models from children data, it turned out to be useful to adapt the feature extraction to children data. For this purpose, the Mel filter bank was optimised. As a result, filter banks were obtained that use less Mel filters (22 instead of 25) since this causes broader filters which are more robust against higher spectral variabilities of the formants. Further, the filterbank is expanded, in order to cover frequencies up to 7500 Hz. For children speech in particular vowels have to be detected in higher frequency bands due to the higher formants. This implies the necessity to recognise e.g. also fricatives in higher frequency regions above the formants. With the improved filter bank, the WER drops significantly on BIRMINGHAM to 23.7%[7.15] (p-value < 0.001) and on YOUTH to 2.9%[7.13] (p-value = 0.048). On top of this, further improvements could be achieved by training two independent codebooks for two feature streams. This approach, however, was not followed up, since it enables further possibilities for codebook adaptation, that could not be investigated in this thesis due to time constraints and provides space for future research.

If little children data is available, it might be necessary to adapt an adult speech recogniser to children. The combination of several approaches led to a significant reduction of WER: In a first step linear VTLN was applied, where simply an expanded filter bank is used to match the children test data with the adult training data (warping with β_{linear}). Then, a piece-wise linear warping factor β was additionally applied to this filter bank. The optimum parameters were searched gender and age dependently on a small validation data set in order to gain a-priori knowledge for different speaker groups. β is smaller for females and for younger children which causes higher resolutions in the higher frequency range. Next, the parameters of the acoustic models trained on adults were adopted to children. The adaptation data was in different scenarios the whole test data, the data of the current speaker (or parts of it e.g. 30 sec. of speech), or the test data of an age group. In some cases the transcription of the test data had to be known, which can be assumed in most pronunciation scoring tasks; in other cases the erroneous hypothesis of a speech recogniser was used. Best results are achieved with MAP adaptation followed by five Baum-Welch re-training iterations; if only a small amount of adaptation data is available, a single Baum-Welch iteration shows better results. Only in few cases, a preceding MLLR is advantageous. In the best case, the WER on YOUTH was reduced by 86 % to 5.7%[7.21] and on BIRMINGHAM by 57 % to 36.9%[7.23] in comparison to the baseline without VTLN and adaptation (p-value < 0.001). It was further shown that inverse VTLN transformed adult data added to the recogniser training can significantly reduce word error rates, if the training is performed on children data. For young children, an enhancement of the ROS of the test data increases recognition rates significantly.

Finally, speech recognisers are trained from different data sets with the target to obtain acoustic models, which are robust as well on native as on non-native speech, and which contain a large set of phonemes. This enables a detection of phone confusions even with phonemes that occur only in the L1 language. The first recogniser is trained from YOUTH, BIRMINGHAM, and non-native children from NONNATIVERC. An evaluation with the NONNATIVE data shows a significant relative reduction of WER by 17 % to 35.9%[7.24] WER (p-value < 0.001). On this recogniser, the BIRMINGHAM children are recognised with 27.6%[7.25], and the YOUTH children with 3.6%[7.26] WER. If additionally German data is added to the training, 31 more phonemes and polyphones can be recognised. However, WER on the NONNATIVE corpus rises to 38.9%[7.27]. Adaptation is not employed for non-native children, since it would adapt the acoustic models to the wrong pronunciation. This might be useful to further improve word recognition but will at the same time eliminate possibilities to detect systematic pronunciation errors in the investigations in the following chapter.

Phoneme recognition is a much harder task. For non-native children, the phoneme error rate (PER) is 56.5%[7.31]. The use of erroneous phoneme recognition for pronunciation scoring is limited. In the following chapter, it is only used additionally to the word recogniser for some features calculated with the *pronfex* module. The most important results of the present chapter are summarised in Appendix E.

In this chapter, results on children recognition are obtained, which corroborate findings from the literature. By a systematic evaluation of VTLN and adaptation useful a priori knowledge was obtained for different age groups. In a new approach the Mel filter bank for the training stage was optimised. Similar to VTLN, error rates could be reduced by expanding the filter bank. However, 8 kHz data is sufficient to recognise children speech. This confirms results from the literature based on higher sampling rates [Li01].

Based on available training data and previous results the best speech recogniser for non-native speech has $35.9\%^{7.24}$ WER (NONNATIVE corpus). It was trained on BIRMINGHAM (optimised filterbank with 22 Mel filters covering 0 – 7.5 kHz), a small amount of YOUTH (covering 0 – 8 kHz), and good non-native readers (NONNATIVERC). $38.9\%^{7.27}$ WER are achieved, if additional German phonemes are added to the speech recognition system (trained with VMGERMAN).

Chapter 8

Automatic Assessment: Experiments

After theoretical basics and the explanation of newly developed scoring algorithms, like the *pronfex* module introduced in Chap. 5, the present chapter focuses on experimental investigations in automatic pronunciation scoring. Automatic pronunciation scoring requires a *ground truth* for training and evaluation, which can be obtained by combining annotations from several experts as discussed in Chap. 6. Basis of all algorithms being evaluated in the following is a robust speech recogniser for non-native speech from children, as developed in Chap. 7 (recognisers with $35.9\%^{7.24}$ and $38.9\%^{7.27}$ WER, cf. Tab. 7.9). The following experiments are divided in word-level, sentence-level, and higher level (text and speaker) assessment. Whereas word level benefits from a large amount of training samples, the higher levels with a rather small size of samples (e.g. 57 speakers) benefit from the fact that lower level classification result can be employed, which might be erroneous, but can be averaged to obtain a more robust hypothesis. In all experiments the German children learning English from the NONNATIVE database (Chap. 4) are investigated.

8.1 Experimental Setup

The NONNATIVE database consists of several subsets. MONT is only annotated by one rater, whereas OHMPLUS has been labelled by up to 14 experts. Thus, the ground truth for MONT is on all levels rater *S*. For OHMPLUS, a more robust reference as discussed in Chap. 6 can be used. This means for word level pronunciation scoring that a word is only considered to be mispronounced, if at least 5 experts agree. An alternative reference needs the agreement of at least 3 out of 8 *experienced teachers*. On the sentence level the OHMPLUS reference is *S*, on the text level it is the average mark of 13 teachers. OHM is a subset of OHMPLUS and contains only students in the first year of English.

In all experiments speech recognisers are employed, which are first and foremost trained on native speakers[1]. None of the speakers from the NONNATIVE corpus has been seen during training; consequently all data can be used for evaluation. Thus, the investigations

---

[1]In some cases additionally little data from VMGERMAN and NONNATIVERC

based on mispronunciation models can be conducted without any additional recogniser training.

However, the experiments on pronunciation features and prosodic features require the training of statistical classifiers. In most experiments, the LDA-classifier as described in Sect. 3.1.2 is employed and only in some cases additionally Gaussian classifiers and neural networks (ANNs require much longer computation time for training). On top of this, feature selection and boosting will be focused on in this chapter (cf. AdaBoost in Sect. 3.1.4)

Parts of the NONNATIVE data are used for training, parts for testing. Training and test are always speaker disjoint. Two possible re-sampling techniques are employed to enable each of the speakers being evaluated once: In 2-fold cross-validation experiments MONT is used for training and OHMPLUS (or OHM) for testing and vice versa. The final result is the average from both evaluations. Additional evaluation is performed using solely the OHM corpus, data with ratings from many experts and children having all the same age 10 – 11. Here, leave-one-speaker-out (*loo*) evaluation as described on page 44 is employed. In each iteration one of 28 speakers is used for testing and the remaining data for training. For *loo*-evaluation, hypotheses of the classifier are accumulated and evaluated in total after all iterations. This way, each speaker is implicitly weighted by the amount of words or sentences he had to read. The results on OHM are in this case directly comparable with evaluation described above, where MONT is used for training and OHM for testing.

All classification results are evaluated in terms of CL as defined in Eq. 3.19 and Eq. 3.21. To further make clear that a K-class problem is involved, CL is often renamed to CL-K, e.g. CL-2 if wrong and correct pronunciation $\mathcal{X}$ and $\mathcal{O}$ are discriminated, or CL-5 if 5 school grades are evaluated. For significance testing, a version of the t-test is employed. A confidence interval for the correlation is received from 1000 correlation values obtained through bootstrap re-sampling (selection with replacement [Bra81]).

8.2 Word-Level Assessment

8.2.1 Word Models

The first approach for word-level pronunciation scoring is text and language dependent, but a valid and easily applicable approach, if a list of expected mispronunciations with respect to content and target group is available. In the following 44 mispronunciation rules (a subset of $e_1 - e_{50}$) are automatically applied as described in Chap. 5.2. An overview of those rules is given in Tab. 2.3 and 5.1. Preliminary experiments on manually designed mispronunciation models have been reported in [Hac07b, Hes06, Hes05]. To enable acoustic modelling of various mispronunciations, the speech recogniser from Tab. 7.9, last line, is employed, where $38.9\%^{7.27}$ WER could be achieved on the NONNATIVE database. The recogniser is trained on British, American, and German speech. This makes rules like

$$e_7: /\textrm{r}/ \rightarrow [\textrm{R}]$$

possible to be applied although the German alveolar /R/ is not contained in the phonetic inventory of English but only the English retroflex variant /r/. When applying systematically all rules, the vocabulary of the speech recogniser grows from 934 to 2698 words and at the same time the WER increases. In the following two approaches will be investigated, to keep the WER on low level:

1. The vocabulary is reduced to the vocabulary of the current sentence, but supplemented with all mispronunciation models, that arise by applying the rules e_i to the sentence vocabulary. The language model is trained on the complete NONNATIVE corpus. One disadvantage of this approach is, that the system would have to know, which sentence is spoken, and cannot deal with any permutation of a list of sentences through the learner.

2. In the second approach, the vocabulary is restricted to the current text, while again a global language model is used. Additionally mispronunciation models for the text based vocabulary are added.

With the first approach the WER (after applying the inverse rule e_i^{-1} to re-map mispronunciation words onto the original word) is 9 % and below in various experiments, in the second approach it rises to around 30 %. The goal, however, is the detection of wrongly pronounced words and not a precise word recognition; mispronounced words should if possible not be recognised. In the following, it will be shown that a low WER is essential to achieve a high correct acceptance rate $\text{REC}_\mathcal{O}$. However, the best result in terms of CL-2 will be obtained with the second approach based on a text dependent vocabulary. First of all, a weighting factor will be introduced.

Weighting Factor. To adjust the balance between the hit-rate for mispronounced words and the false alarm rate (terminology is illustrated in Tab. 3.1) a factor γ_{mispron} is introduced: The n-gram probabilities $P(C_i|C_{i-n+1} \ldots C_{i-1})$ for observed word categories C_i (cf. Eq. 3.34) are estimated from the complete set of reference texts and kept constant in all experiments. However, the set of probabilities $P(w_i|C_i)$ of a word w_i given its category C_i has to be extended to the newly added words which model mispronunciations, as described in Sect. 5.2. Given a set of $0 \leq k \leq N$ words w_i^k describing the word category C_i, with w_i^0 being the correct pronunciation and w_i^k $k \neq 0$ possible mispronunciations, then $P(w_i^0|C_i)$ is estimated from the reference texts, and for all other elements the probability[2] is uniformly set to

$$P(w_i^k|C_i) = \gamma_{\text{mispron}} \cdot P(w_i^0|C_i), \quad 0 < k \leq N \tag{8.1}$$

because the mispronunciation models have not been annotated in the NONNATIVE data and thus their a-priori probabilities cannot be estimated. A smaller γ_{mispron} results in less mispronunciation models occurring in the most likely word sequence, a lower hit-rate $\text{REC}_\mathcal{X}$ and a higher correct acceptance $\text{REC}_\mathcal{O}$. The percentage of mispronunciation models is in both approaches described above around 4 % for $\gamma_{\text{mispron}} = 0.1$ and 18 % for $\gamma_{\text{mispron}} = 1.0$.

---

[2]We again obtain probabilities when normalising for $\sum_k P(w_i^k|C_i) = 1$.

	reduced sentence vocab.			reduced text vocab.		
γ_{mispron}	CL-2	REC_{χ}	$\text{REC}_{\mathcal{O}}$	CL-2	REC_{χ}	$\text{REC}_{\mathcal{O}}$
1.0	58.4	39.6	77.2	63.7	60.0	67.3
0.5	58.9%[8.2]	32.7	85.1	**64.8**[8.3]	55.6	74.0
0.1	56.2	20.3	92.2	63.5	48.5	78.5

Table 8.1: Classification rate using mispronunciation models. Basis are speech recognisers with reduced sentence and text based vocabulary.

Classification Results. The class-wise averaged classification rate CL-2 is between 56.2 % and 58.9%[8.2] in the sentence based approach for $\gamma_{\text{mispron}} \in [0.1; 1.0]$ and between 63.5 % and 64.8%[8.3] CL-2 in the text based approach (cf. Tab. 8.1). In both cases it is maximum for $\gamma_{\text{mispron}} = 0.5$. A mispronounced word counts as detected, if it is substituted by a mispronunciation model, substituted by another word, or deleted by the recogniser. The reference for the evaluation is rater S for the MONT set of the NONNATIVE corpus; for the OHMPLUS set of the corpus at least 5 of the 14 teachers have to agree (cf. Tab. 6.1). In the optimum case with 64.8%[8.3] CL-2, the word error rate (after remapping of mispronunciation models onto the correct pronunciation) is 28.9%[8.1] WER.

In the sentence based approach recalls $\text{REC}_{\mathcal{O}} = 92.2 \%$ and $\text{REC}_{\chi} = 20.3 \%$ is received for $\gamma_{\text{mispron}} = 0.1$, which means that less than 8 % of the larger part of correctly pronounced words are mistakenly marked as wrongly pronounced, whereas 1 of 5 words which are indeed mispronounced have been found by the system. The low $\text{REC}_{\chi} = 20.3 \%$ is a reasonable amount, since also teachers do not reject all mispronunciations. Important is a high $\text{REC}_{\mathcal{O}}$ to avoid rejecting correctly pronounced words. The respective numbers are $\text{REC}_{\mathcal{O}} = 77.2 \%$ and $\text{REC}_{\chi} = 39.6 \%$ for $\gamma_{\text{mispron}} = 1.0$.

In the text based classification, $\text{REC}_{\mathcal{O}}$ never extends 78.5 %, because the WER of the speech recogniser is higher. These results show that classification rates for mispronounced words using speech recognition and mispronunciation models are insufficient, in particular the specifity, if the recogniser's vocabulary is not restricted to such a small context like a sentence. This is due to the fact that the performance of speech recognition for non-native speech from children is too low. Therefore, this approach has to be combined with other methods.

Evaluation of Rules e_i. Unfortunately, the NONNATIVE database has not been annotated on the phone level, which would make a more precise evaluation possible: In how many cases has the correct mispronunciation rule e_i been applied? In the case $\gamma_{\text{mispron}} = 0.1$ with 20.3 % REC_{χ}, only 62 out of 326 correctly detected mispronunciations are recognised due to a mispronunciation rule (the others are substitutions with other words or deletions). For those 62 words, it has been auditorily verified by the author whether the correct rule has been applied. Only in 8 cases the selected rule was wrong. In 74 % the rule identifies the mispronounced phoneme and gives helpful suggestions for an improvement. In 87% at least the right phoneme was identified; there are cases where phonemes are inserted which none of the 50 error rules is able to model, but the localisation alone is a helpful hint. The most frequent correct detected mispronunciations are based on e_{45} (/aI/ → [I]), e_{49} (/u:/ → [u:]$_{\text{german}}$), e_{12} ("sch" → [S]), e_{27} (/@U/ → [o:]), and e_{15} (/Z/ → /S/) in "garage".

8.2.2   Pronunciation Features

The set of 75 word level features for pronunciation scoring has been introduced in Chap. 5.3. The current state of the *pronfex* module is illustrated in Fig. 5.2. Preliminary results on pronunciation scoring with pronunciation features as well as on feature subsets have been reported in [Cin09, Hac07a, Hac05b, Cin04b, Cin04a]. To compute pronunciation features, the following statistics have to be estimated in advance:

- Acoustic models and language model: Here, the speech recogniser from Tab. 7.9, line seven, is employed, where 35.9%[7.24] WER are achieved on the NONNATIVE database. It is able to recognise the full NONNATIVE vocabulary of 934 words. Alternatively, the recogniser from Tab. 7.9, last line is used with reduced text dependent vocabulary as described in Sect. 8.2.1. Here, 28.9%[8.1] WER are achieved. This recogniser additionally integrates mispronunciation word models, so that also the feature *PronAcc-4* (cf. Sect. 5.3.1) can be calculated (75 pronunciation features in total).

- A phoneme recogniser as described in Tab. 7.10 is employed. It is trained on BIRM-INGHAM and has a phone error rate of 61.7%[7.32] PER. The better phoneme recogniser trained on YOUTH (56.5%[7.31] PER) is not used since this would need comparisons of AE phonemes with BE phonemes (word recognition and forced alignment)[3].

- Phoneme bigram models: They are trained on the reference texts from the BIRM-INGHAM and the NONNATIVE database.

- 22 TRAP-classifiers: each is based on TRAPs calculated from the 816 msec time trajectory of a single frequency band by employing a Mel filter bank with 22 filters between 0 and 7500 Hz. The TRAP-classifiers are pure *frame classifiers*; neither of them is taking into account any classification results from neighbouring frames. Using short-time analysis with 10 msec time shift, 81 log-energy values are obtained per TRAP. They are reduced to 23 values through smoothing and sampling, where the distance between the samples and the degree of smoothing is higher at the boundaries of the TRAP, while all information in the centre is kept. The resulting 23-dimensional vectors are input to the frame classifier which discriminates 27 phonemes. Here, the respective voiced and unvoiced versions of fricatives are merged into one class as well as (/d/,/t/), (/b/,/p/), and (/g/,/k/). The classifiers are trained on BIRMINGHAM. A frame based reference is obtained by forced alignment. However, only those frames

---

[3]It will anyway turn out that features based on a phoneme recogniser are outperformed by most other features.

set 1 vs. set 2	reference	d	set 1	set 2	μ
			CL-2 in %		
speech recogniser with full vocabulary (934 words occurring in NONNATIVE*)*					
MONT vs. OHM	S vs. "5 of 14"	74	57.0	64.0	60.5
MONT vs. OHMPLUS	S vs. "5 of 14"	74	58.3	65.0	61.7
reduced text dep. vocabulary and mispronunciation models					
MONT vs. OHM	S vs. "5 of 14"	75	62.9	63.9	63.4
MONT vs. OHMPLUS	S vs. "5 of 14"	75	65.5	66.7	**66.1**
MONT vs. OHM	S vs. S	75	67.1	69.4	68.3
MONT vs. OHMPLUS	S vs. S	75	68.5	70.8	**69.7**[8.4]

Table 8.2: Cross-validation for the classification of $\mathcal{X}$ vs. $\mathcal{O}$ using pronunciation features. μ is the mean of both iterations, d is the dimension of the feature vectors. "5 of 14" means that 5 out of 14 experts had to agree to mark a word with $\mathcal{X}$ (cf. Tab. 6.1).

are used for training, where two time alignments from different BIRMINGHAM speech recognisers agree[4].

- Duration statistics: These statistics are calculated from the BIRMINGHAM data, after forced alignment.

- Phoneme confusion statistics: While M_B after Eq. 5.9 can be easily calculated from BIRMINGHAM assuming all words to be correctly pronounced, the matrices $M_{\mathcal{O}}$ and $M_{\mathcal{X}}$ have to be calculated from parts of the NONNATIVE data that are used for training. This means for 2-fold cross-validation as described in Sect. 8.1 that two different pairs of matrices are required. In the leave-one-speaker-out (*loo*) case, even 28 different pairs of matrices have to be calculated, each excluding exactly one speaker. In each training iteration, new pronunciation features have to be extracted as well for the training as for the test set using phoneme confusion statistics that have never seen the respective test data.

In the following, experiments on feature extraction are compared, which are based on two different speech recognisers as described above. As for the classifier training, the weighting of both classes $\mathcal{O}$ and $\mathcal{X}$ is determined on a validation set (randomly chosen, 10 % of the respective training set) as described on page 47 to obtain CL $\approx$ RR. The reference for the MONT set is rater S. For OHMPLUS different references are being evaluated: a word can be marked with $\mathcal{X}$ if it is marked by at least 5 out of 14 experts, or by 3 out of 8 experienced teachers (cases "5 of 14" and "3 of 8" in Tab. 6.1). In some investigations S is also the reference for OHMPLUS.

---

[4]Speech recognisers are trained on BIRMINGHAM, but based on different feature extraction with different ν_{max}, cf. Fig. 7.7.

speech recogniser	reference	d	CL-2	RR	$REC_{\mathcal{X}}$	$REC_{\mathcal{O}}$
reduced text dep. vocabulary	"5 of 14"	75	67.8	70.0	65.3	70.2
		69 (PCA)	68.4	69.6	67.2	69.7
full vocabulary (934 words)	"5 of 14"	74	68.1	71.1	64.8	71.4
		69 (PCA)	**70.1**$^{8.5}$	**73.5**	66.4	73.8
full vocabulary (934 words)	"3 of 8"	74	69.7	70.5	68.8	71.4
		69 (PCA)	**71.3**$^{8.6}$	72.9	69.5	73.1

Table 8.3: *loo*-evaluation of the OHM data. Classification of $\mathcal{X}$ vs. $\mathcal{O}$ using pronunciation features. d is the dimension of the feature vectors. "5 of 14" means that 5 out of 14 experts had to agree to mark a word with $\mathcal{X}$ and "3 of 8" means that 3 out of the 8 experienced teachers had to agree (cf. Tab. 6.1).

Cross-Validation. Tab. 8.2 shows the results in the cross-validation task. With the text based speech recogniser 66.1 % CL-2 are obtained, with the global recogniser only 61.7 % CL-2. This table shows further that the additional children in OHMPLUS which are not included in OHM and which are from a different age group are useful as additional training data when evaluating MONT. They also increase the classification rate on OHM, which means that they can be more precisely classified than the younger children from the OHM subset. Last but not least, it seems to be better to train with MONT that has been annotated by rater S and to evaluate data annotated with the average teacher ratings "5 of 14", than vice versa. Further, MONT benefits from the lower WER of a recogniser with reduced vocabulary. In a next step also for OHM and OHMPLUS the ratings of S are used to get rid of this mismatch between training and test. Now, CL-2 rises to 69.7%$^{8.4}$. On the OHM set a optimum result of 69.4 % CL (OHMPLUS 70.8 % CL) is reached. However, these numbers only show the agreement with S and are potentially falsified through errors of the human rater. Using the more reliable average rating from 14 experts maximum 64.0 % CL-2 (OHMPLUS 66.7) are obtained in the best case. Next, *loo* evaluation will be conducted on OHM only, to have reliable annotations that are consistent in training and test.

Loo-Evaluation. In comparison to the cross-validation, the classification rate rises when using *loo*-evaluation on OHM to 67.8 % and 68.1 % CL-2 respectively depending on whether the text dependent or the global speech recogniser is used (Tab. 8.3, cases without PCA). This shows that the classification rate rises for matched training and test (only OHM data). Next it was investigated, to which extend the classification is improved, when the highly redundant feature set is reduced to less principal components by means of PCA (cf. page 42). In each *loo* iteration the transformation matrix is estimated on the training data. The optimum CL-2 is obtained in $d = 69$-dimensional feature space[5]. With the

---

[5]The optimum number of principal components is determined on the test set to show the maximum possible classification result.

speech recog. with 934 words		reduced text dep. vocabulary	
best per feature group	CL-2	best per feature group	CL-2
PronRos-1	**60.3**	*PronRos-1*	59.5
PronPauses-2	51.1	*PronPauses-1*	51.7
PronDurLUT-2	**60.9**	*PronDurLUT-2*	**60.3**
PronDurScore-1	59.3	*PronDurScore-1*	58.2
PronLikeli-3	**62.2**	*PronLikeli-3*	**61.4**
PronLikeliRatio-1	57.1	*PronLikeliRatio-1*	58.5
PronTrap-6	55.6	*PronTrap-4*	54.3
PronAcc-1	58.7	*PronAcc-3*	**60.7**
PronPhoneSeq-3	**61.6**	*PronPhoneSeq-3*	**60.7**
PronConfidence-5	59.1	*PronConfidence-5*	58.9
PronPhoneConf-2	**65.5**	*PronPhoneConf-2*	**62.0**
Context = Δ PronPhoneConf-1	59.4	*Context = Δ PronPhoneConf-1*	58.9

Table 8.4: Best pronunciation features based on *loo*-evaluation of the OHM data and classification of $\mathcal{X}$ vs. $\mathcal{O}$. The table shows the best feature per feature group for the speech recogniser with 934 words and the speech recogniser with reduced text dependent vocabulary plus mispronunciation models. Basis is the reference "5 of 14" (cf. Tab. 6.1).

global speech recogniser it rises to 70.1%[8.5], where the hitrate is 66.4 % and the correct acceptance rate 73.8 %; the overall recognition rate is 73.5 %. The classification rate is significantly increased in comparison to the cases without PCA (p-value 0.005) and the case from Tab. 8.2 (64.0 % CL-2) which uses MONT for training (p-value 0.001). If the reference "3 of 8" is used instead of "5 of 14" (3 out of 8 experienced teachers have to vote with $\mathcal{X}$ to cause a label "wrongly pronounced"), CL-2 rises further to 71.3%[8.6]: Using more consistent raters increases classification rates.

By employing additional training data from OHMPLUS or MONT in all *loo*-iterations or additional native data (BIRMINGHAM) the classification result could not be improved but is in all cases greater than 67 %. This means that the approach based on pronunciation features also works well, when different speaker groups are used for training and test (cf. Tab. 8.2), but best results are obtained in the matched condition (cf. Tab. 8.3).

Best Features. Next, 75 classifiers are trained, each based on only one pronunciation feature. Tab. 8.4, left, shows the single best features for each of the 12 feature groups described in Sect. 5.3.1. In experiments based on the speech recogniser with the global vocabulary of 934 words the following features performed best per feature group: ROS × word-duration, length of pauses after the word, observed word-duration, sum of phoneme duration scores, log-likelihood normalised with ROS, likelihood ratio after Eq. 5.13, duration normalised TRAP-score from higher frequency bands, phoneme accuracy, phoneme sequence bigram probability (based on the speech recogniser, not the phoneme recogniser)

reference	d	CL-2	RR	$REC_{\mathcal{X}}$	$REC_{\mathcal{O}}$
"5 of 14"	124	62.6	65.8	59.1	66.1
"3 of 8"	124	**63.1**$^{8.7}$	63.4	62.7	63.4

Table 8.5: *loo*-evaluation of the OHM data. Classification of $\mathcal{X}$ vs. $\mathcal{O}$ using prosodic features. d is the dimension of the feature vectors. "5 of 14" means that 5 out of 14 experts had to agree to mark a word with $\mathcal{X}$ and "3 of 8" means that 3 out of the 8 experienced teachers had to agree (cf. Tab. 6.1).

normalised with ROS, confidence of the reference word, and minimum frame based phone confusion. The optimum context feature is based on phone confusions. This selection of features differs only marginally, when the text based speech recogniser is used (Tab. 8.4, right).

The best result of 65.5 % CL-2 is obtained alone with the phone confusion feature using the global speech recogniser. With the text based speech recogniser 62.0 % CL-2 are obtained. This speech recogniser with lower word error rates achieves yet higher CL-2 with the *PronAcc* features. Lowest results are in both cases obtained with *PronPauses*[6]; it is only significantly better than chance for a p-value ≥ 0.1. If the phone confusion statistics would have been estimated on all NONNATIVE data including the test speaker, CL-2 would rise for the *PronPhoneConf* features up to 68 %. This shows that future experiments on speaker adaptation can further improve the detection of wrongly pronounced words.

8.2.3 Prosodic Features

The computation of prosodic features only requires duration and energy statistics, which are estimated on BIRMINGHAM after forced alignment. The native acoustic models are further used for forced alignment of the NONNATIVE data and are described in Tab. 7.9, line 7: the WER on NONNATIVE is 35.9%[7.24]. Preliminary results on prosodic features for pronunciation scoring have been reported in [Hac07a].

A comparison of Tab. 8.5 and Tab. 8.3 shows worse results when using prosodic features: 62.6 % CL-2 given the reference "5 of 14" and 63.1%[8.7] for the reference "3 of 8". However, in the next section it will be seen that prosody is a useful extension to the pronunciation features. The best features for each of the 9 feature groups described in Sect. 5.4 are summarised in Tab. 8.6. Here, classification is performed with 1-dimensional feature vectors. Optimum results are received with the mean energy of the two succeeding words, the first FFT-coefficient of the energy of the current word, and the onset position of the F_0. Worst results are achieved with jitter and shimmer features. However, the classification rate is for these features still significantly better than chance (p-value = 0.001).

---

[6]Pauses will turn out to be important for sentence level classification.

feature group	best feature [context]	CL-2
Energy	*ProsEneMean* [1,2]	**60.4**
Fourier analysis	*ProsFFT0* [0,0]	**59.4**
Pitch	*ProsF0Min* [1,1]	55.5
Voiced/unvoiced	*ProsVuvDur+Global*	57.5
Duration	*ProsDurNorm* [-1,-1]	55.3
Position of extrema	*ProsPosF0On* [0,0]	**59.2**
Length of pauses	*ProsPauseBefore* [0,0]	55.5
Jitter	*ProsJitMean* [1,1]	53.8
Shimmer	*ProsShimMeanGlobal*	53.3

Table 8.6: Best prosodic features based on *loo*-evaluation of the OHM data and classification of $\mathcal{X}$ vs. $\mathcal{O}$. The table shows the best feature per feature group for the speech recogniser with 934 words. Basis is the reference "5 of 14" (cf. Tab. 6.1).

8.2.4   Feature Selection

In this section pronunciation and prosodic features are combined. By simply concatenating pronunciation and prosodic feature vectors the classification rate unfortunately cannot be increased. The reasons could be the "curse of dimensionality" (too many parameters to train, not enough training data) or the failure of a linear classifier like LDA to utilise the additional information. Therefore it seems reasonable to reduce the large number of feature components to eliminate redundant information. These investigations are in particular welcome, when only parts of the $74 + 124 = 198$ features are re-implemented e.g. for a commercial pronunciation scoring application where computational constraints may be present. Employing the AdaBoost algorithm (cf. Sect. 3.1.4) an optimal subset of these 198 features will be searched. The elements of the resulting feature set are expected to be uncorrelated, each containing supplementary information.

In the following experiments the calculation of pronunciation features is based on the global speech recogniser with a vocabulary of 934 words. In Sect. 8.2.6 the results will be combined with the results based on mispronunciation models from Sect. 8.2.1. This way the text based speech recogniser is additionally employed.

AdaBoost.   Feature selection with AdaBoost is conducted in *loo* mode employing the OHM data as described in [Hac07a]. In each iteration the feature selection is performed on the respective training data set. CL of all *loo* iterations is shown in Fig. 8.1 for different numbers of features. The optimum CL is reached between 40 and 50 features and results in up to 69.7%[8.8] CL. This is the same result which also could have been achieved with 74 pronunciation features using the LDA-classifier in Tab. 8.3 (result without PCA). Best results are obtained in experiments based on a reference where 3 out of 8 experienced teachers had to agree. These results are superior to the results based on the reference "5 of 14". Furthermore, the figure shows that recognition can be improved by using much more features than commonly used in the literature. Even with large feature numbers no over-

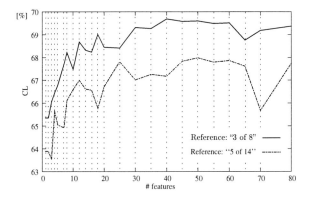

Figure 8.1: Classification rates on the test data dependent on the number of features selected with AdaBoost (*loo*-evaluation on the OHM data).

fitting to the training data is observed (on which the classification rate rises continuously). Also the increase from 20 to 40 features results in a significant rise of the classification rate on the test data (p-value 0.05).

Next, it will be evaluated, which of the 198 features perform best on average over all *loo* iterations. The results of all AdaBoost iterations have to be merged. Thereto, the weights ω^τ from Eq. 3.23 are employed which are determined as follows: Each features c_j has in *loo*-iteration i a weight $\omega_i^{\tau(c_j,i)}$ where $\tau(c_j,i)$ is the rank obtained from the AdaBoost algorithm (c_j is the τ-th feature selected with AdaBoost in *loo*-iteration i). Now, the mean weight

$$\bar{\omega}(c_j) = \sum_{i=1}^{n_{\text{loo}}} \omega_i^{\tau(c_j,i)}, \qquad \tau(c_j,i) \in \mathbb{N} := \text{rank of } c_j \text{ in iteration } i \qquad (8.2)$$

is calculated from all $n_{\text{loo}} = 28$ *loo*-iterations for each feature c_j. The algorithm to merge the selected feature lists (based on weights $\omega_i^{\tau(c_j,i)}$) from all *loo*-iterations is to re-sort the features based on their weights $\bar{\omega}$. Tab. 8.7 shows the top 20 given this new ranking and given the annotations "5 of 14". Results for the reference "3 of 8" are shown in Tab. 8.8.

Best Features. The top 20 best features shown in Tab. 8.7 combine uncorrelated information, including prosody and information from a speech recogniser. The most important features consider phone confusion probabilities that differ in automatic speech recognition for correct and wrong pronunciation (*PronPhoneConf-1*, Δ *PronPhoneConf-1*, and *PronPhoneConf-3*). Log-likelihood scores (minimum and maximum phoneme likelihood: *PronLikeli-5*, *PronLikeli-6*) are obtained by forced alignment whereas confidence measures (*PronConfidence-5*) are received from the speech recogniser. Additional duration is taken into account in 4 features: The ratio of expected duration and observed duration (*PronDurLUT-3*), the normalised duration (*ProsDurNorm*), the observed duration

#	$\bar{\omega}$	group	context	selected feature
1	0.75	*PronPhoneConf-1*	[0,0]	mean phoneme confusion after Eq. 5.14
2	0.32	*PronLikeli-5*	[0,0]	min. phoneme log-likelihood
3	0.30	*PronContext*	[-1,0]	context of *PronPhoneConf-1*
4	0.29	*PronConfidence-5*	[0,0]	confidence of reference
5	0.29	*PronDurLUT-3*	[0,0]	expected duration/observed duration
6	0.27	*ProsEneMean*	[1,2]	mean of energy
7	0.23	*ProsFFT-1*	[0,0]	2nd FFT coefficient
8	0.21	*ProsDurNorm*	[-1,-1]	normalised duration
9	0.20	*ProsFFT-0*	[0,0]	1st FFT coefficient
10	0.20	*ProsPosEneMaxRel*	[1,1]	relative position of max. energy
11	0.18	*PronLikeli-6*	[0,0]	max. phoneme log-likelihood
12	0.18	*PronTrap-1*	[0,0]	mean of band dependent likelihood ratios
13	0.18	*PronDurLUT-1*	[0,0]	observed duration
14	0.15	*ProsPauseAfter*	[1,1]	length of pauses after word
15	0.14	*PronPhoneSeq-1*	[0,0]	prior prob. of phoneme seq. (word recog.)
16	0.13	*ProsF_0RegCoeff*	[-1,0]	regression coefficient of pitch
17	0.12	*ProsF_0Mean*	[1,1]	mean pitch
18	0.12	*ProsPosEneMax*	[-1,-1]	position of max. energy
19	0.12	*PronPhoneConf-3*	[0,0]	maximum phoneme confusion
20	0.12	*PronDurLUT-4*	[0,0]	σ of phoneme dur. deviation

Table 8.7: Top 20 features selected with AdaBoost and ranked with their mean ω-values after Eq. 8.2. Basis is the reference "5 of 14" (cf. Tab. 6.1).

(*PronDurLUT-1*), and an analysis of phoneme duration deviations (*PronDurLUT-4*). A further duration analysis is given by the position of the maximum energy in the preceding word and the relative position in the succeeding word (*ProsPosEneMax, ProsPosEneMaxRel*). The energy of the word itself is analysed with the lowest Fourier-coefficients (*ProsFFT-0* and *ProsFFT-1*) and the mean energy of the succeeding words (*ProsEneMean*). Further important supplementary information is obtained with a TRAP-feature (*PronTrap-1*), the length of pauses after the succeeding word (*ProsPauseAfter*), and the priori probability of the observed phone sequence estimated with bigram statistics (*PronPhoneSeq-1*). The F_0 regression (left context, *ProsF_0RegCoeff*) and its mean (right context, *ProsF_0Mean*) round up this feature set.

Some feature groups are not found at all in the top 20 lists: *PronAcc* is found on rank 28 (confidence of recognised words overlapping with the word under consideration), *ProsShim* on rank 36, *PronDurScore* on 41, *ProsVUV* on rank 43, and *ProsJit* on rank 50. *PronRos* and *PronLikeliRatio* do not occur at all in the top 80. The reason seems to be that ROS is implicitly used in other feature groups and that some features are quite similar to already selected features or exceeded by more powerful features like *PronPhoneConf*. Please note that all features based on the phoneme recogniser are beyond rank 58.

#	$\bar{\omega}$	group	context	selected feature
1	0.51	*PronPhoneConf-2*	[0,0]	minimum phoneme confusion
2	0.48	*PronLikeli-1*	[0,0]	log-likelihood word-score
3	0.27	*PronDurLUT-3*	[0,0]	cf. Tab. 8.7 #5
4	0.23	*ProsEneMean*	[1,2]	cf. Tab. 8.7 #6
5	0.21	*ProsFFT-1*	[0,0]	cf. Tab. 8.7 #7
6	0.20	*PronPhoneConf-1*	[0,0]	cf. Tab. 8.7 #1
7	0.20	*PronPhoneConf-3*	[0,0]	cf. Tab. 8.7 #19
8	0.19	*PronLikeli-5*	[0,0]	cf. Tab. 8.7 #2
9	0.19	*PronConfidence-5*	[0,0]	cf. Tab. 8.7 #4
10	0.19	*PronContext*	[-1,0]	context of *PronConfidence-1*
11	0.17	*ProsDurNorm*	[-1,-1]	cf. Tab. 8.7 #8
12	0.16	*ProsF$_0$RegCoeff*	[-1,0]	cf. Tab. 8.7 #16
13	0.16	*PronAcc-3*	[0,0]	confidence of recognised word
14	0.15	*PronLikeli-6*	[0,0]	cf. Tab. 8.7 #11
15	0.15	*PronTrap-1*	[0,0]	cf. Tab. 8.7 #12
16	0.15	*ProsPauseAfter*	[1,1]	cf. Tab. 8.7 #14
17	0.15	*ProsF$_0$MseReg*	[0,0]	mean square error of F_0 regression
18	0.13	*ProsVUVDur+Global*		duration of voiced segments (sentence)
19	0.13	*ProsFFT-2*	[0,0]	3rd FFT coefficient
20	0.13	*PronContext*	[-1,0]	cf. Tab. 8.7 #3

Table 8.8: Top 20 features selected with AdaBoost and ranked with their mean ω-values after Eq. 8.2. Basis is the reference "3 of 8" (cf. Tab. 6.1).

Tab. 8.8 shows that a very similar feature set is selected when a different reference is used ("3 of 8" experienced teachers). Here, the winners are the minimum instead of the mean phoneme confusion and a different log-likelihood score. *PronAcc* has been selected instead of *PronPhoneSeq*. Further the context of the confidence is taken into account, a higher FFT coefficient of the energy, the mean square error of the regression of the F_0, and a global feature that measures the duration of the voiced segments within the sentence.

In this section interesting subsets of the 198 features have been described. Best classification rate has been achieved with 40 features, but the optimum result from Tab. 8.3 (71.3%[8.6], based on a larger set of 69 pronunciation features) is not exceeded. In the following section, the AdaBoost algorithm is applied using two-fold cross-validation (MONT vs. OHMPLUS).

8.2.5 Comparison of Classifiers

Now, different classifiers are being evaluated for the cross-validation task MONT vs. OHM-PLUS. This setup was chosen, since in particular the training of neural networks (ANN) is very time-consuming. Here, only two training iterations are necessary, whereas for the

set 1 vs. set 2	classifier	d	CL-2 in %		
			set 1	set 2	μ
MONT vs. OHMPLUS	Gauss	80	61.6	66.7	64.2
MONT vs. OHMPLUS	LDA	80	64.9	67.6	66.3
MONT vs. OHMPLUS	AdaBoost	80	65.8	68.7	$67.3^{8.9}$
MONT vs. OHMPLUS	ANN,linear	80	66.8	67.4	67.1
MONT vs. OHMPLUS	ANN, [4,4,4]	80	66.5	68.1	67.3
MONT vs. OHMPLUS	LDA	199	66.7	69.5	68.1
MONT vs. OHMPLUS	LDA after PCA	$199 \rightarrow 69$	67.3	69.7	$\mathbf{68.5}^{8.10}$
MONT vs. OHMPLUS	LDA after PCA	$80 \rightarrow 69$	66.8	69.2	**68.0**
MONT vs. OHMPLUS	Gauss after PCA	$80 \rightarrow 69$	62.3	67.0	64.7

Table 8.9: Comparison of Gauss classifier, LDA classifier, AdaBoost, and Neural Networks (ANN), for the cross-validation task on the word level. μ is the mean of both iterations. Basis is a speech recognition with reduced text-dependent vocabulary plus mispronunciation models. The reference is rater S, d is the dimension of the feature vectors.

loo-experiments on OHM the training of 28 different ANNs for the different training sets in different *loo* iterations would be required. The reference in the cross-validation task is rater S, because in Tab. 8.2 these ratings turned out to be classified best. Basis for feature extraction is the text based speech recogniser with mispronunciation models. In this configuration 199 features (75 pronunciation features + 124 prosodic features) can be calculated. Prior to the extensive training of ANNs, this feature set is reduced with the AdaBoost algorithm.

With AdaBoost a subset of 80 features is selected in each cross-validation iterations. Using this feature set it could be shown that the AdaBoost classifier performs best ($67.3\%^{8.9}$ CL-2, cf. Tab. 8.9). With LDA only 66.3 % CL-2 are obtained and with the simple Gaussian classifier 64.2 % CL-2. The same classification rate as obtained with AdaBoost is reached with ANNs, but never overexceeded, neither with a linear ANN without any hidden layers (67.1 % CL-2), nor with any complex architecture. From many investigated architectures with one, two, or three hidden layers, the configuration [4,4,4] performed best, which stands for three hidden layers with 4 nodes, each. Here, the number of weights $\omega_{i,j}$ that had to be trained is $80 \times 4 + 4 \times 4 + 4 \times 4 + 4 \times 2 = 360$. This results in more than 20 training samples per parameter. However, there are many simple ANN architectures, where the number of samples per parameter drops beyond 10, e.g. with a single hidden layer and more than 10 nodes[7]. The size of the training data seems to be the main restriction and does not allow any more complex ANN architecture.

The performance with the 80 features selected using AdaBoost is good despite the fact that the selection on the training set (e.g. MONT) is different to the optimum selection that would have been obtained on the test set (e.g. OHMPLUS). This again shows that

---

[7]Among the investigated architectures are [4,4], or different configurations with a single hidden layer and up to 12 nodes

reasonable classification rates are also obtained when mismatched data is used for training and testing.

Using all 199 features and an LDA classifier, the classification rate rises to 68.1 % CL-2, with LDA after feature reduction to 69 components with PCA (cf. Tab. 8.3) 68.5%[8.10] CL-2 are achieved. The Gaussian classifier after PCA performs worse[8]. However, the classification rate from Tab. 8.2 where solely pronunciation features are being used (69.7%[8.4] CL-2, 75 features) is not exceeded in all experiments starting in the high dimensional feature space ($d = 199$).

8.2.6 Fusion and Evaluation

In the preceding sections pronunciation and prosodic features already have been combined. In the following, these approaches are additionally brought together with the results based on mispronunciation models (cf. Sect. 8.2.1). The setup of the fusion is outlined in Fig. 8.2; it is based on meta-features (cf. Sect. 5.1), i.e. the output of a classifier is used as feature in a succeeding classification stage.

Meta-Features. The result from the AdaBoost classifier which is based in prosodic and pronunciation features is the a posteriori probability of the class $\mathcal{X}$. From the speech recogniser based on mispronunciation models, unfortunately only discrete values are obtained: correctly recognised words are mapped onto 0 (correct pronunciation), regular substitutions and deletion[9] onto 1, and substitutions with a mispronunciation model onto 2. To obtain a finer granulation of the scores rather than this three discrete values, the results are additionally processed in a filtered form employing a simple hat filter. This is motivated by the assumption that the pronunciation of the neighbouring words is likely to influence also the current word. This very approach is also applied to the AdaBoost scores. This means that the meta-feature c_{meta}^{τ} (category of recognition result $\in \{0, 1, 2\}$ or a posteriori probability) for word τ are replaced with[10]

$$\tilde{c}_{\text{meta}}^{\tau} = \frac{1}{3}c_{\text{meta}}^{\tau-1} + c_{\text{meta}}^{\tau} + \frac{1}{3}c_{\text{meta}}^{\tau+1}. \tag{8.3}$$

Additional input to the meta-classifier is the length of the word (number of graphemes), since the probability of a mispronunciation may differ for short and long words and may also be detected with different accuracy. On top of this, the overall reading and pronunciation

---

[8]When optimising the number of principal components on the test data it was observed that the classification rate rises when using less components (due to the fact that in MONT different and more mispronunciations are observed than in OHMPLUS; "mismatched data"). This increase is stronger for the Gaussian classifier (less robust when using sparse data in high dimensional features space, cf. Sect. 3.1.2). The optimum result for the Gaussian classifier is 67.9 % CL-2 when using 7 principal components and 69.4 % CL-2 for the LDA classifier using 10 components.

[9]Insertions can also be observed in the recognised word sequence, but have no influence on this grading of the reference words (which does in this case not exist).

[10]Normalisation with factor 3/5 is omitted, since it would not change the result of the subsequent classification stage.

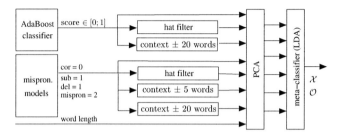

Figure 8.2: Fusion of feature based pronunciation scoring (pronunciation and prosodic features using AdaBoost) and speech recognition based on mispronunciation models. The fusion is based on meta-features which are raw and smoothed results from the previous classification steps, averaged scores to model context and the word length (number of graphemes).

proficiency that depends on the current speaker and the current text is taken into account. It is measured by averaging the word based scores over a long context window of ± 20 words and for the mispronunciation models additionally over a shorter window of ± 5 words (a strong mispronunciation may confuse the speech recogniser within the whole sentence).

Loo Evaluation. The results obtained with the meta-classifier are outlined in Fig. 8.3. It shows the evaluation of the OHM data in *loo* mode. Note that in each *loo* iteration the following calculation steps have to be performed

- The phoneme confusion statistics have to be re-calculated (without using the respective test data) and consequently also the pronunciation features for the training and test data (prosodic features are constant in all *loo*-iterations).

- Feature selection is performed on the training data.

- Training and test data are classified (soft classification) using the selected features (the speech recognition results based on mispronunciation models are constant in each iteration).

- From the training data meta-features are determined to train the PCA transformation (reduction to $d = 6$) and a meta-classifier.

- PCA and meta-classifier are used to classify the test data.

The classification scores for the respective test data in all *loo*-iterations are concatenated; with varying weightings for the classes $\mathcal{X}$ and $\mathcal{O}$ a ROC evaluation is obtained. Details of the approach are explained in Chap. 3.1.3.

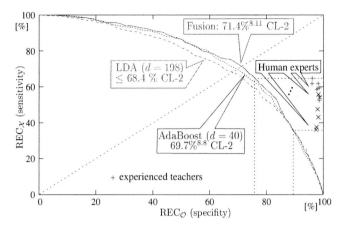

Figure 8.3: ROC evaluation for word level pronunciation scoring on the OHM data (*loo*). Comparison of the meta-classifier (fusion), the LDA classifier using 198 features, the AdaBoost classifier with 80 features, and human raters. Basis is the reference "3 of 8 experts" (cf. Tab. 6.1).

Classification Results. Fig. 8.3 shows the ROC curve based on a the meta-classification results of all *loo* iterations and compares it with an LDA classifier based in 198 pronunciation and prosodic features and with the AdaBoost algorithm which selects 40 features from the same set. The results using mispronunciation models, only, are not shown, since from discrete classification results a computation of ROC is not possible. The result with mispronunciation models is only 64.8%[8.3] CL-2 (cf. Tab. 8.1), with AdaBoost up to 69.7%[8.8] CL-2[11] are reached and with the meta-classifier up to 71.4%[8.11] CL-2[12]. The last improvement[13] is significant for a p-value of 0.05. Using LDA with 198 features does not over-exceed 68.4 % CL-2, here the improvement to 71.4 % is significant for a p-value of 0.001. The main advantage from fusion, however, remains the additional detection of phone level mispronunciation errors with the help of error rules e_i. Human raters (reference "3 of 8") show a high specifity (96.1 % – 98.7 % REC_O) but only a medium sized sensitivity (36.1 – 64.7 % REC_X) as discussed in Chap. 6.3. This corresponds to a CL-2 between 66.8 % and 80.4 % as shown in Tab. 6.5. The experienced teachers show higher REC_X than the other experts. The average CL-2 for this two rater groups is 78.4 % vs. 71.2 %. The classification rate in CL-2 is slightly better for our automatic system than for the average student teacher, when

---

[11]ROC-evaluation shows optimum weights for the test data, which means that even 69.8 % are reached. To improve readability, in the text and the figure 69.7%[8.8] CL-2 from Chap. 8.2.4 are shown.

[12]κ is only 0.15.

[13]From 69.8 to 71.4%[8.11]

the ground truth is defined by a consortium of expert teachers. Two student teachers and rater S are outperformed by the proposed automatic system.

Discussion. If the automatic system has to be set to exactly the same sensitivity as the human experts have, it shows a clearly lower specifity (76 % – 89 % instead of 96.1 % – 98.7 %, dashed lines in Fig. 8.3). Exemplarily the case with 85.0 % $REC_{\mathcal{O}}$ and 47.6 % $REC_{\mathcal{X}}$ is regarded as an acceptable system. For this case it is interesting, which of the words marked with $\mathcal{X}$ are indeed classified with $\mathcal{X}$. It turned out that the correctly classified $\mathcal{X}$ words are on average longer (4.5 phonemes per word) than the missed words with a length of 3.4 phonemes per word (type 2 errors, cf. Tab. 3.1). Not detected is in particular the wrong pronunciation of "is", "the", and "they". Since unfortunately no phone based annotations are available, the two groups of words, *hits* (204 words) and *miss* (225 words), are converted into phonemes in order to investigate which phone occurs more often in which group hoping that clear differences allow to draw conclusions on robustly detected or not detected phoneme based pronunciation errors. The missed words contain often the vowel "i" (/I/, /i:/, /aI/), the semi-vowel /w/, the voiced /z/, as well as /h/ and /m/. In future, classification rates could be improved by considering this knowledge and weighting "i" differently in the classification process or using an additional phoneme based voiced/unvoiced analysis. Robustly classified are mispronounced words containing /@/, /3r/, /A:/, /O:/, and /{/, all plosives, and /T/, /Z/, or /N/.

Another interesting group of words is the number of false alarms (type 1 errors). In the investigated example, 15 % of the correctly pronounced words are wrongly rejected. However, it turned out that 33 % of these words are not arbitrarily rejected but indeed marked by at least one of the 14 experts. In contrast, the correctly accepted words contain only 15 % which have been marked by at least one human rater. In future, the correct acceptance rate could be increased by using a priori knowledge, which words are expected to be correctly pronounced, and which words are new in the respective exercise.

Conclusion on Word-Level Classification. In this section considerable classification performance has been achieved for word based classification by combining different information sources. What is more, for many of the detected mispronunciations reliable hints can be given which phone has been pronounced wrongly and by which phone it was confused by employing mispronunciation models based on mispronunciation rules. This knowledge should of course be mapped onto a set of easily understandable instructions. Best results have been achieved with matched training and test data (same type of school, same age, same human experts) and with ratings from experienced teachers. In this case a global speech recogniser with a vocabulary of 934 words and no mispronunciation models was superior to a recogniser with reduced text dependent vocabulary. The latter, however, performs in particular better when recognising speakers with poor English proficiency, i.e. the children from MONT. Best classification rate of 71.3%[8.6] CL-2 is achieved with 74 pronunciation features. Applying AdaBoost, this results can be approximated even in lower dimensional feature space. The fusion of several moderate performing classifiers with meta-features resulted in a classifier with 71.4%[8.11] CL-2.

8.3 Sentence-Level Assessment

In the following pronunciation will be assessed on the sentence level. This makes e.g. training exercises possible, where the student has to read several sentences and the system picks out few sentences with the worst pronunciation in order to demand a repetition. Within these sentences additionally mispronounced words may be marked. In the same way exercises are thinkable, where one word is trained in varying context. State-of-the-art commercial systems often focus only on the word of interest ignoring mistakes in the remaining sentence. The proposed sentence features can also give a rough assessment of the other words. With a smoothed sequence of sentence level ratings the system is further able to draw conclusions on the progression, i.e. it can recognise whether the student is improving or not.

Evaluation Measures. Preliminary results on sentence level pronunciation scoring have been reported in [Cin09, Hac05a, Hac05b, Cin04b, Cin04a]. The main disadvantage of the following investigations is that only one-dimensional sentence-ratings are available for the NONNATIVE database (rater S)[14]. In contrast to the text-level ratings that will be discussed later in this chapter, the assessment is solely based on 5 discrete school grades. By using the rank-operation no different or finer partition can be obtained to be used as ground truth. This would have been provided by averaging the grades from several human experts. Consequently, only a subset of the measures described in Chap. 6.1 are investigated in the present section. For some measures a continuous score

$$E_\tau(k) = \sum_{k=1}^{K} k\, P(k|\mathbf{c}^\tau) \tag{8.4}$$

is calculated from the soft scores $P(k|\mathbf{c}^\tau)$ over all $K = 5$ classes instead of using discrete classification, where $P(k|\mathbf{c}^\tau)$ is the posterior probability of class k given a feature vector $\mathbf{c}$ representing utterance τ. The following measures are used:

- CL-5, CL-3: classification of 5 or 3 discrete school grades, respectively (cf. Fig. 6.1); comparison with the raw ratings of S.

- δ, ρ: comparison of $E(k)$ with the raw ratings of S.

- ρ_S: conversion of $E(k)$ and the raw ratings of S into ranks, then calculation of ρ

- δ_{nrm}: normalisation of reference and scores $E(k)$ (zero mean)[15], then calculation of δ.

---

[14] Remedy could have been to use the percentage of marked words per sentence to obtain 14 further ratings: however the correlation with the sentence level grading is only low.

[15] The normalisation is performed on the test set to show the minimum error, useful for the interpretation of the classification result. No gliding mean subtraction.

feature group	best feature (CL-3)	CL-3	CL-5	$1 - \delta$	$1 - \delta_{\mathrm{nrm}}$	κ_{rnk}
Rate-Of-Speech	*SentRos-5*	46.6	**30.4**	**68.5**	79.2	0.15
Pauses	*SentPauses-1*	**47.0**	**31.3**	68.1	**79.5**	0.15
Duration	*SentDurLUT-1*	45.4	25.8	67.9	78.7	0.09
Duration Score	*SentDurScore-2*	44.8	26.4	68.4	79.4	0.15
Log-Likelihood	*SentLikeli-5*	**47.0**	**31.7**	**69.2**	**79.7**	**0.21**
Likelihood Ratio	*SentLikeliRatio-1*	**48.5**	28.6	**68.6**	79.1	0.08
Traps	*SentTrap-9*	39.5	24.4	68.0	78.6	0.00
ASR Accuracy	*SentAcc-9*	**47.0**	**30.7**	**68.6**	**79.7**	**0.22**
Phoneme LM	*SentPhoneSeq-6*	40.9	26.2	67.9	79.2	0.18
ASR Confidence	*SentConfidence-2*	40.3	26.1	67.8	78.6	**0.20**
Phone Confusion	*SentPhoneConf-1*	**47.8**	29.0	**70.1**	**80.0**	**0.22**
Context	Δ *PronLikeliRatio-1*	46.3	29.2	68.3	78.7	0.14

Table 8.10: Best sentence pronunciation features based on *loo*-evaluation of the OHM data. The table shows the best feature per feature group using a speech recogniser based on a global vocabulary of 934 words. Reference is rater S; CL-3, CL-5, δ, δ_{nrm} in %.

- κ_{rnk}: classification of 5 discrete school grades; conversion into ranks, then calculation of κ.

Feature extraction is in all cases based on the speech recogniser with the full vocabulary and without mispronunciation models (Tab. 7.9, line seven, 35.9%[7.24] WER). Preliminary experiments have shown lower classification rates when calculating sentence features based on a recogniser using the smaller text dependent vocabulary (cf. Sect. 8.2.1). This means further that only 77 out of 78 sentence features described in Chap. 5.3.2 are used, leaving out the feature *SentAcc-8* which is based on mispronunciation models. Phoneme recogniser, phoneme bigram models, TRAP classifiers, duration statistics, and phoneme confusion matrices used for feature extraction are the same as in Sect. 8.2.2.

8.3.1   Sentence Pronunciation Features

In initial investigations, the set of 77 sentence pronunciation features (cf. Sect. 5.3.2) is investigated. Tab. 8.10 shows the best features for each of the 12 feature groups (cf. Tab. 8.4, left, for word based features). The classification results are based on *loo*-evaluation on the OHM data. The best feature per group shown in the table is optimum with respect to CL-3. The best classification results using only a single feature are 48.5 % CL-3 for *SentLikeliRatio-1* (it compares log-likelihood scores from forced alignment and from word recognition) and 47.8 % CL-3 for *SentPhoneConf-1* (it is the average phone confusion score). Classifying 5 school grades up to 30.7 % CL-3 are achieved. These results correspond to classification accuracy of up to 70.1 % in terms of $1 - \delta$, up to 80.0 % in terms of $1 - \delta_{\mathrm{nrm}}$, and up to 0.22 in terms of κ.

best feature	ρ	best feature	ρ
SentRos-5	-0.17	*SentTrap-1*	-0.08
SentPauses-1	0.17	*SentAcc-2*	-0.19
SentDurLUT-3	-0.08	*SentPhoneSeq-6*	-0.17
SentDurScore-3	-0.15	*SentConfidence-1*	**-0.21**
SentLikeli-8	**-0.20**	*SentPhoneConf-10*	**-0.21**
SentLikeliRatio-3	-0.11	Context of *SentPhoneConf-1*	-0.15

Table 8.11: Correlation of raw sentence pronunciation features with rater S. The table shows the best feature per feature group on the OHM data.

	d ($\rightarrow$: PCA)	CL-3 [%]	CL-5 [%]	$1-\delta$ [%]	$1-\delta_{\text{nrm}}$ [%]	ρ	ρ_S	κ_{rnk}
1. sentence features	$77 \rightarrow 30$	$50.4^{8.12}$	32.6	71.9	75.2	**0.24**	**0.26**	0.21
2. av. word classif.	74	40.7	25.0	37.0	**79.5**	0.22	0.24	0.12
3. meta-features	$5 \rightarrow 4$	46.2	29.2	69.1	76.9	0.22	0.24	0.14
4. min/max/mean of word features	$222 \rightarrow 150$	$\mathbf{50.7^{8.13}}$	**33.4**	**72.9**	73.1	0.23	0.24	**0.22**

Table 8.12: Comparison of the four approaches outlined in Fig. 5.1 for sentence level scoring with pronunciation features; *loo*-evaluation of the OHM data. d is the dimension of the feature vectors. Reference is rater S.

The correlation ρ of the raw features with the marks of rater S (no classification[16]) is up to 0.21 and highest for *SentPhoneConf-10* (maximum phone confusion score based on native phone confusion statistic) and *SentConfidence-1* (minimum frequency of any reference word in the n-best lists) as shown in Tab. 8.11.

8.3.2 Word and Sentence based Pronunciation Features

After the evaluation of single sentence features in the previous section, features are now being combined: In the first experiment all 77 sentence pronunciation features are employed. This approach is compared with 3 alternative sentence scoring approaches that have been introduced in Chap. 5 and are outlined in Fig. 5.1. In all experiments principal component analysis (PCA) is employed for feature reduction to overcome the curse of dimensionality in the case of sparse sentence level data (1.303 sentences) and to decorrelate feature components. All experiments are conducted on the OHM data in *loo* mode (28-fold cross-validation); the PCA transformation is estimated on the respective training sets. Only the number of principal components to be used is optimised on the entire test data. These results show the maximum possible classification rate[17].

---

[16]Phone confusion statistics are estimated on the disjoint MONT part of the database

[17]Optimum number of principal component in steps of 5 (steps of 1 in the meta-feature case). Criterion was CL-3.

(1) Sentence Features. In the first experiment 77 sentence features are reduced to 30 principal components by means of PCA to serve then as input to an LDA classifier. The results are shown in Tab. 8.12. CL-3 is $50.4\%^{8.12}$, CL-5 is 32.6%, the Spearman rank correlation ρ_S is 0.26, and $\kappa = 0.21$. The complement of the error is $1 - \delta = 71.9\%$; it rises after normalisation of the data (same mean for the automatic scores and the human ratings) to $1 - \delta_{nrm} = 75.2\%$. CL-3, CL-5, δ, and κ are outperformed with approach 4, where the results are insignificantly better. The confidence interval for a p-value of 0.05 is in the range of $\pm 4\%$ (percentage points) for CL-3, $\pm 3\%$ for CL-5, and ± 0.06 for ρ.

(2) Average Word Classification. In the second approach the word based classification is averaged. For this purpose the result $71.3^{8.6}$ CL-2 based solely on pronunciation features is used (Tab. 8.3). The word based scores of the classes $\mathcal{X}$ and $\mathcal{O}$ are averaged over the sentence and normalised in order to sum up to 1.0 for each sentence. The score for $\mathcal{X}$ is then used as continuous score. After ranking and division in 5 partitions one yields discrete marks. For this approach Tab. 8.12 shows the lowest classification rates and correlation values. Only after normalisation $1 - \delta_{nrm}$ is high (79.5%).

(3) Meta-Features. The same word classification results are also basis for the approach 3. Now, the classification results are not averaged, but features are extracted that are input to a second meta-classifier. The 5 meta-features are the minimum, maximum, and mean word based classification score of the class $\mathcal{X}$ within the sentence, the total number of words in the sentence, and the number of words that have been classified with $\mathcal{X}$. Tab. 8.12 shows advantages of the meta-classifier in comparison to average word classification for all measures but worse results than reached with the approaches 1 and 4.

(4) Min-Max-Mean Features. In approach number 4 the word based pronunciation features are employed to build sentence based features. For each of the 78 word features the minimum, maximum and the average is determined over all occurring values in a sentence. This results in $3 \times 74 = 222$ features. Features that perform best in a one dimensional classification task are the average of *PronPhoneConf-2*, *PronAcc-1*, *PronPhoneConf-9*, *PronLikeli-3*, and *PronAcc-2* (up to 30.5% CL-5). With the complete feature set $50.7\%^{8.13}$ CL-3 are achieved after feature reduction to 150 principal components. Also CL-5 and κ are higher than in the case of special designed sentence features. Note that 33.4% CL-5 correspond with 68.1% CL-$5^{\pm 1}$, if one tolerates a confusion of neighbouring marks. Using these min/max/mean features, much more principal components are required than in the case of sentence pronunciation features.

Summing up, best results have been obtained with sentence pronunciation features or a large set of sentence features that can be determined directly from word based features. In the following section, these features will be combined with prosodic features.

372 prosodic features	d	CL-3	CL-5	$1 - \delta_{\mathrm{nrm}}$	ρ_{S}	κ_{rnk}
	$(\rightarrow : \text{PCA})$	[%]	[%]	[%]		
+ min/max/mean of word	$594 \rightarrow 150$	49.5	30.3	73.6	0.26	0.23
pronunciation features						
+ sentence pron. features	$449 \rightarrow 110$	**54.8**[8.14]	33.9	74.1	$0.28^{8.17}$	0.23

Table 8.13: Combination of prosodic features and sentence pronunciation features; *loo* evaluation of the OHM data. The sentence prosodic features are obtained by determining maximum, minimum, and mean of the word prosodic features. d is the dimension of the feature vectors. Reference is rater S.

	d	CL-3	CL-5	$1 - \delta_{\mathrm{nrm}}$	ρ_{S}	κ_{rnk}
train vs. test	$(\rightarrow : \text{PCA})$	[%]	[%]	[%]		
MONT vs. OHMPLUS	$449 \rightarrow 15$	54.4	30.0	77.3	0.32	0.27
OHMPLUS vs. MONT	$449 \rightarrow 15$	50.6	33.0	70.8	0.40	0.37
μ	$449 \rightarrow 15$	**52.5**[8.16]	31.5	74.1	**0.36**[8.18]	0.32

Table 8.14: Combination of prosodic and pronunciation features on the sentence level (cross-validation). μ is the mean of both iterations, d is the dimension of the feature vectors. Reference is rater S.

8.3.3 Pronunciation Evaluation with Prosodic Features

For pronunciation scoring with prosodic features the 124 word based features described in Sect. 5.4 are employed, since no special sentence features are available. For sentence level scoring approach 4 from Fig. 5.1 is applied and combined with sentence pronunciation features from approach 1 or 4 in Tab. 8.12.

The results on OHM are shown in Tab. 8.13 for the *loo* case. Optimum classification takes place in 110 dimensional feature space (reduction from 449 components with PCA). In comparison to Tab. 8.12 in particular CL-3 and ρ_{S} are clearly increased when using additional prosodic features ($54.8^{8.14} > 50.7^{8.13}$ CL-3, significant for the p-value 0.05). This corresponds to $69.3\%^{8.15}$ CL-$5^{\pm 1}$ when tolerating a confusion of neighbouring marks. The results for cross-validation MONT vs. OHMPLUS are shown in Tab. 8.14. The difference between both parts of the NONNATIVE database has an impact on the number of feature components used for the evaluation. Classification takes place in 15-dimensional feature space, only, since the lower order principal components seem to contain corpus dependent information; they do not generalise. CL-3 is $52.5\%^{8.16}$. In the cross-validation task a high correlation $\rho_{\mathrm{S}} = 0.36^{8.18}$ is obtained and a high κ_{rnk} of 0.32. The reason is not that this data can be better classified than OHM, but most likely that the marks 4 and 5 are more frequent (cf. Tab. 4.4). Those sentences have – when correctly classified – in particular a positive influence on the correlation (cf. Eq. 2.2): Given variance normalised data it can be easily seen in this equation that values closer to the expectation have a lower influence on ρ.

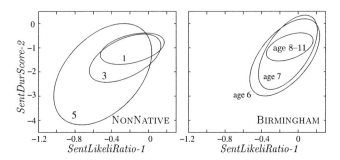

Figure 8.4: Comparison of native and non-native data in pronunciation feature-space. The non-native data is shown in clusters for the marks 1, 3, and 5. The native data is divided into age groups.

8.3.4   Evaluation with Native Models

Fig. 8.4 compares native and non-native data in feature space. For the marks 1, 3, and 5 it is clearly visible that the classes overlap which makes classification hard. The figure shows further higher variances for sentences with mark 5 and for younger native children. Surprisingly, the shift of the classes for worse speakers has the same direction as for the younger native speakers. This means that many young native speakers have a pronunciation which would be judged with mark 3 by an automatic system trained on the NONNATIVE database. The cluster for mark 1 is in the same region as the cluster of native children in the age of 8—11, which complies with the assumption that most natives would be marked with 1. The different pronunciation of good non-native speakers and natives is completely eliminated with these features.

Approach.   Since it was also observed for other feature components that the native 8–11 year-old children are in the same region as the good non-native speakers, or even more distant from the worse marks, it will be investigated next, whether the native data alone is sufficient to train a pronunciation scoring system. Does the distance from the native age-8—11-cluster correlate with the human grading for a non-native learner? This of course would make the expensive recording of non-native training data required for different mother tongues redundant. In the following the Mahalanobis distance is investigated (cf. Chap. 3.1.2). Since it is not known, in which direction of the native cluster the worse marks will be found, non-native data has to be employed additionally for validation. When evaluating the MONT data, OHMPLUS is used for validation and vice versa. The training data is in all cases the BIRMINGHAM corpus. Since it turned out that the PCA is not appropriate for this different kind of training and test data, the validation data will be further used for feature selection with AdaBoost.

#	ω	validation: MONT feature	ω	validation: OHMPLUS feature
1	0.78	*SentPauses-2*	0.53	*SentLikeli-4*
2	0.49	*SentLikeli-2*	0.36	mean (*ProsDurNorm*)
3	0.33	*SentPhoneConf-9*	0.34	*SentPhoneConf-9*
4	0.22	max (*ProsF$_0$Min*)	0.25	*SentLikeli-2*
5	0.19	mean (*ProsEneNorm*)	0.24	max (*ProsVUVDur+Global*)
6	0.17	*SentLikeli-3*	0.21	max (*ProsEneNorm*)
7	0.16	mean (*ProsEneMax*)	0.20	mean (*ProsEneMean*)
8	0.15	mean (*ProsF$_0$Off*)	0.14	mean (*ProsEneNorm*)
9	0.15	*SentContext-5*	0.13	*SentROS-3*
10	0.15	*SentPhoneConf-2*	0.13	mean (*ProsVUVNum+Global*)

Table 8.15: Top 10 sentence features selected with AdaBoost from 453 features and ranked with their ω-values. Basis is the reference of rater S.

AdaBoost. For feature selection the AdaBoost algorithm described in Chap. 3.1.4 is employed. Since this version of AdaBoost is only valid for a 2-class task, on the validation data only the sets {1,2} vs. {3,4,5} are discriminated. The optimum features together with their weights ω are shown in Tab. 8.15. Many features are similar for MONT and OHMPLUS. However *SentPauses* is optimum for MONT whereas duration, ROS, and length of voiced segments are selected on OHMPLUS.

The classification algorithm is the following: For each weak classifier a Gaussian density is trained on BIRMINGHAM. Then the Mahalanobis distance is determined for each sample of the validation data. These values are converted into ranks. Finally, for each sample the distance from the maximum rank is used as score for the class {1, 2} and the distance from the rank 1 as score for the class {3, 4, 5}. Using these scores different ϑ as described on page 49 can be evaluated. On the test data the scores of the class {3, 4, 5} are the basis to calculate ρ_S and $1 - \delta_{nrm}$. For κ and CL, these scores are converted into ranks and divided in partitions. The results with the top $d = 20$ features are summarised in Tab. 8.16. CL-3 and CL-5 are smaller than in Tab. 8.14, but δ, ρ_S, and κ_{rnk} are similar in this approach that is based on a classifier trained on native data.

In this section different sentence features and sentence scoring approaches have been evaluated. Best CL-3 has been achieved on OHM (54.8%[8.14]). Best ρ is obtained with cross-validation (0.36[8.18]).

8.4 Text- and Speaker-Level Assessment

This final experimental section investigates, whether it is possible to use the described approaches to estimate the proficiency in correct pronunciation for a speaker given a small text (text-level assessment), or the speaker's proficiency in general (speaker-level assess-

validation vs. test	d	CL-3 [%]	CL-5 [%]	$1 - \delta_{\mathrm{nrm}}$ [%]	ρ_{S}	κ_{rnk}
MONT vs. OHMPLUS	20	45.4	29.0	80.4	0.28	0.26
OHMPLUS vs. MONT	20	44.9	28.4	70.6	0.39	0.38
μ	20	**45.2**	28.7	75.5	**0.34**[8.19]	0.32

Table 8.16: Combination of prosodic and pronunciation features on the sentence level (cross-validation). μ is the mean of both iterations, reference is rater S. All acoustic models are trained on native data (BIRMINGHAM). On the validation data set $d = 20$ features are selected with AdaBoost.

ment given several texts). Due to a small number of samples in the NONNATIVE database given these higher levels (e.g. 57 speakers), some approaches based on word- or sentence-level features (1 and 4 in Fig. 5.1) are not applicable. In this section the classification results obtained on word or sentence level are averaged for the respective context of interest. Also classification with meta-features is investigated (only on the text level) as well as the additional assessment of reading proficiency by classifying prosodic boundaries as described in Sect. 5.5 (only on the speaker level).

8.4.1 Text Level

Text level scores are obtained on the OHM data in *loo*-mode from word and speaker level scores. The reference is either the mean of the ratings from 13 experts or the mean of 8 experienced teachers. For the MONT part of the database text ratings are not available.

Text level scores are obtained from the sentence level by averaging the sentence based a-posteriori scores for each of the five marks over the whole text. The expectation over all 5 marks (Eq. 8.4) is used for correlation analysis. Discrete text level classification results are obtained after ranking and partitioning. The underlying sentence level scores are the classification results from Tab. 8.13 (54.8%[8.14] CL-3). Further text level scores are calculated from the word level in the same way as described on page 172 ("average word classification"). Here, the word scores are obtained from the classifier described in Sect. 8.2.6 ("Fusion", 71.4%[8.11] CL-2).

Comparing the different annotations, Tab. 8.17 shows best results when using the rating of 8 experienced teachers for training and evaluation. Further, it can clearly be seen that classification rates and correlation indices are higher for scores obtained from the word than from the sentence level. $1 - \delta_{\mathrm{nrm}}$, ρ_{S}, and κ_{rnk} is in all cases noticeably higher than in Tab. 8.13. The results for "combi" are based on the linear combination of the word and sentence based scores (optimum on the test data). These results show only little improvement. The optimum "fair" result is 55.1%[8.20] CL-3 which corresponds to $\rho_{\mathrm{S}} = 0.63\%$[8.24] and $\kappa_{\mathrm{rnk}} = 0.63\%$[8.25]. CL-10$_{\mathrm{rnk}}^{\pm2}$ is in the optimum case 68.2% and $1 - \delta_{\mathrm{nrm}}$ reaches 81.9%. $1 - \delta_{\mathrm{rnk}}$ is always lower than $1 - \delta_{\mathrm{nrm}}$. $1 - \delta$ for unnormalised data is in particular low for scores obtained from the word level.

ref.	basis lev.	CL-3	CL-5	CL-10$^{\pm2}_{rnk}$	$1-\delta$	$1-\delta_{nrm}$	$1-\delta_{rnk}$	ρ	ρ_S	κ_{rnk}
13	word	52.0	34.1	**68.2**	26.3	**81.9**	72.8	0.61	0.62	**0.63**
13	sent.	45.6	25.9	59.6	73.1	81.3	65.0	0.32	0.34	0.34
8	word	**55.1**[8.20]	**36.3**	61.7[8.21]	26.8	80.9[8.22]	**73.3**[8.23]	0.61	**0.63**[8.24]	**0.63**[8.25]
8	sent.	43.9	26.9	59.7	**73.2**	80.8	65.4	0.35	0.37	0.38
8	combi	55.9	33.2	70.2	31.8	81.2	74.4	0.63	0.65	0.65

Table 8.17: Evaluation (*loo*) of the OHM data on the text-level by averaging scores from lower-levels (basis). Reference (Ref.) is the mean of 13 experts or the mean of 8 experienced teachers (cf. Tab. 6.11 and 6.10), respectively. All numbers in % except ρ, ρ_S, and κ_{rnk}

basis	d	CL-3	CL-5	CL-10$^{\pm2}_{rnk}$	$1-\delta$	$1-\delta_{nrm}$	$1-\delta_{rnk}$	ρ	ρ_S	κ_{rnk}
word	$5 \rightarrow 5$	50.8	32.0	70.1	71.3	71.4	70.0	0.62	0.62	0.59
sent.	$16 \rightarrow 3$	55.2	28.2	64.8	71.8	72.0	70.0	0.62	0.63	0.57
combi	$21 \rightarrow 3$	**57.8**[8.26]	30.1	**76.3**[8.27]	**73.1**	**73.3**[8.28]	69.4[8.29]	**0.66**[8.30]	0.64	**0.59**[8.31]

Table 8.18: Evaluation of the OHM data on the text-level using meta-features representing lower-level (basis) recognition results. Reference is the mean of 8 experienced teachers (cf. Tab. 6.11). d shows the dimension of the meta-features before and after PCA. All numbers in % except ρ, ρ_S, and κ_{rnk},

Tab. 8.18 shows increased recognition results when using meta features describing the fluctuation of word and sentence level scores. Among other features, the mean, minimum, and maximum score found within the respective text are input to a second classification step (*loo* mode). From the word level scores five meta-features are extracted as described on page 172 ("meta features"). 16 further meta-features are obtained from the sentence classification: the minimum a posteriori score for each of the 5 classes (marks) within the text, the mean a posteriori scores for 5 classes, scores for the maximum, and finally the number of sentences. Altogether 21 meta-features are extracted. As these features contain highly redundant information, they are reduced to only 3 or 5 principal components with PCA. If the PCA transformation begins in 21 dimensional feature space, the classification and correlation indices are better than the outcome based on either word or sentence scores. Tab. 8.18 summarises the results which are in most cases better than the respective numbers in Tab. 8.17, except for CL-5, $1-\delta_{nrm}$, and κ_{rnk}. CL-3 reaches 57.8%[8.26], which corresponds to 76.3[8.27] CL-10$^{\pm2}_{rnk}$. $1-\delta_{rnk}$ is 69.4%[8.29] while ρ rises to 0.66%[8.30].

The text-level results of the automatic classifier can be compared directly with the agreement of human experts that has been discussed in Chap. 6. The optimum results from Tab. 8.18 will now be compared with Tab. 6.11 (OHM data, the reference is the mean rating of 8 experienced teachers). While the automatic system reaches 57.8%[8.26] CL-3, the agreement among human experts is 74.0%[6.27] (the system reaches 0.78 of the average human performance). The numbers for CL-10$^{\pm2}_{rnk}$ are 76.3%[8.27] vs. 81.2%[6.28] (0.94 of the human performance), for $1-\delta_{nrm}$ 73.3%[8.28] vs. 83.6%[6.25] (0.89 of the human performance), for ρ 0.66[8.30] vs. 0.77[6.23] (0.86 of the human performance), and for κ_{rnk} 0.59[8.31] vs. 0.66[6.29]

(0.89 of the human performance). Except for the coarse measure CL-3 in all cases nearly 90 % of the human agreement are reached. For some measures the automatic system is even better than the worst human expert: The minimum CL-10$_{\mathrm{rnk}}^{\pm2}$ among teachers is 70.1 % (student teacher with average of the 8 experienced teachers), and the worst correlation is 0.58 (again for a student teacher). The worst $1 - \delta_{\mathrm{nrm}}$ is 79.2 %. The confidence interval for a p-value of 0.05 is [0.55;0.77] for ρ and around ±12 % (percentage points) for CL-3.

Since Tab. 6.11 shows very similar numbers for the OHM and the OHMPLUS data, the evaluation result of the automatic system $(1 - \delta, \rho) = (73.1, 0.66)$ can be directly projected into the "agreement-plane" in Fig. 6.4[18]. The system is in the region of the worst human experts[19] N, T_9 and T_{11}; the distance to these experts is smaller than the distance between the first and second rating of those teachers who rated the data half a year later again. For the OHM data, the (CL-10$_{\mathrm{rnk}}^{\pm2}$, ρ_S) agreement plain is shown in Fig. A.1 and A.2.

8.4.2   Speaker Level

In the same way as for the text level scoring, word and sentence scores are now averaged over all utterances of a speaker. Meta-features are not used, since the number of samples (speakers) is too small to train a classifier (e.g. 32 for OHMPLUS). The word and sentence level basis scores used in Tab. 8.19 are the same as in Tab. 8.17. Again, it is better to use the mean rating of the 8 experienced teachers for training and testing, and it is again better to use word level pronunciation scores. The speaker level scores are higher than the text level scores. However, $1 - \delta$ is now rather small when the basis level is the word level and when no normalisation is applied. On the other hand, ρ rises to 0.51 even when using sentence scores. The correlation reaches in the optimum case $0.72^{8.36}$. A comparison with Tab. 6.12 ($\rho = 0.83^{6.46}$ for the 8 experienced teachers on OHM) shows that the automatic system reaches 0.81 of the human performance. The numbers for CL-3 are $69.0\%^{8.32}$ vs. $76.5\%^{6.50}$ (0.90 of the human performance), for CL-10$_{\mathrm{rnk}}^{\pm2}$ $66.7\%^{8.33}$ vs. $86.1\%^{6.51}$ (0.77 of the human performance), and for $1-\delta_{\mathrm{nrm}}$ $81.9\%^{8.34}$ vs. $86.9\%^{6.48}$ (0.94 of the human performance). κ_{rnk} reaches $0.72^{8.37}$ and is between automatic system and average human expert even higher than among the 8 experienced teachers. CL-3, CL-10$_{\mathrm{rnk}}^{\pm2}$, and $1 - \delta_{\mathrm{nrm}}$ are for automatic pronunciation scoring higher than for the *experienced* teacher with lowest agreement.

For speaker-level cross-validation pronunciation scoring is performed on the whole NON-NATIVE corpus. Best results are achieved, when the speaker scores are obtained from word-level scores, when these scores are solely based on 75 pronunciation features (Tab. 8.2, result $69.7\%^{8.4}$ CL-2), and when the reference is consistently rater S (no teacher ratings are available for MONT). Tab. 8.20 shows that CL-3 is in the average $44.7\%^{8.38}$ and ρ_S $= 0.51^{8.40}$. The results are clearly better when training with MONT (higher variability in pronunciation proficiency) and testing with OHMPLUS (more consistent pupils) than the other way round, like also shown in Tab. 8.2. Instead of averaging the results over both

---

[18]When evaluating the automatic system with the mean of all 13 experts $(1 - \delta_{\mathrm{nrm}}, \rho) = (81.9, 0.61)$ are achieved in Tab. 8.17

[19]Note, that N is among the 8 expert teachers with more than 1 year of teaching experience but does not show on all levels high agreement scores, as discussed on page 112 in the footnote.

ref.	basis lev.	CL-3	CL-5	CL-$10^{\pm2}_{\text{rnk}}$	$1-\delta$	$1-\delta_{\text{nrm}}$	$1-\delta_{\text{rnk}}$	ρ	ρ_{S}	κ_{rnk}
14	word	63.1	46.0	68.3	22.0	82.5	75.8	0.67	0.70	0.70
14	sent.	53.7	28.7	**71.7**	73.3	**83.2**	71.1	0.48	0.50	0.50
8	word	**69.0**[8.32]	**49.3**	66.7[8.33]	22.8	81.9[8.34]	**76.3**[8.35]	0.67	**0.72**[8.36]	**0.72**[8.37]
8	sent.	53.7	32.0	71.7	73.2	82.6	70.0	0.51	0.53	0.53

Table 8.19: Evaluation of the OHM data on the speaker-level by averaging scores from lower-levels (basis). Reference (Ref.) is the mean of 14 experts or the mean of 8 experienced teachers (cf. Tab. 6.12), respectively. All numbers in % except ρ, ρ_{S}, and κ_{rnk}

training vs. test *pronunciation evaluation*	CL-3 [%]	CL-5 [%]	CL-$10^{\pm2}_{\text{rnk}}$ [%]	$1-\delta_{\text{nrm}}$ [%]	ρ_{S}	κ_{rnk}
MONT vs. OHMPLUS	55.5	41.2	65.1	73.8	0.59	0.59
OHMPLUS vs. MONT	33.9	34.3	62.9	74.2	0.42	0.42
μ	**44.7**[8.38]	37.8	64.0	74.0[8.39]	**0.51**[8.40]	0.51[8.41]
boundary classification						
NONNATIVERC vs. NONNATIVE	**43.5**[8.42]	29.2	49.9	73.8[8.43]	**0.36**[8.44]	0.36[8.45]

Table 8.20: Pronunciation scoring (cross-validation) and prosodic boundary classification on the speaker-level by averaging scores from the word-levels. Complete NONNATIVE database, reference is rater S. All numbers in % except ρ, ρ_{S}, and κ_{rnk}

cross-validation iterations, the result data can also be concatenated and then evaluated in terms or ρ. Then the correlation is 0.58 and has the confidence interval [0.42;0.73] for a p-value of 0.05.

Prosodic Boundaries. Classification of reading proficiency with prosodic boundaries is performed on the entire NONNATIVE corpus. (Tab. 8.20), since this approach is in particular good for poor readers like the students of the MONT set, and since the approach only works for the speaker level, where enough M_1 and M_2 boundaries occur. Boundaries are rare in those simple sentences read by beginners. Details of the approach were described in Chap. 5.5. First, a classifier for the three classes M_0, $\{M_1, M_2\}$, and M_3 is trained on the NONNATIVERC data which contains good readers who are expected to read most boundaries correctly. 75.3 % CL-3 of the expected boundaries are classified correctly (*loo* on NONNATIVERC). The recall of M_3 is even 84.1 %, since these boundaries are especially easy to detect. Most of them occur at the end of a sentence which often coincides with the end of the audio-file; words followed by M_3 have on the investigated databases in most cases no neighbouring word on the right side. The recall of $\{M_1, M_2\}$ is 68.1 %. When evaluating a classifier trained on NONNATIVERC on the NONNATIVE corpus, still 72.9 % CL-3 of the expected boundaries are detected correctly.

In the second step, only the word based a posteriori score of $\{M_1, M_2\}$ is used to assess the children of the NONNATIVE database. It is averaged over all words where a prosodic boundary is expected to follow. Then it is evaluated, whether this average score is appropriate for pronunciation scoring. It correlates with $0.36^{8.44}$ with the rater S. CL-3 is $43.5\%^{8.42}$ and nearly reaches the result based on pronunciation features ($44.7^{8.38}$). Note that only with rater S these good results could be obtained. The ratings of S seem to encode information about the students' reading proficiency and not only pronunciation issues.

8.5   Discussion

In the present chapter, the pronunciation of non-native children has been evaluated on the phoneme, word, sentence, text, and speaker level. Different algorithms have been evaluated and combined; results from lower (finer) levels are downsampled to obtain appropriate results for the coarser level. It has been found that best results are obtained when using consistent data for training and testing, e.g. the OHM data which contains only children from the same school and of the same age. Best results are further obtained when using only the ratings from the 8 experienced teachers (T_1– T_7, N). The OHM data was evaluated in *loo* mode; further evaluations with more data were performed on the whole NONNATIVE corpus using cross-validation (OHMPLUS vs. MONT). Here it turned out that best results are obtained when using rater S as reference (Tab. 8.2). This makes the data again more consistent, since she is the only human experts who annotated the MONT part of the corpus. In Tab. 8.9 also different classifiers are compared: Gauss, LDA, AdaBoost, and ANN. Due to sparse data the LDA (after feature reduction with principal component analysis) could not be outperformed with any more sophisticated classifier.

For pronunciation evaluation, common approaches like mispronunciation models are compared with newly developed approaches, like many of the pronunciation features, meta-classifiers, evaluation with native models, and boundary classification scores. For classification in high dimensional feature space prosodic and pronunciation features are combined. Employing the AdaBoost algorithm different optimum feature subsets have been extracted for word and sentence level pronunciation scoring. The optimum feature list on the word level (averaged over all *loo* iterations) is headed by a phoneme confusion feature and followed by a log-likelihood score, duration features, energy features, a confidence score, and several pitch measures. Besides the newly developed phoneme confusion features, also TRAP-features, energy FFT coefficients, or phoneme sequence scores, which all never have been applied before in the field of pronunciation scoring, are among the top twenty features (cf. Tab. 8.7 and 8.8). None of the features based on a phoneme recogniser is among the top 40. Best pronunciation features on the sentence level are — besides phoneme confusion and log-likelihood — based on pauses, likelihood-ratio, and word accuracy (cf. Tab. 8.10). AdaBoost selects from 453 components[20] (cf. Tab. 8.15) additionally features analysing the duration of voiced segments or the sentence mean of word based energy features.

Different evaluation measures like the classification rate CL, δ, ρ, and κ (described in Chap. 6.1) are employed to evaluate the system. But what exactly does 60 % agreement or a correlation of 0.6 mean? In fact, the numbers alone are not meaningful. The approach

---

[20]2 class problem: {1,2} vs.{3,4,5}

in this thesis is, to compare the system with human experts *and* to compare the human experts among each other (cf. Chap. 6). The actual evaluation is then the comparison of both numbers for different measures with the goal that preferably all measures show in both cases values of the same magnitude.

The basis of pronunciation scoring is a speech recognition system. Speech recognition is more difficult for children and non-native speakers (cf. Chap. 7). In the present chapter the word accuracy was increased by using recognisers with reduced text dependent vocabulary. It turned out that the pronunciation scoring with pronunciation features could in most cases not be improved when using a speech recogniser with increased word accuracy. Only for pronunciation scoring with mispronunciation models high word accuracy is indispensable. Robust classification is also more important for the worse speakers (MONT).

For word and phone level pronunciation assessment mispronunciation models were added to the vocabulary of the speech recogniser. A factor was introduced to adjust the a-priori probability of these words. With a reduced text dependent vocabulary, $64.8\%^{8.3}$ CL-2 (mispronounced $\mathcal{X}$ vs. correctly pronounced $\mathcal{O}$) was achieved on the NONNATIVE corpus. On a small subset it was found that the mispronunciation rule identifies not only the mispronounced word, but in 87 % also the right phoneme. Using word level pronunciation features, up to $71.3\%^{8.6}$ CL-2 was achieved on OHM in *loo* mode (when optimising the required number of principal components on the test data); with prosodic features $63.1\%^{8.7}$ CL-2 were reached. Since after fusion of prosodic and pronunciation features the classification rate in 198-dimensional feature space decreased, the AdaBoost algorithm was employed for feature selection and classification. The optimum result on OHM is $69.7\%^{8.8}$ CL-2 and after fusion with the mispronunciation models (meta-classifier in 8-dimensional feature space, cf. Fig. 8.2) it rises to $71.4\%^{8.11}$ CL-2 (without any optimisation on the test data). The last improvement is significant for a p-value of 0.05. CL-2 for human experts is on average $75.6\%^{6.3}$. Some of the student teachers and rater S are even outperformed by the automatic system when the ground truth is defined by a consortium of expert teachers. However, all human experts have a very high specifity ($\text{REC}_{\mathcal{O}} > 96.1\%$) but do not interfere for all occurrences of mispronounced words ($36.1\% < \text{REC}_{\mathcal{X}} < 64.7\%$). The automatic system has for $\text{REC}_{\mathcal{X}} = 47.6\%$ only a specifity of $\text{REC}_{\mathcal{O}} = 85.0\%$. The correctly classified $\mathcal{X}$-words are on average longer than the missed words. Robustly classified mispronounced words containing /@/, /3r/, /A:/, /O:/, and /{/, all plosives, and /T/, /Z/, or /N/. From the wrongly rejected words 33 % are not arbitrarily rejected, but marked by at least one of the 14 experts.

On the sentence level marks 1 – 5 have been annotated only by rater S. Results with sentence level pronunciation features and min/max/mean word features are better than the average word classification or the extraction of meta-features form the word-level classification scores (for details on these 4 approaches see Fig. 5.1). When combining sentence level pronunciation features and min/max/mean word level prosodic features $54.8\%^{8.14}$ CL-3 were achieved. On the sentence level the combination of pronunciation features and prosody results in a significant improvement (p-value 0.05). This corresponds to $69.3\%^{8.15}$ CL-$5^{\pm1}$ when tolerating a confusion of neighbouring marks; the correlation ρ_S is $0.28^{8.17}$ (*loo*-evaluation on OHM). To avoid expensive collection of non-native training data, a new approach was introduced, which uses the Mahalanobis distance between native training data and the non-native test data for pronunciation scoring in combination with AdaBoost feature selection. The correlation with rater S is $0.34^{8.19}$ in the cross-validation task.

For text level pronunciation scoring, 21 meta-features were calculated from the underlying word and sentence level classification scores. In comparison with the average rater (from the 8 experienced teachers) CL-3 reaches $57.8\%^{8.26}$, which corresponds to $76.3^{8.27}$ CL-$10_{rnk}^{\pm 2}$, $1 - \delta_{rnk} = 69.4\%^{8.29}$, $\rho = 0.66^{8.30}$, and $\kappa_{rnk} = 0.59^{8.31}$. The respective numbers for the agreement of human experts are $74.0\%^{6.27}$, $81.2\%^{6.28}$, $83.6\%^{6.25}$, $0.77^{6.23}$, and $0.66^{6.29}$. Except for the coarse measure CL-3 in all cases nearly 90 % of the human agreement are reached. For some measures the automatic system is even better than the worst human expert. Word level scores are a better basis for text and speaker level assessment than sentence level scores.

For the speaker level, no sufficient data is available to train a meta-classifier. Here, the pronunciation scores were simply calculated by averaging the word or sentence level classification scores. The agreement with the human experts rises now to $69.0\%^{8.32}$ CL-3, $66.7\%^{8.33}$ CL-$10_{rnk}^{\pm 2}$, $1 - \delta_{nrm} = 81.9\%^{8.34}$, $\rho_S = 0.72^{8.36}$, and $\kappa_{rnk} = 0.72^{8.37}$. The respective numbers for the agreement of human experts are $76.5\%^{6.50}$, $86.1\%^{6.51}$, $86.9\%^{6.48}$, $0.83^{6.46}$, and $0.70^{6.52}$. Some measures are for automatic pronunciation scoring even higher than for some *experienced* teachers. Additional information on prosodic boundaries was applied for speaker level pronunciation scoring, too. As described in Sect. 5.5, the scores of a boundary classifier were averaged over all words that are annotated with a succeeding M_1 or M_2 boundary. This new approach results in a score that correlates with $\rho_S = 0.36^{8.44}$ with rater S.

To conclude, it should be highlighted that on all levels the automatic classification system can compete with human teachers. It reaches at least the performance of the human expert with lowest agreement. Although many of the results suggest an only intermediate performance of an automatic system for pronunciation evaluation, the system could reach – dependent on the evaluation measure – up to 94 % of the human performance. Also humans do by far not agree with 100 %.

Based on the available data and based on the agreement measures ρ_S and CL-3, best results are achieved on the speaker level, when the automatic system observes a large context: The correlation with human experts is $0.72^{8.36}$ ($0.83^{6.46}$ among human experts) and CL-3 reaches $69.0\%^{8.32}$ ($76.5\%^{6.50}$ among humans). Wrongly pronounced words are detected with $71.4\%^{8.11}$ CL-2 ($75.6\%^{6.3}$ among experts) when combining mispronunciation models, pronunciation features, and prosodic features. On the sentence level the best result is achieved with prosodic features and sentence pronunciation features ($54.8\%^{8.14}$ CL-3; $\rho_S = 0.28^{8.17}$).

Chapter 9

Contributions to Multimodal Extensions of the System

9.1 Outline of an Elaborated Multimodal System

The focus of the present thesis has been the recognition of non-native English from children and the automatic assessment of their pronunciation. Both aspects are essential for developing an automatic tuition system like those systems introduced in Chap. 2.3. The demonstration system developed in the context of this thesis is *Caller* (cf. Chap. 2.4). Besides the development of pedagogically valuable content and appropriate feedback, there are several aspects which will distinguish future generations of tuition systems: it will not only be recognised what the children are saying, and how correct they pronounce the words, but also how they behave and interact with the system. This comprises many aspects whose automatic detection can be improved with multimodality, i.e. by combining information obtained with the microphone, with a camera, or from haptic interaction, e.g. when using a touch screen. It can be classified whether the student is angry or happy, frustrated, bored, or motivated. The system could react by adapting the content and the feedback. The system could additionally detect whether the student interacts with the computer, discusses exercises with other students, or if he/she does something totally different.

To mention only some research from the literature, [Kra04] analyses the uncertainty of children and adults using audio and video information, and [Aru01] or [Yil05] recognise politeness and frustration in child-machine interaction. Different eye-tracking systems can already be found on the market, some systems are comfortable to use and require only a stereo-camera system attached to the computer monitor. The *LME* has long-term experience in emotion recognition. In various research projects the set of classic emotions were extended to a set of emotional user-states that can differ according to the application and may e.g. include also reprimanding which is actually not an emotion [Bat03b, Bat08]. Advantages of the use of multimodal information when classifying emotional user states and analysing human-machine interaction are discussed in [Not07]. The focus of the present chapter is the multimodal classification of the focus of attention and the classification of emotional user states.

9.2   Classification of the Focus of Attention

9.2.1   Push-to-Talk vs. Off-Talk Detection

Results and findings from the *SmartWeb* project[1] [Rei05, Wah04] can be considered as fundamental contributions to an elaborated CALL system. In this project a multimodal system was developed that recognises the user's focus of attention. The user is interacting with the Internet via a PDA in order to get information, on e.g. points of interest. To overcome the tedious use of devices such as push-to-talk but still be able to tell whether the user is addressing the system or talking to himself or to a third person, *On-Talk* vs. *Off-Talk* was classified automatically with the help of the camera of the device directed towards the user, and the speech input addressed to the speech recognition engine. This classification is used additionally to a voiced/unvoiced detection which determines the time interval where speech can be observed. On-Talk means that the spoken sentences are addressed to the system, and Off-Talk that the user speaks to someone else [Opp01, Sie01, Bat02]. In SmartWeb the category Off-Talk was further subdivided into *Read Off-Talk* (the user was reading aloud from the display), *Paraphrasing Off-Talk* (the user was reporting results from SmartWeb to another person), and *Spontaneous Off-Talk* which comprises speaking to oneself, swear words, and short responses to an interruption by anther person. A detailed description of the multimodal recognition of the focus of attention (*On-Focus* vs. *Off-Focus*) – algorithms and the corpus – can be found in [Hac06, Bat06, Not07, Bat07, Bat09]. Also in human–human communications, the partners do not always focus on the interaction itself. They can be distracted by other thoughts or by other people being present and interrupting.

The classification of the focus of attention is based on the results from face detection per frame, prosodic analysis per word, and linguistic analysis. Results from 3 classifiers are combined using meta-features as described in Chap 5.1 and Chap. 8.2.6.

Face Detection.   For face detection a robust classifier after Viola and Jones [Vio04] was employed, which uses Haar-like wavelets shown in Fig. 9.1, top, left (complete set of wavelets, up to scaling). The algorithm is based on AdaBoost, as described in Chap. 3.1.4. From all possible wavelets per 24×24 subi-mage, a few hundred are selected containing as complementary information. as possible. The best seven features obtained on the training set of the SmartWeb corpus are shown in Fig. 9.1, together with randomly selected images from the database in the background. On the test set, *On-View* (looking into the camera) and *Off-View* (not looking into the camera) are detected with 88 % CL-2. Note, that *Off-View* is neither a sufficient nor a necessary formal condition for *Off-Focus*: we can listen to our partner while looking away. The meta-features obtained from the frame based

---

[1] http://www.smartweb-projekt.de/

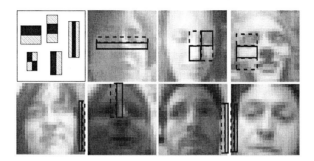

Figure 9.1: Haar wavelets for face detection on 24 × 24 sub-images after [Vio04], and the top 7 features selected with AdaBoost for the SmartWeb corpus when classifying the focus of attention.

classification are among others the proportion of On-View frames in the beginning and end of the utterance, and the global proportion of On-View frames with and without time smoothing of the 0/1-contour (On-/Off-View), to cope with poor face detection occurring due to strong backlight.

Prosodic Analysis. The prosodic analysis is performed with prosodic features as described in Chap. 5.4. Prosody enables a discrimination of different speaking registers: durations are longer for read speech; for On-Talk energy is higher, pauses are shorter, and the F_0-range is wider. The meta-features are built from the word based classification scores from 4 On/Off-Talk classes similar as in Sect. 8.4.1.

Linguistic Analysis. Each recognised word is converted into a part-of-speech tag. It was found that for *Read Off-Talk* and *Paraphrasing Off-Talk*, more nouns, adjectives, and participles occur, and in contrast for *Spontaneous Off-Talk*, more particles, articles, and interjections. Meta features are among others the number of content words and the number of function words per sentence.

The fusion is performed with a meta-classifier and results in sentence level scores for On-Talk and Off-Talk. On the spontaneous SmartWeb corpus, where 100 subjects had to test a prompting system in different environments while being from time to time disturbed by another person, 84.5 % CL-2 have been achieved (72.3 % CL-4, when evaluating different Off-Talk categories). Also for a CALL application it might be useful to automatically classify the focus of attention, e.g. whether the learner talks to the system, discusses with another student, or asks questions to a human teacher present in the class room. This way a push-to-talk button would become redundant. Face detection and prosody could be an important basis to classify the focus off attention, even if the Off-Talk utterances are expected to be often spoken in the L1 language. Additionally language identification will be helpful.

9.3 Emotions

Recent investigations on emotion recognition at the *LME* are based on the *Aibo*-corpus and on the *SympaFly*-corpus [Bat08]. The first of the two corpora was recorded in parallel to the NONNATIVE corpus (Chap. 4) and from the same speakers. In Appendix A the speaker IDs from the *Aibo* and the NONNATIVE corpus are related to each other.

The *Aibo* corpus contains emotional spontaneous speech from children playing with the Sony's AIBO (dog-like) pet robot and is described in [Bat05a, Bat04a]. The basic idea is to combine a new type of corpus (children's speech) with natural emotional speech within a Wizard-of-Oz task. The children had to navigate the AIBO through a parcours painted on a carpet and were led to believe that the robot is responding to their commands. However, it was actually being controlled by a human operator via wireless LAN; the existing AIBO speech recognition module was switched off. The robot performed a predetermined, fixed sequence of actions, no matter what the child was saying. This way, real emotions could be evoked. For this databases the emotional user states neutral, joyful, surprised, emphatic, helpless, touchy (i.e. irritated), angry, motherese, bored, and reprimanding were observed and annotated by several labellers and are analysed in [Bat05b, Bat05c, Ste05a, Sch07, Bat08, Ste09].

The SympaFly-corpus was recorded using a fully automatic speech dialogue telephone system for flight reservation and booking. Besides neutral, the observed user states are (from positive to negative): joyful, emphatic, surprised, ironic, compassionate, helpless, touchy, angry, and panic. Additionally, prosodic peculiarities are analysed (e.g. pauses, emphasis, hyper-articulation, and syllable lengthening) as well as the dialogue step success. Automatic classification results are reported in [Bat03a, Bat04b, Ste04a, Bat08].

Also in a CALL application the classification of user states might be helpful. First of all, it would be a benefit for didactic reasons: the system can adapt content and feedback to the user-state, for example, if the learner is bored or frustrated. The system can even react to uncertainty or surprise, or counteract to extremely negative states such as panic in the SympaFly task. Anger might be an indication that the automatic system does not work correctly, e.g. if the speech recognition engine fails repeatedly on a certain phrase. Additional exercises in a CALL application could further include real dialogue tasks like the proposed flight reservation system. A natural dialogue can also react to positive and negative user states or even try to irritate the learner on purpose.

After this short outline of an elaborated system, in the next chapter a more general outlook concerning the entire thesis will be given.

Chapter 10

Outlook

The two experimental parts in this thesis concentrated on the recognition of children speech and on automatic pronunciation scoring. However, the problems occurring when recognising young children are by far not solved, and similar problems occur also when recognising elderly people – a hot topic in research focusing on the aging society. In this thesis, it was shown that a recogniser trained on age dependent data succeeds with high recognition rates. However, there will not be enough training data available for all age groups, in particular not in all existing languages. Given an application where enough data is available, a huge pool of features, e.g. MFCC from different filterbanks, PLP, and TRAP features, could be provided and the training of the speech recognition system could be combined with feature selection approaches. In the case of insufficient training data, further progress will be necessary in adaptation and selective training: a pool of speakers from different age groups could be sufficient if at the same time various acoustic transformations are provided; the training algorithm could then automatically select the appropriate training data.

To evaluate pronunciation scoring, it will remain necessary to collect and annotate further training data in different L1/L2 language pairs for many years. The goal in this thesis was to create a system which imitates a teacher's way of grading. Thus the teachers had only a minimum set of instructions when annotating the NonNative corpus: they should mark those words where they also would have stopped the student in class. A large spectrum of possibly wrong pronunciations is received when combining the diverse set of annotations from many labellers. For future research it is recommended to let some of the experts additionally mark really *all* occurring mistakes, and also specialised errors like reading errors or errors meeting criteria from [Cuc00b]. Then, a two stage evaluation of the system would be possible: firstly, how many samples are correctly classified, and secondly, which words remain classified as mispronounced (if possible, the same words as a teacher would mark in class) if some thresholds are changed to reduce the total number of rejections. Furthermore, exercise dependent knowledge should be used in addition (e.g. this exercise concentrates on the pronunciation of "th", another exercises on fluent reading, and yet another one on the new vocabulary). A large corpus with several hundreds of exercises would be required to evaluate the additional use of such computer readable a-priori knowledge.

In this thesis the NONNATIVE corpus has been evaluated in detail on different levels. A larger corpus would be required to systematically evaluate the fusion of these results and the additional adaptation to the learner. The next step would be to evaluate the algorithms with another corpus (e.g. ISLE) and to focus on the phone level assessment. Here, it could be evaluated for categories of phone level mistakes, which assessment approaches (i.e. which pronunciation features) work best, and which effect different categories have on the higher level (word, sentence) classification results. On the other hand, algorithms developed on other sites could be evaluated on the NONNATIVE corpus with its singular amount of ratings.

The algorithms based on pronunciation features, prosodic features, and rule based mispronunciation modelling have to be combined with other newly developed promising approaches (cf. Chap. 2.2.2), above all Hidden Articulatory Markov Models (HAMM). The result of further investigations could be a pronunciation software development kit, where different features and algorithms can be easily combined to the desired evaluation module, or even a knowledge based system, where the designers of the exercise need simply to define different goals in detail; the pronunciation evaluation layer of the software would automatically apply the right algorithms and adapt them, dependent on the feedback of the system tester.

The next steps to reach such a goal are currently made at the *LME* in the C-AuDiT project[1]. The assessment algorithms are further developed and language independence is investigated. In this project the industrial partner will make the integration in a professional language learning framework possible[2]. Focus in this research project is also the development of a fully automatic speech dialogue which serves as new type of pronunciation exercise, where the learner has to fulfil small tasks like, e.g. to book a flight.

Finally putting aside all the sophisticated algorithms from the field of automatic pattern recognition we will find: the only three things which the user of a CALL-system will notice, is the content and design of the exercises, the feedback after a speech input, and the benefit he gets from spending hours with the software. These are pedagogical questions, which are the focus and will be the focus of other dissertations. An important issue in future research will be the mapping from the automatic score to the appropriate feedback.

---

[1]C-AuDiT: "computerunterstütztes Aussprache- und Dialogtraining" http://www.c-audit.org/, funded by German Federal Ministry for Research and Education (BMBF)

[2]digital publishing AG, Munich, http://www.digitalpublishing.de/english/

Chapter 11

Summary

Computer-aided language learning (CALL) enables the training of a foreign language even without a human teacher. An important aspect is the training of the *spoken* language, which is more and more being integrated into commercial software, but in most cases only based on rather simple algorithms. The present thesis focuses on computer-aided pronunciation training (CAPT), in particular to support children learning English as a second language (L2) in school. The L1 of the children recorded within the *Pf-Star* project and investigated in the present thesis is German (NONNATIVE corpus). Since many of the algorithms in automatic pronunciation scoring are based on automatic speech recognition (ASR) and forced time alignment, a robust ASR system is required which also yields acceptable word accuracy for children. Children speech, however, is known to be recognised with up to 170 % higher error rates than adult speech.

In the beginning of this thesis, a phonetic analysis of English and German has been given. Most pronunciation errors occur in the case of an unknown phoneme, unknown phoneme sequences, or the unfamiliar terminal voicing. In Chap. 2 pronunciation errors known from the literature are summarised and in Chap. 5 extended with typical errors found in the NONNATIVE data. The resulting synopsis defines mispronunciation rules that are used to build automatically special acoustic mispronunciation models which are added to the ASR system for pronunciation scoring.

A literature overview on pronunciation scoring is found in Chap. 2. Different measures are explained, like the reliability of a rater, the Pearson correlation ρ between raters (metric ratings), the Spearman correlation (ordinal data, for pronunciation scoring similar to ρ as shown in Chap. 6), and the classification rate. In Chap. 6, additionally the deviation δ is introduced. Multiple raters are evaluated in terms of Cohen κ and Krippendorff α; both indices subtract the chance agreement from the observed agreement. However, the similarity of both measures makes in the experimental part an analysis with both indices obsolete. The overview of the state-of-the-art describes numerous scoring algorithms from the literature, among others mispronunciation models, Hidden Articulatory Markov Models, prosodic features, GOP (goodness of pronunciation), log-likelihood features, and log-likelihood ratio. Then, selected systems like the ISLE project (German and Italian adults learning English) are described and an overview of commercial systems is given. *Caller* is a client/server system developed at the Chair of Pattern Recognition (*LME*). Only a minimal installation is required locally on the computer and all complex speech recognition and scoring modules described in this thesis run on a server.

Chap. 3 describes fundamental algorithms from the field of pattern recognition, which are relevant for the experimental part, i.e. LDA classification, Neural Networks, and ASR. AdaBoost can improve the performance of a classifier by assigning higher weights to the wrongly classified training samples in the next iteration. In the end, classifiers of all iterations are combined. Similarly as in the Viola and Jones algorithm for face detection, a modified algorithm is used for feature selection in this thesis. An appropriate evaluation measure for the classification of unbalanced data is the class-wise averaged classification rate (CL); speech recognition results are usually evaluated with the word error rate (WER). Concerning ASR, in particular the *LME*-recogniser is described in detail. Feature extraction is based on 24 MFCC features; alternative feature extraction approaches like TRAPs are described, but only used for some newly developed features for pronunciation scoring. The ASR system is based on semi-continuous Hidden Markov Models. The acoustic models are employed for forced alignment of the spoken utterance with the expected word sequence (known in the case of a reading test for pronunciation scoring), as well as for speech recognition. In the second case acoustic modelling and language modelling are combined using two parameters (linguistic weight and insertion penalty) which are optimised for different databases in Chap. 7.

After this, the peculiarities of children speech are described, and an overview of state-of-the-art approaches for children speech recognition is given (VTLN, MLLR, MAP, CMLSN, SAT, etc.). Differences between children and adults are the shorter vocal tract, the resulting higher formants, lower speaking rate, and the amount of extraneous speech and breathing noises. Higher inter- and intra-speaker variabilities are analysed in Chap. 7 separate for different frequency bands. Vocal tract length normalisation, and the adaptation algorithms MAP and MLLR are described in detail since they are applied to different children corpora in the experimental part.

To compare children with adult speech, different databases are investigated: VERB-MOBIL contains speech from American adults, YOUTH from American children. Since in German schools mainly British English is taught, the children from the BIRMINGHAM corpus (also recorded within Pf-Star) are additionally used for training, when evaluating non-native English speakers from Germany (NONNATIVE). Another advantage of the BIRMINGHAM corpus is that it contains children from different age groups (4 – 14) which allows an age dependent evaluation of the data. The NONNATIVE corpus is annotated on the word level with $\mathcal{O}/\mathcal{X}$ (correctly/wrongly pronounced), as well as on the sentence-, text-, and speaker-level (marks from 1 – 5) by up to 14 experts. Additional labels annotate different categories of syntactic boundaries.

For automatic scoring different approaches are presented in Chap. 5. A common approach for L1- and *text dependent* pronunciation scoring is to add mispronunciation models to the speech recognition engine. Those models are automatically build from 50 rules. If the speech decoder decides for a mispronunciation model, conclusions can be drawn to the phone level mistakes. *Text independent* approaches are based on feature extraction and classification. In addition to 124 prosodic features per word, 75 novel pronunciation features are used, where most of them have been newly developed for this thesis. For sentence and higher level pronunciation scoring, 4 approaches are presented which are based on the word level scores: (i) averaging word based classification results, (ii) combination of word based features, (iii) extraction of meta-features from word based classification results that are input to a second classification step, and (iv) the design of special sentence level features. For this purpose 78 sentence pronunciation features have been developed. A last approach uses the word based boundary classification scores to draw conclusions on the pronunciation.

The agreement of human raters is analysed in Chap. 6. It was shown that the strictness (% words marked with $\mathcal{X}$) is for all raters around 5 %. On the word level the average pairwise inter-rater agreement is 71.8%[6.1] CL-2. The intra-rater agreement is obtained when comparing raters with their second rating that took place half a year later (79.5 %). The open CL-2 is 79.3%[6.2]. On the text-level, the pairwise evaluation shows 0.63[6.7]/75.7%[6.8] in terms of $\rho/(1-\delta)$ in the inter-rater case and 0.77/84.3 % in the intra-rater case. The open inter-rater $\rho/(1 - \delta)$ is 0.78[6.9]/79.9[6.10]. On the speaker level it rises to 0.80[6.32]/82.6%[6.33]. κ increases from 0.43[6.6] on the word to 0.67[6.38] on the speaker level (all numbers for the OHMPLUS subset). There are other measures investigated which lead finally to an illustration where each rater is shown in the "agreement-plane", which is spanned by the first two principal components over all measures. The experts have not been calibrated; a system being able to achieve high correlations with those calibrated reference ratings would only detect mispronunciations specified in the rater instructions and never imitate the true marking of teachers.

The baseline recognition rates for BIRMINGHAM and YOUTH are 26.1%[7.6] and 3.3%[7.4] WER using a 4-gram language model (LM). With a unigram LM 52.2%[7.5] and 23.8%[7.3] are achieved. A strong increase of WER can be observed when evaluating the data with adult acoustic models trained on VERBMOBIL (85.3%[7.8] and 41.3%[7.7] WER with 4-gram LM). For the NONNATIVE data, the best baseline is obtained when evaluating with BIRMINGHAM models (43.5%[7.10] WER).

If enough training data is available to train acoustic models from children, ASR can be improved when adapting the feature extraction to children data by optimising the Mel filter bank. This way, WER was reduced significantly, e.g. on BIRMINGHAM to 23.7%[7.15] WER (4-gram LM). It is further shown that inverse VTLN transformed adult data added to the recogniser training can significantly reduce word error rates. An enhancement of the ROS for very young speakers also reduces WER. For the case that *not* enough data is available, different algorithms are investigated to adapt the adult speech recogniser to children. Best results are achieved with a combination of linear VTLN, piece-wise linear VTLN, MAP, and 5 supervised Baum-Welch iterations. Only in some cases an additional MLLR adaptation step before MAP reduces WER. This way, the WER for BIRMINGHAM is reduced by 57 % to 36.9%[7.23], and for Youth by 86 % to 5.7%[7.21].

The optimum speech recogniser for NONNATIVE is trained with data from YOUTH and BIRMINGHAM and additional good non-native readers from NONNATIVERC (35.9%[7.24] WER). When mispronunciation models are added to the ASR engine, the system has to be able to recognise additional German phones. Thus, adult German speakers from VMGERMAN are added (after inverse VTLN) to the training. The resulting recogniser achieves $38.9\%^{7.27}$ WER, and with a reduced text dependent vocabulary and additional mispronunciation models, $28.9\%^{8.1}$. For pronunciation scoring based on mispronunciation models, a very precise ASR system is essential, whereas it turned out that moderate speech recognition is sufficient for the approach based on pronunciation features. The phoneme error rate of a phone recogniser required for pronunciation feature extraction is $56.5^{7.31}$.

For pronunciation evaluation, common approaches like mispronunciation models are compared in Chap. 8 with newly developed approaches, like many of the pronunciation features, meta classifiers, evaluation with native models, and boundary classification scores. For classification in high dimensional feature space, prosodic and pronunciation features are combined. Employing the AdaBoost algorithm, different optimum feature subsets could be selected. The best feature is the phoneme-confusion which is the a-priori probability of the observed confusion given forced alignment and word recognition. This probability is obtained during training from all mispronounced words and is normalised with the likelihood of this confusion given correctly pronounced words. Further optimum features are log-likelihood scores, duration, energy, and confidence features, as well as novel features based on TRAPs, FFT coefficients, and phoneme sequence scores. On the sentence level also pauses, likelihood-ratio, and word accuracy achieve good results.

With mispronunciation models, $64.8\%^{8.3}$ CL-2 are achieved on the word level. The mispronunciation rule identifies for correct detected mispronunciations in 87% also the exact phoneme. With the AdaBoost classifier based on prosodic and pronunciation features, $69.7\%^{8.8}$ CL-2 are reached, and after fusion with the mispronunciation models, the accuracy rises to $71.4\%^{8.11}$ CL-2. CL-2 for human experts is on average $75.6\%^{6.3}$ but some of the experts are outperformed by the automatic system. However, all teachers have a very high specifity ($\text{REC}_{\mathcal{O}} > 96.1\%$) and only a moderate sensitivity ($36.1\% < \text{REC}_{\mathcal{X}} < 64.7\%$) since they do not reject every mispronunciation in order to not frustrate the student. The automatic system has for a moderate $\text{REC}_{\mathcal{X}} = 47.6\%$ only a specifity of $\text{REC}_{\mathcal{O}} = 85.0\%$. However, from the wrongly rejected words, 33% are not arbitrarily rejected, but marked by at least one of the 14 experts.

On the sentence level, the system reaches $69.3\%^{8.15}$ CL-$5^{\pm 1}$ (tolerating a confusion of neighbouring marks) and $\rho = 0.288^{8.17}$. On the text level CL-$10^{\pm 2}$ reaches $76.3\%^{8.27}$, which corresponds to $1 - \delta = 69.4\%^{8.29}$, $\rho = 0.66^{8.30}$, and $\kappa = 0.59^{8.31}$. The respective numbers for human experts for the OHM subset are $81.2\%^{6.28}$, $83.6\%^{6.25}$, $0.77^{6.23}$, and $0.66^{6.29}$; nearly 90% of the human agreement are reached. For some measures the automatic system is even better than the worst expert. On the speaker level the agreement with the experts rises now to $66.7\%^{8.33}$ CL-$10^{\pm 2}$, $1 - \delta = 81.9\%^{8.34}$, $\rho = 0.72^{8.36}$, and $\kappa = 0.72^{8.37}$ (human experts for OHM: $86.1\%^{6.51}$, $86.9\%^{6.48}$, $0.83^{6.46}$, and $0.70^{6.52}$).

Future CALL-systems require an appropriate mapping from the automatic score to a helpful feedback. They also will be improved by integrating multimodal aspects like the detection of the user's focus of attention instead of using a push-to-talk button. Automatic scoring accuracy can be further improved by adaptation to the learner and his knowledge.

Appendix A

Addendum to the Speech Corpora

A.1 Data Sets MONT and OHMPLUS

The tables Tab. A.1 and Tab. A.2 show the ID of the speakers recorded for the NONNATIVE database. It consists of a letter ('m' for male or 'w' for female), one digit that denotes school and grade and 2 digits for the speaker number. The digit '0' denotes the 5th grade of the Ohm-Gymnasium (subset OHM), '1' denotes the children from the 6th and 7th grade that are additionally contained in OHMPLUS, and '2' denotes the 5th or 6th grade of the Montessori-Schule. Additionally, recordings of the same children playing with the Aibo pet robot [Bat04a] and reading German sentences [Rus03, Mai06b] were performed. These databases are denoted as "Aibo" and "Ohm8000" (also "extended fluency corpus") and are not investigated in this thesis. The tables, however, show a mapping between NONNATIVE, "Aibo", and "Ohm8000" which might be useful for future research, e.g. a comparison of spontaneous and read children speech.

The format of the audio files of the NONNATIVE data is {SPKR}{TEXT}.{TURN}, where SPKR is the speaker ID as described above, TEXT a text ID with the initial letter 'T' and TURN the turn number starting for each text with '000'.

ID	ID$_{\mathrm{Aibo}}$	ID$_{\mathrm{Ohm8000}}$	gender	age	annotations % $\mathcal{X}$ rater S	speaker rater S
w201	Mont_01	w201	f	11^-	24	4
w202	Mont_02	w202	f	10	22	4
w203	Mont_03	w203	f	11	10	3
m204	Mont_04	m204	m	10	20	5
w205	Mont_05	w205	f	11	19	3
w206	Mont_06	w206	f	11^-	26	4
w207	Mont_07	w207	f	11^+	4	2
w208	Mont_08	w208	f	11	17	3.5
w209	Mont_09	w209	f	11	16	3
m210	Mont_10	m210	m	12^-	10	2
m211	Mont_11	m211	m	12	14	4
w212	Mont_12	w212	f	12^-	15	3
w213	Mont_13	w213	f	12	9	3
w214	Mont_14	w214	f	12	12	4
w215	Mont_15	w215	f	11^+	14	4
w216	Mont_16	w216	f	12	12	3
m217	Mont_17	m217	m	11	11	3
m218	Mont_18	m218	m	11	12	3.5
m219	Mont_19	m219	m	11^+	21	5
m220	Mont_20	m220	m	12	15	4
m221	Mont_21	m221	m	12^-	9	2
w222	Mont_22	w222	f	12^-	7	3
w223	Mont_23	w223	f	13^-	11	3
w224	Mont_24	w224	f	12	16	3
w225	Mont_25	w225	f	12^-	4	2

Table A.1: MONT Data: German children reading English sentences: ID, gender and age. $-/+$ denotes birthday within two months before/after the recoding. ID$_{\mathrm{Aibo}}$: for the respective speaker, also German spontaneous, emotional speech data is available [Bat05a, Bat04a, Rus03]. ID$_{\mathrm{Ohm8000}}$: for the respective speaker, also German read speech data is available [Bat05a, Rus03]. The last two columns show the percentage of words marked by rater S, and the speaker rating.

ID	ID$_{Aibo}$	ID$_{Ohm8000}$	gender	age	annotations		
					% $\mathcal{X}$	text	speaker
					av. rater	av. rater	rater S
w001	Ohm_01	w001	f	10	5.5	2.2	3
m002	Ohm_02	m002	m	10$^+$	4.6	1.8	2
w003	Ohm_03	w003	f	10	5.5	3.0	3
w004	Ohm_03	w004	f	11	8.7	3.3	5
m005	Ohm_05	m005	m	11	6.1	2.0	2
w006	Ohm_06	w006	f	11$^-$	1.5	1.3	2
m007	Ohm_07	m007	m	11$^-$	7.9	3.4	3
m008	Ohm_08	m008	m	10	3.4	2.1	2
m009		m009	m	11	5.0	2.8	3
w010	Ohm_10	w010	f	11	8.8	3.5	4
m011	Ohm_11	m011	m	11	9.1	3.3	2.5
m013	Ohm_13	m013	m	10	5.3	2.5	3
w014	Ohm_14	w014	f	11	1.9	1.6	1
w016	Ohm_16	w016	f	11	8.2	3.0	4
w018	Ohm_18	w018	f	11	4.3	1.9	2
m019	Ohm_19	m019	m	10	9.3	2.8	4
w020	Ohm_20	w020	f	10$^+$	6.7	2.7	2
m021	Ohm_21	m021	m	11	3.7	2.3	3
w022	Ohm_22	w022	f	11$^-$	4.6	2.9	3
m023	Ohm_23	m023	m	10$^+$	1.6	1.5	2
w024	Ohm_24	w024	f	10	7.1	2.6	3
m025	Ohm_25	m025	m	10	3.1	2.2	2
m027	Ohm_27	m027	m	10	2.9	2.0	2
w028	Ohm_28	w028	f	10	3.4	2.1	2
m029	Ohm_29	m029	m	11$^-$	7.1	2.9	3
m030		m030	m	11	4.5	2.4	2
m031	Ohm_31	m031	m	11	3.2	1.9	1
w032	Ohm_32	m032	f	10	3.0	1.9	3
m101			m	13$^-$	4.1	2.3	1
m102			m	12$^+$	9.0	3.2	2
m103			m	12$^+$	8.2	3.7	3
w104			f	14	8.2	3.2	3

Table A.2: OHMPLUS Data: German children reading English sentences. ID, gender and age. $-/+$ denotes birthday within two months before/after the recoding. ID$_{Aibo}$: for the respective speaker, also German spontaneous, emotional speech data is available [Bat05a, Bat04a, Rus03]. ID$_{Ohm8000}$: for the respective speaker, also German read speech data is available [Bat05a, Rus03]. The three last columns show the percentage of words marked on average by the 13 experts, the average text level rating from 13 experts, and the speaker rating from rater S.

A.2   Annotations of the Corpus

All annotations of the NONNATIVE corpus are described in Sect. 4.1.2. Word level-annotations of mispronounced words are found in Tab. 4.2. Labelling of syntactical boundaries are summarised in Tab. 4.3.

On the sentence level, S labelled with marks 1 (best) – 5 (worst), cf. Tab. 4.4. Text level annotations of 13 teachers can be found in Tab. 4.5 for the OHMPLUS subset of the data. The ratings of 5 experts who graded the data again half a year later are shown in Tab. A.3. Text level ratings for the OHM-subset are summarised in Tab. A.4. Speaker level gradings are available from S. The corresponding expert ratings T_1 – T_{12}, and N are calculated automatically by averaging the text level ratings of each speaker. All speaker level ratings can be found in Tab. A.5.

expert	1	$1 + x$	2	$2 + x$	3	$3 + x$	4	$4 + x$	5	μ
first pass:										
T_2	11	18	22	21	30	11	8	0	2	2.5
T_3	27	0	40	0	42	0	12	0	2	2.4
T_4	25	14	27	20	23	5	8	1	0	2.2
T_6	10	28	30	28	10	8	7	2	0	2.2
T_8	7	0	25	0	66	0	22	0	3	2.9
second pass:										
T_2	11	34	23	18	19	10	5	1	2	2.2
T_3	34	16	37	10	17	1	5	3	0	2.0
T_4	26	34	25	10	15	10	3	0	0	1.9
T_6	6	62	16	32	5	1	1	0	0	1.8
T_8	3	0	23	0	68	2	22	0	5	3.0

Table A.3: Text level annotation: marks 1 (best) to 5 (worst) for OHMPLUS from 5 experts who rated the data again in a second pass half a year later, $x \in \{0.3, 0.5, 0.7\}$. All other text level ratings can be found in Tab. 4.5.

expert	1	$1 + x$	2	$2 + x$	3	$3 + x$	4	$4 + x$	5	μ
first pass:										
T_1	12	0	35	0	41	1	8	0	0	2.5
T_2	11	16	19	19	22	9	1	0	0	2.3
T_3	26	0	37	0	28	0	6	0	0	2.1
T_4	22	12	21	18	15	3	5	1	0	2.1
T_5	5	0	20	0	35	0	31	0	6	3.1
T_6	10	23	27	21	8	3	5	0	0	2.1
T_7	0	5	13	24	27	13	11	2	2	2.9
T_8	7	0	21	0	56	0	13	0	0	2.8
T_9	11	0	41	0	39	0	6	0	0	2.4
T_{10}	9	10	30	19	15	8	4	2	0	2.3
T_{11}	14	0	43	8	20	3	9	0	0	2.3
T_{12}	25	1	36	5	28	0	2	0	0	2.1
N	11	35	15	11	15	8	1	1	0	2.0
second pass:										
T_2	11	32	17	13	15	7	2	0	0	2.0
T_3	31	14	29	9	11	1	2	0	0	1.8
T_4	24	32	16	7	11	6	1	0	0	1.8
T_6	6	57	9	22	2	1	0	0	0	1.7
T_8	3	0	23	0	56	1	13	0	1	2.9

Table A.4: Text level annotation: marks 1 (best) to 5 (worst) for the OHM subset from 13 experts, $x \in \{0.3, 0.5, 0.7\}$. 5 experts rated the data again in a second pass half a year later.

corpus	expert	1	2	3	4	5	μ
Mont	S	0	4	10	9	2	3.4
Ohm	S	2	11	11	3	1	2.6
OhmPlus	S	3	12	13	3	1	2.6
OhmPlus	T_1	0	13	15	4	0	2.6
OhmPlus	T_2	5	13	13	1	0	2.4
OhmPlus	T_3	5	13	13	3	0	2.3
OhmPlus	T_4	6	14	11	1	0	2.2
OhmPlus	T_5	1	4	12	12	3	3.3
OhmPlus	T_6	6	17	7	2	0	2.2
OhmPlus	T_7	0	6	18	7	1	3.1
OhmPlus	T_8	1	5	21	5	0	2.9
OhmPlus	T_9	1	12	18	1	0	2.6
OhmPlus	T_{10}	1	18	9	4	0	2.5
OhmPlus	T_{11}	1	14	12	5	0	2.7
OhmPlus	T_{12}	6	14	10	2	0	2.3
OhmPlus	N	12	10	9	1	0	2.0
second pass:							
OhmPlus	T_2	6	14	11	1	0	2.2
OhmPlus	T_3	11	12	8	1	0	2.0
OhmPlus	T_4	10	14	7	1	0	2.0
OhmPlus	T_6	10	17	5	0	0	1.8
OhmPlus	T_8	0	6	19	7	0	3.0

Table A.5: Speaker level annotation: marks 1 (best) to 5 (worst) from 14 experts after rounding. 5 experts rated the data again in a second pass half a year later. Average rating μ has been calculated without previous rounding.

A.3 Agreement of the Ratings

The agreement of the 13 experts on the word level, text level, and the speaker level is analysed in Chap. 6. For the word level and the text level, detailed values are given per expert for various agreement measures. These detailed numbers on the speaker level are shown in the following tables.

	S	T_1	T_2	T_3	T_4	T_5	T_6	T_7	T_8	T_9	T_{10}	T_{11}	T_{12}	N	μ
ρ	*0.54*	**0.73**	0.69	**0.77**	0.70	0.67	0.66	**0.73**	0.62	*0.53*	**0.72**	0.61	0.70	0.62	0.66
$1-\delta$	74.7	**81.6**	**80.6**	**80.8**	78.5	*67.2*	77.2	74.9	76.9	78.5	**80.7**	79.4	78.8	*73.8*	77.40

Table A.6: Pair-wise agreement of the experts on the speaker level and average μ per line (OHMPLUS data): mean correlation ρ and deviation δ. Maxima are shown in bold, minima in italics.

	S	T_1	T_2	T_3	T_4	T_5	T_6	T_7	T_8	T_9	T_{10}	T_{11}	T_{12}	N	μ
ρ	*0.64*	**0.89**	0.84	**0.94**	0.85	0.80	0.80	**0.88**	0.75	*0.63*	**0.87**	0.72	0.84	0.75	0.80
$1-\delta$	79.5	**90.6**	88.0	87.4	83.5	*67.7*	81.8	*77.8*	80.8	84.2	**87.9**	86.3	83.6	*76.9*	82.6
$1-\delta_{\text{rnk}}$	*75.7*	**85.1**	82.2	**90.6**	85.8	82.3	82.3	**85.5**	78.6	*73.5*	**85.4**	79.7	83.4	*76.2*	81.9

Table A.7: Agreement of the experts on the speaker level and average μ per line (OHMPLUS data): open-correlation ρ and open-deviation δ. Maxima are shown in bold, minima in italics.

	S	T_1	T_2	T_3	T_4	T_5	T_6	T_7	T_8	T_9	T_{10}	T_{11}	T_{12}	N	μ
CL-3	81.2	78.1	**87.5**	**93.8**	81.2	*59.4*	71.9	*65.6*	*68.8*	71.9	84.4	**90.6**	**87.5**	81.2	78.8
CL-10$_{\text{rnk}}^{\pm 2}$	*69.2*	**87.5**	80.8	**96.7**	**88.3**	76.7	84.2	85.0	*75.0*	*75.0*	**94.2**	80.8	85.8	81.7	82.9

Table A.8: Agreement of the experts on the speaker level and average μ per line: classification rate CL-3, CL-5, and CL-10$_{\text{rnk}}^{\pm 2}$. Maxima are shown in bold, minima in italics.

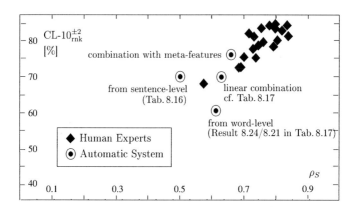

Figure A.1: Text level results on the OHM data. Comparison of human experts and the automatic system. The best result is obtained after combining sentence and word level results using meta-features as presented in Tab. 8.18. Here, the sentence level results are based on the results from Tab. 8.16, where the distance from the BIRMINGHAM data is used as pronunciation score.

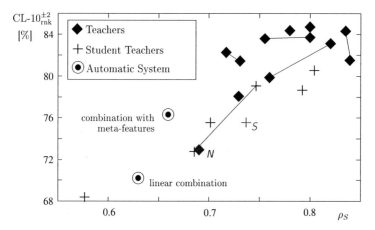

Figure A.2: Text level results on the OHM data. Magnified evaluation space from Tab. A.1. The lines connect the first and second rating of some human experts.

Appendix B

The Phonetic Inventory

B.1 The Phonetic Alphabet SAMPA

In the following table an overview of English and German phones is given. All phonetic transcription is in SAMPA, for comparison also the TIMIT notation, that is well known in the speech recognition community, is shown (only defined for American English). All information is from [Sampa] and [Hie93] as well as from the Beep dictionary [Beep] for British English and the CMU Pronunciation Dictionary [CmuDict] for American English. Related phones in both languages are compared in [Bon00b].

The first column of the table shows the SAMPA notation, the second the TIMIT notation used in the CMU Pronunciation Dictionary [CmuDict]. The third column indicates which phones are used for acoustic modelling of the speech recognisers used in this thesis. Here, for each phone either the phonetic category (cf. Sect. 3.2, Isadora) is given or a mapping to a different similar phone. The broad categories are P+ (plosives), F+ (fricatives), N+ (nasals and liquids), and V+ (vowels and diphthongs). The + discriminates e.g. the category V+ from the vowel /V/. In the 4th and the 5th row it is shown whether the respective phone exists in American (AE) and British English (BE). The last two columns give examples for English (British, if the respective phone is defined in BE) and German.

SAM.	TIM.	cat.	BE	AE	English		German	
Plosives								
/p/	p	P+	√	√	pin	/pIn/	Pein	/paIn/
/b/	b	P+	√	√	bin	/bIn/	Bein	/baIn/
/t/	t	P+	√	√	tin	/tIn/	Teich	/taIC/

continued on next page

SAM.	TIM.	cat.	BE	AE	English		German	
/d/	d	P+	√	√	din	/dIn/	Deich	/daIC/
/k/	k	P+	√	√	kin	/kIn/	Kunst	/kUnst/
/g/	g	P+	√	√	give	/gIv/	Gunst	/gUnst/
Affricates								
/pf/	-	F+					Pfahl	/pfa:l/
/ts/	-	F+					Zahl	/tsa:l/
/tS/	ch	F+	√	√	chin	/tSIn/	deutsch	/dOItS/
/dZ/	jh	F+	√	√	gin	/dZIn/	Dschungel	/dZUNl/
Fricatives								
/f/	f	F+	√	√	fin	/fIn/	fast	/fast/
/v/	v	F+	√	√	vim	/vIm/	was	/vas/
/s/	s	F+	√	√	sin	/sIn/	Tasse	/tas@/
/z/	z	F+	√	√	zing	/zIN/	Hase	/ha:z@/
/S/	sh	F+	√	√	shin	/SIn/	sein	/SaIn/
/Z/	zh	F+	√	√	measure	/meZ@/	Genie	/Zeni:/
/h/	hh	F+	√	√	hit	/hIt/	Hand	/hant/
/T/	th	F+	√	√	thin	/TIn/		
/D/	dh	F+	√	√	this	/DIs/		
/C/	-	F+					sicher	/zIC6/
/x/	-	F+					Buch	/bu:x/
Nasals								
/m/	m	N+	√	√	mock	/mQk/	mein	/maIn/
/n/	n	N+	√	√	knock	/nQk/	nein	/naIn/
/N/	ng	N+	√	√	thing	/TIN/	Ding	/dIN/
Liquids								
/l/[1]	l	N+	√	√	long	/lQN/	Leim	/laIm/
/r/	r	N+	√	√	wrong	/rQN/		
/R/[2]	-	N+					Reim	/RaIm/
Semi-vowels								
/j/	y	F+	√	√	yacht	/jQt/	ja	/ja:/
/w/	w	F+	√	√	wasp	/wQsp/		
Schwa								
/@/[3]	ax	V+	√		another	/@nVD@/	bitte	/bIt@/

continued on next page

---

[1] There are different [l] in English: clear and dark [l]. The latter is unknown in the German language, in British English used before consonants and in American in principle.

[2] Since all recordings took place in southern Germay, the alveolar [r] is pronounced and not the velar [R] (northern Germany) nor the retroflex English variant of [r]; however, to discriminate the phoneme /r/ from the English phoneme in "wrong", we rename it to /R/.

[3] No Schwa is used in the CMU Pronunciation Dictionary [CmuDict]: "corner" ends with TIMIT "er", "appraisal" begins with TIMIT "ah"

SAM.	TIM.	cat.	BE	AE	English		German	
/@'/[4]	ax	V+		√	corner	/kOrn@'/		
/6/	-	V+					besser	/bEs6/
Checked Vowels[5]								
/a/	-	V+					Satz	/zats/
/V/	ah	V+	√	√	cut	/kVt/		
/{/[6]	ae	V+	√	√	pat	/p{t/		
/E/	eh	V+		√	pet[7]	/pEt/	Gesetz	/g@zEts/
/e/	eh	V+	√		pet	/pet/		
/I/	ih	V+	√	√	pit	/pIt/	Sitz	/zIts/
/Q/	_[8]	V+	√		pot	/pQt/		
/A/[9]	aa	V+		√	pot	/pAt /		
/O/	-	V+					Trotz	/trOts/
/U/	uh	V+	√	√	put	/pUt/	Schutz	/SUts/
/9/[10]	-	V+					Hölle	/h91@/
/Y/	-	V+					hübsch	/hYpS/
Free Vowels (incl. Diphthongs)								
/i/[11]	-	→ /i:/	√		happy	/h{pi/		
/o/	-	→ /o:/					o.k.	/oke:/
/u/[12]	-	→ /u:/	√		into	/Intu/		
/A:/	aa	V+	√		stars	/stA:z/[13]		
/a:/	-	V+					Tat	/ta:t/
/E:/	-	V+					spät	/SpE:t/
/e:/	-	V+					Beet	/be:t/
/i:/	iy	V+	√	√	ease	/i:z/	Lied	/li:t/
/O:/[14]	ao	V+	√	√	caused	/kO:zd/		

continued on next page

---

[4] [@'] can be analyzed as [@r] [Sampa]. In [CmuDict] TIMIT "er" is used instead. It corresponds to /3'/.

[5] Must be followed by a consonant

[6] Some Americans distinguish between "jazz" and "has". They use [E@] vs. [e@] instead of [{] [Sampa]. In [Del00] /{/ is grouped with other free monophthongs as long vowels.

[7] [E] instead of [e] is also widely spread in Britain [Sampa]

[8] "oh" is used in [Beep]

[9] Americans pronounce "stars" with [stArz] instead of BE [stA:z] [CmuDict]. Many Americans (and most Canadians) further do not distinguish between /A/ and /O:/ [Sampa]

[10] Some sites use /8/

[11] /i:/ varies in unstressed syllables between [i] and [I] [Sampa]. [Beep] and [CmuDict] use /i:/ instead of /i/

[12] /u:/ varies in unstressed syllables between [u] and [U] [Sampa]. [Beep] and [CmuDict] use /u:/ instead of /u/

[13] AE: [stArz] [CmuDict]

[14] Many Americans (and most Canadians) do not distinguish between /O:/ and /A/. "cause" is pronounced as [kAz]. However, before /r/ it is recommended to write /O:/(/kO:rn@'/) [Sampa]

SAM.	TIM.	cat.	BE	AE	English		German	
/o:/	-	V+					rot	/ro:t/
/}/[15]	-	→ /u:/	√		suit	/s}t/		
/u:/	uw	V+	√	√	lose	/lu:z/	Blut	/blu:t/
/2:/[16]	-	V+					Höhle	/h2:l@/
/y:/	-	V+					süß	/zy:s/
/3r/	er	V+	√		furs	/f3rz/		
/3'/[17]	er	→ /3r/		√	furs	/f3'z/		
/@U/	ow	V+	√		nose	/n@Uz/		
/oU/[18]	ow	V+		√	nose	/noUz/		
/aI/	ay	V+	√	√	rise	/raIz/	Eis	/aIs/
/aU/	aw	V+	√	√	rouse	/raUz/	Haus	/haUs/
/eI/	ey	V+	√	√	raise	/reIz/		
/OI/	oy	V+	√	√	noise	/nOIz/		
/OY/[19]	-	V+					Kreuz	/krOYts/
/I@/	-[20]	V+	√		fears	/fI@z/[21]		
/e@/	-[22]	V+	√		stairs	/ste@z/[23]		
/U@/	-[24]	V+	√		cures	/kjU@z/[25]		
/i:6/	-	V+					Tier	/ti:6/
/I6/	-	V+					Wirt	/vI6t/
/y:6/	-	V+					Tür	/ty:6/
/Y6/	-	V+					Türke	/tY6k@/
/e:6/	-	V+					schwer	/Sve:6/
/E6/	-	V+					Berg	/bE6k/
/E:6/	-	V+					Bär	/bE:6/
/2:6/	-	V+					Föhr	/f2:6/
/96/	-	V+					Wörter	/v96t6/
/a:6/	-	V+					Haar	/ha:6/
/a6/	-	V+					hart	/ha6t/
/u:6/	-	V+					Kur	/ku:6/

continued on next page

---

[15][Beep] uses /u:/ instead of /}/
[16]Some sites use /7:/
[17][3'] can be analysed as [@r] [Sampa]. /3'/ is transcribed instead of [@'] in [CmuDict]

[18]/@U/ and /oU/ are only notational variants and not denoting differences in phonetic substance
[19]/OI/ and /OY/ are only notational variants and not denoting differences in phonetic substance

[20]"ia" is used in [Beep]
[21]AE: /fIrz/ [CmuDict]
[22]"ea" is used in [Beep]
[23]AE: /stErz/ [CmuDict]
[24]"ua" is used in [Beep]
[25]AE: /kjUrz/ [CmuDict]

SAM.	TIM.	cat.	BE	AE	English		German	
/U6/	-	V+					kurz	/kU6ts/
/o:6/	-	V+					Ohr	/o:6/
/O6/	-	V+					dort	/dO6t/
Glottal stop								
/?/	q	-[26]	√	√	network	/ne?w3:k/	Verein	/fE6?aIn/[27]

Table B.1: SAMPA (SAM.) for British English (BE), American English (AE) and German with examples. Additional TIMIT (TIM.) symbols for AE. The third row shows either mappings to other phonetic symbols or phonetic categories (cat.).

B.2 Sub-Phonemic Units

Here the subphonemic labels for BE, AE and German phonemes that are used in the ISADORA system are described. Each HMM consists of 1–4 states, each state corresponds to a sub-phonemic label. "S" denotes sequential states, "A" atomic states, details in [Sch95, pp. 281]

```
S: /3r/  [3] [3] [3] ;
S: /A:/  [A] [A] [A] ;
S: /D/   [D] [D] [D] ;
S: /I/   [I] [I] [I] ;
S: /N/   [N] [N] [N] ;
S: /O:/  [O] [O] [O] ;
S: /OI/  [O] [O] [O] [I] ;
S: /S/   [S] [S] [S] ;
S: /T/   [T] [T] [T] ;
S: /U/   [U] [U] [U] ;
S: /V/   [V] [V] [V] ;
S: /Z/   [Z] [Z] [Z] ;
S: /aI/  [a] [a] [a] [I] ;
S: /aU/  [a] [a] [a] [U] ;
S: /b/   [B] [b] [b] ;
S: /d/   [O] [d] [d] ;
S: /dZ/  [O] [d] [Z] ;
S: /eI/  [e] [e] [e] [I] ;
S: /f/   [f] [f] [f] ;
S: /g/   [G] [g] [g] ;
```

---

[26]not used in any transcriptions in the present thesis

[27]In German /?/ occurs usually in the beginning of words, that start with a vowel: [?a:b6] ("aber")

```
S: /h/   [h] [h] [h] ;
S: /i:/  [i] [i] [i] ;
S: /j/   [j] [j] [j] ;
S: /k/   [K] [k] [4] ;
S: /l/   [l] [l] [l] ;
S: /m/   [m] [m] [m] ;
S: /n/   [n] [n] [n] ;
S: /p/   [P] [p] [5] ;
S: /r/   [r] [r] [r] ;
S: /s/   [s] [s] [s] ;
S: /t/   [+] [t] [1] ;
S: /tS/  [+] [t] [S] ;
S: /u:/  [u] [u] [u] ;
S: /v/   [v] [v] [v] ;
S: /w/   [w] [w] [w] ;
S: /z/   [z] [z] [z] ;
S: /{/   [{] [{] [{] ;
```

Only for British English:
```
S: /@/   [@] [@] ;
S: /@U/  [@] [U] [U] [U] ;
S: /I@/  [I] [I] [I] [@] ;
S: /Q/   [Q] [Q] [Q] ;
S: /U@/  [U] [U] [U] [@] ;
S: /e/   [e] [e] [e] ;
S: /e@/  [e] [e] [e] [@] ;
```

Only for American English:
```
S: /E/   [E] [E] [E] ;
S: /oU/  [o] [U] [U] [U] ;
S: /A/   [q] [q] [q] ;[28]
```

Silence, non-verbal noise, and breathing:
```
S: /-/   [-] ;
S: /#/   [W] [W] [W] [W] ;
S: /NV/  [X] ;
S: /ATM/ [H] ;
```

Additional phones required to model German speech:
```
S: /pf/  [P] [p] [f] ;
S: /ts/  [+] [t] [s] ;
```

---

[28] only if /A:/ and /A/ are discriminated, otherwise [A]

```
S: /C/  [C] [C] [C] ;
S: /x/  [x] [x] [x] ;
S: /R/  [R] [R] [R] ;
S: /6/  [6] [6] ;
S: /a/  [a] [a] [a] ;
S: /a:/ [a] [a] [a] ;
S: /9/  [9] [9] [9] ;
S: /Y/  [Y] [Y] [Y] ;
S: /E:/ [E] [E] [E] ;
S: /e:/ [e] [e] [e] ;
S: /o:/ [o] [o] [o] ;
S: /O/  [O] [O] [O] ;
S: /2:/ [2] [2] [2] ;
S: /y:/ [y] [y] [y] ;
S: /u:/^29 [u] [u] [u] ;
S: /OY/ [O] [O] [O] [Y] ;
S: /i6/ [i] [i] [i] [6] ;
S: /I6/ [I] [I] [I] [6] ;
S: /y6/ [y] [y] [y] [6] ;
S: /Y6/ [Y] [Y] [Y] [6] ;
S: /e6/ [e] [e] [e] [6] ;
S: /E6/ [E] [E] [E] [6] ;
S: /26/ [2] [2] [2] [6] ;
S: /96/ [9] [9] [9] [6] ;
S: /a6/ [a] [a] [a] [6] ;
S: /u6/ [u] [u] [u] [6] ;
S: /U6/ [U] [U] [U] [6] ;
S: /o6/ [o] [o] [o] [6] ;
S: /O6/ [O] [O] [O] [6] ;
```

---

[29]/u:/$_{German}$ is in this thesis denoted as /U:/

Appendix C

Systems for Pronunciation Training

From the website of the Bavarian Ministry of Education[1] the Bavarian School-Server[2] can be addressed. Here, information on available software that is appropriate to be used in class can be found[3]. In the following an overview of this software is given together with other systems discussed in Chap. 2.3

1. American Slang
   United Soft Media, Munich
   `http://www.usm.de`

2. ARTUR: ARTiculation TUtoR
   Center of Technology, KTH, Stockholm [Bes04, Gra05]
   cf. Chap. 2.3

3. Autograder[TM]
   SRI international[Neu96, Kim97, Neu98, Fra99, Neu00, Fra00, Tei00]
   `http://www.speech.sri.com/projects/language_instruction.html`
   cf. Chap. 2.3

4. AzAR: Automat zur Akzent Reduktion
   `http://www.ias.et.tu-dresden.de/institut/jb2005.pdf`
   TU Dresden, voice INTER connect GmbH `http://voiceinterconnect.de`
   cf. Chap. 2.3

5. Caller: Computer Assisted Language Learning from Erlangen)
   Chair of Pattern Recognition, University of Erlangen-Nuremberg
   cf. Chap. 2.4

6. C-AuDiT: "computerunterstütztes Aussprache- und Dialogtraining"
   digital publishing, University of Erlangen-Nuremberg, BMBF

---

[1] `http://www.km.bayern.de`
[2] Bayerischer Schulserver, `http://www.schule.bayern.de/`
[3] `http://www.schule.bayern.de/unterricht/schulfaecher/Englisch/software_englisch.htm`

`http://www.c-audit.org/`
cf. Chap. 10

7. Colorado Literacy Tutor
   Center for spoken Language Research, Colorado
   `http://www.colit.org/`
   cf. Chap. 2.3

8. Der grosse Kurs für Anfänger Englisch
   Pons
   speech analysis by acapela
   `http://www.pons.de/`

9. Easy Language
   IMSI
   `http://www.imsisoft.com/`

10. EduSpeak®
    SPEECH@SRI
    `http://www.speechatsri.com/products/eduspeak.shtml`
    cf. Chap. 2.3

11. English Coach 2000
    Cornelsen
    `http://www.cornelsen.de`

12. English One & Two
    United Soft Media, Munich
    `http://www.usm.de`

13. Englisch voll easy!
    Pons
    `http://www.pons.de/`

14. Fluency
    Carnegie Mellon University [Esk98, Esk00]
    cf. Chap. 2.3

15. Grips!
    Augustus-Verlag

16. ISLE: Interactive Spoken Language Education
    Universities of Leeds, Milan, and Hamburg, Didael, Ernst Klett Verlag, Entropic
    `http://nats-www.informatik.uni-hamburg.de/~isle/`
    cf. Chap. 2.3

17. Interaktive Sprachreise Englisch
    digital publishing, Munich
    http://www.digitalpublishing.de/english/
    cf. Chap. 2.3

18. learn2speak
    http://learn2speak.eu
    online platform

19. Learn to Speak™
    MenusSoft®, Toledo, OH
    http://www.menussoft.com/

20. Lernvitamine Englisch
    Cornelsen, digital publishing
    http://www.lernvitamine.de/cgi/WebObjects/Lernvitamine
    cf. Chap. 2.3

21. Listen (Reading tutor)
    Carnegie Mellon University [Ban03]
    http://www.cs.cmu.edu/~listen/ cf. Chap. 2.3

22. Mango
    http://www.trymango.com/
    free online platform

23. Multilingua Movie Talk
    Systhema Verlag GmbH

24. NativeAccent™
    Carnegie Speech
    http://www.carnegiespeech.com/speech_products.html
    cf. Chap. 2.3

25. OpenVOC
    TU Dresden [Hof05]
    cf. Chap. 2.3

26. Parling (CALL system for children)
    ITC-irst, Trento [Mic04]
    cf. Chap. 2.3

27. Perfekt!
    Cornelsen

28. PhonePass (Automated English test on the telephone [Ber04])
    Ordinate, Versant^{TM}
    http://www.versanttest.de/
    cf. Chap. 2.3

29. Professional English
    Technik und Medien GmbH, Berlin
    http://www.tm-online.de

30. SLIM project
    http://project.cgm.unive.it/slimpage/slim
    University of Venice 1992 - 1996[Del00]
    cf. Chap. 2.3

31. STAR project
    DRA Malvern 1990 [Rus00]
    cf. Chap. 2.3

32. Talk to Me
    Auralog, Cornelsen
    speech analysis by Nuance
    http://www.abitz.com/cornelsen/tellmemore_englisch.php3
    cf. Chap. 2.3

33. Tell Me More
    Auralog, Cornelsen
    http://www.abitz.com/cornelsen/tellmemore_englisch.php3
    cf. Chap. 2.3, review in [Ner03]

34. The Multimedia English Course
    Hueber, Ismaning; YDP Multimedia
    http://www.hueber.de

35. TripplePlayPlus
    Syracuse Language Systems
    review in [Ner03]

36. VILTS^{TM}
    SRI international[Neu96, Kim97, Neu98, Fra99, Neu00, Fra00, Tei00]
    http://www.speech.sri.com/projects/language_instruction.html
    cf. Chap. 2.3

37. Vokabel- & Wortschatztrainer
    Langenscheidt
    speech analysis by LingCom
    http://www.langenscheidt.de

38. WriteToLearn^{TM}
Center for spoken Language Research, Colorado
Pearson Knowledge Technologies `http://www.pearsonkt.com/`
cf. Chap. 2.3

Appendix D

Variables and Symbols

D.1 Indices and Frequently Used Numbers

c	index for classes
i	index
j	index
k	index for classes
l	index
m	index for densities
n	index, number
r	index for raters
υ	index of samples
τ	discrete point of time

B	size of filter bank
d	dimension of the feature vector
K	# of classes
t	total # of discrete time intervals
L	length of words sequence
M	# of Gaussian mixtures
Q	# phonemes
R	# of raters
N	number

D.2 General Variables and Symbols

$\mathcal{B}$	class label for all native British pronounced words
$\mathcal{D}$	distribution
$\mathcal{N}$	normal distribution

$\mathcal{O}$	class label for correct pronunciation
$\mathcal{X}$	class label for wrong pronunciation
$\boldsymbol{c}, \boldsymbol{c}^{\tau}, \boldsymbol{c}^{\upsilon}$	feature vector (at time τ; number υ)
$\mathrm{cov}(X_i, X_j)$	covariance
$\dim(.)$	dimension of a vector
$E(X)$	expectation of random variable X
$\boldsymbol{f}$	speech signal, input pattern or function
f_{τ}	sample of the speech signal
F_0	fundamental frequency
F_i	i-th formant
$P(.)$	probability or discrete probability distribution
$p(.)$	probability density function
q	phoneme
q_i^{a}	reference phoneme, position i in forced alignment
q_i^{r}	recognised phoneme, position i in recognition result
q_{τ}	observed phoneme in frame τ
q^i	phoneme i out of Q phonemes
$\boldsymbol{w}$	sentence, list of words w_i
$\boldsymbol{q}$	sentence, list of words q_i
$\boldsymbol{x}, \boldsymbol{x}^{(r)}$	vector of annotations (of rater r)
$x_i^{(r)}$	annotation of rater r: value for sample i
$\bar{x}_i$	average annotation of sample i from many raters
x_i^{rnk}	annotation of sample i after conversion to ranks
X_i	random variable
ϑ	threshold
$\boldsymbol{\lambda}$	HMM
$\boldsymbol{\lambda}_0$	HMM, silence model
$\boldsymbol{\mu}, \boldsymbol{\mu}_m$	mean vector (density m)
μ	mean (e.g. of CL over all cross-validation iterations)
σ	standard deviation
$\boldsymbol{\Sigma}, \boldsymbol{\Sigma}_m$	covariance matrix (density m)
$\chi_c(.)$	characteristic function

D.3 Pronunciation Scoring

Evaluation measures. The following variables and functions are used for the evaluation of ratings as defined in Chap. 2 and applied in Chap. 6 and for the evaluation of automatic pronunciation scoring (Chap 8):

CL-$K_{\mathrm{rnk}}^{\pm\vartheta}$	class-wise averaged classification rate (K classes): after conversion to ranks. A confusion of neighbouring classes $\pm\vartheta$ are tolerated
CL-2	class-wise averaged classification rate (2 classes $\mathcal{O}, \mathcal{X}$)

CL-3	class-wise averaged classification rate (3 marks)
CL-5	class-wise averaged classification rate (5 marks)
err	error-measure between ratings
rel_r	reliability of rater r
$\text{cov}(X_i, X_j)$	covariance
$\text{dist}(c, k)$	distance measure between two ordinal class labels c and k
$k_{\max}$	maximum of class labels (ordinal or interval data)
$k_{\min}$	minimum of class labels (ordinal or interval data)
$\mathcal{M}$	set of marks, e. g. school grades $\{x \in \mathbb{R} \mid 1 \leq x \leq 6\}$
$\boldsymbol{x}^{(r)}$	sequence of ratings from rater r
σ_r	standard deviation of annotations by rater r
$_{\text{testlet}}\sigma_r^j$	standard deviation of rater r in testlet j
$_{\text{test}}\sigma_r$	standard deviation of rater r in a test $\boldsymbol{x}_{\text{test}}^{(r)}$ that consists of several testlets
α	Cronbach α, reliability
α_{krip}	Krippendorff α, reliability
δ_{nrm}	error-measure between ratings
δ	error-measure between ratings (after normalisation of raters)
δ_{rnk}	error-measure between ratings (after conversion to ranks)
κ	inter-rater reliability
κ_{rnk}	inter-rater reliability (after conversion to ranks)
ρ	Pearson correlation
ρ_{S}	Spearman's rank correlation
ρ_{SB}	correlation after Spearman-Brown
ρ_{Witt}	correlation after Witt et al. [Wit00]
ρ_{cor}	correlation using Spearman's correction for attenuation
$\omega_{c,k}$	weighting of the confusion of classes c and k

Pronunciation scores (literature). The following pronunciation scores and features are described in Chap. 2:

S_i	pronunciation score, pronunciation feature
S_{GOP1}	goodness of pronunciation (GOP)
S_{GOP2}	GOP, penalises common errors
S_{GOP3}	GOP, different models for correctly and wrongly pronounced words
S_{Dur1}	total duration of speech plus pauses
S_{Dur2}	a-priori probability of observed duration
S_{ROS1}	number of speech segments per duration
S_{ROS2}	number of speech segments per duration without pauses

S_{LR}	likelihood ratio
S_{PTR}	phonation-time-ratio
$S_{\text{LikeliGlob}}$	global log-likelihood
$S_{\text{LikeliLoc}}$	local log-likelihood
$S_{\text{LikeliNorm}}$	normalised log-likelihood
$S_{\text{Posterior}}$	log-posterior score
S_{Acc}	phone-accuracy
S_{Acc2}	syllable-accuracy
S_{SylTime}	timing between syllables
S_{CDiff}	difference of confidence values
S_{CNorm}	normalised difference of confidence values

Symbols in Chap. 2. The following variables and symbols are additionally used in Chap. 2:

D	difference between highest and lowest mark
d_i	duration of segment i
$\bar{d}_i$	duration of segment i, normalised by ROS
e_i	rule for mispronunciation error i
n_c	# elements in class c
$n_c^{(r)}$	# items rated with c by rater r
$n_{c,k}$	# of double ratings with c and k over all pairs of raters
$n_{c,k}^{(r,l)}$	# items rated with c by rater r and k by rater k
N_{testlet}	# of testlets
P_{o}	observed agreement
P_{c}	agreement by chance
$\bar{P}_{\text{o}}$	observed disagreement
$\bar{P}_{\text{c}}$	disagreement by chance
$P_{\text{o}}^{(r,l)}$	observed agreement between raters r and l
$P_{\text{c}}^{(r,l)}$	agreement by chance between raters r and l
$P_{c,ney}^{(r,l)}$	agreement by chance after [Kut03]
R^i	number of raters for item i
$\boldsymbol{x}_{\text{test}}^{(r)}$	evaluation of a test. Each component is a rating obtained form several testlets
$\boldsymbol{X}_{\text{testlet}}^{(r)}$	testlets (lines) with ratings from rater r each column represents a candidate/speaker
Z	# of speakers

Symbols in Chap. 5 and Chap. 8. The following variables and symbols are additionally used in Chap. 5 and Chap. 8:

$\boldsymbol{c}_{\text{word}}^{v}$	feature vector for the vth word

$\boldsymbol{c}_{\text{sent}}$	sentence feature vector
$\boldsymbol{c}_{\text{meta}}$	meta-feature vector
$c_{i,\text{meta}}$	meta features, component i
$c_{i,\text{sent}}$	sentence features, component i
$D_{\text{s+p}}$	duration of sentence incl. pauses
D_{s}	duration of sentence without pauses
D_{w}	duration of word
d_i	duration of segment i
$\bar{d}_i$	duration of segment i, normalised by ROS
d_{word}	dimension of word based feature vector
d_{sent}	dimension of sentence based feature vector
$d_{\text{LUT}}(q)$	duration of phoneme q in look-up-table
$L_\tau^{\text{a}}(\boldsymbol{f})$	likelihood score in frame τ for
	the reference given speech signal $\boldsymbol{f}$
$L_\tau^{\text{r}}(\boldsymbol{f})$	likelihood score in frame τ from
	the recogniser given speech signal $\boldsymbol{f}$
$\mathbf{M}_{\mathcal{B}}$	phoneme confusion matrix (British pronounced words)
$\mathbf{M}_{\mathcal{O}}$	phoneme confusion matrix (correctly pronounced words)
$\mathbf{M}_{\mathcal{X}}$	phoneme confusion matrix (mispronounced words)
$m_{\mathcal{B}}^{i,j}$	entry of the matrix $\mathbf{M}_{\mathcal{B}}$
$m_{\mathcal{O}}^{i,j}$	entry of the matrix $\mathbf{M}_{\mathcal{O}}$
$m_{\mathcal{X}}^{i,j}$	entry of the matrix $\mathbf{M}_{\mathcal{X}}$
N	number of frames
$n_{\text{p}}^{(\text{sent})}$	number phonemes in sentence
$n_{\text{w}}^{(\text{sent})}$	number words in sentence
$P_{\text{LUT}}(d|q)$	prob. of duration d given phoneme q
	(from the look-up-table)
$R^{(\text{phone})}, R^{(\text{word})}$	rate-of-speech
$R_j^{(\text{local})}$	rate of speech in word j
q_i	phoneme number i
q_i^{a}	phoneme i in reference (alignment)
q_i^{r}	phoneme i obtained from the speech recogniser
$\boldsymbol{q}^{\text{a}}$	phoneme sequence (reference)
$\boldsymbol{q}^{\text{r}}$	phoneme sequence (recognition)
q_τ	phoneme in time frame τ
q^i	i-th phoneme in a set of Q phonemes
w_v	word number v
γ_{mispron}	weighting for mispronunciation models
$\delta_i^{(\text{phon})}$	phoneme based duration deviation

D.4   Classification and Speech Recognition

Evaluation measures.   The following variables and symbols are defined in Chap. 3 to evaluate classifiers and speech recognisers:

CL	class-wise averaged recognition rate
PREC_k	Precision of class k
$\text{REC}_\mathcal{X}$	Recall of class "wrongly pronounced"
$\text{REC}_\mathcal{O}$	Recall of class "correctly pronounced"
REC_k	Recall of class k
RR	overall recognition rate
WA	word accuracy
WC	word correctness
WER	word error rate
PER	phoneme error rate
ω_k	weighting of class k
n_{del}	# deletions
n_{fa}	# false alarms
n_{fn}	# false negatives
n_{all}	# words/phones in reference
n_{ins}	# insertions
n_{sub}	# substitutions
n_{tn}	# true negatives
n_{tp}	# true positives

Neural Networks.   . The following further variables and symbols are defined in Chap. 3 (Classification and speech recognition). First, variables to describe ANN:

$a_i(\tau)$	activation state of node i at time τ
o_i	output of node i
u_i	output of node i of the output layer
$\text{net}_i(\tau)$	net input of node i at time τ
f_{act}	activation function
f_{out}	output function
J	number
$\boldsymbol{W}$	matrix of weights $\omega_{i,j}$
$\omega_{i,j}$	weight for link between nodes i and j

Hidden Markov Models.   . The following variables describe HMM:

$\boldsymbol{A}$	HMM transition matrix
a_{ij}	HMM transition probability
$\boldsymbol{b}$	HMM output distribution

b_i	output distribution in HMM state s_i
$b_i^{(\text{cont})}$	output distribution of continuous HMM in state s_i
$b_i^{(\text{semi})}$	output distribution of semi-continuous HMM in state s_i
$c_{i,m}$	weighting for mixture m in in HMM state s_i
I	number of HMM states
o_τ	observation at time τ (HMM)
q_τ	HMM state at time τ (variable)
s_i	name of HMM state i
$\boldsymbol{\pi}$	HMM initial state probabilities
π_i	initial state probability of HMM state s_i

AdaBoost. The following variables are used to describe AdaBoost:

$h(\boldsymbol{c})$	weak classifier
$h^+(\boldsymbol{c})$	strong classifier
n_{loo}	number of loo-iterations
x^v	label of sample v
ϵ_τ	error in boosting iteration τ
τ	AdaBoost iteration, index/rank of the selected feature
$\tau(c_j, i)$	index of feature c_j in loo iteration i
$\phi_{\tau,v}$	weighting of sample v at time τ
ω^τ	weight in boosting iteration τ
$\bar{\omega}(c_j)$	mean weight of feature c_j over all loo iterations
ω_i^τ	weight of boosting iteration τ in loo iteration i

Symbols in Chap. 3. Those further variables and symbols are used in Chap. 3:

A	size of area
c_m^k	weighting for mixture m in GMM for class k
C_i	category of word i
$\boldsymbol{c}_{\text{stat}}^\tau$	static components of the MFCC feature vector
$\boldsymbol{c}_{\text{dyn}}^\tau$	dynamic components of the MFCC feature vector
d	dimension of the feature vector
ν	frequency value
ν_{max}	maximum frequency covered by the filterbank
ν_{b}	boundary frequency for bi-linear VTLN
$H(.,.)$	crossentropy
$\boldsymbol{I}$	identity matrix
M_i	# Gaussian mixtures for feature stream i
P_k	a-priori probability of class k
$p(k|\boldsymbol{c})$	conditional density for the posterior probability of class k

	given the features $\boldsymbol{c}$
$p(k\|l)$	confusion probability density
	class k instead of l
$P_{\mathrm{LM}}(.)$	posterior probability obtained from the
	language model
$p_{\mathrm{AM}}(.)$	posterior probability density obtained from the
	acoustic models
$p_{\mathrm{Viterbi}}(.)$	Viterbi probability density obtained from the
	acoustic models
r_{kl}	costs for the wrong decision k
r	# partitions for cross-validation
t	total number i of time steps τ_i
$u_k(\boldsymbol{c})$	test variable for class k
$V(\delta)$	risk of a decision rule
V	size of volume
$\boldsymbol{w}$	word sequence
$\boldsymbol{w}^{(\mathrm{opt})}$	optimal word sequence
w_i	i-th word
z	length
$\alpha_\tau(i)$	forward probability: at time τ in state i
β	VTLN warping factor (piecewise linear)
β_{linear}	VTLN warping factor (linear)
γ_{ip}	insertion penalty
γ_{lw}	language weight
$\gamma_{\mathrm{mispron}}$	weighting for mispronunciation models
$\delta(k\|\boldsymbol{c})$	decision rule
η	normalisation constant (MLLR)
η_m	normalisation constant for Gaussian density m (MLLR)
$\boldsymbol{\theta}$	Parameter vector
$\theta_\tau(i)$	Viterbi probability: at time τ in state i
$\boldsymbol{\Sigma}_{\mathrm{w}}$	within class scatter
$\boldsymbol{\Sigma}_{\mathrm{b}}$	between class scatter
τ_i	discrete time step i
ϕ_{MAP}	weight of old parameters in MAP adaptation
Ω_k	class k

Appendix E

List of Results

Results in % for WER, PER, CL-2, CL-3, CL-$5^{\pm 1}$, CL-$10_{\mathrm{rnk}}^{\pm 3}$ CL-$10_{\mathrm{rnk}}^{\pm 2}$, $1 - \delta$, $1 - \delta_{\mathrm{nrm}}$, $1 - \delta_{\mathrm{rnk}}$.

result number	description	result		page
	Word Level Expert Agreement			112
6.1	Expert ratings: mean pairwise CL-2 on OHMPLUS	71.8	CL-2	112
6.2	Expert ratings, $\theta = 5$, open-CL-2 on OHMPLUS	79.3	CL-2	114
6.3	Expert ratings, $\theta = 3$, open-CL-2 on OHM	75.6	CL-2	114
6.4	Expert ratings, $\theta = 3$, open-CL-2 on OHMPLUS	76.8	CL-2	114
6.5	Expert ratings, κ on OHM	0.39	κ	115
6.6	Expert ratings, κ on OHMPLUS	0.43	κ	115
	Text Level Expert Agreement			115
6.7	Expert ratings: mean pairwise ρ on OHMPLUS	0.63	ρ	115
6.8	Expert ratings: mean pairwise $1 - \delta$ on OHMPLUS	75.7	$1 - \delta$	115
6.9	Expert ratings: open ρ on OHMPLUS	0.78	ρ	116
6.10	Expert ratings: open $1 - \delta$ on OHMPLUS	79.9	$1 - \delta$	116
6.11	Expert ratings: open $1 - \delta_{rnk}$ on OHMPLUS	82.9	$1 - \delta_{nrm}$	116
6.12	Expert ratings: open $1 - \delta_{nrm}$ on OHMPLUS	80.7	$1 - \delta_{rnk}$	116
6.13	Expert ratings: open CL-$10_{rnk}^{\pm 2}$ on OHMPLUS	82.0	CL-$10_{rnk}^{\pm 2}$	116
6.14	Expert ratings: open CL-$10_{rnk}^{\pm 3}$ on OHMPLUS	91.8	CL-$10_{rnk}^{\pm 3}$	116
6.15	Expert ratings: κ_{rnk} on OHMPLUS	0.64	κ_{rnk}	117
6.16	Experienced teachers: open ρ on OHMPLUS	0.79	ρ	117
6.17	Experienced teachers: open $1 - \delta$ on OHMPLUS	79.0	$1 - \delta$	117
6.18	Experienced teachers: open $1 - \delta_{nrm}$ on OHMPLUS	83.2	$1 - \delta_{nrm}$	117
6.19	Experienced teachers: open $1 - \delta_{rnk}$ on OHMPLUS	81.2	$1 - \delta_{rnk}$	117
6.20	Experienced teachers: CL-3 on OHMPLUS	71.8	CL-3	117
6.21	Experienced teachers: open CL-$10_{rnk}^{\pm 2}$ on OHMPLUS	82.7	CL-$10_{rnk}^{\pm 2}$	117
6.22	Experienced teachers: κ_{rnk} on OHMPLUS	0.68	κ_{rnk}	117
6.23	Experienced teachers: open ρ on OHM	0.77	ρ	117
6.24	Experienced teachers: open $1 - \delta$ on OHM	80.2	$1 - \delta$	117
6.25	Experienced teachers: open $1 - \delta_{nrm}$ on OHM	83.6	$1 - \delta_{nrm}$	117

6.26	Experienced teachers: open $1 - \delta_{rnk}$ on OHM	80.7	$1 - \delta_{rnk}$	117
6.27	Experienced teachers: open CL-3 on OHM	74.0	CL-3	117
6.28	Experienced teachers: open CL-$10^{\pm2}_{rnk}$ on OHM	81.2	CL-$10^{\pm2}_{rnk}$	117
6.29	Experienced teachers: κ_{rnk} on OHM	0.66	κ_{rnk}	117
	Speaker Level Expert Agreement			118
6.30	Expert ratings: mean pairwise ρ on OHMPLUS	0.66	ρ	118
6.31	Expert ratings: mean pairwise $1 - \delta$ on OHMPLUS	77.4	$1 - \delta$	118
6.32	Expert ratings: open ρ on OHMPLUS	0.80	ρ	118
6.33	Expert ratings: open $1 - \delta$ on OHMPLUS	82.6	$1 - \delta$	118
6.34	Expert ratings: open $1 - \delta_{nrm}$ on OHMPLUS	86.3	$1 - \delta_{nrm}$	118
6.35	Expert ratings: open $1 - \delta_{rnk}$ on OHMPLUS	81.9	$1 - \delta_{rnk}$	118
6.36	Expert ratings: open CL-3 on OHMPLUS	78.8	CL-3	118
6.37	Expert ratings: open CL-$10^{\pm2}_{rnk}$ on OHMPLUS	82.9	CL-$10^{\pm2}_{rnk}$	118
6.38	Expert ratings: κ_{rnk} on OHMPLUS	0.67	κ_{rnk}	118
6.39	Experienced teachers: open ρ on OHMPLUS	0.83	ρ	118
6.40	Experienced teachers: open $1 - \delta$ on OHMPLUS	81.4	$1 - \delta$	118
6.41	Experienced teachers: open $1 - \delta_{nrm}$ on OHMPLUS	87.1	$1 - \delta_{nrm}$	118
6.42	Experienced teachers: open $1 - \delta_{rnk}$ on OHMPLUS	82.9	$1 - \delta_{rnk}$	118
6.43	Experienced teachers: open CL-3 on OHMPLUS	76.6	CL-3	118
6.44	Experienced teachers: open CL-$10^{\pm2}_{rnk}$ on OHMPLUS	85.7	CL-$10^{\pm2}_{rnk}$	118
6.45	Experienced teachers: κ_{rnk} on OHMPLUS	0.73	κ_{rnk}	118
6.46	Expert ratings: open ρ on OHM	0.83	ρ	118
6.47	Expert ratings: open $1 - \delta$ on OHM	81.8	$1 - \delta$	118
6.48	Expert ratings: open $1 - \delta_{nrm}$ on OHM	86.9	$1 - \delta_{nrm}$	118
6.49	Expert ratings: open $1 - \delta_{rnk}$ on OHM	82.0	$1 - \delta_{rnk}$	118
6.50	Expert ratings: open CL-3 on OHM	76.5	CL-3	118
6.51	Expert ratings: open CL-$10^{\pm2}_{rnk}$ on OHM	86.1	CL-$10^{\pm2}_{rnk}$	118
6.52	Expert ratings: κ_{rnk} on OHM	0.70	κ_{rnk}	118
	Speech Recognition			125
7.1	VERBMOBIL baseline 4-gram	34.6	WER	132
7.2	VERBMOBIL baseline unigram	52.3	WER	132
7.3	YOUTH baseline unigram	23.8	WER	133
7.4	YOUTH baseline 4-gram	3.3	WER	133
7.5	BIRMINGHAM baseline unigram	52.2	WER	133
7.6	BIRMINGHAM baseline 4-gram	26.1	WER	133
7.7	YOUTH 4-gram on VERBMOBIL	41.3	WER	134
7.8	BIRMINGHAM 4-gram on VERBMOBIL	85.3	WER	134
7.9	NONNATIVE 4-gram on VERBMOBIL	72.6	WER	135
7.10	NONNATIVE 4-gram on BIRMINGHAM	43.5	WER	135
7.11	NONNATIVE 4-gram on YOUTH	50.3	WER	135
7.12	YOUTH unigram, fb 7 kHz	22.2	WER	135
7.13	YOUTH 4-gram, fb 7 kHz	2.9	WER	135
7.14	BIRMINGHAM unigram, fb 7.5 kHz	49.7	WER	135
7.15	BIRMINGHAM 4-gram, fb 7.5 kHz	23.7	WER	135
7.16	YOUTH unigram, 2 streams	19.3	WER	136

8.27	Meta-features, loo, reference: experienced teach.	76.3	CL-$10^{\pm 2}_{rnk}$	176
8.28	Meta-features, loo, reference: experienced teach.	73.3	$1 - \delta_{nrm}$	176
8.29	Meta-features, loo, reference: experienced teach.	69.4	$1 - \delta_{rnk}$	176
8.30	Meta-features, loo, reference: experienced teach.	0.66	ρ	176
8.31	Meta-features, loo, reference: experienced teach.	0.59	κ	176
	Speaker Level Pronunciation Scoring			178
8.32	Av. word score, loo, reference: experienced teach.	69.0	CL-3	178
8.33	Av. word score, loo, reference: experienced teach.	66.7	CL-$10^{\pm 2}_{rnk}$	178
8.34	Av. word score, loo, reference: experienced teach.	81.9	$1 - \delta_{nrm}$	178
8.35	Av. word score, loo, reference: experienced teach.	76.3	$1 - \delta_{rnk}$	178
8.36	Av. word score, loo, reference: experienced teach.	0.72	ρ	178
8.37	Av. word score, loo, reference: experienced teach.	0.72	κ	178
8.38	Av. word score, cross-vali, reference S	44.7	CL-3	179
8.39	Av. word score, cross-vali, reference S	74.0	$1 - \delta_{nrm}$	179
8.40	Av. word score, cross-vali, reference S	0.51	ρ	179
8.41	Av. word score, cross-vali, reference S	0.51	κ	179
8.42	Score from boundary classification, reference S	43.5	CL-3	179
8.43	Score from boundary classification,, reference S	73.8	$1 - \delta_{nrm}$	179
8.44	Score from boundary classification, reference S	0.36	ρ	179
8.45	Score from boundary classification, reference S	0.36	κ	179

Bibliography

[All94]   J. Allen. "How Do Humans Process and Recognize Speech". *IEEE Transactions on Speech and Audio Processing*, Vol. 2, No. 4, pp. 567–577, 1994.

[Aru01]   S. Arunachalam, D. Gould, E. Andersen, D. Byrd, and S. Narayanan. "Politeness and Frustration Language in Child-Machine Interactions". In: ISCA, Ed., *Proc. European Conference On Speech Communication and Technology (Eurospeech)*, Aalborg, 2001.

[Asa05]   S. Asakawa, N. Minematsu, T. Isei-Jaakkola, and K. Hirose. "Structural Representation of the Non-Native Pronunciation". In: ISCA, Ed., *Interspeech 05 - Proc. 9th European Conference On Speech Communication and Technology (Eurospeech)*, pp. 165–168, Lisbon, 2005.

[Atl04]   L. Atlas, Q. Li, and J. Thompson. "Homomorphic Modulation Spectra". In: IEEE, Ed., *Proc. Int. Conf. on Acoustics, Speech and Signal Processing (ICASSP)*, pp. 761–764, Montreal, Canada, 2004.

[Atw99]   E. Atwell, D. Herron, P. Howarth, R. Morton, and E. Wick. "Pronunciation Training: Requirements and Solutions. ISLE Deliverable D1.4". Tech. Rep., ISLE, Interactive Spoken Language Education, Hamburg, 1999. http://nats-www.informatik.uni-hamburg.de/~isle/public/D14/D14.pdf.

[Bag94]   P. C. Bagshaw. *Automatic Prosodic Analysis for Computer Aided Pronunciation Teaching*. PhD thesis, University of Edinburgh, Center for Speech Technology Research, 1994. http://www.cstr.ed.ac.uk/research/projects/fda/Bagshaw_PhDThesis.pdf.

[Ban03]   S. Banerjee, J. E. Beck, and J. Mostow. "Evaluating the Effect of Predicting Oral Reading Miscues". In: ISCA, Ed., *Proc. European Conference On Speech Communication and Technology (Eurospeech)*, pp. 3165 – 3168, 2003.

[Bat00]   A. Batliner, A. Buckow, H. Niemann, E. Nöth, and V. Warnke. "The Prosody Module". In: W. Wahlster, Ed., *Verbmobil: Foundations of Speech-to-Speech Translations*, pp. 106–121, Springer, Berlin, 2000.

[Bat01]   A. Batliner, J. Buckow, R. Huber, V. Warnke, E. Nöth, and H. Niemann. "Boiling down Prosody for the Classification of Boundaries and Accents in German and English". In: ISCA, Ed., *Proc. European Conference On Speech Communication and Technology (Eurospeech)*, pp. 2781–2784, Aalborg, 2001.

[Bat02]   A. Batliner, V. Zeißler, E. Nöth, and H. Niemann. "Prosodic Classification of Offtalk: First Experiments". In: P. Sojka, I. Kopecek, and K. Pala, Eds., *Proc. 5th Int. Conf. on Text, Speech, Dialogue (TSD)*, pp. 357–364, Lecture Notes in Artificial Intelligence, Springer, Berlin, 2002.

[Bat03a] A. Batliner, C. Hacker, S. Steidl, E. Nöth, and J. Haas. "User States, User Strategies, and System Performance: How to Match the One with the Other". In: ISCA, Ed., *Proc. of an ISCA Tutorial and Research Workshop on Error Handling in Spoken Dialogue Systems*, pp. 5–10, Chateau d'Oex, 2003.

[Bat03b] A. Batliner, K. Fischer, R. Huber, J. Spilker, and E. Nöth. "How to Find Trouble in Communication". *Speech Comm.*, Vol. 40, pp. 117–143, 2003.

[Bat04a] A. Batliner, C. Hacker, S. Steidl, E. Nöth, S. D'Arcy, M. Russell, and M. Wong. "'You Stupid Tin Box' - Children Interacting with the AIBO Robot: A Cross-Linguistic Emotional Speech Corpus.". In: ELRA, Ed., *Proceedings of the 4th International Conference of Language Resources and Evaluation LREC 2004*, pp. 171–174, Lisbon, 2004.

[Bat04b] A. Batliner, C. Hacker, S. Steidl, E. Nöth, and J. Haas. "From Emotion to Interaction: Lessons from Real Human-Machine-Dialogues". In: E. Andrè, L. Dybkiaer, W. Minker, and P. Heisterkamp, Eds., *Affective Dialogue Systems, Proceedings of a Tutorial and Research Workshop, Kloster Irrsee*, pp. 1–12, Lecture Notes in Artificial Intelligence, Springer, Berlin, 2004.

[Bat05a] A. Batliner, M. Blomberg, S. D'Arcy, D. Elenius, D. Giuliani, M. Gerosa, C. Hacker, M. Russell, S. Steidl, and M. Wong. "The PF-STAR Children's Speech Corpus". In: ISCA, Ed., *Interspeech 05 - Proc. 9th European Conference On Speech Communication and Technology (Eurospeech)*, pp. 2761–2764, Lisbon, 2005.

[Bat05b] A. Batliner, S. Steidl, C. Hacker, E. Nöth, and H. Niemann. "Private Emotions vs. Social Interaction - towards New Dimensions in Research on Emotion". In: S. Carberry and F. de Rosis, Eds., *Adapting the Interaction Style to Affective Factors*, Edinburgh, 2005. (8 pages, no pagination).

[Bat05c] A. Batliner, S. Steidl, C. Hacker, E. Nöth, and H. Niemann. "Tales of Tuning - Prototyping for Automatic Classification of Emotional User States". In: ISCA, Ed., *Interspeech 05 - Proc. 9th European Conference On Speech Communication and Technology (Eurospeech)*, pp. 489–492, Lisbon, 2005.

[Bat06]   A. Batliner, C. Hacker, and E. Nöth. "To Talk or not to Talk with a Computer: On-Talk vs. Off-Talk". In: K. Fischer, Ed., *How People Talk to Computers, Robots, and Other Artificial Communication Partners*, pp. 79–100, Bremen, 2006.

[Bat07]   A. Batliner, C. Hacker, M. Kaiser, H. Mögele, and E. Nöth. "Taking into Account the User's Focus of Attention with the Help of Audio-Visual Information: Towards less Artificial Human-Machine-Communication". In: *Proc. Int. Conf. on Auditory-Visual Speech Processing (AVSP)*, Hilvarenbeek, 2007.

[Bat08]   A. Batliner, S. Steidl, C. Hacker, and E. Nöth. "Private Emotions Versus Social Interaction: a Data-Driven Approach towards Analysing Emotion in Speech". *User Modelling and User-Adapted Interaction - The Journal of Personalization Research (umuai)*, Vol. 18, pp. 175–206, 2008.

[Bat09]   A. Batliner, C. Hacker, and E. Nöth. "To Talk or not to Talk with a Computer". *submitted to: J. on Multimodal User Interfaces (JMUI)*, 2009.

[Bat96]   A. Batliner, R. Kompe, A. Kießling, H. Niemann, and E. Nöth. "Syntactic-Prosodic Labelling of Large Spontaneous Speech Databases". In: IEEE, Ed., *Proc. Int. Conf. on Spoken Language Processing (ICSLP)*, pp. 1712–1715, Philadelphia, 1996.

[Bat98]   A. Batliner, R. Kompe, A. Kießling, M. Mast, H. Niemann, and E. Nöth. "M = Syntax + Prosody: A Syntactic-Prosodic Labelling Scheme for Large Spontaneous Speech Databases". *Speech Communication* , Vol. 25, pp. 193–222, 1998.

[Bat99]   A. Batliner, M. Nutt, V. Warnke, E. Nöth, J. Buckow, R. Huber, and H. Niemann. "Automatic Annotation and Classification of Phrase Accents in Spontaneous Speech". In: ISCA, Ed., *Proc. European Conference On Speech Communication and Technology (Eurospeech)*, pp. 519–522, Budapest, 1999.

[Bau66]   L. Baum and T. Petrie. "Statistical Inference for Probabilistic Functions of Finite State Markov Chains". *Ann. Math. Statist.*, Vol. 37, pp. 1554–1563, 1966.

[Beep]   "British English Example Pronunciation Dictionary (BEEP)". http:// mi.eng.cam.ac.uk/~ajr/wsjcam0/node8.html ,Download: ftp://svr-ftp. eng.cam.ac.uk/pub/comp.speech/dictionaries/beep.tar.gz, last visited October 2007.

[Bel03]   L. Bell and J. Gustafson. "Child and Adult Speaker Adaptation during Error Resolution in a Publicly Available Spoken Dialogue System". In: ISCA, Ed., *Proc. European Conference On Speech Communication and Technology (Eurospeech)*, pp. 613–616, Geneve, 2003.

[Ber04]   J. Bernstein, I. Barbier, E. Rosenfeld, and J. de Jong. "Theory and Data in Spoken Language Assessment". In: S. Kim and D. Youn, Eds., *Interspeech 2004 - Proc. 8th Int. Conf. on Spoken Language Processing (ICSLP)*, pp. 1685–1688, Jeju Island, Korea, 2004.

[Ber90]   J. Bernstein, M. Cohen, H. Murveit, D. Rtischev, and M. Weintraub. "Automatic Evaluation and Training in English Pronunciation". In: ISCA, Ed., *Proc. Int. Conf. on Spoken Language Processing (ICSLP)*, pp. 1185–1188, Kobe, 1990.

[Bes04]   J. Beskow, O. Engwall, B. Granström, and P. Wik. "Design Strategies for a Virtual Language Tutor". In: S. Kim and D. Youn, Eds., *Interspeech 2004 - Proc. 8th Int. Conf. on Spoken Language Processing (ICSLP)*, pp. 1693–1696, Jeju Island, Korea, 2004.

[Bha43]   A. Bhattacharyya. "On a Measure of Divergence between two Statistical Populations Defined by their Probability Distributions". *Bull. Calcutta Mathematical Society*, Vol. 35, No. 3, pp. 99–110, 1943.

[Bie02]   S. Biersack. "Systematische Aussprachefehler deutscher Muttersprachler im Englischen – eine phonetisch-phonologische Bestandsaufnahme". *Forschungsberichte des Instituts für Phonetik und Sprachliche Kommunikation der Universität München (FIPKM)*, Vol. 39, pp. 37–130, 2002.

[Bon00a] P. Bonaventura, P. Herron, and W. Metzel. "Phonetic Rules for Diagnosis of Pronunciation Errors". In: *Konvens 2000, Tagungsband 5. Konferenz Verarbeitung natürlicher Sprache*, pp. 225 – 230, Ilmenau, 2000.

[Bon00b] P. Bonaventura, P. Howarth, and W. Metzel. "Phonetic Annotation of a Non-Native Speech Corpus". In: *Proc. Conf Integrating Speech Technologies in Learning (InSTIL)*, pp. 10 – 17, Dundee, 2000.

[Bra81]   E. Bradley. "Nonparametric estimates of standard error: The jackknife, the bootstrap and other methods". *Biometrika*, Vol. 68, No. 3, pp. 589–599, 1981.

[Bur96]   D. Burnett and M. Fanty. "Rapid Unsupervised Adaptation to Children's Speech on a Connected-Digit Task". In: *Proc. Int. Conf. on Spoken Language Processing (ICSLP)*, pp. 1145–1148, Philadelphia, 1996.

[Che03]   B. Chen, Q. Zhu, and N. Morgan. "Learning Long-Term Temporal Features in LVCSR Using Neural Networks". In: *Proc. European Conference On Speech Communication and Technology (Eurospeech)*, pp. 853–856., Geneva, 2003.

[Che04]   B. Chen, S. Chang, and S. Sivadas. "Learning Discriminative Temporal Patterns in Speech: Development of Novel TRAPS-Like Classifiers". In: *Interspeech 2004 - Proc. 8th Int. Conf. on Spoken Language Processing (ICSLP)*, Jeju Island, Korea, 2004.

[Cic72]   D. Cicchetti. "Assessing Inter-Rater Reliability for Rating Scales: Resolving some Basic Issues". *British Journal of Psychiatry*, Vol. 129, pp. 452 – 456, 1972.

[Cin04a]   T. Cincarek. "Pronunciation Scoring for Non-Native Speech". Diplomarbeit, Lehrstuhl für Mustererkennung (Informatik 5), Universität Erlangen-Nürnberg, 2004.

[Cin04b]   T. Cincarek, R. Gruhn, C. Hacker, E. Nöth, and S. Nakamura. "Pronunciation Scoring and Extraction of Mispronounced Words for Non-Native Speech". In: *Proceedings of the Acoustical Society of Japan*, pp. 165–166, Okinawa, 2004. in Japanese.

[Cin09]   T. Cincarek, R. Gruhn, C. Hacker, E. Nöth, and S. Nakamura. "Automatic Pronunciation Scoring of Words and Sentences Independent from the Non-Native's First Language". *Computer Speech & Language*, Vol. 23, pp. 65–88, 2009.

[Cla98]   T. Claes, I. Dologlou, L. ten Bosch, and D. Compernolle. "A Novel Feature Transformation for Vocal Tract Length Normalization in Automatic Speech Recognition". *IEEE Trans. on Speech and Audio Processing*, Vol. 6, pp. 549 – 557, 1998.

[CmuDict] "The CMU Pronouncing Dictionary, Version 0.6". http://www.speech.cs.cmu.edu/cgi-bin/cmudict, last visited October 2007.

[Coh60]   J. Cohen. "A Coefficient of Agreement for Nominal Scales". *Educational and Psychology Measurement*, Vol. 20, pp. 37–46, 1960.

[Cos05]   P. Cosi and B. L. Pellom. "Italian Children's Speech Recognition for Advanced Interactive Literacy Tutors". In: ISCA, Ed., *Interspeech 05 - Proc. 9th European Conference On Speech Communication and Technology (Eurospeech)*, pp. 2201 – 2204, Lisbon, 2005.

[Cro51]   L. Cronbach. "Coefficient Alpha and the Internal Structure of Tests". *Psychometrika*, Vol. 16, pp. 297 – 334, 1951.

[Cuc00a]   C. Cucchiarini, H. Strik, D. Binnenpoorte, and L. Boves. "Pronunciation Evaluation in Read and Spontaneous Speech: A Comparison between Human Ratings and Automatic Scores". In: *Proceedings of New Sounds*, Klagenfurt, 2000.

[Cuc00b]   C. Cucchiarini, H. Strik, and L. Boves. "Different Aspects of Expert Pronunciation Quality Ratings and Their Relation to Scores Produced by Speech Recognition Algorithms". *Speech Comm.*, Vol. 30, pp. 109–119, 2000.

[DAr04] S. D'Arcy, L. Wong, and M. Russell. "Recognition of Read and Spontaneous Children's Speech Using two new Corpora". In: *Interspeech 2004 - Proc. 8th Int. Conf. on Spoken Language Processing (ICSLP)*, pp. 1473–1476, Jeju Island, Korea, 2004.

[Das98] S. Das, D. Nix, and M. Picheny. "Improvements in Children's Speech Recognition Performance". In: IEEE, Ed., *Proc. Int. Conf. on Acoustics, Speech and Signal Processing (ICASSP)*, pp. 433 – 436, Seattle, WA, 1998.

[Dav82] M. Davies and J. Fleiss. "Measuring Agreement for Multimodal Data". *Biometrics*, Vol. 38, pp. 1047 – 1051, 1982.

[Del00] R. Delmonte. "SLIM Prosodic Automatic Tools for Self-Learning Instruction". *Speech Comm.*, Vol. 30, pp. 145–166, 2000.

[Dre85] B. Dretzke. *Fehlerbewertung im Aussprachebereich: Objektive Fehlerbeurteilung versus subjektive Fehlerbewertung – eine Untersuchung von Aussprachefehlern deutscher Anglistikstudenten in der Zielsprache Englisch*. Buske, Hamburg, 1985.

[Eck93] W. Eckert, T. Kuhn, H. Niemann, S. Rieck, A. Scheuer, and E. Schukat-Talamazzini. "A Spoken Dialogue System for German Intercity Train Timetable Inquiries". In: ISCA, Ed., *Proc. European Conference On Speech Communication and Technology (Eurospeech)*, pp. 1871–1874, Berlin, 1993.

[Eid96] E. Eide and H. Gish. "A Parametric Approach to Vocal Tract Length Normalization". In: IEEE, Ed., *Proc. Int. Conf. on Acoustics, Speech and Signal Processing (ICASSP)*, pp. 346–348, Atlanta, 1996.

[Ele05] D. Elenius and M. Blomberg. "Adaptation and Normalization Experiments in Speech Recognition for 4 to 8 Year old Children". In: ISCA, Ed., *Interspeech 05 - Proc. 9th European Conference On Speech Communication and Technology (Eurospeech)*, pp. 2749 – 2752, Lisbon, 2005.

[Esk00] M. Eskenazi, Y. Ke, J. Albornoz, and K. Probst. "The Fluency Pronunciation Trainer: Update and User Issues". In: *Proc. Conf Integrating Speech Technologies in Learning (InSTIL)*, Dundee, 2000.

[Esk02] M. Eskenazi and G. Pelton. "Pinpointing Pronunciation Errors in Children's Speech: Examining the Role of the Speech Recognizer". In: *Pronunciation Modeling and Lexicon Adaptation for Spoken Language Technology Workshop*, Colorado, 2002.

[Esk96] M. Eskenazi. "Detection of Foreign Speakers' Pronunciation Errors for Second Language Training - Preliminary Results". In: ISCA, Ed., *Proc. Int. Conf. on Spoken Language Processing (ICSLP)*, pp. 1465–1468, Philadelphia, 1996.

[Esk98]   M. Eskenazi and S. Hansma. "The Fluency Pronunciation Trainer". In: *Proc. Speech Technology in Language Learning (STILL)*, pp. 77 – 80, Marholmen, 1998.

[Esk99]   M. Eskenazi. "Using a Computer in Foreign Language Pronunciation Training: What Advantages?". *Tutors that Listen: Speech Recognition for Language Learning, Special Issue, CALICO Journal*, Vol. 16, pp. 447–469, 1999.

[Fei90]   A. Feinstein and D. Cicchetti. "High agreement but low kappa: I. The problem of two paradoxes". *Journal of Clinical Epidemiology*, Vol. 43, No. 2, pp. 543 – 549, 1990.

[Fer71]   G. Ferguson. *Statistical Analysis in Psychology and Education. Series in Psychology*, McGraw-Hill, Tokyo, third Ed., 1971.

[Fis97]   J. Fiscus. "A Post-Processing System to Yield Reduced Word Error Rates: Recogniser Output Voting Error Reduction". In: IEEE, Ed., *Proc. of the Automatic Speech Recognition and Understanding Workshop (ASRU)*, pp. 347–352, Santa Barbara, 1997.

[Fle53]   H. Fletcher. *Speech and Hearing in Communication*. Krieger, New York, 1953.

[Fle69]   J. Fleiss, J. Cohen, and B. Everitt. "Large Sample Standard Errors of Kappa and Weighted Kappa". *Psychological Bullettin*, Vol. 72, pp. 323 – 327, 1969.

[For05]   K. Forbes-Riley and D. Litman. "Correlating Student Acoustic-Prosodic Profiles with Student Learning in Spoken Tutoring Dialogues". In: ISCA, Ed., *Interspeech 05 - Proc. 9th European Conference On Speech Communication and Technology (Eurospeech)*, pp. 157–160, Lisbon, 2005.

[Fra00]   H. Franco, L. Neumeyer, V. Digalakis, and O. Ronen. "Combination of Machine Scores for Automatic Grading of Pronunciation Quality". *Speech Comm.*, Vol. 30, pp. 121–130, 2000.

[Fra99]   H. Franco, L. Neumeyer, M. Ramos, and H. Bratt. "Automatic Detection of Phone-Level Mispronunciation for Language Learning". In: ISCA, Ed., *Proc. European Conference On Speech Communication and Technology (Eurospeech)*, pp. 851–854, Budapest, 1999.

[Fre95]   Y. Freund and R. E. Schapire. "A Decision-Theoretic Generalization of On-Line Learning and an Application to Boosting". In: *EuroCOLT '95: Proceedings of the Second European Conference on Computational Learning Theory*, pp. 23–37, Springer-Verlag, London, UK, 1995.

[Fre99a]   Y. Freund and R. Schapire. "A Short Introduction to Boosting". *Journal of Japanese Soc. for Artif. Intel.*, Vol. 14, pp. 771–780, 1999.

[Fre99b]   Y. Freund. "A Adaptive Version of the Boost by Majority Algorithm". In: *Proc of the 12thAnnual Conf. on Computational Learning Theory*, pp. 102–113, Santa Cruz, 1999.

[Fri89]   J. Friedman. "Regularized Discriminant Analysis". *Journal of the American Statistical Association*, Vol. 84, pp. 165–175, 1989.

[Gal01]   M. Gales. "Adaptive Training for Robust ASR". In: IEEE, Ed., *Proc. of the Automatic Speech Recognition and Understanding Workshop (ASRU)*, pp. 15 – 20, Trento, 2001.

[Gal97]   M. Gales. "Maximum Likelihood Linear Transformations for HMM-based Speech Recognition". In: *Technical Report CUED/F-INFENG/TR291*, Cambridge University Engineering Dept., 1997.

[Gal98]   M. Gales. "Maximum Likelihood Linear Transformations for HMM-based Speech Recognition". *Computer Speech and Language*, Vol. 12, pp. 75 – 98, 1998.

[Ger04a]   M. Gerosa and D. Giuliani. "Investigating Automatic Recognition of Nonnative Childrens Speech". In: *Interspeech 2004 - Proc. 8th Int. Conf. on Spoken Language Processing (ICSLP)*, pp. 1521–1524, Jeju Island, Korea, 2004.

[Ger04b]   M. Gerosa and D. Giuliani. "Preliminary Investigations in Automatic Recognition of English Sentences Uttered by Italian Children". In: *Proc. Symposion on InSTIL/ICALL (Integrating Speech Technologies in Learning and intelligent CALL)*, Venice, 2004.

[Ger06]   M. Gerosa. *Acoustic Modeling for Automatic Recognition of Children's Speech*. PhD thesis, International Doctorate School in Information and Communication Technologies, University of Trento, 2006.

[Gil89]   L. Gillick and S. Cox. "Some Statistical Issues in the Comparison of Speech Recognition Algorithms". In: IEEE, Ed., *Proc. Int. Conf. on Acoustics, Speech and Signal Processing (ICASSP)*, pp. 532–535, Glasgow, 1989.

[Giu03]   D. Giuliani and M. Gerosa. "Investigating Recognition of Children's Speech". In: IEEE, Ed., *Proc. Int. Conf. on Acoustics, Speech and Signal Processing (ICASSP)*, pp. 137–140, Hongkong, 2003.

[Giu04]   D. Giuliani and M. Giuliani. "Speaker Normalization through Constrained MLLR Based Transforms". In: *Interspeech 2004 - Proc. 8th Int. Conf. on Spoken Language Processing (ICSLP)*, pp. 2893–2897, Jeju Island, Korea, 2004.

[Gra05]   B. Granström. "Speech Technology for Language Training and e-Inclusion". In: ISCA, Ed., *Interspeech 05 - Proc. 9th European Conference On Speech Communication and Technology (Eurospeech)*, pp. 449 – 452, Lisbon, 2005.

[Gre97]   S. Greenberg and B. E. Kingsbury. "The Modulation Spectrogram: In Pursuit of an Invariant Representation of Speech". In: IEEE, Ed., *Proc. Int. Conf. on Acoustics, Speech and Signal Processing (ICASSP)*, pp. 1647–1650, Munich, 1997.

[Gru04]   R. Gruhn, T. Cincarek, and S. Nakamura. "A Multi-Accent Non-Native English Database". In: *Proc. Acoustical Society of Japan*, 2004.

[Grz]   J. Grzega. "Sprachwissenschaft für den Sprachunterricht – Einige Hinweise für Englischlehrer, Proseminar 2003, Universität Eichstätt–Ingolstadt". http: //www1.ku-eichstaett.de/SLF/EngluVglSW/schule14.pdf, last visited October 2007.

[Gus02]   J. Gustafson and K. Sjolander. "Voice transformations for Improving Children's Speech Recognition in a Publicly Available Dialogue System". In: *Proc. Int. Conf. on Spoken Language Processing (ICSLP)*, pp. 297 – 300, Denver, 2002.

[Hac01]   C. Hacker. "Optimierung der Merkmalberechnung für die automatische Spracherkennung". Studienarbeit, Lehrstuhl für Mustererkennung (Informatik 5), Universität Erlangen-Nürnberg, 2001.

[Hac03]   C. Hacker, G. Stemmer, S. Steidl, E. Nöth, and H. Niemann. "Various Information Sources for HMM with Weighted Multiple Codebooks". In: A. Wendemuth, Ed., *Proceedings of the Speech Processing Workshop*, pp. 9–16, Magdeburg, 2003.

[Hac05a]   C. Hacker, A. Batliner, S. Steidl, E. Nöth, H. Niemann, and T. Cincarek. "Assessment of Non-Native Children's Pronunciation: Human Marking and Automatic Scoring". In: G. Kokkinakis, N. Fakotakis, E. Dermatas, and R. Potapova, Eds., *Proc. 10th Int. Conf. on SPEECH and COMPUTER (SPEECOM)*, pp. 123 – 126, Patras, 2005.

[Hac05b]   C. Hacker, T. Cincarek, R. Gruhn, S. Steidl, E. Nöth, and H. Niemann. "Pronunciation Feature Extraction". In: W. Kropatsch, R. Sablatnig, and A. Hanbury, Eds., *Pattern Recognition, 27th DAGM Symposium, Proceedings*, pp. 141–148, Lecture Notes in Computer Science, Springer, Berlin, 2005.

[Hac06]   C. Hacker, A. Batliner, and E. Nöth. "Are You Looking at Me, are You Talking with Me – Multimodal Classification of the Focus of Attention". In: P. Sojka, I. Kopecek, and K. Pala, Eds., *Proc. 9th Int. Conf. on Text, Speech, and Dialogue (TSD)* , pp. 581 – 588, Lecture Notes in Artificial Intelligence, Springer, Berlin, Heidelberg, 2006.

[Hac07a]   C. Hacker, T. Cincarek, A. Maier, A. Heßler, and E. Nöth. "Boosting of Prosodic and Pronunciation Features to Detect Mispronunciations of Non-Native Children". In: IEEE, Ed., *Proc. Int. Conf. on Acoustics, Speech and Signal Processing (ICASSP)*, pp. 197 – 200, Honolulu, 2007.

[Hac07b]   C. Hacker, A. Maier, A. Hessler, U. Guthunz, and E. Nöth. "Caller: Com-
           puter Assisted Language Learning from Erlangen – Pronunciation Training
           and More". In: *Proc. Int. Conf. Interactive Computer Aided Learning (ICL)*,
           Villach, 2007. (6 pages, no pagination).

[Had07]   T. Haderlein. *Automatic Evaluation of Tracheoesophageal Substitute Voices*.
           Vol. 25 of *Studien zur Mustererkennung*, Logos Verlag, Berlin, 2007.

[Hag04]   A. Hagen, B. Pellom, S. van Vuuren, and R. Cole. "Advances in Children's
           Speech Recognition within an Interactive Literacy Tutor". In: A. for Computa-
           tional Linguistics, Ed., *Proc. Human Language Technology Conference - North
           American Chapter of the Association for Computational Linguistics, Annual
           Meeting (HLT-NAACL)*, pp. 25–28, Boston, 2004.

[Hag05]   A. Hagen and B. Pellom. "Data Driven Subword Unit Modeling for Speech
           Recognition and its Application to Interactive Reading Tutors". In: ISCA, Ed.,
           *Interspeech 05 - Proc. 9th European Conference On Speech Communication and
           Technology (Eurospeech)*, pp. 2757 – 2760, Lisbon, 2005.

[Hel03]   R. Hellyer-Jones, M. Horner, and R. Parr. *Green Line New 1*. Klett, Stuttgart,
           2003.

[Her00]   D. Herron and W. Metzel. "Error diagnosis for spoken language. ISLE Deliver-
           able D4.5". Tech. Rep., ISLE, Interactive Spoken Language Education, Ham-
           burg, 2000. http://nats-www.informatik.uni-hamburg.de/~isle/public/
           D45/D45.pdf.

[Her03]   H. Hermansky and P. Jain. "Band-Independent Speech-Event Categories for
           TRAP based ASR". In: ISCA, Ed., *Proc. European Conference On Speech
           Communication and Technology (Eurospeech)*, pp. 1013–1016, Geneva, 2003.

[Her90]   H. Hermansky. "Perceptual Linear Predictive (PLP) Analysis of Speech". *J.
           Acoust. Soc. Am.*, Vol. 87, No. 4, pp. 1738–1752, 1990.

[Her91]   H. Hermansky, N. Morgan, A. Bayya, and N. Kohn. "Compensation for the
           Effect of the Communication Channel in Auditory-Like Analysis of Speech
           (RASTA-PLP)". In: ISCA, Ed., *Proc. European Conference On Speech Com-
           munication and Technology (Eurospeech)*, pp. 1367–1370, Genova, 1991.

[Her98]   H. Hermansky and S. Sharma. "TRAPs - Classifiers of Temporal Patterns".
           In: *Proc. Int. Conf. on Spoken Language Processing (ICSLP)*, pp. 1003–1006,
           Sydney, Australia, 1998.

[Her99a]   H. Hermansky and S. Sharma. "Temporal Patterns (TRAPs) in ASR of Noisy
           Speech". In: IEEE, Ed., *Proc. Int. Conf. on Acoustics, Speech and Signal Pro-
           cessing (ICASSP)*, pp. 289–292, Phoenix, 1999.

[Her99b] D. Herron, W. Metzel, E. Atwell, R. Bisiani, F. Daneluzzi, R. Morton, and J. Schmidt. "Automatic Localization and Diagnosis of Pronunciation Errors for Second-Language Learners of English". In: ISCA, Ed., *Proc. European Conference On Speech Communication and Technology (Eurospeech)*, pp. 855–858, Budapest, 1999.

[Hes05] A. Heßler. "Entwicklung einer Englisch-Lernsoftware mit integrierter Spracherkennung". Studienarbeit, Lehrstuhl für Mustererkennung (Informatik 5), Universität Erlangen-Nürnberg, 2005.

[Hes06] A. Heßler. "Eine Client-Server Anbindung zur automatischen Aussprachebewertung für das Projekt 'Caller'". Diplomarbeit, Lehrstuhl für Mustererkennung (Informatik 5), Universität Erlangen-Nürnberg, 2006.

[Hie93] J. Hieronymus. "Ascii Phonetic Symbols for the World's Languages: Worldbet". *Journal of the International Phonetic Association*, 1993.

[Hof05] M. Hofmann and O. Jokisch. "OpenVOC - Open Platform for Multilingual Vocabulary Training Integration Speech Technology Components". In: G. Kokkinakis, N. Fakotakis, E. Dermatas, and R. Potapova, Eds., *Proc. 10th Int. Conf. on SPEECH and COMPUTER (SPEECOM)*, pp. 745 – 748, Patras, 2005.

[Hon04] F. Hönig. "Modifications of Perceptual Linear Prediction and the Mel-Frequency Cepstrum". Diplomarbeit, Lehrstuhl für Mustererkennung (Informatik 5), Universität Erlangen-Nürnberg, 2004.

[Hon05] F. Hönig, G. Stemmer, C. Hacker, and F. Brugnara. "Revising Perceptual Linear Prediction (PLP)". In: ISCA, Ed., *Interspeech 05 - Proc. 9th European Conference On Speech Communication and Technology (Eurospeech)*, pp. 2997–3000, Lisbon, 2005.

[Hua01] X. Huang, A. Acero, and H.-W. Hon. *Spoken Language Processing – A Guide to Theory, Algorithm, and System Development*. Prentice Hall, Upper Saddle River, 2001.

[Hub02] R. Huber. *Prosodisch-linguistische Klassifikation von Emotion*. Vol. 8 of *Studien zur Mustererkennung*, Logos Verlag, Berlin, 2002.

[Hub99] J. Huber, E. Stathopoulos, G. Curione, T. Ash, and K. Johnson. "Formants of children, Women, and Men: The Effects of Vocal Intensity Variation". *J. Acoust. Soc. Am.*, Vol. 106, pp. 1532–1542, 1999.

[Imo00] K. Imoto, M. Dantsuji, and T. Kawahara. "Modeling the Perception of English Sentence Stress For Computer-Assisted Language Learning". In: *Proc. Int. Conf. on Spoken Language Processing (ICSLP)*, pp. 175–178, Bejing, 2000.

[Jai03]   P. Jain and H. Hermansky. "Beyond a Single Critical-Band in TRAP Based ASR". In: ISCA, Ed., *Proc. European Conference On Speech Communication and Technology (Eurospeech)*, pp. 437–440, Geneva, Switzerland, 2003.

[Kaj99]   S. Kajarekar, N. Malayath, and H. Hermansky. "Analysis of Speaker and Channel Variability in Speech". In: IEEE, Ed., *Proc. of the Automatic Speech Recognition and Understanding Workshop (ASRU)*, pp. 59–65, Colorado, 1999.

[Kie96]   A. Kießling, R. Kompe, A. Batliner, H. Niemann, and E. Nöth. "Classification of Boundaries and Accents in Spontaneous Speech". In: R. Kuhn, Ed., *Proc. of the 3rd CRIM / FORWISS Workshop* , pp. 104–113, Montreal, 1996.

[Kie97]   A. Kießling. *Extraktion und Klassifikation prosodischer Merkmale in der automatischen Sprachverarbeitung. Berichte aus der Informatik*, Shaker, Aachen, 1997.

[Kim97]   Y. Kim, H. Franco, and L. Neumeyer. "Automatic Pronunciation Scoring of Specific Phone Segments For Language Instruction". In: ISCA, Ed., *Proc. European Conference On Speech Communication and Technology (Eurospeech)*, pp. 633 – 636, Rhodes, Greece, 1997.

[Kra04]   E. Krahmer and M. Swerts. "Signaling and Detecting Uncertainty in Audiovisual Speech by Children and Adults". In: *Interspeech 2004 - Proc. 8th Int. Conf. on Spoken Language Processing (ICSLP)*, Jeju Island, Korea, 2004.

[Kri03]   K. Krippendorff. *Content Analysis, An Introduction to Its Methodology*. Sage Publications, Thousand Oaks, CA, 2nd Ed., 2003.

[Kri05]   K. Krippendorff. "Computing Krippendorff's Alpha-Reliability". 2005. http://www.asc.upenn.edu/usr/krippendorff/webreliability2.pdf, last visited October 2007.

[Kru99]   F. Krummenauer. "Erweiterungen von Cohen's kappa-Maß für Multi-Rater-Studien: Eine Übersicht". *Informatik, Biometrie und Epidemiologie in Medizin und Biologie*, Vol. 30, pp. 3–20, 1999.

[Kul02]   A. Kulicke. "Schnelle Sprecheradaption". Diplomarbeit, Lehrstuhl für Mustererkennung (Informatik 5), Universität Erlangen-Nürnberg, 2002.

[Kut03]   M. Kutschmann. "Der Kappa-Koeffizient: Diskussion eines Missverständnisses und ein Modifizierungsvorschlag". 2003. 49. Biometrisches Kolloquium, http://epi.klinikum.uni-muenster.de/StatMethMed/2002/Berlin/Kutschmann.pdf, last visited October 2007.

[Lan98]   P. Langlais, A.-M. Öster, and B. Granström. "Phonetic Level Mispronunciation Detection in Non-Native Swedisch Speech". In: *Proc. Int. Conf. on Spoken Language Processing (ICSLP)*, pp. 1743–1746, Sydney, 1998.

[Lee99]   S. Lee, A. Potamianos, and S. Narayan. "Acoustics of Children's Speech: Developmental Changes in Temporal and Spectral Parameters". *J. Acoust. Soc. Am.*, Vol. 105, pp. 1455–1468, 1999.

[Leg95]   C. Leggetter and P. Woodland. "Maximum Likelihood Linear Regression for Speaker Adaptation of Continuous Density Hidden Markov Models". *Computer Speech and Language*, Vol. 9, pp. 171–185, 1995.

[Lev66]   V. Levensthein. "Binary Codes Capable of Correcting Deletions Insertions and Reversals". *Cybernetics and Control Theory*, Vol. 10, pp. 707–710, 1966.

[Li01]   Q. Li and M. Russell. "Why is Automatic Recognition of Children's Speech Difficult". In: ISCA, Ed., *Proc. European Conference On Speech Communication and Technology (Eurospeech)*, pp. 2671–2674, Aalborg, 2001.

[Li02]   Q. Li and M. Russell. "An Analysis of the Causes of Increased Error Rates in Children's Speech Recognition". In: *Proc. Int. Conf. on Spoken Language Processing (ICSLP)*, pp. 2337–2340, 2002.

[Li07]   X. Li, Y.-C. Ju, L. Deng, and A. Acero. "Efficient and Robust Language Modeling in an Automatic Children's Reading Tutor System". In: IEEE, Ed., *Proc. Int. Conf. on Acoustics, Speech and Signal Processing (ICASSP)*, pp. 193 – 196, Honolulu, 2007.

[Lin05]   B. Lindtfert and K. Schneider. "Acoustic Correlates of Contrastive Stress in German Children". In: ISCA, Ed., *Interspeech 05 - Proc. 9th European Conference On Speech Communication and Technology (Eurospeech)*, pp. 1177 – 1180, Lisbon, 2005.

[Lin95]   R. Linn and N. Gronlund. *Measurement and Assessment in Teaching*. Prentice Hall, Upper Saddle River, seventh Ed., 1995.

[Mai05a]   A. Maier. "Recognizer Adaptation by Acoustic Model Interpolation on a Small Training Set from the Target Domain". Diplomarbeit, Lehrstuhl für Mustererkennung (Informatik 5), Universität Erlangen-Nürnberg, 2005.

[Mai05b]   A. Maier. "Robust Speech Recognition of Noisy or Reverberated Data Using Multiple Recognizers in Different Energy Bands". Studienarbeit, Lehrstuhl für Mustererkennung (Informatik 5), Universität Erlangen-Nürnberg, 2005.

[Mai05c]   A. Maier, C. Hacker, S. Steidl, and E. Nöth. "Helfen 'Fallen' bei verrauschten Daten? - Spracherkennung mit TRAPs". In: H. Fastl and M. Fruhmann, Eds., *Fortschritte der Akustik: Plenarvorträge und Fachbeiträge der 31. Deutschen Jahrestagung für Akustik DAGA*, pp. 315–316, Deutsche Gesellschaft für Akustik e.V., Munich, 2005.

[Mai06a] A. Maier. "PEAKS - Programm zur Evaluation und Analyse Kindlicher Sprach-störungen - Bedienungsanleitung: http://www5.informatik.uni-erlangen. de/Forschung/Publikationen/2006/Maier06-PPZ.pdf". Tech. Rep. 1, FAU, Erlangen, 2006.

[Mai06b] A. Maier, C. Hacker, E. Nöth, E. Nkenke, T. Haderlein, F. Rosanowski, and M. Schuster. "Intelligibility of Children with Cleft Lip and Palate: Evaluation by Speech Recognition Techniques". In: Y. Tang, S. Wang, G. Lorette, D. Yeung, and H. Yan, Eds., *Proc. 18th Int. Conf. on Pattern Recognition*, pp. 274–277, IEEE, Hong Kong, 2006.

[Mai06c] A. Maier, T. Haderlein, C. Hacker, E. Nöth, F. Rosanowski, U. Eysholdt, and M. Schuster. "Automatische internetbasierte Evaluation der Verständlichkeit". In: M. Gross and F. Kruse, Eds., *Aktuelle phoniatrisch-pädaudiologische As-pekte*, pp. 87–90, Heidelberg, 2006.

[Mai06d] A. Maier, T. Haderlein, and E. Nöth. " Environmental Adaptation with a Small Data Set of the Target Domain ". In: P. Sojka, I. Kopecek, and K. Pala, Eds., *Proc. 9th Int. Conf. on Text, Speech and Dialogue (TSD)*, pp. 431–437, Lecture Notes in Artificial Intelligence, Springer, Berlin Heidelberg, 2006.

[Mai06e] A. Maier, E. Nöth, E. Nkenke, and M. Schuster. "Automatic Assessment of Children's Speech with Cleft Lip and Palate". In: T. Erjavec and J. Gros, Eds., *Proc. Int. Language Technologies Conference (IS-LTC)* , pp. 31–35, Ljubljana, 2006.

[Mai09] A. Maier. *Speech of Children with Cleft Lip and Palate: Automatic Assessment*. Vol. 29 of *Studien zur Mustererkennung*, Logos Verlag, Berlin, 2009.

[Mak89] A. Makhoul, El-Jaroudi, and R. A., Schwartz. "Formation of Disconnected Decision Regions with a Single Hidden Layer". In: *Proc. Int. Joint Conf. on Neural Networks*, pp. 455 – 460, Washington DC, 1989.

[Mar02] K. Martel. "Mutual Knowledge and Prosody in Young Children". In: *Proc. Speech Prosody 2002, Int. Conf.*, pp. 479–482, Aix-en-Provence, 2002.

[McG88] R. S. McGowan and S. Nittrouer. "Differences in Fricative Production Between Children and Adults: Evidence from an Acoustic Analysis of /f/ and /s/ ". *J. Acoust. Soc. Am.*, Vol. 83, pp. 229–236, 1988.

[Men00] W. Menzel, D. Herron, P. Bonaventura, and R. Morton. "Automatic Detection and Correction of Non-Native English Pronunciation". In: *Proc. Conf Integrat-ing Speech Technologies in Learning (InSTIL)*, pp. 49 – 56, Dundee, 2000.

[Mer95] L. Mervis. "Assessment Handbook - A Guide for Developing Assessment Programs in Illinois Schools". Tech. Rep., Illinois state board of education,

Springfield, 1995. http://www.gower.k12.il.us/Staff/ASSESS/index.htm, last visited October 2007.

[Mic04]   O. Mich, D. Giuliani, and M. Gerosa. "Parling, a CALL System for Children". In: R. Delmonte, P. Delclouque, and S. Tonelli, Eds., *Proceedings of NLP and Speech Technologies in Advanced Language Learning Systems Symposium*, pp. 169–172, Venice, 2004.

[Min04a]   N. Minematsu. "Pronunciation Assessment Based upon the Compatibility between a Learner's Pronunciation Structure and the Target Language's Lexical Structure". In: S. Kim and D. Youn, Eds., *Interspeech 2004 - Proc. 8th Int. Conf. on Spoken Language Processing (ICSLP)*, pp. 1317 –1320, Jeju Island, Korea, 2004.

[Min04b]   N. Minematsu. "Pronunciation Assessment Based upon the Phonological Distortions Observed in Language Learner's Utterances". In: S. Kim and D. Youn, Eds., *Interspeech 2004 - Proc. 8th Int. Conf. on Spoken Language Processing (ICSLP)*, pp. 1669 – 1672, Jeju Island, Korea, 2004.

[Mol00]   S. Molau, S. Kanthak, and H. Ney. "Efficient Vocal Tract Normalization in Automatic Speech Recognition". In: *Konf. Elektronische Sprachsignalverarbeitung (ESSV)*, pp. 209–216, Cottbus, 2000.

[Mol01]   S. Molau, M. Pitz, R. Schlüter, and H. Ney. "Computing Mel-frequency Cepstral Coefficients on the Power Spectrum". In: IEEE, Ed., *Proc. Int. Conf. on Acoustics, Speech and Signal Processing (ICASSP)*, pp. 73–76, Salt Lake City, 2001.

[Mor04]   N. Morgan, B. Chen, Q. Zhu, and A. Stolcke. "Trapping Conversational Speech: Extending TRAP/TANDEM Approaches to Conversational Telephone Speech Recognition". In: IEEE, Ed., *Proc. Int. Conf. on Acoustics, Speech and Signal Processing (ICASSP)*, pp. 537 – 540, Montreal, 2004.

[Mou06]   M. Moustroufas and V. Digalakis. "Automatic Pronunciation Evaluation of Foreign Speakers Using Unknown Texts". *Computer Speech and Language*, Vol. 21, No. 1, pp. 219–230, 2006.

[Nar02]   S. Narayanan and A. Potamianos. "Creating Conversational Interfaces for Children". *IEEE Transactions on Speech and Audio Processing*, Vol. 10, No. 2, pp. 65 – 78, 2002.

[Ner02a]   A. Neri, C. Cucchiarini, H. Strik, and L. Boves. "A Pedagogy-Technology Interface in Computer Assisted Pronunciation Training". *Computer Assisted Language Learning*, Vol. 15, pp. 441–467, 2002.

[Ner02b] A. Neri, C. Cuchiarini, and C. Strik. "Feedback in Computer Assisted Pronunciation Training: Technology Push or Demand Pull?". In: *Proc. Int. Conf. on Spoken Language Processing (ICSLP)*, pp. 1209–1212, Denver, 2002.

[Ner02c] A. Neri, C. Cuchiarini, and C. Strik. "Feedback in Computer Assisted Pronunciation Training: When Technology meets Pedagogy". In: *Proceedings of the CALL Conference "CALL professionals and the future of CALL research"*, pp. 179–188, Antwerp, 2002.

[Ner03] A. Neri, C. Cuchiarini, and C. Strik. "Automatic Speech Recognition for Second Language Learning: How and why it Actually Works". In: *Proc. of 15th Int. Congress of Phonetic Sciences*, pp. 1157–1160, Barcelona, 2003.

[Neu00] L. Neumeyer, H. Franco, V. Digalakis, and M. Weintraub. "Automatic Scoring of Pronunciation Quality". *Speech Comm.*, Vol. 30, pp. 83–93, 2000.

[Neu96] L. Neumeyer, H. Franco, M. Weintraub, and P. Price. "Automatic Text-independent Pronunciation Scoring of Foreign Language Student Speech". In: *Proc. Int. Conf. on Spoken Language Processing (ICSLP)*, pp. 1457–1460, Philadelphia, PA, 1996.

[Neu98] L. Neumeyer, H. Franco, V. Abrash, L. Julia, O. Ronen, H. Bratt, and J. Bring. "WebGrader: A Multilingual Pronunciation Practice Tool". In: *Proc. Speech Technology in Language Learning (STILL)*, Marholmen, 1998.

[Nie03] H. Niemann. *Klassifikation von Mustern.* available online, second Ed., 2003. http://www5.informatik.uni-erlangen.de/en/our-team/niemann-heinrich/books/.

[Nie90] H. Niemann. *Pattern Analysis and Understanding.* Vol. 4 of *Springer Series in Information Sciences*, Springer, Heidelberg, 1990.

[Nil82] N. Nilsson. *Principles of Artificial Intelligence.* Springer–Verlag, Berlin, 1982.

[Not02] E. Nöth, A. Batliner, V. Warnke, J. Haas, M. Boros, J. Buckow, R. Huber, F. Gallwitz, M. Nutt, and H. Niemann. "On the Use of Prosody in Automatic Dialogue Understanding". *Speech Comm.*, Vol. 36, No. 1-2, pp. 45 – 62, 2002.

[Not07] E. Nöth, C. Hacker, and A. Batliner. "Does Multimodality Really Help? The Classification of Emotion and of On/Off-Focus in Multimodal Dialogues - Two Case Studies.". In: *Proc. 49th International Symposium ELMAR-2007*, Zadar, 2007.

[Oh06] Y. Oh, J. Yoon, and H. Kim. "Acoustic Model Adaptation Based on Pronunciation Variability Analysis for Non-Native Speech Recognition". In: IEEE, Ed., *Proc. Int. Conf. on Acoustics, Speech and Signal Processing (ICASSP)*, pp. 137 – 140, Toulouse, 2006.

[Oht05] K. Ohta and S. Nakagawa. "A Statistical Method of Evaluating Pronunciation Proficiency for Japanese Words". In: ISCA, Ed., *Interspeech 05 - Proc. 9th European Conference On Speech Communication and Technology (Eurospeech)*, pp. 2233–2236, Lisbon, 2005.

[Opp01] D. Oppermann, F. Schiel, S. Steininger, and N. Beringer. "Off-Talk – a Problem for Human-Machine-Interaction". In: *Proc. European Conf. on Speech Communication and Technology*, pp. 2197–2200, Aalborg, 2001.

[Pal90] D. Pallett, W. Fisher, and J. Fiscus. "Tools for the Analysis of Benchmark Speech Recognition Tests". In: IEEE, Ed., *Proc. Int. Conf. on Acoustics, Speech and Signal Processing (ICASSP)*, pp. 97–100, Albuquerque, 1990.

[Pal96] S. Palethorpe, R. Wales, J. E. Clark, and T. Senserrick. "Vowel Classification in Children ". *J. Acoust. Soc. Am.*, Vol. 100, pp. 3843–3851, 1996.

[Par04] J. Park and S.-C. Rhee. "Development of the Knowledge-based Spoken English Evaluation System and it's Application". In: S. Kim and D. Youn, Eds., *Interspeech 2004 - Proc. 8th Int. Conf. on Spoken Language Processing (ICSLP)*, pp. 1681–1684, Jeju Island, Korea, 2004.

[Pet53] G. Peterson and H. Barney. "Control Methods used in a Study of the Vowels". *J. Acoust. Soc. Am.*, Vol. 24, pp. 175–184, 1953.

[Pit03] M. Pitz and H. Ney. "Vocal Tract Normalization as Linear Transformation of MFCC". In: ISCA, Ed., *Proc. European Conference On Speech Communication and Technology (Eurospeech)*, pp. 1445–1448, Geneva, 2003.

[Pot03] A. Potamianos and S. Narayanan. "Robust Recognition of Children's Speech". *IEEE Transactions on Speech and Audio Processing*, Vol. 11, No. 6, pp. 603–616, 2003.

[Pot97a] A. Potamianos, S. Narayanan, and S. Lee. "Automatic Speech Recognition for Children". In: ISCA, Ed., *Proc. European Conference On Speech Communication and Technology (Eurospeech)*, pp. 2371–2374, Rhodes, 1997.

[Pot97b] A. Potamianos and R. Rose. "On Combining Frequency Warping and Spectral Shaping in HMM Based Speech Recognition". In: IEEE, Ed., *Proc. Int. Conf. on Acoustics, Speech and Signal Processing (ICASSP)*, pp. 1275–1278, Munich, 1997.

[Rei05] N. Reithinger, S. Bergweiler, R. Engel, G. Herzog, N. Pfleger, M. Romanelli, and D. Sonntag. "A Look Under the Hood - Design and Development of the First SmartWeb System Demonstrator". In: *Proc. of the Seventh Int. Conf. on Multimodal Interfaces (ICMI)*, pp. 159–166, Trento, 2005.

[Rie94]   M. Riedmiller and H. Braun. "RPROP – Description and Implementation Details". 1994. Technical Report. Universität Karlsruhe.

[Rie95]   S. Rieck. *Parametrisierung und Klassifikation gesprochener Sprache*. Vol. 10 of *Fortschrittberichte Informatik/Kommunikationstechnik no. 353*, VDI Verlag, Düsseldorf, 1995.

[Rij79]   C. V. Rijsbergen. *Information Retrieval*. Butterworths, London, 1979.

[Roo93]   E. Rooney, R. Vaughan, S. Hiller, F. Carraro, and J. Laver. "Training Vowel Pronunciation Using a Computer-Aided Teaching System". In: ISCA, Ed., *Proc. European Conference On Speech Communication and Technology (Eurospeech)*, pp. 1347–1350, Berlin, 1993.

[Rus00]   M. Russell, R. Series, J. Wallace, C. Brown, and A. Skilling. "The STAR System: an Iterative Pronunciation Tutor for Young Children". *Computer, Speech and Language*, Vol. 14, pp. 161–175, 2000.

[Rus03]   M. Russell. "WP5: Speech Technologies for Children. Deliverable D10". Tech. Rep., PF-STAR, Preparing for Future Multisensorial Interaction Research, Birmingham, 2003. http://pfstar.itc.it/public/docs.htm.

[Rus04]   M. Russell. "WP5: Speech Technologies for Children. Deliverable D14". Tech. Rep., PF-STAR, Preparing for Future Multisensorial Interaction Research, Birmingham, 2004. http://pfstar.itc.it/public/docs.htm.

[Sampa]   "SAMPA: a Computer Readable Phonetic Alphabet". http://www.phon.ucl. ac.uk/home/sampa/home.htm, last visited October 2007.

[Sch05]   M. Schuster, E. Nöth, T. Haderlein, S. Steidl, A. Batliner, and F. Rosanowski. "Can you Understand him? Let's Look at his Word Accuracy - Automatic Evaluation of Tracheoesophageal Speech". In: IEEE, Ed., *Proc. Int. Conf. on Acoustics, Speech and Signal Processing (ICASSP)*, pp. 61–64, Philadelphia, 2005.

[Sch07]   B. Schuller, D. Seppi, A. Batliner, A. Maier, and S. Steidl. "Towards more Reality in the Recognition of Emotional Speech". In: IEEE, Ed., *ICASSP, 2007 IEEE International Conference on Acoustics, Speech, and Signal Processing, Proceedings*, pp. 941–944, Bryan, TX, 2007.

[Sch86]   G. Scherer and A. Wollmann. *Englische Phonetik und Phonologie*. Schmidt, E., Berlin, 1986.

[Sch90]   R. Schapire. "The Strength of Weak Learnability". *Machine Learning*, Vol. 5, No. 2, pp. 197–227, 1990.

[Sch95]   E. G. Schukat-Talamazzini. *Automatische Spracherkennung – Grundlagen, statistische Modelle und effiziente Algorithmen.* Vieweg, Braunschweig, 1995.

[Sch96]   M. Schüßler. "Realisierung von Spracheradaptionsverfahren für ein sprecherunabhängiges Spracherkennungssystem". Diplomarbeit, Lehrstuhl für Mustererkennung (Informatik 5), Universität Erlangen-Nürnberg, 1996.

[Sel05]   M. Seltzer and A. Acero. "Training Wideband Acoustic Models Using Mixed-Bandwidth Training Data via Feature Bandwidth Extension". In: IEEE, Ed., *Proc. Int. Conf. on Acoustics, Speech and Signal Processing (ICASSP)*, pp. 921 – 924, Philadelphia, 2005.

[Sha99]   S. Sharma. *Multi-Stream Approach to Robust Speech Recognition.* PhD thesis, Oregon Graduate Institute of Science and Technology, 1999.

[Sie01]   R. Siepmann, A. Batliner, and D. Oppermann. "Using Prosodic Features to Characterize Off-Talk in Human-Computer-Interaction". In: M. Bacchiani, J. Hirschberg, D. Litman, and M. Ostendorf, Eds., *Proc. of the Workshop on Prosody and Speech Recognition 2001*, pp. 147–150, Red Bank, NJ, 2001.

[Ste01]   G. Stemmer, C. Hacker, E. Nöth, and H. Niemann. "Multiple Time Resolutions for Derivatives of Mel-Frequency Cepstral Coefficients". In: IEEE, Ed., *Proc. of the Automatic Speech Recognition and Understanding Workshop (ASRU)*, pp. 37 – 40, Trento, 2001.

[Ste02]   G. Stemmer, S. Steidl, E. Nöth, H. Niemann, and A. Batliner. "Comparison and Combination of Confidence Measures". In: P. Sojka, I. Kopecek, and K. Pala, Eds., *Proc. 5th Int. Conf. on Text, Speech, and Dialogue (TSD)*, pp. 181–188, Lecture Notes in Artificial Intelligence, Springer, Berlin, 2002.

[Ste03a]   S. Steidl, G. Stemmer, C. Hacker, E. Nöth, and H. Niemann. "Improving Children's Speech Recognition by HMM Interpolation with an Adults' Speech Recognizer". In: B. Michaelis and G. Krell, Eds., *Pattern Recognition, 25th DAGM Symposium, Proceedings*, pp. 600–607, Lecture Notes in Computer Science, Springer, Berlin, Heidelberg, New York, 2003.

[Ste03b]   G. Stemmer, C. Hacker, S. Steidl, and E. Nöth. "Acoustic Normalization of Children's Speech". In: ISCA, Ed., *Proc. European Conference On Speech Communication and Technology (Eurospeech)*, pp. 1313–1316, Geneva, 2003.

[Ste03c]   G. Stemmer, V. Zeißler, C. Hacker, E. Nöth, and H. Niemann. "A Phone Recognizer Helps to Recognize Words Better". In: IEEE, Ed., *Proc. Int. Conf. on Acoustics, Speech and Signal Processing (ICASSP)*, pp. 736–739, Hong Kong, 2003.

[Ste03d] G. Stemmer, V. Zeißler, C. Hacker, E. Nöth, and H. Niemann. "Context-Dependent Output Densities for Hidden Markov Models in Speech Recognition". In: *Proc. European Conference On Speech Communication and Technology (Eurospeech)*, pp. 969–972, Geneva, 2003.

[Ste04a] C. Steidl, S. Hacker, C. Ruff, A. Batliner, E. Nöth, and J. Haas. "Looking at the Last two Turns, I'd Say this Dialogue is Doomed - Measuring Dialogue Success". In: P. Sojka, I. IKopecek, and K. Pala, Eds., *Proc. 7th Int. Conf. on Text, Speech, and Dialogue (TSD)*, pp. 629–636, Lecture Notes in Artificial Intelligence, Springer, Berlin, Heidelberg, 2004.

[Ste04b] S. Steidl, G. Stemmer, C. Hacker, and E. Nöth. "Adaption in the Pronunciation Space for Non-Native Speech Recognition". In: S. Kim and D. Youn, Eds., *Interspeech 2004 - Proc. 8th Int. Conf. on Spoken Language Processing (ICSLP)*, pp. 318–321, Jeju Island, Korea, 2004.

[Ste05a] S. Steidl, M. Levit, A. Batliner, E. Nöth, and H. Niemann. "'Of All Things the Measure is Man' – Automatic Classification of Emotions and Inter-Labeler Consistency". In: IEEE, Ed., *Proc. Int. Conf. on Acoustics, Speech and Signal Processing (ICASSP)*, pp. 317–320, Philadelphia, 2005.

[Ste05b] G. Stemmer. *Modeling Variability in Speech Recognition*. Vol. 19 of *Studien zur Mustererkennung*, Logos Verlag, Berlin, 2005.

[Ste09] S. Steidl. *Automatic Classification of Emotion-Related User States in Spontaneous Children's Speech*. Vol. 28 of *Studien zur Mustererkennung*, Logos Verlag, Berlin, 2009.

[Sto06] F. Stouten and J.-P. Martens. "On the Use of Phonological Features for Pronunciation Scoring". In: IEEE, Ed., *Proc. Int. Conf. on Acoustics, Speech and Signal Processing (ICASSP)*, pp. 329 – 332, Toulouse, 2006.

[Suz04] Y. Suzuki, M. Muto, K. Shirai, and Y. Sagisaka. "Analysis of the Phone Level Contribution to Objective Evaluation of English Speech by Non-Natives". In: S. Kim and D. Youn, Eds., *Interspeech 2004 - Proc. 8th Int. Conf. on Spoken Language Processing (ICSLP)*, pp. 1673–1676, Jeju Island, Korea, 2004.

[Tei00] C. Teixeira, H. Franco, E. Shriberg, K. Precoda, and K. Sonmez. "Prosodic Features for Automatic Textindependent Evaluation of Degree of Nativeness for Language Learners". In: *Proc. Int. Conf. on Spoken Language Processing (ICSLP)*, pp. 187–190, Bejing, 2000.

[Tep05a] J. Tepperman and S. Narayanan. "Automatic Syllable Stress Detection Using Prosodic Features for Pronunciation Evaluation of Language Learners". In: IEEE, Ed., *Proc. Int. Conf. on Acoustics, Speech and Signal Processing (ICASSP)*, pp. 937–940, Philadelphia, 2005.

[Tep05b]   J. Tepperman and S. Narayanan. "Hidden-Articulator Markov Models for Pronunciation Evaluation". In: IEEE, Ed., *Proc. of the Automatic Speech Recognition and Understanding Workshop (ASRU)*, pp. 174 – 179, San Juan, 2005.

[Tib97]   S. Tibrewala and H. Hermansky. "Multi-Stream Approach in Acoustic Modeling". In: *Proc. LVCSR-Hub5 Workshop (Large Vocabulary Continuous Speech Recognition)*, 1997.

[Tru05]   K. Truong, A. Neri, F. de Wet, C. Cucchiarini, and H. Strik. "Automatic Detection of Frequent Pronunciation Errors Made by L2-Learners". In: ISCA, Ed., *Interspeech 05 - Proc. 9th European Conference On Speech Communication and Technology (Eurospeech)*, pp. 1345–1348, Lisbon, 2005.

[Vio04]   P. Viola and M. J. Jones. "Robust Real-Time Face Detection". *Int. J. Comput. Vision*, Vol. 57, No. 2, pp. 137–154, 2004.

[Wah00]   W. Wahlster, Ed. *Verbmobil: Foundations of Speech-to-Speech Translations*. Springer, Berlin, 2000.

[Wah04]   W. Wahlster. "Smartweb: Mobile Application of the Semantic Web". In: *KI 2004: Advances in Artificial Intelligence*, pp. 50–51, Springer, Berlin, Heidelberg, 2004.

[Wah06]   W. Wahlster, Ed. *SmartKom: Foundations of Multimodal Dialogue Systems*. Springer, Berlin, 2006.

[Wak77]   H. Wakita. "Normalization of Vowels by Vocal Tract Length and its Application to Vowel Identification". *IEEE Trans. on Acoustics, Speech and Signal Processing*, Vol. 25, pp. 183–192, 1977.

[Wal77]   P. Wald and R. Kronmal. "Discriminant Functions when Covariances are Unequal and Sample Sizes are Moderate". *Biometrics*, Vol. 33, pp. 479–484, 1977.

[War03]   V. Warnke. *Integrierte Segmentierung und Klassifikation von Äußerungen und Dialogakten mit heterogenen Wissensquellen*. Vol. 9 of *Studien zur Mustererkennung*, Logos Verlag, Berlin, 2003.

[Wer88]   P. Werbos. "Backpropagation: Past and Future". In: *Proceedings of the IEEE International Conference on Neural Networks*, pp. 343–353, San Diego, 1988.

[Wil96]   J. Wilpon and C. Jacobsen. "A Study of Speech Recognition for Children and the Elderly". In: IEEE, Ed., *Proc. Int. Conf. on Acoustics, Speech and Signal Processing (ICASSP)*, pp. 349–352, Atlanta, 1996.

[Wit00]   S. Witt and S. Young. "Phone-level Pronunciation Scoring and Assessment for Interactive Language Learning". *Speech Comm.*, Vol. 30, pp. 95–108, 2000.

[Wit97]   S. Witt and S. Young. "Language Learning Based on Non-Native Speech Recognition". In: ISCA, Ed., *Proc. European Conference On Speech Communication and Technology (Eurospeech)*, pp. 633 – 636, Rhodes, 1997.

[Wit99]   S. Witt. *Use of Speech Recognition in Computer-Assisted Language Learning*. PhD thesis, Cambridge University Engineering Department, Cambridge, UK, 1999.

[Woo01]   P. Woodland. "Speaker Adaptation for Continuous Density HMMs: A Review". In: ISCA, Ed., *Proc. ITRW on Workshop Adaptation Methods for Speech Recognition*, pp. 11–19, Sophia Antipolis, 2001.

[Yam05]   Y. Yamashita, K. Kato, and K. Nozawa. "Automatic Scoring for Prosodic Proficiency of English Sentences Spoken by Japanese Based on Utterance Comparison.". *IEICE Transactions*, Vol. 88-D, No. 3, pp. 496–501, 2005.

[Yil05]   S. Yildirim, C. Lee, S. Lee, A. Potamianos, and S. Narayanan. "Detecting Politeness and Frustration State of a Child in a Conversational Computer Game". In: ISCA, Ed., *Interspeech 05 - Proc. 9th European Conference On Speech Communication and Technology (Eurospeech)*, pp. 2209 – 2212, Lisbon, 2005.

[Zaj05]   K. Zajdo, J. van der Stelt, T. Wempe, and L. Pols. "Cross-Linguistic Comparison of Two-year-old Children's Acoustic Vowel Spaces: Contrasting Hungarian with Dutch". In: ISCA, Ed., *Interspeech 05 - Proc. 9th European Conference On Speech Communication and Technology (Eurospeech)*, pp. 1173 – 1176, Lisbon, 2005.

[Zei06]   V. Zeißler, J. Adelhardt, A. Batliner, C. Frank, E. Nöth, R. Shi, and H. Niemann. "The Prosody Module". In: W. Wahlster, Ed., *SmartKom: Foundations of Multimodal Dialogue Systems*, pp. 139–152, Springer, Berlin, 2006.

[Zei10]   V. Zeißler. "Robuste Erkennung der prosodischen Phänomene und der emotionalen Benutzerzustände in einem multimodalen Dialogsystem". PhD thesis, Lehrstuhl für Mustererkennung (Chair of Pattern Recognition), Universität Erlangen–Nürnberg, Erlangen (Germany), 2010. To appear.

[Zel95]   A. Zell and et al. "SNNS, Stuttgart Neural Network Simulator, User Manual, Version 4.1.". 1995. Institute for parallel and distributed high performance systems, Universität Stuttgart.

[Zel97]   A. Zell. *Simulation Neuronaler Netze*. Addison Wesley Longman Verlag, München, 1997.

[Zma05]   C. Zmarich and S. Bonifacio. "Phonetic Inventories in Italian Children aged 18 - 27 Months: a Longitudinal Study". In: ISCA, Ed., *Interspeech 05 - Proc. 9th European Conference On Speech Communication and Technology (Eurospeech)*, pp. 757 – 760, Lisbon, 2005.

[Zor05]   D. Zorn. "Vergleichende Klassifikation des Benutzerzustands Müdigkeit in der Sprache". Studienarbeit, Lehrstuhl für Mustererkennung (Informatik 5), Universität Erlangen-Nürnberg, 2005.

Index